# I WONDER AS I WANDER

# OTHER BOOKS BY LANGSTON HUGHES

**POETRY**

    The Weary Blues
    The Dream Keeper
    Fine Clothes to the Jew
    Shakespeare in Harlem
    Fields of Wonder
    One-Way Ticket
    Montage of a Dream Deferred

**FICTION**

    Not Without Laughter
    The Ways of White Folks
    Laughing to Keep From Crying
    The Sweet Flypaper of Life
    Simple Speaks His Mind
    Simple Takes a Wife

**AUTOBIOGRAPHY**

    The Big Sea
    I Wonder as I Wander

**JUVENILES**

    Famous American Negroes
    Famous Negro Music Makers
    First Book of the West Indies
    First Book of Rhythms
    First Book of Negroes
    First Book of Jazz

# I WONDER AS I WANDER

## AN AUTOBIOGRAPHICAL JOURNEY

## by LANGSTON HUGHES

**RINEHART & COMPANY, INC.**

*NEW YORK • TORONTO*

POEMS BY LANGSTON HUGHES FROM HIS BOOKS, "THE WEARY BLUES," "THE DREAM KEEPER," AND "SHAKESPEARE IN HARLEM," USED IN SECTION 2, "MAKING POETRY PAY," ARE REPRINTED BY PERMISSION OF, AND BY SPECIAL ARRANGEMENT WITH, ALFRED A. KNOPF, INC.

PUBLISHED SIMULTANEOUSLY IN CANADA BY
CLARKE, IRWIN & COMPANY, LTD., TORONTO

**TO ARTHUR AND MARION SPINGARN**

# CONTENTS

**4  SOUTH TO SAMARKAND**

**5  SPRING BESIDE THE KREMLIN**

**6  COLOR AROUND THE GLOBE**

## 7 WRITING FOR A LIVING

## 8 WORLD WITHOUT END

# I WONDER AS I WANDER

*I am debtor both to the Greeks and to the barbarians; both to the wise and to the unwise.* Romans 1:14

# 1

# IN SEARCH
# OF SUN

**LESS THAN LYRIC**

WHEN I was twenty-seven the stock-market crash came. When I was twenty-eight, my personal crash came. Then I guess I woke up. So. when I was almost thirty, I began to make my living from writing. This is the story of a Negro who wanted to make his living from poems and stories.

For ten years I had been a writer of sorts, but a writer who wrote mostly because, when I felt bad, writing kept me from feeling worse; it put my inner emotions into exterior form, and gave me an outlet for words that never came in conversation.

Now I found myself in the midst of a depression. I had just lost my patron. Scholarships, fellowships and literary prizes became scarce. I had already gotten several awards that were not to be had a second time. Jobs were very hard to find. The WPA had not yet come into being. If I were to live and write, at all, since I did not know how to do anything else, I had to make a living from writing itself. So, of necessity, I began to turn poetry into bread.

But this earning of bread did not come about in easy direct steps. First, it was Mary McLeod Bethune who suggested to me that I travel through the South reading my poems. And my conversations with Mary McLeod Bethune came about because I went to Haiti.

I went to Haiti to get away from my troubles. I had intended to go from Cleveland, where I spent Christmas with my mother, to Key

West by bus, thence to Cuba and Haiti. But in Cleveland, I met at Karamu House a fellow named Zell Ingram who was going to the Cleveland School of Art, but who did not like it, so he wanted to quit classes and travel. He borrowed his mother's car; she gave him three hundred dollars, and we set out. I had three hundred dollars left from the Harmon Award granted me for my novel, *Not Without Laughter*, having given my mother one hundred of the four-hundred-dollar grant. On a morning in March, Zell and I began our journey to the South.

As soon as I got rid of the last dollar of the money left from my estranged patron's allowances, I felt immensely better. My stomach, that for weeks had turned over and over since my relations with the kind and elderly lady on Park Avenue had ended so abruptly, now stopped turning over altogether.

I came out of college in 1929, the year of the Stock Market crash and the beginning of the Great Depression. I had written my first novel, *Not Without Laughter*, as a student on the campus of Lincoln University. I had had a scholarship to college. After graduation a monthly sum from my patron enabled me to live comfortably in suburban New Jersey, an hour from Manhattan, revising my novel at leisure. Propelled by the backwash of the "Harlem Renaissance" of the early 'twenties, I had been drifting along pleasantly on the delightful rewards of my poems which seemed to please the fancy of kind-hearted New York ladies with money to help young writers. The magazines used very few stories with Negro themes, since Negro themes were considered exotic, in a class with Chinese or East Indian features. Editorial offices then never hired Negro writers to read manuscripts or employed them to work on their staffs. Almost all the young white writers I'd known in New York in the 'twenties had gotten good jobs with publishers or magazines as a result of their creative work. White friends of mine in Manhattan, whose first novels had received reviews nowhere nearly so good as my own, had been called to Hollywood, or were doing scripts for the radio. Poets whose poetry sold hardly at all had been offered jobs on smart New York magazines. But they were white. I was colored. So in Haiti I began to puzzzle out how I, a Negro, could make a living in America from writing.

There was one other dilemma—how to make a living from *the kind of writing I wanted to do*. I did not want to write for the pulps, or turn out fake "true" stories to sell under anonymous names as Wallace Thurman did. I did not want to bat out slick non-Negro short stories in competition with a thousand other commercial writers trying to make *The Saturday Evening Post*. I wanted to write seriously and as well as I knew how about the Negro people, and make *that* kind of writing earn for me a living.

I thought, with the four hundred dollars my novel had given me, I had better go sit in the sun awhile and think, having just been through a tense and disheartening winter after a series of misunderstandings with the kind lady who had been my patron. She wanted me to be more African than Harlem—primitive in the simple, intuitive and noble sense of the word. I couldn't be, having grown up in Kansas City, Chicago and Cleveland. So that winter had left me ill in my soul. I could not put my mind on writing for months. But write I had to—or starve—so I went to sit in the sun and gather my wits.

In Cleveland that winter it had been cold and damp, and it looked as though spring had no intention of coming. I knew it would be warm in Haiti. When Zell and I reached North Carolina, we were already out of the snow belt. And, speeding down the Florida coast, we met the sun, friendly and warm.

We stopped at Daytona Beach to visit Bethune-Cookman College of which that most distinguished of Negro women, Mary McLeod Bethune, was president. We reached Daytona about eight o'clock in the evening. It took us some time to find the campus. When we did, we stopped before the first building where we saw lights burning. It was warm, so the doors and windows were all open. We heard a group of girls singing in a second-floor room. Zell went upstairs to inquire the way to Mrs. Bethune's home. As a teacher answered his knock on the classroom door, I heard the singing stop. Then I heard a woman's voice exclaim, "No more class tonight, girls—the poet, Langston Hughes, is here!"

I was struck dumb with shyness. I had no idea my name would be known in Florida—other than to Mrs. Bethune herself whom I had once met at Columbia University. Some of the students came running down the stairs, followed by the teacher, and I was greeted with open arms. We were shown to Mrs. Bethune's house across the campus where she welcomed us graciously, although she was not forewarned of our visit. Food was prepared and a guest room put at our disposal. But before I went to bed I sat for a long time on the front porch talking to Mrs. Bethune, motherly and kind and wise as she was toward me, a very puzzled young man.

The next day I read some of my poems to the English classes on her campus. That was the beginning of my learning how to make a living from writing—for it was Mrs. Bethune who said to me the night before, "Why don't you tour the South reading your poems? Thousands of Negro students would be proud and inspired by seeing you and hearing you. You are young, but you have already made a name for yourself in literary circles, and you can help black students to feel that a Negro youth can amount to something in this world in spite of our problems."

I kept thinking about what Mrs. Bethune said as I drove southward down the long straight Florida road toward Miami.

## HAVANA NIGHTS

IN Miami, Zell and I put the Ford in a garage. We went by rail to Key West, thence by boat to Cuba. It was suppertime when we got to El Moro with Havana rising white and Moorish-like out of the sea in the twilight. The evening was warm and the avenues were alive with people, among them many jet-black Negroes in white attire. Traffic filled the narrow streets, auto horns blew, cars' bells clanged, and from the wineshops and fruit-juice stands radios throbbed with drumbeats and the wavelike sounds of maracas rustling endless rumbas. Life seemed fluid, intense, and warm in the busy streets of Havana.

Our hotel was patronized mostly by Cubans from the provinces, with huge families. Its inner balconies around an open courtyard were loud with the staccato chatter of stout mamas and vivacious children. Its restaurant on the first floor—with the entire front wall open to the street—was as noisy as only a Cuban restaurant can be, for, added to all the street noises, were the cries of waiters and the laughter of guests, the clatter of knives and forks, and the clinking of glasses at the bar.

I liked this hotel because, since tourists never came there, the prices were on the Cuban scale and low. None of the rooms had any windows, but they had enormous double doors opening onto the tiled balconies above the courtyard. Nobody troubled to give anyone a key. The management simply took for granted all the guests were honest.

I went the next day to look up José Antonio Fernandez de Castro to whom, on a previous trip to Cuba, I had been given a letter of introduction by Miguel Covarrubias. José Antonio was a human dynamo who at once set things in motion. A friend of many American artists and writers, he drank with, wined and dined them all; fished with Hemingway; and loved to go to Marianao—the then nontourist amusement center. He knew all the taxicab drivers in town—with whom he had accounts—and was, in general, about the best person in Cuba to know, if you'd never been there before.

José Antonio was a newspaperman on the *Diario De La Marina*. He later became an editor of *Orbe*, Cuba's weekly pictorial magazine. Then he went into the diplomatic service to become the first secretary of the Cuban Embassy in Mexico City, and from there to Europe. Painters, writers, newsboys, poets, fighters, politicians and rumba dancers were all José's friends. And, best of all for me, he knew the Negro musicians at Marianao, those fabulous drum beaters who use their bare hands to beat out rhythm, those clave knockers and maraca shakers who somehow have saved—out of all the centuries of slavery and all the miles and miles from Guinea—the heartbeat and songbeat of Africa. This ancient heartbeat they pour out into the Cuban night from a little row of café hovels at Marianao. Or else they flood with song those smoky low-roofed dance halls where the poor of Havana go for entertainment after dark.

Most Cubans who lived in Vedado, Havana's fashionable section, had no idea where these dance halls were. That is why I liked José Antonio. He lived in Vedado, but he knew *all* Havana. Although he was a white Cuban of aristocratic background, he knew and loved Negro Cuba. That first night in town we went straight to Marianao.

This was my third trip to Cuba. Once I had been there as a sailor, and I had known the life of the water front and San Isidro

Street. The winter preceeding my present trip, I had come in search of a Negro composer to do an opera with me at the behest of my New York patron. So I had by now many friends in Havana, including the then unknown Nicolás Guillén, who later became a famous poet. My own poems had been published in Spanish in a number of Cuban magazines and papers, and I had given readings of them previously for Havana cultural organizations. The Club Atenas, leading club of color, had entertained me.

The Club Atenas occupied a large building with a staircase of marble, beautiful reception rooms, a ballroom, a comfortable library, a fencing room and a buffet. I had been astonished and delighted with its taste and luxury, for colored people in the United States had no such club. Diplomats, politicians, professional men and their families made up its membership—and a cultured and charming group they were. Then no rumbas were danced within the walls of the Atenas, for in Cuba in 1930 the rumba was not a respectable dance among persons of good breeding. Only the poor and declassé, the sporting elements, and gentlemen on a spree danced the rumba.

Rumbas and sones are essentially hip-shaking music—of Afro-Cuban folk derivation, which means a bit of Spain, therefore Arab-Moorish, mixed in. The tap of claves, the rattle of gourds, the dong of iron bells, the deep steady roll of drums speak of the earth, life bursting warm from the earth, and earth and sun moving in the steady rhythms of procreation and joy.

A group of young business and professional men of Havana once gave a rumba party in my honor. It was not unlike an American fraternity or lodge smoker—except that women were present. The women were not, however, wives or sweethearts of the gentlemen giving the rumba. Far from it. They were, on the whole, so a companion whispered to me, younger and prettier than most of their wives. They were ladies of the demimonde, playgirls, friends and mistresses of the hosts, their most choice females invited especially for zest and decorativeness.

The party was held in a large old Spanish colonial house, presided over by a stout woman with bold ways. It began about four in the afternoon. At dusk dinner was served; then the fiesta went on far into the night. It was what the Cubans call a *cumbancha*. Spree, I suppose, would be our best word.

When I arrived a Negro rumba band was playing in the court-yard, beating it out gaily, with maracas beneath the melody like the soft undertow of sea waves. Several kegs of wine sat on stools in the open air, and a big keg of beer decorated one end of the patio. Hidden in a rear court was a bar from which waiters emerged with Bacardi or whatever else one wished to drink that was not already in sight.

A few lovely mulatto girls sat fanning in wicker chairs. One or two couples were dancing as I came in, but the sun still shone in the courtyard and it was not yet cool enough for much action. Gradually more and more people began to arrive, girls in groups, men in ones or twos, but no men and women together. These were the women men kept, but did not take out. I had become acquainted with this custom of the mistress in Mexico and other Latin lands, where every man who was anybody at all had both a wife and a pretty mistress.

As the sun went down beyond the skyline, life began to throb in the cool enclosure. The taps on the wine kegs flowed freely. Lights were lighted in the patio, more chairs brought, and I was given a seat of honor near the orchestra. Most of the dancing pairs sat down, or disappeared inside the house. But the music seemed to take a new lease on life. Now various couples, one or two at a time, essayed the rumba in the center of the court as the rest of the party gathered to watch. I could not make out whether it was a dance contest or not, and my hosts were slightly tipsy by then so not very coherent in their explanations. But when the dancing couples seemed to tire, others took the floor. Sometimes a short burst of applause would greet an especially adept pair as the man swept around the woman like a cock about a hen, or the woman without losing a beat of the rhythm, went very slowly down to the floor on firm feet and un-dulated up again. Tirelessly the little Negro band played. Like a mighty dynamo deep in the bowels of the earth, the drums throbbed, beat, sobbed, grumbled, cried, and then laughed a staccato laugh. The dancing kept up until it was quite dark and the first stars came out.

Glass after glass was thrust into my hands as I sat looking and listening with various friends about me. Then after a while, a little tired of sitting still so long, I got up and moved to the other end of the courtyard. As soon as I rose, the music stopped. People began to drink and chatter, but there was no more exhibition dancing. Later

I learned that I, as the guest of honor, controlled that part of the entertainment. By rising, I had indicated a lack of further interest, so the rumba stopped. Had I known, I might have not risen so soon.

After supper—delicious sea food served with boiled bananas and Spanish rice—the general dancing began again. Several pretty girls did their best to teach me to rumba. Cuban dancing is not as easy as it looks, but I had a good time trying to learn, and I was interested in trying to understand the verses the musicians sang as they played. Some of the men who spoke English translated for me. Most of the songs were risqué in an ingenious folk way. One thing that struck me was that almost all the love lyrics were about the charms of *mi negra*, my black girl, *mi morena*, my dark girl, my chocolate sweetie or my mulatto beauty, plainly described as such in racial terms. These dusky nuances, I notice, are quite lost in the translations that Broadway makes of Cuban songs for American consumption.

As the night laughed on and big stars sparkled lazily over the festive courtyard, some of the men of the party explained to me that within the house there were rooms with big old-fashioned beds to which one might retire. "And here are girls," they said. "You are the guest of honor. Take your choice from any. Our women are your women, tonight."

So it goes at a rumba party in Havana to which one does not invite one's wife, one's mother, or one's sweetheart.

## CUBAN COLOR LINES

IN spite of the fact that Cuba is distinctly a Negroid country, there exists there a sort of triple color line. This triple line, in varying degrees of application, is common to all the West Indies. At the bottom of the color scale are the pure-blooded Negroes, black or dark brown in color. In the middle are the mixed bloods, the light browns, mulattoes, golden yellows and near whites with varying textures of Indian-Spanish hair. Then come the nearer whites, the octoroons, and the pure white of skin. In Cuba, although these three distinct divisions exist, the lines are not so tightly drawn as in some of the other islands of the Caribbean. The British Islands are the worst in this respect. The Latin Islands are more careless concerning racial matters.

But in Cuba one quickly notices that almost all the clerks in the bigger shops are white or near white; that in the daily papers almost all the photographs of society leaders are white, or light enough to pass for white; that almost all the gentlemen who represent the people and sit on government commissions and staff the Cuban consulates and ministries abroad are white, or at least "meriney," as American Negroes term that reddish blond border line between colored and white. But this scale is not 100% true. Occasionally a very dark Negro occupies a very high position in Cuba. That is what misleads many visitors from the United States—particularly colored visitors who are looking anixously for a country where they can say there is no color line—for Cuba's color line is much more flexible than that of the United States, and much more subtle. There are, of course, no Jim Crow cars in Cuba, and at official state gatherings and less official carnivals and celebrations, citizens of all colors meet and mingle. But there are definite social divisions based on color— and the darker a man is, the richer and more celebrated he has to be to crash those divisions.

The use of Havana as a winter playground by American tourists has, of course, brought its quota of Southern racial prejudice from the mainland. Hotels that formerly were lax in their application of the color line now discourage even mulatto Cubans, thus seeking the approval of their American clientele. But the purely Cuban hotels, with no eye out for tourists, cater to guests of all shades of complexion and the service is most courteous.

My single unpleasant experience in Havana took place at the entrance to the Havana Beach. The Cubans later explained to me that the only wide clean stretch of bathing beach near the city had been leased by politicians to an American concern that built there handsome pavilions and bathing houses for the use of tourists, charged a dollar to go on to the beach—a prohibitive sum then to most Cubans —and proceeded to draw the color line, as well. But since, in Havana, it is very difficult for even North Americans to draw a strict color line, the beach often had mulatto politicians and plutocrats sporting thereon. But entrance to the beach then seemed to depend, if you were colored, largely on whether you had enough political pull or social prestige to force the management to sell you a season ticket. At the gate, I discovered to my discomfort, that they would not sell colored people the customary dollar entrance tickets at all, although they were sold quite freely to whites for a single afternoon's bathing. If you were colored, the gatekeeper demanded a season ticket.

My friend, José Antonio Fernandez de Castro, and a group of journalists one Saturday had planned a beach party to which Zell Ingram and I were invited. Zell and I, since we had a lot of free time, decided to go the the beach early and spend the whole morning there in the sun until our friends arrived. We got off the street car in front of the tropical entrance pavilion and went to the window to purchase tickets. The young woman at the window said she was sorry there were no tickets. Zell and I stepped back and studied the tariff list posted beside the window. In both English and Spanish the rates for entrance tickets, season tickets, the renting of bathing suits, etc. were clearly printed. Since I speak Spanish I again approached the young lady.

"It says tickets are a dollar each. I'll take two."

She shoved the money back through the wicket. "You'll have to see the manager. I can't sell them to you."

The same sort of treatment had been meted out to me so often in my own country from Kansas to New York, Boston to Birmingham, that I began to understand.

I went to the entrance gate and asked the attendant there to kindly call the manager for me. Instead the attendant called a bouncer. The bouncer was an old American boxer—white, of course—with cauliflower ears and a flat nose.

"What do you guys want? This place ain't run for you," he said. "You can't come in."

"Do you mean to tell me that you're drawing the color line on a Cuban beach against American citizens—and you're an American yourself?"

"Don't start no arguments," he growled, drawing back his fist.

By now Zell had doubled up his fists, too, and squared off for a fight. Zell was a big fellow, but it seemed better to me not to attempt to settle the matter by a brawl, so I said, "Don't hit him, Ingram." But the ex-pug had already backed up beyond reach.

"Get out," he yelled from within the enclosure, "or I'll send for the police."

"Go ahead," I said, "send for them."

The bouncer retired. A Cuban attendant permitted me to enter the lobby where there was a telephone. I called up José Antonio who asked us to wait there for him; he would be right out by taxi. As a newspaperman he no doubt scented a story. Zell and I sat down in the lobby to wait. Just then a policeman, at the instigation of the bouncer, came up to us. He was a pleasant young officer, a white Cuban, with apparently little relish for his task.

"No pueden sentarse aqui," he said. "You can't sit here."

"Why?" I asked.

"The manager says you can't."

Zell, who spoke no Spanish, kept asking, "Shall I hit him, man?"

"No," I said. "Let's not give them any cause to arrest us. Let José Antonio, who is a Cuban, get at the bottom of this."

"Please get the manager for me then," I requested of the officer.

He went away and shortly returned with the manager, a tall patronizing American white man. I began to explain to the manager why we had come to the beach, but he interrupted to say that we would not be allowed within and insisted that we leave the lobby at once. I said that since it was a public lobby, we would wait there for our friends. The manager declared he would have us ejected.

He went away. Zell and I sat in the big wicker chairs and waited, knowing that it would take perhaps an hour for José Antonio to arrive. Shortly a car sped rapidly up to the entrance, screeched to a halt, and four policemen with drawn sabres jumped out. They came running toward us as if they intended to slice us to mince meat.

"Out!" cried the cops, waving their swords in the air and descending upon us. "Get out!"

In the face of such ferocious weapons there was nothing to do but withdraw, so Zell and I went outside to the platform in front of the pavilion where the street cars stopped. Apparently satisfied the police got back into their car and sped away as we stood by the tracks to wait for our Cuban friends. But shortly the ex-pug appeared again and commanded us to leave the area at once, "Scram! Get going!"

"I'll report this to the American consulate," I said, stubborn and angry by now.

"Report it," cried the pug with a series of oaths. "Go ahead. They won't do nothing."

I knew American consulates had seldom been known to fight the battles of colored citizens abroad if Jim Crow were involved.

"I'll do something," said Zell as his fists doubled up again. This time the bouncer slammed the gate and retreated for good into the beach-house. He did not want to fight. Then, in a few moments, with a wail of sirens a large police van swept down the road, stopped in front of us, and a dozen cops leaped out armed to the teeth. This time we were surrounded, hustled into the patrol wagon, and carried off to the nearest station. It happened that the station was in charge of a Negro captain, an enormous, very dark, colored man who listened to the officers' charges against us, wrote them down in his book— and refused to lock us up.

"Wait here for your friends," he said gently. "This is outrageous, but it is what happens to colored people in Cuba where white Americans are in control! This is not the first time there has been trouble at the Havana beach."

Out of breath and quite red in the face after not finding us at the beach, José Antonio arrived shortly, and Zell and I were released from the police station to appear for a hearing on the morrow. To court the next morning the beach authorities sent several Cuban attendants whom we had never seen to present their side of the case to the judge. The attendants swore that Mr. Ingram and I had come into the beach café in our wet bathing suits, had put our feet upon the tables, had used profane langauge, and had otherwise misbehaved to the discomfort of all the more genteel tourists and bathers.

The judge, a kindly old mulatto gentleman—who might have been termed a Negro had he lived in the United States, but who was "white" in Havana—looked at the beach attendants sternly and said, "These gentlemen, I am sure, never set foot on your beach at all. They had no opportunity to change into their bathing suits. They had not been in the water. The police report indicates that they were arrested fully clothed on the street car platform outside. I believe their statement—that you refused to sell tickets to them—and I do not believe your fabrications. What you have done is against all the tenets of Cuban hospitality and against Cuban law, which recognizes no differences because of race or color. These guests on our shores have suffered enough at your hands and deserve an apology. Case dismissed!"

When Zell and I moved on that week to Haiti, our Cuban friends who had invited us to a beach party that never came off, gave instead a farewell lobster supper with wine, music and dancing—so we left Cuba with the rumba throbbing in our ears.

## WATER FRONT HOTEL

HAITI, land of blue sea and green hills, white fishing boats on the sea, and the hidden huts of peasants in the tall mountains. People strong, midnight black. Proud women whose heads bear burdens, whose backs are very straight. Children naked as nature. Nights full of stars, throbbing with Congo drums. At the capital lovely ladies ambergold, mulatto politicians, warehouses full of champagne, banks full of money. A surge of black peasants who live on the land, and the foam of the cultured elite in Port au Prince who live on the peasants.

Port au Prince, city of squalid huts, unattractive sheds and shops near the water front, but charming villas on the slopes that rise behind the port. A presidential palace gleaming white among palm trees with the green hills for a backdrop. A park where bands play at night. An enormous open-air market.

"Ba moi cinc cob," children beg of tourists in the street. Cinc cob means a nickle. They speak a patois French. The upper classes, educated abroad, speak the language of Paris. But I met none of the upper class Haitians. Knowing that my very limited funds would hardly permit such socializing, I did not use the letters of introduction Walter White, William Seabrook, Arthur Spingarn and James Weldon Johnson had given me to the cultural and political elite. In Port au Prince, Zell and I did not go to one of the fashionable hotels back of the city. We went instead to a distinctly nontourist hotel near the port, patronized entirely by Haitians. There were no screens on the windows, but the beds were canopied with thick mosquito netting. It was late April and quite warm. We stayed in Port au Prince about a week, then boarded a dilapidated bus and started out for the storied Citadel. The Citadel at Cap Haitien had always been my goal. Blair Niles and Vandercook, in their excellent books about Haiti, had been filled with wonder regarding this great relic of Negro pride. One of the most astonishing ruins in the New World, the books said, this Citadel on a mountaintop. I had read of Toussaint L'Ouverture, Dessalines, King Christophe, proud black names, symbols of a dream—freedom—building a citadel to guard that freedom.

There are no railroads to Cap Haitien. There was then merely a dirt road from Port au Prince, rebuilt, but badly, by the American Marines. Loaded to the gills, our open bus started out. Its narrow benches made for six people, each held eight or ten persons. Bags and bundles occupied all the floor space. Coops of chickens and boxes of town-bought goods were stacked on top the vehicle. Overloaded until its fenders sank almost onto the tires, the bus started on its twelve-hour trip to the Cape. But it was three weeks before it finally arrived. At St. Marc, midway the island, the road had been completely washed out. A river flowed merrily across it and down to the sea. No traffic could pass. Did this indicate on the part of the U.S. Marines a lack of capacity to build a decent road? Or was it just nature in a primitive country where rains are heavy and the waterslopes steep? Or did the hungry peasants, as some folks whispered, make a change in the water's course and deflect the flood so that it would destroy the road—and thus give them a week or so of well-paid work repairing it again?

Anyhow, our bus drew up at the raging stream roaring across the road, and stopped. A hundred yards or so ahead, across the muddy water, was the highway again, but we couldn't reach it. On both banks peasants had gathered with enormous bunches of bananas for sale, piles of hard-boiled eggs on plantain leaves, and bowls of hot soup. Everybody piled out of the bus. The driver inspected the depth and swiftness of the water. Various plans for crossing were discussed. Men waded into the stream and went down to their knees in mud. It was impossible to cross even on foot or horseback. Finally, as the afternoon wore away, it was decided to give up the bus trip until the flood ceased and the road was mended. The driver would return his whole load of people to Port au Prince. Zell and I decided to remain in St. Marc where, we felt, native life would be more interesting than that of the capital. So the busman drove us to a big frame house on the main road with a sort of New Orleans balcony facing the beach. There we secured rooms.

Our double doors opened directly onto the balcony with a view across a field of golden flowers down to the sea. The whole beach front at St. Marc was covered with brightly yellow blossoms for whose name in patois I found no translation in my French-English dictionary. When we went down to the sea to bathe, I discovered, buried among the bright flowers, the barrels of old cannon and here and there heavy, round iron shot left over, no doubt, from some battle that had taken place on this coast in the distant days when Napoleon's troops had attempted to crush the slave revolt that freed the people and gave them their own rulers.

After three weeks, when the rains at St. Marc had stopped and the road was mended, our bus came back, and its driver remembered to pick us up. He suddenly halted without warning one day, at noon, at the door of our house. This time the bus was so full of people that there did not seem to be an inch in which to crowd another soul. Folks were even riding on top of piles of luggage. Somehow, Ingram and I, with our baggage, pushed in among the chickens, pigs and people, and off we sped in a cloud of dust along the sea road and up into the mountains. The scenery was thrilling, blue ocean far below as we climbed, bright birds, thatched villages, wild coffee plants, sailing white clouds.

Late afternoon came, sunset, dusk, then night. High in the mountains, how far we were from the city of Cap Haitien nobody seemed to know. Then, too, the patois our friendly fellow passengers spoke prevented me from gleaning any clear information. The French I had learned during a year in Paris didn't work here at all. Only a very few words of the friendly chatter about me did I understand. The bus driver spoke a more conventional French, but he was occupied with his steaming motor. The overloaded bus was very rickety and very slow. It made a great noise as it ran, and its springs seemed ready to give away at any time. A few hours after sundown, in the pitch-black of night we ran out of gas. The bus sputtered to a complete halt near the top of a mountain pass. It was quite dark, but the glimmer of starshine was enough for us to discern eventually that all around lay only loneliness and mountain jungle. Not a house or a light. And it was cold high in those hills.

The bus driver got out and inspected his tank. There was a great argument in patois that we couldn't understand. But literal understanding was not necessary to gather from the hubbub that the passengers were angry. To the irate babble of the Haitians, Zell added a few loud and disgusted four-letter words in Harlem English. But there was nothing to do about it. We were stuck there for the night.

Finally the driver and a few of the men took a lantern and went in search of some sign of human habitation. Long after midnight they came back with a couple of sleepy peasants who stood and discussed the situation for an hour. Finally one of the peasants took an empty gasoline can that dangled from the back of the bus and went off in the night in search of gas. When the moon rose over the mountains, it shone with a cool golden light through the heavy foliage. There was no traffic on the road that night. Nothing came or went. Except for the disgusted mutter of an occasional passenger and sharp answer from the driver who must have been as put out as the rest of us, all was quiet.

The high, chill night air penetrated to the bone. Zell and I put on our raincoats but they did not make us any warmer. Finally Zell got on top of the bus and went to sleep between the sacks of rice and the boxes of goods. As I walked up and down the road in the moonlight to keep warm, a few hundred yards away from the stalled bus I came across some large clay culvert pipes. These, I suppose, were there to be placed under the road as drains for the mountain streams that developed during the rainy season. Crawling into one of these pipes as a refuge from the cold, I lay down and went to sleep.

It was long after sunup when the peasant returned lugging a can of gasoline. He had walked I don't know how many kilometers to get it. We greeted him warmly and the driver gave him a few coins. Everybody piled back into the bus and we rattled on up the mountain and down the mountain through thickly wooded country. In midafternoon, we came around a curve on the side of a steep hill and suddenly found ourselves looking at the Atlantic, blue and far away, across a fertile plain of rippling green. But before our bus got down out of the hills it began to rain, without warning. Water suddenly descended in sheets—a heavy tropical cloudburst. Everybody in the bus began to pray that the road *please* be not washed out again within a few miles of our destination.

The open bus had no sides, the top leaked, so we were all drenched to the skin in a matter of minutes. At this point Zell, who had never traveled before outside the confines of the U.S.A., said he wished he had stayed home in Cleveland. Taking three weeks to go less than a hundred miles from Port au Prince to Cap Haitien, sleeping on top of a bus all night in the mountain cold, and eating nothing but bananas all day, Zell said he could stand. But *why in the hell* didn't the bus driver have waterproof curtains for the sides of his no-good conveyance? Why did paying passengers have to sit fully exposed to the wind and weather in a tropical downpour of solid water—like riding through a swimming pool?

"The Haitians are poor people," I said. "Waterproof curtains cost money; that's why the bus driver hasn't got any."

Zell was not interested in Caribbean economics. He was tired, hungry, wet, homesick and mad when we reached Cap Haitien. Water poured through the streets. Rain hit the tin roofs of the houses with a roar like artillery. Each time the bus stopped to discharge drenched passengers, who removed drenched chickens and soaked baggage, it looked as if water would wash the whole world away. Cap Haitien's streets were like rivers.

The bus man kindly took us to the very entrance of a small hotel on the ocean front, all of whose doors and windows were at that moment tightly locked against the storm. The driver kicked on the door. Finally a forlorn and very dark little maid opened it a crack. The driver threw our waterlogged baggage down from the top of the bus and we went in. The hotel wasn't much to look at inside, but it felt good to be out of the rain. We were given a room overlooking the ocean. It had a window with no window panes, only heavy solid wooden shutters, which were tightly closed then, so the room was very dark. We took off our wet clothes and wrung the water out of them. Disgusted, Ingram went to bed. But I was hungry, so I went downstairs to see what time supper would be ready.

This little hotel had only one other guest, a Santo Dominican revolutionary in exile. He was a very fat gentleman in white drill. As soon as I set foot in the bar, he began to tell me, in Spanish, about himself and his political prowess in his homeland across the border. He was overtalkative, but useful. Since I knew Spanish, by medium of that language, when the proprietor came, he translated for me from the Creole the answers to my inquiries about rates and meals. The proprietor of the hotel declared he spoke French, but to my ears it sounded like patois. And to him my French, although it had served me well in Paris, was not understandable. Therefore, the Santo Dominican revolutionary came in handy. Naturally, in return for his services as an interpreter, I offered him a drink.

One of the first things he told me was, "No hay nada a divertirse aquí." There's nothing to do here. "Nothing, but drink." I gathered from him that Cap Haitien was a dull place indeed, and the hotel in which we lived even duller. His description of the hotel was a single dirty word, more polite in French than in Spanish, and not at all acceptable in English.

Certainly that particular afternoon was depressing. The rain continued to come down in torrents until darkness fell. But there was a supper of excellent fresh fish, rice and boiled plantains. After dark things livened up a bit. One or two men and a few girls came in to dance and drink. A talking machine in one corner of the dining room played rumbas, sones, congas, and beguines if someone put a coin in it. The political exile had no money, but he indicated what pieces he liked, and was willing to waddle from the bar to the machine and drop the coins in.

A thin tan-brown girl came and sat down at our table. Her name was Coloma. She was beautiful in a frail wild way, like a brown swamp orchid. She, too, was from Santo Domingo, but she was not a political exile. She was living with a German trader who, at that moment, was away down the coast somewhere. Coloma spoke only Spanish—and from that evening on Zell began to learn Spanish. But I devoted myself to the local patois, for, a few days after the cloudburst, Coloma introduced me to a friend of hers, a chubby little Haitian girl who spoke only patois. This she helped me to learn. Between them, Coloma and Clezie-Anne did their best to make life at Cap Haitien pleasant for us.

The morning sunlight, blazing with a clear white brilliance that hurt the eyes, woke us early every day. Our one window faced directly onto the harbor. Fishing boats dotted the bay, but there were seldom steamers in port. The big French shuttered doors of our room opened onto a balcony that ran entirely around two sides of the hotel, located on a corner. In front of our balcony was a wide grassy area dotted with very tall palm trees. Here fishermen spread their nets to dry in the sun, and market women sometimes stopped to unload their burros and sort out their wares before proceeding to the main part of town. A short distance away was the jail, and early on our first morning, prisoners in stripes were out working on the roads that had overflowed with water the night before.

There was a tap at the door of our room which gave onto an inner balcony overlooking the kitchen and servant's patio below. This tapping was followed by the entrance of Serfina, the barefooted little maid of all work, who came bringing us a pot of coffee, steaming black, that is a pre-breakfast custom in Haiti.

The coffee, the sun, and the view of sea and palms made us feel better after our drenching of the day before. We hung our still-wet clothes on the balcony, and put our damp baggage out there on the floor in the sun, too. Downstairs there was a simple breakfast of rolls and coffee. While Zell took a stool to the balcony to sketch, I went exploring up the main street toward the business section—on which there was but little business—and back along the sea wall to the wide parklike space before our hotel. I sat down with the market women and the fishermen and listened to their chatter, of which I understood not a word for many days. But I began at once to like "au Cap" as the Haitians call that city where the slaves, years ago, planned the revolt that shook the foundations of human bondage in the Western world.

I came to know well the fishermen who beached their boats at the foot of our street, and sometimes I went out with them on the sunny sea to fetch in their haul. I spent hours investigating the ruins of old forts on rocky heights overhanging the sea, and whole days lying in the sunshine on the beach. Almost every night I could hear distant drums far away on the plains across the bay, or possibly very near at hand in some outdoor clearing at the edge of town itself. Not often were these drums playing for voodoo ceremonies—as foreign visitors always seemed to believe. They were usually playing for the conga, or pleasure dances of the peasants, who gathered to scoot barefooted back and forth across the ground, or circle in one spot around each other in movements as old as Africa, to a rhythm as old as the earth.

The Haitian conga dance is, of course, a sex dance undisguised, but the men and women never touch each other. Standing a foot or two apart, solemnly enticing each other as though in a trance. The dancing is too self-centered to be vulgar. Haitian peasant dancing is serious in mood, almost ritualistic, without laughter, and lacking the verve and variety of the Cuban rumba with its humor and inventiveness. The Haitians do not attempt to entertain anyone except themselves. Each man and each woman, even when they dance in couples, seems to be dancing alone.

Of course I am speaking of the barefoot Haitians who dance to the drums. Those who wear shoes and belong to the clerical classes, and who dance indoors to an orchestra with trumpets and strings, dance very much as people do in the United States. And the upperclass Haitians who have lived abroad know all the steps of Broadway and of Paris. But the black Haitians of the soil seem to remember Africa in their souls and far-off ancestral tribes where each man and each woman danced alone.

Real voodoo dances are not easy for tourists to see. I saw only one, deep in the woods near Milot one night in the dark of the moon. The songs were monotonous chants punctuated by long wails. The dancers danced themselves into a kind of trance, not unlike that of our own Deep South revivals. They often leaped high into the air, and came down whirling. And the women kept singing, *"Damballa s'enva a Dondee! Damballa s'enva a Dondee!"* The deep call of the drums shook the air until almost dawn.

Wakes I found more interesting than dances. Death in Haiti is an occasion for joy, or so it would seem to one who did not understand what takes place at a wake. In Cap Haitien often I saw a canopy spread across the street in front of some poor house. Tables of food and drink were set beneath the canopy, gay lights burned, and people gathered for games and refreshments. And at first I would ask, "A party?"

"No," my fishermen friends would answer. "Someone is dead." They explained that the companions of the deceased gathered to play the games and sing the songs the dead person liked, and to eat the food and drink the drinks he would have drunk in life.

Once I went with a fisherman, Destin, to a wake for one of the men from the crew of his own boat. It was at a very small house, too poor to spread a canopy, or to have long tables in the yard, but there was food and drink. The one room of the house had been cleared of furniture. There the dead man lay. Around him stood the men from his fishing boat. Destin joined them. They were singing a song, in patois, about the sea. Over and over they sang the same refrain, joining hands and swinging their arms back and forth like a boat rocking on the waves. Destin translated into French for me what they were saying. It was a very simple song:

> Donne-lui la main pour naviger.
> Mer profonde! Mer profonde!
> Donne-lui la main pour naviger. . . .

> Give him a hand to go to sea.
> Sea so deep! Sea so deep!
> Give him a hand to go to sea.

> Give him a hand to go to sea.
> Sea so blue! Sea so blue!
> Give him a hand to go to sea. . . .

Over and over, as the various attributes of the sea were chanted by the lead singer in short phrases, the deep male voices of the fishermen came in like the boom of waves to cry, "Give him a hand to go to sea."

## DON'T CARRY PARCELS

AT our water-front hotel the food served, although well-cooked, was monotonous in its lack of variety. Fish, rice, beans and boiled plantains over and over. Since we were paying only twenty-five dollars a month for room and board, and since all the other guests ate the same menu and enjoyed it, we had no grounds for complaint. But, tired of this Haitian fare, Zell and I occasionally went to the large general store on Cap Haitien's main street and loaded up with tins of sardines, salmon, baked beans, corn and other supplies of our own, which the cook would prepare for us.

The manager of the hotel did not object to this. He even dined with us at times. But he did object violently to our carrying groceries *in our own hands* down the street. One day he and the Revolutionary Exile sat down at a table with me in the bar and carefully explained that no gentleman should be seen carrying even so much as a loaf of bread in Haiti. Indeed, I had noticed that those persons who wore shoes—a mark of the upper classes—always had trailing behind in the street an adult servant, or a small black boy or girl, to bear their parcels, usually on the head. Even a bar of soap—when persons of the best Haitian society bought soap—the clerk handed, not to the customer, but to a waiting servant. The servant put the soap on his noggin and trotted along barefooted behind his empty-handed master or mistress. The hotel manager seemed shocked to observe that two American gentlemen—evidently young men of means, since we possessed both coats and shoes—should be seen in the public streets with packages in our arms. He had long wanted to warn us about it, he said earnestly. It was something we *must* stop.

"Don't carry parcels."

While he was engaged in correcting my manners, since I took his admonition amiably, he went on to say that furthermore he had noticed both Mr. Ingram and myself sitting in the grassy open space in front of the hotel *on the ground* talking with market women and fishermen, and even playing with their children—or worse, engaged in dominoes with the barefooted wharf workers who hung out on the sea wall! These things, the hotel manager explained, simply *were not done* in Haiti by persons of our standing. He, the manager, who was also a lawyer, would be glad to introduce us to his friends with whom, he was sure, we would have much more in common.

I was pleased to accept the manager's offer, I said politely. But at the same time, I argued with him that I did not see why, since I was interested in the folk life of the Haitian people, I should not associate with whom I pleased—especially since the better-class Haitians neither knew how to play drums nor dance the conga. The parties at the homes of his friends, I was sure, were very much like the parties of educated people everywhere. I tried to tell the hotel manager that one can drink champagne and talk about Proust or Gide in New York. But one cannot see a conga dance there or attend a wake with tables set in the yard for games of cards. But he got up and went away shaking his head.

I did meet some of his friends, however, and found them pleasant fellows, a few of whom had studied English and read American Negro newspapers and magazines. I was afraid then that someone might recognize my name or know my poetry, for I did not want to be lionized in Haiti, nor have my days filled with invitations to dine with people who could not play drums. I wanted to be lazy, lie on the beach as long as I liked, talk with whom I pleased, go to cockfights on Sundays, sail with the fishermen, and never wear a coat.

Coats and shoes in Haiti! With the mercury at a hundred in the shade, our hotel manager went around all day with his coat on. For an educated Haitian to dress otherwise was unheard of at the Cap. If you *possessed* a coat and a pair of shoes, you *always* wore them—for fear people would think you had none, and thus class you with the peasants whose incomes never encompassed such finery.

Another thing which disturbed me and made me shy away from formal Haitian society was the color line between the mulattoes and the blacks. In this, and in the aloofness with which the "best people" held themselves away from the workers, I was reminded strongly of my years in Washington where Negro society, too, was stratified—the government workers, college professors and schoolteachers considering themselves much better than the usually darker (although not always poorer) people who work with their hands. I hated this attitude. And, in Haiti of all places—with its thrilling history of the slaves who drove the French into the ocean and freed themselves—to find people divided by the lightness or darkness of one's skin, and whether or not one was able to afford shoes—well, I personally preferred the people without shoes.

When the manager brought up the subject again, I smiled and gently reminded him that he had a shoeless mistress—for he often spent the night at the hotel with a very pretty barefooted girl instead of going home to his wife and family. His mistress, a lithe chocolate-brown teen-ager from the hills, had not been in the city long.

"Ah, but women—that is different," said the hotel manager. "They are young, vigorous, sweet as mangoes, these little peasant girls! But I never go on the street with her! Never!"

The servants at the hotel were all former peasants. One day Zell and I sat on the inner balcony around the courtyard, pounding away on two big voodoo drums we had bought, trying to learn to play them with our bare fingers as the Haitians do. Just when we were beginning to master a simple rhythm, the manager came rushing up the stairs scolding in his patois French. "S'il vous-plaît, messieurs! Kindly do not play the drums! Please! It upsets the servants. They hear the drums and they cannot work. Drums are not for gentlemen, anyway."

"Let's get out of this hotel," Zell said to me in English, "before I paste him one."

By then we had been in Haiti most of the summer. Our money was running low—we had less than a hundred dollars left between us—but we had seen everything of interest in and around Cap Haitien. Zell had made a large number of sketches, water colors, and figures in wood, and had designed a wood-block cover for my one and only privately printed book of poems, Dear Lovely Death, which Amy Spingarn was preparing on her hand press at Troutbeck. I had lain in the Haitian sun day after day baking out all the cold and confusion of a bewildering New York winter. Now I was ready to write again. Just where I would get the money to sit down at home and write, I did not know, but in the back of my head was Mrs. Bethune's suggestion, "Read your poems to the students of the South." Perhaps I could earn enough from such programs to plan for a period of writing. In August, Zell and I decided to make one more pilgrimage to the Citadel where we had been twice, then head for home.

## PEOPLE WITHOUT SHOES

THE Citadel is in ruins. But it is one of the lustiest ruins in the world, rearing its husky shoulders out of a mountain with all the strength of the dreams that went into its making more than a century ago.

The immensity of the Citadel, towering on a mountain peak whose slopes would create a problem for modern builders, is beyond belief. A hundred years ago, when motors and machinery were lacking, the transporting of its gigantic stones from the plain below, and the rearing of its walls, was one of the great feats in the history of human energy and determination. The fact that beauty as well as strength went into its making is cause for further wonderment, for the Citadel is majestic, graceful in every proportion, with wide inner staircases and noble doorways of stone, curving battlements, spacious chambers and a maze of intricate cellars, dungeons, terraces and parade grounds.

Dessalines began the Citadel, and it was sixteen years in the building. In 1804, standing before his troops with the tricolor of blue, white and red in his hands, Dessalines suddenly tore the French flag into three parts and let the white part fall to the ground. Haiti, he said, would never again be dominated by whites. When Dessalines was killed, Christophe carried on the building of the Citadel. Three thousand feet above sea level the fortress rose stone by stone, cannon by cannon, passed by hand up the steep slopes. When Christophe died, Haiti became a republic. But its upper classes developed a political caste that ruled badly—yet no worse than many another ruling class in other lands. But in 1915 the American Marines came to Haiti to collect American loans, and were there when I came. Haiti was a land of people without shoes—black people, whose feet walked the dusty roads to market in the early morning, or trod softly on the bare floors of hotels, serving foreign guests. Barefooted ones tending the rice and cane fields under the hot sun, climbing mountain slopes, picking coffee beans, wading through surf to fishing boats on the blue sea. All of the work that kept Haiti alive, paid the interest on American loans, and enriched foreign traders, was done by people without shoes.

Yet shoes were things of great importance in Haiti, as our hotel manager indicated. Everyone of any social or business position *must* wear them. To be seen barefooted marked one a low-caste person of no standing. In a country where the climate would permit everyone to go naked in comfort, officials, professional men, clerks and teachers had to swelter in dignity with coats buttoned about their bellies on even the hottest days. Strange, bourgeois and a little pathetic, I found this accent on clothes and shoes in an undeveloped land, where the average wage was then thirty cents a day, and where the sun blazed like fury. Articles of clothing in Haiti were not cheap. Taxes were high, jobs scarce, wages low, so the doubtful step upward to the dignity of leather between one's feet and the earth, or a coat between one's body and the sun, was a step not easily to be achieved. But perhaps a coat and a pair of shoes had more meaning than that inherent in their mere possession. And perhaps that meaning was something carried over from the long-ago days of the white masters, who wore coats and shoes —and had force and power. Perhaps they were symbols.

Most of Haiti's people without shoes could not read or write, and had no power. They lived in thatched huts or rickety houses; rose with the sun; went to sleep with the dark. They washed their clothes in running streams with lathery weeds—too poor to buy soap. On holidays they danced to the Saints and the Voodoo Gods all mixed up together. Foreign ships came into Haitian harbors, dumped goods, and sailed away with the raw materials of black labor—cocoa beans, coffee, sugar, dyewoods, fruits and rice. The mulatto upper classes educated their sons and daughters abroad. And because black hands touched the earth, gathered in the fruits, and loaded the ships, the elite became richer and more cultured, taught their children to read and write, to travel, to be superior, to wear coats and shoes.

It was in Haiti that I first realized how class lines may cut across color lines within a race, and how dark people of the same nationality may scorn those below them. Certainly the upper-class Haitians I observed at a distance seemed a delightful and cultured group. No doubt, many of the French slave owners were delightful and cultured, too— but the slaves could not enjoy their culture.

On my first Sunday evening in Port au Prince, in the Champs de Mars, before the Presidential Palace a band played immortally outworn music while well-dressed people strolled round and round the brilliance of the lighted bandstand. Lovely chocolate and amber girls in cool dresses, and brown men in white suits, passed and repassed. But I saw no peasants.

I asked a Haitian in the crowd that night, "Where are all the people without shoes? I don't see any of them."

"Oh, they can't walk here," he said. "The police would drive them away."

## OFFICIAL DELEGATION

JACQUES ROUMAIN, the poet, was then one of the few cultured Haitians who appreciated native folklore, and who became a friend of the people without shoes. Walter White had given me a letter to Jacques Roumain for, since he was a writer, I wanted to meet him. (Years later I translated his *Masters of the Dew*.) Of an aristocratic Haitian family, Roumain held a post in the cabinet and was a friend to the President. So when I found myself again in Port au Prince, feeling that I had to dress up for the occasion, I put on my only coat to go and meet him and had my shoes shined.

Zell and I were returning from Cap Haitien to Cuba on a Dutch boat, traveling as deck passengers with no accommodations, neither food nor shelter, since our passage provided for nothing save space in the open air, where we might lie down on the hard iron deck. Usually none but sugar-cane cutters traveled this way from port to port. To unload cargo, the boat stopped only a day in the Haitian capital, so I decided to present the letter Walter White had given me to Roumain. It was blazing hot; nevertheless, besides my coat I put on a white shirt and tie. Zell, declaring it was too warm to go ashore, stayed aboard ship stretched out on the afterdeck in nothing more than a pair of old trousers.

On the way to Roumain's home I stopped to see a girl I had met on my previous visit to Port au Prince, and with whom I had spent a few days. She remembered me and seemed overjoyed to see me back, but melancholy to know that I was sailing at sunset. As I left her, she said she would be on the dock to see me off.

When I got to Jacques Roumain's house, he was not at home, but his charming and very pretty wife, Nicole, received me. Jacques, she said, was at the Palace, but she would telephone him to come at once. She did. And shortly he arrived, a handsome copper-brown young man with the deep fiery eyes of a picture-book poet. For an hour, in French

—mine halting, and in English—his bad, we talked about poetry and people. Jacques showed me his excellent library in many languages with the cloth and board bindings of America and England mingling with the bright paper covers of France and Germany. From his hill-side windows we looked out on the town and harbor of Port au Prince, and the slums of the port were beautiful from so far away.

My host wanted me to meet the President of the Republic and other officials of the government, as well as the various writers of the capital, so he was distressed to hear that I was sailing that very after-noon. That I had been in Haiti all summer and he had not known it disturbed him even more. He invited me to come again to the island and to accept the hospitality of himself and his friends. And he made me a present of his poems. I descended the hill thinking that if the delightful Roumains were typical representatives of the Haitian elite, then I regretted not having met more of them.

Down in the sweltering town again, I took off my coat and tie. I stopped at the market and bought a couple of loaves of French bread, a long greasy sausage, some cheese and some tinned sardines because, since Zell and I had only deck passage, we could not even purchase bread from the ship's dining salon. We had to have enough to eat all the way to Cuba, and there was no telling how many ports a cargo ship might stop at en route, perhaps anchoring miles out in the water with no way of going ashore to buy food. I bought fruit, too, and a bottle of wine. Thus laden, back I started toward the wharf. The sun, heading west, was still blazing. Sweat poured from me. For cinq cob a street urchin offered to help me, so gratefully I let him put the bread and sausage under his sweaty arms, and the cheese on his head, and he trotted behind me toward the pier.

As I went up the rickety gangplank, the winches were rattling and the cranes lifting swinging crates of cargo through the air. I found Zell on deck aft, where I dumped my packages on a closed hatch and pro-ceeded to undress, putting my clothes in my suitcase in exchange for the oldest and dirtiest pair of trousers I had—in preparation for a night on the bare deck. It was so hot that I removed both shirt and under-shirt. If the iron deck had not seemed like a griddle, I would have taken off my shoes. As it was, I removed my socks and rolled up my pants legs.

We were both hungry, so while I had stripped down to my ragged trousers, Zell spread on a newspaper our supper of cheese, sausage, bread and wine, with a bunch of bananas for dessert. He filled a couple of tin cups with tepid water from the tap, and we sat down on a shady corner of the deck to eat while cargo winches clanked and bales of sisal swung overhead. The sausage was good but greasy. We had neither forks nor napkins. Our hands were greasy and our bodies sweaty as we dined.

In the midst of the meal a ship's officer appeared and asked our names. "Hughes?" he queried. "I have been looking all over the cabin passenger lists for a Hughes. Which is he?"

I admitted to owning that name. "Why?"

"There's a delegation here to see you," said the officer. "I thought they were looking for a first-class passenger. But I'll send them back here."

Wending his way between swinging cargo and shouting stevedores, ducking and watching his head as hampers of coffee beans swung up and over and across the deck then down into an open hatch, the ship's officer disappeared up the iron steps to the main deck. In a few seconds he reappeared at the top of the steps and pointed through a heat haze at Zell and me, half-naked on the afterdeck. Then to my amazement, descending those iron stairs to wend their way through stevedores and cargo, I saw approaching a long line of elegantly dressed gentlemen, some in tail coats and gloves, followed by a number of dark porters and barefoot boys bearing parcels and baskets. I had no idea who they were, but as they approached, I recognized among them Jacques Roumain. As a member of the Ministry of Education, he had assembled a group of Haitian writers and government officials to pay me honor at the last moment and to present me with bon voyage gifts. To receive these gentlemen, I had hardly time even to wipe my mouth, let alone put on a shirt or coat. I was caught greasy-handed, half-naked—and soxless—by an official delegation of leading Haitians.

I arose from my table on the cargo hatch, wiped my hands on my trousers, and was introduced by Roumain as "the greatest Negro poet who had ever come to honor Haitian soil." Each man bowed gravely. I bowed, too. We shook hands, and I introduced them all to Zell Ingram. Then from their package bearers, they took baskets of fruit, bottles of Babancourt rum, books of verse and gifts of Haitian handicraft, which were presented to me. In the midst of this ceremony another guest arrived, but she was not allowed aboard ship. Instead my girl of the morning stood at the dockside calling my name in an insistent feminine voice. I waved, blew a kiss at her, and asked Zell to go to the ship's rail as my emissary—since I was at that moment engaged with an official delegation. The girl looked with astonishment at the elegant gentlemen surrounding me on deck and waited until later to present her gifts. Meanwhile, someone made a little speech in French, welcoming me to Haitian soil and, at the same time, bidding me good-bye, for by now the winches had stopped rattling, the last hatch was being closed, and the stevedores were going ashore. The boat was about to sail.

Jacques Roumain and his friends in government and the arts withdrew to the pier. I went to the ship's rail where, until the boat pulled out, I talked alternately with them and with the Haitian girl whose presents of guava jelly and fruit I put on the hatch along with my other bon voyage gifts.

As the boat lifted anchor to glide slowly out into the Caribbean, the sun was setting behind the hills. I stood on the poop deck over the churning rudder to wave farewell to the folks on the dock—Jacques Roumain, who was to become Haiti's most famous writer, the elegant gentlemen of his delegation, and the girl of the town who had come to see me off.

When the dock was quite out of sight, with Haiti and the sunset almost lost on the rim of the horizon, Zell and I went back to our supper on the hatch. The ship headed for the open sea.

## IT WASN'T MALARIA

ZELL and I had very little money left between us when we sighted Cuba—scarcely forty dollars—and it is a long way from the Caribbean to New York. Six months before, we had started out with about three hundred dollars each, and we had been all summer in Haiti. We had intended to start back sooner, but lingered and lazed at the Cap instead. In July, when we had bestirred ourselves to inquire about deck passage to Cuba, Zell announced that he'd spent all his money. He had written his mother for an additional hundred dollars, but got no answer. August came and we were down to far less than that amount between us, stuck in Cap Haitien.

Zell's mother was a wonderful little woman who adored her only son and was quite willing to help him become the artist he wanted to be. In Cleveland she had worked for the same white family for many years. She kept a little apartment for herself and Zell in the Central Avenue district, and had a small car which she had lent Zell to go to Haiti. She also gave him the money she had intended for his second year in art school. This, he assured her, was enough for the round trip to the Caribbean, as well as for paints and paper. Zell's mother, who had learned to read and write after her son was in his teens, and who eventually graduated from evening school, did not have the least idea where Haiti was. So when Zell ran out of funds at midsummer and wrote his mother for an additional amount to come home, she felt enough was enough! She simply wrote back:

Son:

I give you Three Hundred Dollars once. I lent you my car. You drove to Haiti. Now you get in my car and drive on back home.

Your mother,

Daisy

Zell was depressed by this reply. Since I did not have enough money to pay both of our passages, he simply resigned himself to remaining in Haiti and urged me to go on without him. I, in turn, urged him to write his mother one more time, explaining to her that Haiti was across the water, that the car was a sea span away in Florida, and would she please forgive his miscalculation and send him post haste enough to reach the mainland. In fact, I even dictated the letter.

It worked, at least partially. Zell's mother sent him fifty dollars. But by then the boat we had planned to take from Cap Haitien had come and gone. No other vessel accepting deck passengers was due for weeks. We had to wait. When the next cargo boat finally arrived from Holland via the Virgin Islands, Puerto Rico and the Dominican Republic, it came into port way behind schedule, and before it got there, no one knew from day to day exactly when it was coming.

When the ship did not arrive on schedule, Zell decided to spend the extra time until it came at the home of the pretty and passionate Dominican, Coloma, whose German lover had recently died of the fever. Indeed, Coloma urged him to move in with her, bag and baggage. Zell, who had never lived in sin in residence with a woman before, vowed he would make love to her every night until the boat arrived. But neither he nor Coloma expected this interlude to last as long as it did. Nineteen days and nineteen nights went by before the Dutch boat finally reached Haiti. When Zell and I embarked from the Cap, his girl, Coloma, and mine, Clezie-Anne, were weeping at the dockside. As a lighter took us out to the steamer anchored in the harbor, they sobbed aloud.

The next morning we were at Port au Prince, then Leogane and Jeremie for a day each, before heading for Santiago de Cuba. Crossing the Windward Passage, in the middle of the night while we were asleep on deck, the ship ran headlong into a sudden September squall. The clouds burst and the wind whistled. With dozens of other deck passengers, we were rain-soaked, wind-tossed, and in danger of being washed off the open deck into the sea by the mounting waves. Finally the chief mate allowed us all a crowded shelter between decks where the ship's supplies, ropes and chains, were stored. There, with some fifty seasick peasants squatting in the dark waiting for day, the heat and stench were almost unbearable. But at least we were not whipped by wind and rain as we had been.

At Santiago de Cuba, the immigration authorities did not know what to make of two American Negroes traveling on the open deck, unable to display between us as much as fifty dollars. They argued that only sugar cane workers traveled in that fashion. Therefore, since we had no working permits, they refused to allow us on Cuban soil until we posted bonds. We were consigned to Santiago's "Ellis Island," a jail-like fortress in the harbor, zooming with mosquitoes, crawling with bedbugs, and alive with fleas. I indignantly dispatched a note to the American consul, but it was three days before that worthy found time to row out in a small boat to the Immigration Station and rescue us. We were released only on the condition that we cross the island immediately, embark at once for Florida, and not stop anywhere to work in Cuba.

When Zell and I reached Havana, we were dog-tired, having gotten almost no sleep for the past week on the iron boat deck or in that vermin-infested Immigration Station. We went to the same hotel we'd stopped at before, intending to leave Havana the next day for Key West. But the following morning at breakfast time, Zell did not move from his bed.

"Come on, let's eat," I called. "Get up, old man."

Zell groaned, "I can't get up."

"What?" I cried. "How come you can't get up?"

"I'm weak," he said in a remote voice. "I can't get up. I think I've got the fever."

I felt his brow, but in that hot climate, anyone's head would feel hot, so I was unable to tell whether he had a fever or not. Zell was a healthy fellow who, during our entire trip, had never behaved like this. I was worried.

"Maybe you'll feel better later," I said as I went downstairs for coffee. When I came back Zell was still in bed. He looked up at me like a dying calf.

"Lang, I swear I can't get up."

Frightened, I asked if he thought he needed a doctor. He whispered, "Yes."

Since Zell spoke almost no Spanish, I phoned José Antonio and asked him to recommend a physician who understood English. I requested that he explain to the doctor that we were not wealthy tourists —in fact, that we were almost broke. About noon an English-speaking Cuban physician arrived. He examined Zell, and promptly announced that he had a bad attack of malaria—fever and ague as my grandmother called it in Kansas. I concluded that the mosquitoes at Santiago's "Ellis Island" had done Zell in. The doctor gave me two prescriptions to have filled, and ordered an ice pack for the patient's head. His bill was five dollars. The prescriptions and ice bag cost another six dollars. An additional night in the hotel became necessary, too, since by sunset Zell had not yet gotten enough strength to get out of bed. All of this unexpected expense meant that we would have scarcely twenty dollars left to get all the way from Havana to New York.

A big husky young Negro like Zell—why did he have to get sick at this point? He had been a football player at my high school, Central, in Cleveland. He had been graduated several years after my class, but he knew all my former teachers and we enjoyed talking about our Alma Mater. He had painted scenery for Karamu and worked in the arts and crafts department, teaching youngsters in the late afternoons after his own classes at the Cleveland School of Art were over. Russell and Rowena Jelliffe, the executives of Karamu House, had introduced me to Zell, saying they considered him a very talented young man.

He was a solid, amiable, easygoing fellow who had grown up, as I had, in the slums of Cleveland. Seldom aroused to anger, but of a rambunctious nature when he was aroused, Zell had had to be restrained from fighting the bouncer at the Jim Crow beach in Havana. And, shortly after our arrival at Cap Haitien, Coloma had to employ intense persuasion to keep him from attacking her German lover, when that peddler returned unexpectedly to find his mistress not at home. Hearing that she was having an affair with some foreigner, but not knowing whom, the German headed for our water front hotel to spend the better part of the night in the lobby with a pistol in his pocket. The Revolutionary Exile came upstairs and whispered to Coloma what was in the offing. Zell immediately wanted to challenge him to a "let the best man win" fist fight, but Coloma, knowing on which side her bread was buttered and who paid her rent, did not wish this to happen. In rapid Spanish she asked me to translate to Zell that wisdom demanded other action. She would climb over the balcony, slide quietly down a pillar, follow the water front home, and be there when the German returned. Thus Coloma made her exit. A few weeks later the man died. After that, Coloma had no friend but Zell, whom she loved, and whose departure for home left her dissolved in tears.

"*Que homre, este negro!*" she often said. "Tell him I said, '*What a man!*'"

"Translate to her she's a sweet chick," Zell said, so I did the best I could with that colloquialism. Coloma and Clezie-Anne giggled at our linguistic difficulties.

In the hotel bar there was one record, "*Lamento Esclavo*," that we all liked a lot. It was a haunting kind of beguine with a strange sad lyric about slavery and freedom set against insistent drums and voluptuous maracas:

> Soy Lucumi cautivo
> Sin la libertad no vivo.
> Ay, mi negra Pancha,
> Vamos a bailar—
> Que los negros libres
> Algun dia sera,
> Los negros libres sera!

Often to this music and the ecstatic rolling of the beguine, the Haitian midnights came to the little bar in our hotel on the water front. As the barefoot housekeeper began to turn out the lights to lock up for the night, she would shout in patois, "All's not going out, get in some stall till morning,"—her way of saying to the girls, "Go on upstairs with your boy friends." But when Zell thought the boat was coming to take him to Cuba, not wanting to waste a moment, he moved across the street with Coloma.

In Havana, I had to go a long way to the pharmacy to fill the prescriptions the doctor had given to Zell. As I waited at the drugstore and walked back to the hotel, I thought of those nights in Cap Haitien. On my return to our room I gave my ailing companion his medicine and put an ice bag on his head. He slept most of the day until I left in the evening for dinner with Fernandez de Castro. When I returned about midnight, Zell was still sleeping like a log, so I did not wake him up to give him his medicine. But bright and early the next morning he bounded out of bed seemingly as good as new, ate an enormous breakfast, threw the ice bag away, and never took another dose of the two prescriptions that had cost almost a third of our meager funds to secure. It turned out that Zell had neither fever or ague.

"I reckon I was just tired," he said. "You know—a woman like Coloma! Man, who would've thought it would take that boat nineteen days to show up at Cap Haitien?"

# 2

# POETRY TO
# THE PEOPLE

**MARY McLEOD BETHUNE**

WHEN Zell and I got to Miami, we found the car unmovable. In storage through the long summer heat, the tires had gone flat. The rims of the wheels had cut through one of them and damaged the others. To get the car out, buy a secondhand tire and four new inner tubes, took all the money we had. We had to pawn my camera and everything else, except the two Haitian voodoo drums we had lugged from the Cap. These drums we would not part with under any circumstances. The pawnshops did not consider Zell's paintings of any cash value. Neither did the secondhand tire dealer. I had thirty-four dollars in the bank in New York, but I knew no one in Miami through whom I could cash a check. We were broke—and exactly 1,383 miles from New York.

"All I know to do," I said, "is use what little change we have left for a few gallons of gas to get to Daytona. There I'm sure Mrs. Bethune will cash a check for me at her college."

We starved all the way to Daytona, more than half the length of Florida. But once there, Mrs. Bethune received us cordially, sat us down to dinner, and cashed a thirty-dollar check without question.

"Boys," said Mrs. Bethune, "I was intending to go North myself in a few days by train, so I might as well ride with you and save that fare."

Our little Ford coupe had only one seat, a rather small seat at that. Mrs. Bethune was no small woman. Zell was stocky, too. How the three of us, in hot September weather, would fare on a single seat in a small car all the way from Daytona to Manhattan, I could not surmise.

"We'll make it," Mrs. Bethune said.

With America's leading Negro woman as our passenger, we hit the road early the next morning and drove all day toward the Carolinas. What luck for us! All along the highway, Mary McLeod Bethune had friends. So whenever we got hungry on the road, we stopped at the home of some friends of hers in some Southern village. According to a popular saying in Florida, before Mrs. Bethune reached the wayside home of any friend anywhere, the chickens, sensing that she was coming, went flying off frantically seeking a safe hiding place. They knew some necks would surely be wrung in her honor to make a heaping platter of Southern fried chicken. Colored folks all along the Eastern seaboard spread a feast whenever Mary McLeod passed their way. Zell and I ate well on that trip. We didn't have to spend a penny for food or lodging. When nightfall came, the leading Negroes in the nearest town on the highway, with no advance warning other than a knock on the door, would roll out the red carpet for Mrs. Bethune and ourselves.

"A poet! An artist! What an honor! You always were interested in young people, Mary McLeod. Come in, make yourselves at home! Have you eaten yet? Do you want a bath? We'll get the beds ready whenever you-all get sleepy." And so it went, genial Southern hospitality all the way to Washington.

Mrs. Bethune, aside from her fame in educational circles, was a power in lodge and club activities. She was known far and wide at conclaves, conventions and church meetings. She had spoken at every colored school in the South, too. People loved her, so they showed it by offering her their best. That best, tired and hungry Zell and I shared on this journey. We shared Mrs. Bethune's wit and wisdom, too, the wisdom of a jet-black woman who had risen from a barefooted field hand in a cotton patch to be head of one of the leading junior colleges in America, and a leader of her people. She was a wonderful sport, riding all day without complaint in our cramped, hot little car, jolly and talkative, never grumbling.

We avoided segregation by not having to seek food or sleeping accommodations in public places along the Southern highways. But we did have to get gas and sometimes use the gas-station rest rooms, usually one for MEN, one for LADIES—and a single one marked COLORED somewhere away out in the back for both men and women, if Negro. To the attendant at such stations, Mrs. Bethune would usually say, "Young man, do I have to avail myself of that shanty rest room away around there in the bushes?"

If there were no whites about, the embarrassed attendant might say, "Ma'am, just use the one marked LADIES." But if the station were busy, he would indicate that the COLORED toilet was meant for her. Then Mrs. Bethune would say gently, "Aren't you ashamed, young man?"

The young man would usually turn red and answer, "Yes, ma'am, I really am."

We arrived one day at Cheraw, South Carolina, just before noon. Mrs. Bethune said, "Let's stop at Coulter Academy and dine with the teachers, Langston, and you read some of your poems for the students."

We pulled up before a large frame building. As soon as the teachers and students saw Mrs. Bethune getting out of the car, word spread and commotion began. Classes greeted her with applause and an assembly for the whole school was ordered. She made a warmhearted little talk, then introduced me as a poet whom she wanted the South to know better. I read the students a few of my poems, and was gratified at the warm response they received.

"You see," said Mrs. Bethune as we drove away, "you must go all over the South with your poems. People need poetry."

## TRAGEDY AT HAMPTON

IN New York the depression was in full sway. Had I started looking for work, a job would have been hard to find. Thousands were out of work. But I did not want a job. I wanted to continue to be a poet. Yet sometimes I wondered if I was barking up the wrong tree. I determined to find out by taking poetry, my poetry, to my people. After all, I wrote about Negroes, and primarily for Negroes. Would they have me? Did they want me?

Mrs. Bethune had said, "They need poetry."

Sitting half hungry in my tiny room in the West 135th Street Y in Harlem, her words encouraged me to do something about it. I got a *Negro Year Book* from the nearest library. In it is a list of educational institutions, so I began to write to the presidents of all the Negro colleges in the South. Almost immediately answers came back from several institutions, offering to book me. My next problem would be how to get to these colleges. I had heard of the Rosenwald Fund to aid Negro education, so I wrote a letter outlining my plan for a tour of the South. The Rosenwald Fund granted me a thousand dollars toward the reading of my poems at educational centers.

I bought a Ford. But I could not drive and I had no license. I found a former classmate of mine at Lincoln University, Radcliffe Lucas, who was then a part-time Red Cap at the Pennsylvania Station. He could drive, and had a good business head, I knew, because he had worked his way through college running a weekend taxi service from Lincoln's campus in the country to South Street in Philadelphia.

"Raddie, how would you like to make a tour of the South with me reading poetry and you driving?" I proposed. "You can be my business manager, and we'll share the profits."

Raddie said, "It beats being a Red Cap in these tipless times. Let's go."

So we set out about five o'clock one October morning, headed South. The back seat of the car was filled with luggage and books of mine to sell on tour. I carried along also a large number of books by other contemporary Negro writers for a cultural exhibit. As we left Harlem, the sun was rising. All was well.

My first engagement Monday was at Downingtown, a colored boarding school in Pennsylvania. The youngsters, mostly country kids, seemed to like my poetry. They gave me a big hand. We spent the night at Downingtown, but had to get up at dawn the next morning for a ten o'clock assembly at Morgan College in Baltimore—a very early hour for people to be listening to poetry. But they gave me a big hand, too. That afternoon I read my poems to some English classes at Howard University in Washington. Then we drove into Virginia through the bright red and gold of autumn. At Richmond the students of Union were cordial. And at Virginia State College in Ettrick I saw hanging in a place of honor a large picture of my great-uncle, John Mercer Langston, first president of the college. At Hampton Institute, Booker T. Washington's alma mater, on Friday night, I faced my first large audience, more than a thousand Negro students, a sea of dark faces before me. Spontaneous applause followed many of my poems, and at the end of the program the students gave me an ovation. Thus ended my first week on tour.

Hampton is the most beautiful of Negro campuses, green and lovely, surrounded by inlets from the bay. I was invited to spend the weekend there. It was that weekend that I first met Dorothy Maynor, then a chubby teen-age student choir singer with long black curls. My meeting with her was the beginning of a realization that I was in the South, the troubled Jim Crow South of ever-present danger for Negroes. That weekend two tragic things happened.

Juliette Derricotte, former traveling YWCA executive, beloved of all girl students and then Dean of Women at Fisk University, away from her campus on a speaking trip, had been seriously injured in an automobile wreck on a country road in Georgia. She had been denied treatment at the nearest hospital, a white hospital, and had died before she could be driven to a colored hospital miles away. And that Saturday afternoon a former Hampton athlete, just graduated the spring before and now coaching at Alabama Normal College for Negroes, had been beaten to death by a Southern mob on the way to see his football team play their first game of the season. Dorothy Maynor had known and admired both these people, as had the entire Hampton student body, so the whole campus mourned—and all were horrified at the manner in which their friends had died, victims of Southern prejudice.

Early on Saturday evening it was Dorothy Maynor who brought me the news of these tragic events. I had never seen Miss Maynor before word came to my rooms in Holly Tree Inn that a student wished to see me in the lobby. There stood Dorothy with a troubled face. When the news of the two deaths, with segregation and mob violence involved, had reached Hampton, a group of students had met after supper and decided to hold a memorial protest meeting in the chapel. Dorothy Maynor had been chosen to come and ask if I would speak. As the leading soloist of the student chorus under Nathaniel Dett, Dorothy Maynor was a popular campus figure, but her voice was not yet known in the great concert halls, and I had never heard her name.

Now she stood before me almost in tears, protesting, "A woman like Juliette Derricotte, such a noble woman! How could any hospital refuse to take her in, injured, bleeding—just because she's colored? And one of our football stars beaten to death by an Alabama mob because he parked his car in a white parking lot by mistake!"

Juliette Derricotte I had known in New York and Paris, and I had found her a charming and cultured woman. That she should die of injuries, neglected on a Georgia road because the medical facilities of the South were segregated, horrified me, too. It just did not make sense—not *decent, humane* sense, at any rate. Of course, I would speak at the student protest meeting. Just let me know what time, I told Miss Maynor.

But no such meeting was held at Hampton. The elderly white and Negro heads of the Institute would not permit the students to hold a protest meeting. They—and I—were told at a student committee gathering, "That is not Hampton's way. We educate, not protest."

So on Sunday I left Hampton, sadder and wiser concerning Southern Negro education. The further I penetrated into the Deep South, the sadder I became in this regard. The old abolitionist spirit out of which, during the Civil War and in Reconstruction times, many Negro colleges had grown, had now turned strangely conservative in regard to contemporary problems. It was the year of the Scottsboro case, 1931, yet on many Negro campuses the nine black teen-agers on trial for their lives in Alabama were not even to be mentioned.

"We educate, not protest."

## COLOR AT CHAPEL HILL

IN Virginia I ran into an incident of Jim Crowism more amusing than serious. It was a very warm day driving, and Raddie and I became thirsty. We spotted a roadside refreshment hut so I suggested we pull up there and I would jump out and get some cold sodas. Since I knew we could not eat or drink inside—there is legal Jim Crow in Virginia —it was my intention to purchase the cool drinks and bring them out to the car. But when I put my hand on the knob of the screen door it did not open. I pulled on the door again and discovered to my amazement that a white man just inside was holding the door.

He shouted through the screen, "What do you want?"

I said, "I'd like some sodas."

He said, "Get 'em through the hole."

Puzzled, I said, "What hole?"

He answered, "We got a hole cut for you-all people on the side."

He continued determinedly to hold the door, so I went around the side of the little frame building and there, sure enough, with a sign marked COLORED above it, was a square hole in the wall through which Negroes were served. I did not buy, but I had to laugh. The strange, silly pathetic South!

In North Carolina I spent almost the whole month of November giving programs of my poems. And from the playwright, Paul Green, and the sociologist, Guy B. Johnson, I received a cordial invitation to appear at the University of North Carolina. About a week before I was scheduled to arrive at Chapel Hill, I received a note from a student, Anthony Buttita, asking me to be the guest of himself and his roommate, Milton Abernathy. Buttita said that since the white state University would not house a Negro on the campus, being dyed-in-the-wool Southern, he wanted to show me there were students who did not believe in such stupidities. I accepted Buttita's invitation. He and Abernathy ran a little bookshop near the campus and published an unofficial student paper called Contempo. In connection with my coming, they had requested a poem or an article of mine to publish in their paper. I promptly sent them a poem and an article, both about the then famous Scottsboro Case. They printed my two contributions on the front page of Contempo which was distributed all over the campus the day I arrived. I was as surprised as were most of the Southerners at Chapel Hill, to see my work in Contempo.

My article, a satirical one, was called "Southern Gentlemen, White Women, and Black Boys." Since the Scottsboro Case concerned nine Negro youths accused of raping two white prostitutes in an open coal car on a freight train traveling through Alabama, I inquired in the piece why chivalrous Southern gentlemen allowed their women to ride in a coal car in the first place, even if the women were of doubtful character. By the time I reached the town of Chapel Hill the daily papers had reproduced my "inflammatory" lines, and the white citizenry were claiming mortal insult. When they learned that I was to stop overnight with two white students, Buttita and Abernathy had been promptly ejected from their lodgings, and had nowhere to stay themselves.

My poem, "Christ in Alabama," on the front page of Contempo created even more excitement than did my article. It was an ironic poem inspired by the thought of how Christ, with no human father, would be accepted were He born in the South of a Negro mother, and it ended:

> Most Holy Bastard
> Of the bleeding mouth:
> Nigger Christ
> On the cross of the South!

The theatre of the University at Chapel Hill was packed to the doors the night I read my poems there, and special police were on guard to prevent trouble since considerable pressure had been put upon the University to cancel my lecture. Courageously, the University refused to do so. But a leading politician of the town attempted to get police protection for the program withdrawn, stating that I should be run out of town before I had a chance to speak. "It's bad enough to call Christ a bastard," he cried, "but to call Him a nigger— that's too much!"

Buttita and Abernathy were delighted at the commotion their student paper, Contempo, had caused. So they greeted me, the center of it all, with open arms. They ordered luncheon brought in to the bookshop from a nearby restaurant and invited several liberal white students to share the food. That went so well that, in defiance of Southern custom, they decided to take me to a public restaurant for dinner. Since I could not be their house guest—for they themselves evicted, had nowhere to lay their heads except on the floor of their shop—I would at least, they said, be their guest for meals. I had by afternoon been housed with the leading Negro family of the town. But that evening I dined with my two intrepid white hosts at a *white* café on the main street in the company of several other white students. If they were willing to go through with dinner in a public restaurant in the tense atmosphere of that small town, I was willing, too.

After dinner, when I got back to my stopping place to dress for the lecture, my Negro hosts asked me where I had dined. When I told them at a downtown restaurant, the man of the house said, "What a shame you had to eat in the kitchen."

I said, "No, I ate at a table in the dining room."

His mouth flew open in astonishment. "It's the first time such a thing ever happened in Chapel Hill," he said.

The next morning all the newspapers in the state carried dispatches concerning the excitement attendant upon my appearance at Chapel Hill. At succeeding stops in other Carolina towns my audiences were overflowing. Negroes were delighted at my having, so they said, "walked into a lion's den, and come out, like Daniel, unscathed."

## PLANTATION HOSPITALITY

ON I went, driving down the road, deeper and deeper into Dixie with poetry as a passport. That fall and winter I covered every state in the South. Thousands of students heard me, and I sold many books. Alfred A. Knopf issued a special dollar edition of *The Weary Blues* for me to sell on tour. And, because it was depression times—even a dollar was a lot of money to some people—I prepared a smaller booklet of some of my newer poems to sell for a quarter. Its title poem was "The Negro Mother." Prentiss Taylor, a young artist in Greenwich Village, designed the booklet, endowed it with a dozen handsome black and white drawings, and supervised the printing of it. Since Prentiss Taylor was white, a Southerner from Virginia, and I, colored, I thought maybe such a book, evidence in itself of interracial collaboration and good will, might help democracy a little in the South where it seemed so hard for people to be friends across the color line. Few white people bought our book. But to Negroes I sold three large printings.

Poetry took me into the hearts and homes of colored people all over the South. But it took me into no more white colleges after Chapel Hill, and into very few white homes. However, I did go to call on a white lady one day on an enormous plantation in South Carolina. The lady was the writer, Julia Peterkin, whom I had met at literary gatherings in New York at the Knopfs' and at Carl Van Vechten's. A charming woman then very much in the literary news, Mrs. Peterkin and I had gotten on well at Manhattan cocktail parties. She had been awarded in 1928 the Pulitzer Prize for her novel of Negro plantation life, *Scarlet Sister Mary*. From this novel a drama had been made in which Ethel Barrymore starred, playing Mary in blackface. Julia Peterkin had written other novels of Negro life, too, *Green Thursday*, *Black April* and *Bright Skin*, and later a text for a lovely picture book about her Dixie plantation, *Roll, Jordan, Roll*. The materials of Mrs. Peterkin's distinguished literary career were entirely derived from Negro life in the Deep South, so, when we met, we talked about Negroes and about writing. Graciously—in New York—Mrs. Peterkin had invited me to stop and see her plantation if ever I came to South Carolina.

It was a sunny autumn afternoon when Raddie drove me to the village of Fort Mott and we inquired the whereabouts of Lang Syne Plantation. When we found its entrance, we drove some distance on the plantation grounds through fields of cotton before we located the Big House. In front of a wide veranda my car came to a stop and I got out. There on the high porch alone sat a tall, middle-aged white man.

"Good afternoon," I said, as I mounted the steps.

The man stared at me in unfriendly surprise, and did not reply.

"I'm from New York," I said, "where I knew Mrs. Peterkin, who suggested I stop by, if ever I passed this way, and see the plantation she writes about."

"She's not home," he said.

"My name's Langston Hughes," I volunteered, still on the steps. "Would you be so kind as to tell her that I called?"

"She's not home," he growled a second time. And that is all I ever got out of the man on the porch.

"Please give Mrs. Peterkin my message then and tell her I'm sorry to have missed her," I said.

"She's not home," he insisted.

As we drove away, I looked back to see the man staring at me openmouthed.

But, in contrast to this strange behavior, at Columbia a distinguished collector of Negro folk lore, the venerable physician, Dr. A. C. L. Adams, came to my program, sat on the front row in the auditorium and invited me out to his plantation the next day. My Negro host, Dr. Green, who knew Dr. Adams professionally, offered to drive me to his country place. When I told some of the colored citizens of Columbia where I was going, they said, "Oh, old Dr. Adams will introduce you to a lot of his colored relatives. That plantation is run by the doctor's relatives on the colored side. And he is a fine old white man himself."

He was a fine old man, exactly my idea of what a *true* Southern gentleman should be. Dr. Adams' *Congaree Sketches* and other vignettes I had enjoyed very much, as I had relished his Negro dialogues and bits of folklore that had frequently appeared in *Harper's*. When we arrived on his plantation, he greeted us cordially in front of the Big House and invited us in. My host from Columbia, the colored doctor, got out of the car as he spoke to Dr. Adams, but did not come into the house. He remained outside, smoking in the car. There was nothing inhibiting or self-consciously Southern about Dr. Adams, in so far as I could tell. He invited me to have a seat in the living room, sat down himself, conversed most cordially, and made me feel quite at home. Presently he sent to the fields for the plantation hands whose dialogues he featured in his stories. They came and they, too, seemed perfectly at home, joking and telling tales. One of them brought a guitar and hit a few tunes. We had a very good time that afternoon, but my Negro host from Columbia puzzled me by remaining in the yard. A buxom colored woman in a neat headrag and spotless apron brought in food and drinks, and served the white doctor and myself as the taletelling and music went on. I was having a wonderful time, but did not wish to keep my colored driver-host waiting too long, so finally I begged away and started back to town. Dr. Adams and all his Negroes waved to us from the porch.

On the road to Columbia, I got up the courage to ask Dr. Green why he had not come into Dr. Adams' plantation house with me. Dr. Green said, "Well, in the South, there are some things colored people who live here just can't do. Dr. Adams is a fine man. To him my coming in would mean nothing. But had I gone through the front door of that house as a guest, and word of it got around among the white people of Columbia, it could ruin my hospital. The white drugstores might refuse to honor my prescriptions, and no more white businessmen would contribute to our building fund for the new hospital Negroes hope to erect. That is why I stayed outside, Mr. Hughes, and did not come in."

## WARNING IN MISSISSIPPI

ON the Sunday afternoon when I read my poems at Bethune-Cookman College with Mary McLeod Bethune presiding, I closed with "The Negro Mother" from my new booklet. "Imagine," I said, "a black woman of old in her starched white apron and bright bandanna."

> Children, I come back today
> To tell you a story of the long dark way
> That I had to climb, that I had to know
> In order that our race might live and grow.
> Three hundred years in the deepest South:
> But God put a dream and a song in my mouth.
> God put a dream like steel in my soul.
> Now, through my children, I'm reaching my goal.
> Now, through my children, young and free,
> I realize the blessings denied to me. . . .
> I nourished the dream that nothing could smother
> Deep in my breast, the Negro Mother. . . .

"My son, my son!" cried Mrs. Bethune, rising with tears in her eyes to embrace me on the platform. In closing, her choir sang, "We Are Climbing Jacob's Ladder," as the largely white audience of winter visitors from the big Daytona Beach hotels filled the baskets with checks and greenbacks.

Mrs. Bethune knew how to get things done. She once told me, "People wonder how I can move into action these poor colored women's clubs in some of our backward towns, get them building their own clubhouses and community centers and setting up libraries, and doing something else besides just meeting and eating. Well, when I am presiding over a district meeting, I simply tell these women what I want done. I say, 'Now, I want Sister So-and-So to make a motion to do this, that or the other thing, whatever it is . . . Now, I want you, Sister, over there to second this motion . . . Now I want everybody here—I said everybody—to vote, Aye!—Let's vote . . . Motion carried.' "

In Miami, I gave a program in an undertaker's parlor, since Negroes had no auditorium there. Then from Florida we drove along the Gulf to New Orleans where I was presented at Straight College. After the program a teen-age girl came up to me with a sheaf of poems, which I glanced at quickly, between shaking hands and autographing books that Raddie was selling. I took the poems to be the usual poor output so often thrust into my hands at public gatherings. Then, almost immediately, I saw that these poems showed talent, so I spent an hour after the program going over them with the girl and pointing out to her where I thought they might be improved. The youngster's name was Margaret Walker. A dozen years later her first book of poems, *For My People*, received the Yale University Younger Poets Award. The author sent me an advance copy inscribed:

> To Langston—in gratitude
> for his encouragement even
> when the poems were no good.
>           Sincerely,
>           Margaret Walker

Southern University on the Mississippi near Baton Rouge, with its charming old campus beneath the live oaks and hanging moss, was our next stop. Then into the State of Mississippi, to Jackson, Piney Woods, Holly Springs and Meridian. At Meridian a kindly old white gentleman in the audience came up and said gently, "I just want to warn you that you shouldn't be reading those race-equality poems in Meridian, and you'd better be careful selling your books. There are folks in this state who wouldn't like what you say."

I knew that there were towns in Mississippi where Negro news-papers from the North were not allowed to be sold openly. Vendors had to bootleg Negro papers containing democracy-for-all editorials, and one man I'd met had been run out of town for selling *The Chicago Defender*. Mississippi was a state where few Negroes then dared to vote for fear of violence. In that year, 1931, there had been twelve lynchings in the South. Several of my poems were about voting and lynching; and I always read some of them on each program, as well as one or two poems about the Scottsboro Case. It was my poetry of this type which caused the kindly old white man to warn me about his fellow Mississippians. But, in contrast, at Greenville, Mississippi, in the very heart of the levee country, the leading white poet of the state, Will Alexander Percy, acted as the chairman of my program at a Negro church. He introduced me most graciously to the audience. Later he sent me an inscribed copy of his autobiography, *Lanterns on the Levee,* and over the years that followed I had several beautiful letters from him. But I met less than half a dozen such gentlemanly Southerners on my winter-long tour. Instead, I found a great social and cultural gulf between the races in the South, astonishing to one who, like myself, from the North, had never known such uncompromising prejudices. Of course, a Negro traveler soon got accustomed to—even if never able to accept emotionally—the many visible evidences of legal segregation: the WHITE and COLORED signs everywhere from station waiting rooms to public water fountains, the Jim Crow cars on the trains, the COLORED ENTRANCE placards in the alleys where movie stairways led up to the highest gallery, the restaurants where Negroes could not eat, and so on. But the unpredictable and unexpected things that suddenly happened are the things I never forget.

Once I was late for an evening engagement because, at a river crossing where the bridge was under repair, a ferry was being used. But all the Negro cars on the road had to wait until *all* the white cars in line, no matter how far back, had gotten on the boat. The ferry captain would fill his boat up with white automobiles and leave the Negro cars standing there. By the time the boat crossed the river and came back, more white drivers had gathered. The ferry master would again motion the whites onto the boat ahead of the Negroes. Finally I was allowed to get across the river.

A less irritating but more fantastic incident happened in Savannah. In New York every Sunday, due especially to my interest in the *Book Review* section, I always bought the *Times*. It was not always easy to find a Sunday *Times* in the South. But whenever I stopped in a large city, I tried to find it.

In Savannah I learned that the *Times* might be purchased at a newsstand in one of the railway stations, so I walked down to the station one afternoon to secure a copy. In the colored waiting room there was no newsstand, so I went outside on the sidewalk and around into the white waiting room where I bought the *Sunday Times* without incident. But, coming out of the station, just at the door, a white policeman stopped me.

He yelled, "You can't come in and out this door."

"There's no newsstand in the colored waiting room," I explained.

"I don't care nothing about that!" he barked. "You can't come in this door. This is for white folks."

"Oh," I said, "I am going out now."

"You can't go out this way neither," said the cop as I started through the door.

This puzzled me, as there was no other way out of the station except through the train sheds. "I just came in this way," I said.

"Well, you can't go out this way," barked the cop. "Niggers can't use this door."

"How do I get out then?" I asked.

"Only way I see," said the cop seriously, "is for you to walk the tracks."

In order to get out of the Savannah station with the *New York Times* that day, I had to go through the train gates and follow the railroad tracks to the nearest crossing to reach the street. I had never experienced anything so absurd before. The seriousness of that white policeman and the utter stupidity of being at a door, but not permitted to go *through* it, made me burst out laughing as I walked along with my paper from Manhattan.

I remembered, when I was in my teens, coming up from a summer in Mexico on my return to school in Cleveland, I had gone into the dining car one evening as the train was heading through Texas. I was seated alone when a white man came in. Without looking, he sat down opposite me. When I glanced across the table, I saw that the man was staring at me with a look of utter amazement. Suddenly the man jumped as though he had been shot and cried, "Why, you're a nigger, ain't you?" Then the man fled from the dining car as though he had sat down in front of a lion by mistake. As many Negroes as there are in Texas, what could there be about just one at a table in a public dining car that could so startle a white man? The colored waiters who saw the incident laughed, and so did I.

This was the sort of thing that continually puzzled and amused me in the South. Certainly the much lauded Southern gentility and aristocratic good manners are seldom shown toward Negroes. The man on Julia Peterkin's porch never did rise to greet me, a stranger, as would almost anyone in the North. The Savannah policeman did not say, "Sir, I am sorry, but you are in the wrong place." He simply barked, "You can't come in here!" When I thought about these things seriously, they were not funny. They were boorish and stupid. Some years later when I asked Carson McCullers, the Georgia writer, why white people in the South behaved so badly toward Negroes, Mrs. McCullers said, "Their hind brains don't work."

## PERSONAL AUTOGRAPH

MY standard fee for a program was one hundred dollars. This seemed like a very large amount of money to me—simply for reading from a book of poems—especially since I was completely without platform experience. But most of the larger Negro colleges were willing to pay that amount; and some of the biggest ones would pay even more.

On the other hand, not all of my sponsors, by any means, could pay a hundred dollars. But Raddie and I worked out a technique of letter writing that nine times out of ten brought an engagement of some sort. Using The Negro Year Book's listing of schools and colleges as a starting point for selecting the area we intended to cover, we would, in our first letters to prospective sponsors, state that within a given period I expected to be in the vicinity, and that my fee for a program was one hundred dollars, plus board and lodging, although shelter was taken for granted, anyway, since in the South public accommodations for Negro travelers are very poor, or often lacking altogether. As an afterthought, we would add that, of course, some adjustment of the fee might be made if one hundred dollars seemed exorbitant, since our main purpose was the spreading of culture through poetry. Should a reply plead poverty, my second letter would suggest seventy-five dollars in lieu of one hundred. Should this turn out to be too much, Raddie would then write that, since we would be in the vicinity, anyhow, as a *special* concession Langston Hughes would come for fifty dollars.

However, should even fifty dollars prove too large a fee—and in that depression era it was a considerable sum to some communities —I would instruct my tour manager on my behalf to say that, being nearby and having a free evening, I would give a program for expenses, say twenty-five dollars. If the school or church wrote back that they could not afford even that meager sum, we still did not give up. If I was without a speaking date to fill an empty evening in the area, we would reply that we were planning to stop in their town overnight, and so would—contingent, of course, upon being permitted to offer my books for sale—give a *free* program for culture's sake. When all other offers failed, that one almost always worked. The end result was that almost every evening for months was booked solid, and sometimes Sunday afternoons, as well. In this way we kept a full itinerary, driving several hundred miles a week, and I introduced my poems to every major city, town, and campus in the South that year. No matter how small a dot on the map a town was, we did not scorn it, and my audiences ranged all the way from college students to cotton pickers, from kindergarten children to the inmates of old folks homes.

Entertainment was the hardest part of my tour. White authors and lecturers on a similar tour could always take refuge at a hotel after a program. Negro speakers, barred out of hotels, were at the mercy of private hosts in private homes from whom there was no escape. If the house was small and a party was given in my honor, there was no possibility of going to bed until the last guest had gone. Southerners are great ones for hospitality. Warm and amiable and friendly as it was, I was nevertheless almost killed by entertainment, drowned in punch, gorged on food, and worn out with handshaking. I must have eaten at least a thousand chickens that winter. And I lost a great deal of sleep being entertained from town to town so continuously.

My name I must have written a million times that season on printed programs, in books, on scraps of paper, and even on paper napkins at rural receptions. But, my most personal autograph is, I suppose, obliterated by now. I inscribed it unawares in a small town in Mississippi near the Alabama state line. I was reading my poems that evening for a colored church. I was housed with one of the pillars of the church in a tiny home, spotlessly clean and filled, when I arrived, with the fumes of wonderful cooking. Tired and dusty after a day-long drive, I wanted nothing so much as a good hot bath before dinner. My hostess in preparation for my coming had done a little painting, freshening up all the baseboards and things with white paint. At the very last moment, it seemed, in her zeal to have everything spick-and-span, she had even freshly painted the bathtub, outside and *in*, with white enamel. Unfortunately, the enamel had not quite dried when I arrived. But, unaware of this fact, I blithely ran the bath tub full of hot water and sat down therein, soaking myself happily as I lathered my hair. But ten minutes later, when I started to get up, I could not tear myself loose. I was stuck to the bottom of the tub! With great deliberateness, slowly and carefully pushing myself upward, I finally managed to rise without leaving any skin behind. But I certainly left imprinted on that bath tub a most personal autograph.

That evening as I sat stiffly in the seat of honor at church, I was covered with enamel where I sat. But I didn't tell my hostess what had happened, not wishing to embarrass her. In the next town I bought a gallon of turpentine and took a bath in it.

## MAKING POETRY PAY

BY midwinter I had worked out a public routine of reading my poetry that almost never failed to provoke, after each poem, some sort of audible audience response—laughter, applause, a grunt, a groan, a sigh, or an "Amen!" I began my programs quite simply by telling where I was born in Missouri, that I grew up in Kansas in the geographical heart of the country, and was, therefore very American, that I belonged to a family that was always moving; and I told something of my early travels about the Midwest and how, at fourteen, in Lincoln, Illinois, I was elected Class Poet for the eighth-grade graduating exercises, and from then on I kept writing poetry.

After this biographical introduction I would read to my audiences the first of my poems, written in high school, and show how my poetry had changed over the years. To start my reading, I usually selected some verses written when I was about fifteen:

> I had my clothes cleaned
> Just like new.
> I put 'em on but
> I still feels blue.
>
> I bought a new hat,
> Sho is fine,
> But I wish I had back that
> Old gal o' mine.
>
> I got new shoes,
> They don't hurt my feet,
> But I ain't got nobody
> To call me sweet.

Then I would say, "That's a sad poem, isn't it?" Everybody would laugh. Then I would read some of my jazz poems so my listeners could laugh more. I wanted them to laugh a lot early in the program, so that later in the evening they would not laugh when I read poems like "Porter":

> I must say,
> Yes, sir,
> To you all the time.
> Yes, sir!
> Yes, sir!

All my days
Climbing up a great big mountain
Of yes, sirs!

Rich old white man
Owns the world.
Gimme yo' shoes to shine.

Yes, sir, boss!
Yes, sir!

By the time I reached this point in the program my nonliterary listeners would be ready to think in terms of their own problems. Then I read poems about women domestics, workers on the Florida roads, poor black students wanting to shatter the darkness of ignorance and prejudice, and one about the sharecroppers of Mississippi:

Just a herd of Negroes
Driven to the field,
Plowing, planting, hoeing,
To make the cotton yield.

When the cotton's picked
And the work is done,
Boss man takes the money
And you get none.

Just a herd of Negroes
Driven to the field.
Plowing, planting, hoeing,
To make the cotton yield.

Many of my verses were documentary, journalistic and topical. All across the South that winter I read my poems about the plight of the Scottsboro boys:

Justice is a blind goddess.
To this we blacks are wise:
Her bandage hides two festering sores
That once perhaps were eyes.

Usually people were deeply attentive. But if at some point in the program my audience became restless—as audiences sometimes will, no matter what a speaker is saying—or if I looked down from the platform and noticed someone about to go to sleep, I would pull out my ace in the hole, a poem called "Cross." This poem, delivered dramatically, I had learned, would make anybody, white or black, sit up and take notice. It is a poem about miscegenation—a very provocative subject in the South. The first line—intended to awaken all sleepers— I would read in a loud voice:

> My old man's a white old man. . . .

And this would usually arouse any who dozed. Then I would pause before continuing in a more subdued tone:

> My old mother's black.

Then in a low, sad, thoughtful tragic vein:

> But if ever I cursed my white old man
> I take my curses back.
>
> If ever I cursed my black old mother
> And wished she were in hell,
> I'm sorry for that evil wish
> And now I wish her well.
>
> My old man died in a fine big house,
> My ma died in a shack.
> I wonder where I'm gonna die,
> Being neither white nor black.

Here I would let my voice trail off into a lonely silence. Then I would stand quite still for a long time, because I knew I had the complete attention of my listeners again.

Usually after a résumé of the racial situation in our country, with an optimistic listing of past achievements on the part of Negroes, and future possibilities, I would end the evening with:

I, too, sing America.

I am the darker brother.
They send me
To eat in the kitchen
When company comes,
But I laugh,
And eat well,
And grow strong.

Tomorrow
I'll sit at the table
When company comes.
Nobody'll dare
Say to me,
"Eat in the kitchen,"
Then.

Besides,
They'll see
How beautiful I am
And be ashamed.

I, too, am America.

## DEATH HOUSE AT KILBY

AS a child in Lawrence, my grandmother had carried me to hear
Booker T. Washington speak at the University of Kansas, so I had a
vague memory of that great Negro educator and of the packed auditorium listening to him. Later, when I read his *Up From Slavery* I was
deeply moved. I had long wanted to spend some time at the school
that he had built, Tuskegee, in one of the most backward areas of
Alabama, so I was delighted when I was invited there.

The president, Robert Russa Moten, received me cordially. And
George Washington Carver showed me about his private laboratory
where he carried on his famous experiments. I not only gave an assembly program at Tuskegee, but talked to a number of English classes as
well, and met many of the students and almost all of the teachers.

And I heard Dr. Moten tell a story in chapel one day that I shall never forget, illustrating "the better part of wisdom" in the South.

Dr. Moten said that once, returning from a vacation in the North, he had to change trains at Atlanta to board a Jim Crow car for Tuskegee. From New York to Georgia he had traveled as a first-class passenger. When he stepped from his Pullman to the platform in the early morning at the Atlanta station, Dr. Moten said, he heard a scream behind him. He turned and saw that a woman stumbled at the top step of the coach and was falling forward. Naturally, his first impulse was to reach out his arms and catch her. But when he looked up and saw that she was white, he dropped his arms.

The student audience in chapel roared with laughter. Every one of those Tuskegee students knew that for a black man—and Dr. Moten was very black—to catch a *white* woman in his arms in Georgia might mean a lynching. Naturally, he dropped his arms, and the woman landed headfirst on the platform. But, at least, she did not have a chance to cry, "Rape!" The irony of Dr. Moten's split-second dilemma amused Tuskegee students greatly. But somehow I could not laugh. It seemed to me one of the saddest stories I had ever heard.

Over Alabama that winter lay the shadow of Scottsboro. But I heard no discussion whatsoever of the case at Tuskegee, although at nearby Kilby eight of the nine Negro boys involved were in the death house where I went to see them. (The ninth boy, only thirteen years old, had had a mistrial and was in prison at Birmingham.) Their chaplain, a small-town Negro minister, said it might cheer the boys up if I would read them some of my poems. So at Kilby Prison I went down the long corridor to the death house to read poetry to the Scottsboro boys. In their grilled cells in that square room with a steel door to the electric chair at one end, in their gray prison uniforms, the eight black boys sat or lay listlessly in their bunks and paid little attention to me or to the minister as we stood in the corridor, separated from them by bars. Most of them did not even greet us. Only one boy came up to the bars and shook hands with me.

I selected mostly my humorous poems to read to them, and I did not mention the South or their problems, because I did not know what to say that might be helpful. So I said nothing of any seriousness, except my hope that their appeals would end well and they would soon be free. The youngest boy, Andy Wright, smiled. The others hardly moved their heads. Then the minister prayed, but none of the boys kneeled or even changed positions for his prayer. No heads bowed.

It was almost Christmas then and the colleges were closing for the holidays. My last program for the year was at Oakwood Junior College near Huntsville, Alabama, the town from which one of the Scottsboro girls, Ruby Bates, had come. Having helped to send eight colored youngsters to the death house, she was now at home again in Huntsville. Folks around town said that Ruby Bates had stated that she lied in court; that nobody had raped her. Later under oath she recanted her rape testimony, declaring the whole story had been a fabrication. She said the boys had not touched either her or Victoria Price, the other white girl. But the Negro youths still remained, at Christmas, in the death house.

I wanted to interview Ruby Bates in Huntsville, but the Negro teachers at Oakwood thought I must be crazy. They would take no part in helping me to locate her, and none of them would accompany me to see her. Finally, they dissuaded me from the attempt on the grounds that I would be taking my life in my hands, as well as endangering the college.

## HILLTOP IN SAN FRANCISCO

READING poetry that spring, I covered the whole enormous state of Texas, and at Texas College in Tyler, I met the cutest little freckled-faced twin ever, one Ina Qualls, who had an identical sister named Youra. Catty girls at the various colleges where Ina and Youra have worked—for theirs is the academic life—have told me that Ina's name is not really Ina at all—it was I'm-a before she changed it. The story is that since her father had a large and ever-growing family, he was at a loss for names for all of his offspring, so when the twins came he named one, You're-a Qualls and the other I'm-a Qualls. And subsequent brothers and sisters had names like He's-a Qualls and She's-a Qualls—written Hesa, Shesa. At any rate, Ina is chic and charming and bakes delicious cakes and writes wonderfully sparkling little notes. Of all my memories of the whole vast state of Texas that spring, Ina's freckles and the prairie flowers are the most vivid.

From Houston I headed westward to San Antonio, then took the long trek across the prairies to El Paso. I think I am the only Negro poet who has ever given a program in the frontier town. In El Paso it was strange to find that just by stepping across an invisible line into Mexico, a Negro could buy a beer in any bar, sit anywhere in the movies, or eat in any restaurant, so suddenly did Jim Crow disappear, and Americans visiting Juarez, who would not drink beside a Negro in Texas, did so in Mexico. Funny people, Southerners!

I did not mind leaving the South when my sturdy little Ford headed across the desert through New Mexico and Arizona toward the Coast. In Los Angeles, Loren Miller introduced me to the audience as "The first Negro poet in America to span the continent, coast to coast, with his poetry!" I found no colored colleges in California, but Negro churches and clubs gave me audiences.

Some weeks previously, when I had read my poems at Arkansas A. and M. College for Negroes, I met a young instructor, Arthur Williams, and his wife. When they learned that I was continuing my tour as far as California, they said, "You must meet our friend, Noel Sullivan, there." Mrs. Williams said, "I will write my sister in San Francisco and tell her that you are coming." Her sister, Mrs. Pharr, was the housekeeper for the California friend whom this young couple wanted me to meet and of whom they gave a devoted description.

"He's almost like a saint," they said. "But not a solemn saint. He's witty and wise, rich and kind—and not only has a colored staff in his home, but many colored friends in Paris, London, New York, everywhere. He's so human, when you know him, you forget he's white."

I had never heard of Noel Sullivan, but I said I would be happy to meet him, so the Williamses wrote of my coming. In Los Angeles, I received a letter inviting me to be his guest when I reached San Francisco. His housekeeper, Eulah Pharr, kindly arranged for a Negro settlement house committee, of which she was a member, to present me in a program, so I had two friends in San Francisco even before I arrived. I learned that Noel Sullivan was of a distinguished family and a nephew of the late Senator Phelan. One of San Francisco's earliest skyscrapers was the Phelan Building, and the family estate at Montalvo had long been a show place of the Coast. His house on Hyde Street, I was told, was one of the city's cultural centers. An old mansion at the top of Russian Hill, it had formerly been the home of Robert Louis Stevenson of *Treasure Island* fame, and so was a landmark.

When I drove up to the Sullivan house in San Francisco with its sweeping view of the city and bay, and looked up at its ivied walls, flowered balconies, and window boxes in bright bloom, I was, of course, intrigued at the prospect of being a guest there. A bevy of friendly colored servants greeted me and helped bring in my luggage. Noel Sullivan was not at home, but arrived shortly. He was a tall, rugged-looking man, a bachelor, shy and rather slow of speech. Quietly witty and charming in a most unpretentious way, he at once made a guest feel at ease. Nelson Eddy, then a rising young motion-picture star, was also at Hyde Street that weekend. At my first luncheon Lawrence Tibbett was present, and to dinner came Leslie and Leon Roos, two of Noel Sullivan's favorite San Francisco friends. Shortly, too, I met the distinguished professor of English at Berkeley, Ben Lehman, who later married Judith Anderson, for every day there were new guests at meals.

As housekeeper at Hyde Street, Eulah Pharr, helped to make house guests feel at home, too, and supervised all their comforts. Eulah had a wonderfully warm and outgoing personality, and we became friends immediately. Her husband, Eddie, was one of the butlers, Charles was the other, and Glenn was the chauffeur. These efficient and amiable Negroes aided in making my first visit atop Russian Hill most enjoyable. After a long winter of touring across the whole country, I was more weary than I realized. To sink into a marvelously comfortable bed with sea breezes blowing in the window and be awakened the next morning by fresh orange juice and steaming coffee, then breakfast on the flowered terrace, with a car at my disposal later if I wished to see the city—all this exceeded any dreams of comfort I had ever had. There was even a house secretary to whom I might dictate letters if I chose, and two gardeners who would cut whatever flowers a guest might wish for his bedroom vases. This well-ordered house that I was invited to use became my base during my month of lecturing on the Coast.

I gave a program of my poems at the Women's City Club in San Francisco. Sara Bard Field, Charles Erskine Scott Wood, and the motion-picture actor, Ramon Navarro, were in the audience. I spoke at the University of California at Berkeley, at Oakland, at San Jose, Fresno, Bakersfield, and at Ted Custer's rustic Playhouse at Carmel-by-the-Sea. Meanwhile, to cover my return to New York, I had booked a few programs across the Middle West. But while I was in California a wire came which caused my plans to change. A Negro motion-picture group was being organized in Harlem to go to Russia to make a film. I was invited to be a part of such a group as a writer, to do the English dialogue for the film on a four-month contract. We were to sail from Brooklyn in June.

This unexpected chance to work in films in Russia seemed to open a new door to me. At that time Hollywood did not employ Negro writers. Many young white writers whom I knew had well-paid Hollywood writing jobs, but I had never been offered such a job, nor had any of my work been purchased for motion pictures. To Negro writers, Hollywood was still a closed shop—with the Negroes closed out. It was my intention to try very hard to make a living as a professional writer, so I was interested in all fields of writing. But I thought if I were ever to work in motion pictures or learn about them, it would have to be abroad, so I canceled the few engagements I had pending in the Middle West to sail for Europe.

The day after I had read my poems at Carmel, I spent an hour with an old friend of Noel Sullivan's, Lincoln Steffens. When I told Steffens I was going to Russia, he proceeded, in the light of his experiences there, to give me some "good advice." It consisted mostly in warning me to be prepared *not* to like anything in the Soviet Union—except what he called "its potential." Steffens informed me that the physical facts of life in the USSR might well appall an American like myself accustomed to at least having in sight—if not possession—all the heart desires, from groceries selling caviar to drugstores filled with mousetraps and waterproof watches.

Steffens' parting words were, "Be sure to take soap and toilet paper for yourself—don't part with it!—and lipsticks and silk stockings to give the girls. The Bolsheviks asked for—and seized—everything, in order to get a little. From that little, they expect in time to build a lot. I think they will. But thinking and *having* are two different things. So you do as I say—have your own soap and toilet paper—and maybe you won't be too unhappy."

As I left him on the steps of his home within earshot of the Pacific surf, the frail little old journalist with the white goatee and the twinkling eyes stretched out his hand in the misty Carmel sunlight and wished me well.

"I'm glad you're going to Russia," Steffens said. "It's time Negroes were getting around the world. Can you tell me why in the hell they stay home so much?"

That weekend as I drove up the Coast for engagements in the Northwest, midnight caught us in a strange town in Oregon, too tired to drive any further. We stopped at the first hotel we saw on the main street and asked for rooms. We were refused. We tried another, then another. At each the same reception, "We don't take Negroes." None would accommodate colored travelers. Finally we went to the police station and asked where Americans of color might stay in that city. The police were puzzled, but agreed to try to find us a sleeping place. Unfortunately, the desk sergeant said, there were no Negro families in town. Finally, after several phone calls, a police car escorted us to a dingy hotel on the outskirts—a kind of rooms-by-the-hour assignation house where men take pick-ups or bar girls. There, by special request of the police, we Negroes were allowed accommodations until dawn.

After Portland and Seattle, it was pleasant to get back to San Francisco for a few more restful days with Noel Sullivan and his many friends so often dining at Hyde Street. There a group of mischievous little dachshunds woke me up in the mornings, tripping on their tiny legs across the deep bedroom rug, rushing about the butler's feet to leap on my bed and lap at the cream in the silver pitcher on the break-fast tray. There was a bright parrot squawking in a big cage some-where, too, and canaries singing in the sunlight on the balconies. Animals, birds, people, growing plants and flowers were all over the house. That Hyde Street corner was full of life. Outside my windows the funny little San Francisco cable cars hummed up from the city to the crest of the street, then rattled down the steep grade toward Fisherman's Wharf. Such was the lovely home on Russian Hill where, at the end of May, I began to pack to go East, thence to Moscow. Within the month, I was in quite another world, that of the USSR, a rapid transition in no uncertain terms from the best of American capitalism to the show place of Soviet communism—from Russian Hill to Russia itself.

# 3

# MOSCOW
# MOVIE

DRIVING as fast as I could from coast to coast, I got to New York just in time to pick up my ticket, say goodbye to Harlem, and head for the North German Lloyd, loaded down with bags, baggage, books, a typewriter, a victrola, and a big box of Louis Armstrong, Bessie Smith, Duke Ellington and Ethel Waters records. I was the last passenger up the gangplank, missing all the friends who had come to see me off, for when I arrived visitors had been put ashore.

Crossing the Atlantic on the *Bremen*, it was wonderful weather. My first two days aboard, I did nothing but sleep. After almost nine months of continuous travel, lecturing from Baltimore to Bakersfield, Miami to Seattle, then a breakneck trip by Ford across the whole country, I was pretty tired. The boat was full of young people, and when I did wake up, the voyage was fun. I practiced German, studied Russian, played deck games, and danced.

I had not before known most of the group going to make the Moscow movie. When I became acquainted with them on board, it turned out that the majority were not actors at all, as I had supposed they would be. Of the twenty-two Negroes headed for Moscow, most were youthful intellectuals—recent college graduates curious about the Soviet Union—or youngsters anxious to see Europe, but whose feet had never set foot on any stage and whose faces had never been before a motion-picture camera. There were only two professional theater people in the group. The one really seasoned actor accompanying us was Wayland Rudd, and the other Thespian was Sylvia Garner who had played a minor role in *Scarlet Sister Mary*, having been one of the few Negroes in that "Negro" drama as performed by Ethel Barrymore, Estelle Winwood and other whites in blackface. These two professionals were also the only really mature people in our group, everyone else being well under thirty and some hardly out of their teens. There were no middle-aged or elderly folks, should there be such roles in the film we were to make. It turned out, however, that as yet no one had seen the scenario, or even knew the story. But that worried none of us. It was fun to be traveling. Besides, at home, jobs were hard to get and wages were low.

Among these young Negroes were an art student just out of Hampton, a teacher, a girl elocutionist from Seattle, three would-be writers other than myself, a very pretty divorcée who traveled on alimony, a female swimming instructor, and various clerks and stenographers—all distinctly from the white-collar or student classes. Although we had heard that the film was to be about workers, there was not a single worker—in the laboring sense—except perhaps the leader of the group (the one Communist Party member, so far as I knew), and he did not look much like a worker. But, at least, he had not been to college, and had no connection with the arts. That most of our group were not actors seems to have been due to the fact that very few professional theater people were willing to pay their own fares to travel all the way to Russia to sign contracts they had never seen. Only a band of eager, adventurous young students, teachers, writers and would-be actors were willing to do that, looking forward to the fun and wonder of a foreign land as much as to film-making. There were a few among them who said they wanted to get away from American race prejudice forever, being filled up with Jim Crow. These hoped to remain abroad. But most of the twenty-two simply thought they had found an exciting way to spend the summer. An exciting summer it turned out to be, too.

When we got to Berlin, we ran into the first of our experiences with the famous Russian red tape: permission for our visas had not been okayed. In fact, it seemed the Russian Consulate had not been alerted as to our coming at all, so it would have to cable Moscow to find out if an American Negro group really had been invited to the Soviet Union to work in a film. In Berlin, Negroes were received at hotels without question, so we settled down to await visas. We ate in any restaurant we could afford. In the German capital, I could not help but remember my recent experiences in the South with restaurants that served whites only, and autocamps all across America that refused to rent me a cabin in which to sleep. Nevertheless, in spite of racial freedom, Berlin seemed to me a wretched city. Its beautiful buildings and wide avenues in the center of the town were ringed with grey slums.

Our hotel was near one of the big railroad stations. There I put a coin into what I thought was a candy-bar machine, but a package of prophylactics came out instead. The streets nearby teemed with prostitutes, pimps, panderers and vendors of dirty pictures. Some of the young men in our group got acquainted for the first time with what Americans in the pre-Kinsey era termed "perversions." Unusual sex pleasures from beautiful girls were openly offered in no uncertain phraseology on every corner and at pathetically low prices. Some of the young men, not having much money, bargained rather sharply to satisfy their curiosity as cheaply as possible. Data was exchanged in the hotel lobby.

"Man, do you know what a girl just offered to do for me for a quarter—a blonde, too."

"Aw, fellow, you'd be cheated at that rate. See the chick outside the door? She does what you're talking about for fifteen cents—or a pack of Camels."

The pathos and poverty of Berlin's low-priced market in bodies depressed me. As a seaman I had been in many ports and had spent a year in Paris working on Rue Pigalle, but I had not seen anywhere people so desperate as these walkers of the night streets in Berlin. The only amusing incident I remember about my stay there occurred in the Haus Vaterland, a big amusement center of bars, restaurants and dancing halls in the center of town. Among its attractions was a Wild West Bar on the lower floor, and a Turkish Coffee House with red hassocks and rich rugs on an upper floor. There thick muddy black coffee was served in graceful brass pots with long spouts. A blackamoor in baggy velvet trousers, gold embroidered jacket, and a red fez, poured coffee. He looked like a Nubian slave from Cairo, and it did not occur to us to try to talk to him. But as he poured our coffee, he overheard us speaking English. He almost dropped the pot as he cried, "I'm sure glad to see some of my folks!" He was from Harlem. "Say, what's doing on Lenox Avenue?"

All of a sudden one day, our Soviet visas came through. The Russian Consulate phoned our various hotels, saying the visas were ready and that we must leave on the afternoon boat train for Stettin. At the time of the phone call, I was looking at paintings in a museum. I was almost left behind, for when I reached the hotel, the others had departed for the Consulate to pick up their visas, and from there had gone on to the railroad station. I rushed my baggage, books, typewriter, records and victrola into a cab and headed for the Consulate. There, for once, with dispatch (so many things are done in slow motion in the Soviet orbit) my passport was stamped, and I sped for the station. On the way, my taxi ran into a delivery boy on a bicycle. The police had to take down names and numbers and inspect the taxi license. I barely made the train, throwing bags, boxes, and records in the windows to my anxious companions, and leaping on as it was pulling out.

At Stettin we went directly aboard a Swedish boat—beautiful, very clean and spotlessly white outside and in. I have never seen such a white boat. And all the other people were white, too. We were the only dark passengers. But voyagers and crew were so cordial and friendly to us that we might well have been royal guests. The trip across the Baltic to Helsinki was almost like a fairy-tale journey on a boat filled with amiable people. The only thing they neglected— being Scandinavians, I guess they did not know—was to tell us about smörgasbord. Nobody told us that all the creamed potatoes, smoked ham, sardines, salads, sturgeon, hot dumplings, stuffed rolls and other beautiful things to eat, spread buffet style on a long white table in the big white dining room preceding dinner, were not intended for dinner. So, at our first meal, we made the mistake which many foreign travelers in Scandinavia make—while everybody else waited for us to finish, we ate our fill of these wonderful foods intended merely for appetizers. Then dinner was served!

It was June and the time of the "white nights." The further

north we got, the longer the days became. On reaching Finland, it was daylight at midnight. Helsinki was a plainly pleasant town with music and dancing in the parks in the long white twilights. The people were friendly there, too. They did not seem to look upon Negroes as curiosities—not even twenty-two together—though some Finns had never before seen so many colored folks, and some had never seen any.

In Helsinki, we stayed overnight and the next day we took a train headed for the land of John Reed's *Ten Days That Shook the World*, the land where race prejudice was reported taboo, the land of the Soviets. At the border were young soldiers with a red star on their caps. Spread high in the air across the railroad tracks, there was a banner: WORKERS OF THE WORLD UNITE. When the train stopped beneath this banner for passports to be checked, a few of the young black men and women left the train to touch their hands to Soviet soil, lift the new earth in their palms, and kiss it.

## SCENARIO IN RUSSIAN

IN Moscow we were quartered in the Grand Hotel, a block from the Kremlin, in the heart of the capital. It had enormous rooms with huge pre-tzarist beds, heavy drapes at the windows and deep rugs on the floors. It had a big dark dining room with plenty to eat in the way of ground meats and cabbage, caviar, and sometimes fowl, but not much variety. Most of the guests at the Grand seemed to be upper-echelon Russians—industrial plant managers and political personages, checking in for a few days then gone—with whom we never became acquainted.

Most of the tourists then coming to Russia were housed at the New Moscow or the National. And sometimes a few Americans stayed at the Metropol, but that aristocratic old hotel seemed to be reserved largely for important political visitors from lands other than the U.S.A., ballet dancers, and beautiful but mysterious girls whom some said were secret-service agents. At any rate, the Metropol seemed to be the only hotel in Moscow with any bar-stool girls about. It was also the only hotel with a jazz band, and pretty women available with whom to dance.

"All spies," said some of the fellows in our group, who found the Metropol an agreeable but expensive hangout. "Spies who can't be seduced."

"Spies or not, they sure look good to me," said others. "And dance!"

"I'm teaching one to lindy-hop," declared one of our fellows on his second day in town, "and she can out-lindy me already. They sure got some fine dancing spies in this town!"

I never found out exactly what was the function of the young Russian beauties at the Metropol. They definitely were not prostitutes, as are many such bar-stool lovelies in other European cities. Prostitutes in Russia were few and far between, since the Russian women, like everybody else, had jobs. Anyhow, the Russians said, prostitution was not "sovietski"—meaning it just wasn't the proper thing to do. "Ne sovietski" was a phrase one heard often. If somebody pushed too brusquely into a bus or streetcar, others would turn around and say, "Citizen, that's not sovietski." If two men got into a brawl in the street, the police would say, "Stop! Ne sovietski!" If a child snatched another's candy away, the mother would scold, "Ne sovietski!" Any form of rudeness or misbehavior might be characterized as not being "sovietski," in other words, not worthy of a Soviet citizen.

Of all the big cities in the world where I've been, the Muscovites seemed to me to be the politest of peoples to strangers. But perhaps that was because we were Negroes and, at that time, with the Scottsboro Case on world-wide trial in the papers everywhere, and especially in Russia, folks went out of their way there to show us courtesy. On a crowded bus, nine times out of ten, some Russian would say, "Negrochanski tovarish—Negro comrade—take my seat!"

On the streets queuing up for newspapers, for cigarettes, or soft drinks, often folks in the line would say, "Let the Negro comrade go forward." If you demurred, they would insist, "Please! Visitor to the front." Ordinary citizens seemed to feel that they were all official hosts of Moscow.

The first thirty days or so in Moscow were all free days, because the scenario had not yet been completed. Our actors, therefore, were at leisure, although being paid for the time. The contracts had been signed a few days after we arrived. But mine, a special contract as a writer, was held up a week or so while it was being drawn in detail. When it was finally handed to me in triplicate at the studio, it was entirely in Russian. I said, "I can't read a word of it, and I won't sign something I can't read."

The officials of Meschrabpom Films assured me it was all right— "*Horashaw!*"

"That may be," I said, "but I will sign only a contract I can read, in English. I have just come from California where I heard about people signing contracts in Hollywood which they had not read carefully, and——"

"Don't mention Hollywood in the same breath with the film industry of the Workers' Socialist Soviet Republics," shouted the Meschrabpom executive with whom I was dealing. "That citadel of capitalism escapism—Hollywood! Bah!"

"Don't yell at me," I said. "I'll go right back home to New York and never sign your contract."

So I went back to the hotel, leaving the documents on his desk. A week later English copies were sent me, and I signed them—at a salary which, in terms of Russian buying power, was about a hundred times a week as much as I had ever made anywhere else. I had paid my own fare to Moscow, as had each of the others in our group. On my way across the United States, I had left several hundred dollars with my mother in Cleveland to help on her expenses while I was in Europe. Meschrabpom Films refunded all travel expenses to us in dollars once we had gotten to Moscow, and I held on to mine to use on the return trip home.

In looking back at the saga of the twenty-two American Negroes who spent their own money to go several thousand miles to make a picture with no contracts in front, and, on the other hand looking at a film concern that would bring to its studios such a group without exercising any sort of selectivity beforehand, I am amazed at the naïveté shown on both sides. But I must say there was never any temporizing regarding work or money. We arrived in Moscow ready to work, and we were promptly paid all monies due. Nevertheless, our expedition ended in an international scandal and front-page headlines around the world, with varying degrees of truth in the news stories, depending on the politics of the home paper or its Moscow correspondent.

The script of the film we were to make consisted of an enormous number of pages when I first saw it—entirely in Russian! Just like my contract, it had to be translated. This took two or three weeks. Meanwhile, all of us "Negro-worker-comrades," as Muscovites called us, were almost nightly guests of one or another of the great theaters, the Moscow Art Theatre, the Vakhtangov, the Meyerhold, the Kamerny, or the Opera, where we saw wonderful performances and met their distinguished actors. There was sight-seeing by day, or nude bathing in the Park of Rest and Culture on the banks of the Moscow River. Finally, after weeks of shows, parties and pleasure, I received an English version of the scenario and retired to my room in the Grand Hotel to read it.

At first I was astonished at what I read. Then I laughed until I cried. And I wasn't crying really because the script was in places so mistaken and so funny. I was crying because the writer meant well, but knew so little about his subject and the result was a pathetic hodgepodge of good intentions and faulty facts. With his heart in the right place, the writer's concern for racial freedom and decency had tripped so completely on the stumps of ignorance that his work had fallen as flat as did Don Quixote's valor when good intentions led that slightly demented knight to do battle with he-knew-not-what.

Although the scenario concerned America, it was written by a famous Russian writer *who had never been in America*. At that time, only a very few books about contemporary Negro life in our country had been translated into Russian. These the scenarist had studied, and from them he had put together what he thought was a highly dramatic story of labor and race relations in the United States. But the end result was a script improbable to the point of ludicrousness. It was so interwoven with major and minor impossibilities and improbabilities that it would have seemed like a burlesque on the screen. At times that night as I read, I could not keep from laughing out loud, to the astonishment of my two roommates, lying at that moment half asleep in their beds, dreaming about being movie actors. But the situation really wasn't funny when I started thinking about my companions and the others from Harlem who'd come so far to perform in a film. But, not wishing to upset them immediately, I said nothing about the absurd script, since I had no idea what position the studio might take concerning my report on it.

I simply took the scenario back to the Meschrabpom officials the next morning to tell them that, in my opinion, no plausible film could possibly be made from it since, in general, the script was so mistakenly conceived that it was beyond revision.

"It is just simply *not true* to American life," I said.

"But," they countered indignantly, "it's been approved by the Comintern."

The Comintern was, I knew, the top committee of the Communist Party concerned with international affairs.

"I'm sorry," I said, "but the Comintern must know very little about the United States."

"For example?" barked the Meschrabpom officials.

To convince them, I went through the scenario with the studio heads page by page, scene by scene, pointing out the minor nuances that were off tangent here, the major errors of factual possibility there, and in some spots the unintentional portrayal of what amounted to complete fantasy—the kind of fantasy that any European merely reading cursorily about the race problem in America, but knowing nothing of it at first hand, might easily conjure up. I made it clear that one could hardly blame the scenarist who had had, evidently, very meager facts available with which to work.

Having red-penciled all of the errors, I said, "Now what is left from which to make a picture?"

The Russians are in general a talkative people, very argumentative and often hard to convince. I had to go over and over it all again, not only with the first officials that day, but several other sets of officials in the studio on subsequent days. They in turn, no doubt, checked with their political higher-ups. These political higher-ups, so I heard, months later, fired about half of the studio executive staff for permitting the mistakes of the scenario to happen in the first place. Meanwhile, as the days went by, nothing was said to the cast concerning the script difficulties. I left up to the studio official announcement of its problems. So our twenty-one actors continued to enjoy the pleasures of Moscow, although most of them began to be a bit restive and a little bored.

The film in English was to have been called, *Black and White*. Its locale was Birmingham, Alabama. Its heroes and heroines were Negro workers. The men were stokers in the steel mills, the women domestics in wealthy homes. The white leading role was that of a progressive labor organizer, presumably a member of a union like the incipient CIO, who wanted Negroes and whites to be organized fraternally together. Its villains were the reactionary white bosses of the steel mills and the absentee owners, Northern capitalists, who aroused the poor white Southern workers against both the union and the Negroes. Its general outline was plausible enough, but almost *all* of its details were wrong and its accents misplaced.

There was, for example, an important scene intending to show how a poor but beautiful colored girl might be seduced by a wealthy young white man in Alabama. The girl was pictured serving a party in the home of the director of the steel mill whose son became entranced by their lovely dark-skinned servant. This hot-blooded white aristocrat, when the music started, simply came up to the beautiful Southern colored girl passing drinks and said gently, "Honey, put down your tray; come, let's dance."

In Russia, old Russia of the Tzars or Soviet Russia, in a gay mood, master and maid quite naturally might dance together in public without much being made of it. But *never* in Birmingham, if the master is white and the maid colored—not even now in this democratic era of integration.

Later, to show what the scenarist imagined to be the delusions of the possibilities of capitalism in the minds of Negroes wealthy enough to have escaped from the working class, and to indicate how, nevertheless, such Negro capitalists because of race must eventually ally themselves with the workers, the scenario had some fabulously wealthy colored men portrayed as owning their own radio studios and broadcasting towers in Birmingham. When, at the film's climax, a mob of poor white workers have been falsely aroused against their fellow Negro workers, and the white union organizer has been stoned out of town, a great race riot breaks out in which the poor whites attack both rich and poor Negroes alike, stoning them and bombing their homes. Then it is that the rich Negroes rush to their radio station and start broadcasting to the North for help. Who comes to their rescue? Not the Northern white liberals or philanthropists who simply shake their heads and say, "These things take time, education, patience." It is the white workers of the industrial North, already unionized and strong, who jump into their cars and buses and head straight for Alabama to save their Negro brothers. These pages of the scenario presented a kind of trade-union version of the Civil War all over again, intended as a great sweeping panorama of contemporary labor battles in America. It would have looked wonderful on the screen, so well do the Russians handle crowds in films. Imagine the white workers of the North clashing with the Southern mobs of Birmingham on the road outside the city, the red fire of the steel mills in the background, and the militant Negroes eventually emerging from slums and cabins to help with it all! But it just couldn't be true. It was not even plausible fantasy—being both ahead of and far behind the times.

"All I can see to do for this film," I said, "is to start over and get a new one, based on reality, not imagination."

"Will you write it?" the Russian executives asked me.

"I couldn't," I said. "I've never lived in the South, never worked in a steel mill, and I know almost nothing about unions or labor relations. For this kind of film you need somebody who knows a great deal about what he is writing. The only thing I know anything at all about in this script are the work songs and spirituals—and of those there is already a good selection."

"We'll keep the songs," said the officials, "and get a new scenario. The cast can start rehearsing the music immediately."

So that is what partially happened. The following week, after a month of leisure, our twenty-two Negroes—including myself—started rehearsing songs. The first rehearsal of the music was funnier than anything in the script. The director, who had been especially imported from abroad for this film, was a young German named Karl Yunghans, who spoke neither Russian nor English well, so he had to work with us mostly through an interpreter. Yunghans had been brought from Berlin for this Negro film because he had successfully directed a recent African travelogue. Like the scenarist, Yunghans had never been in the United States and had never known any Negroes other than Africans. He knew nothing at all about race relations in Alabama, or labor unions, North, South or European. He was an artist. But he was an eager and ambitious young man, very worried about the current delays in his picture, and most anxious to begin to create in cinema what Meschrabpom intended to be the first great Negro-white film ever made in the world. An enormous budget, millions of rubles, had been allotted to its making. Money was no problem. Yunghans had been in Russia several months now, waiting to begin. Meanwhile he had married one of the prettiest women in Moscow, a simple girl with the blondest of blonde hair and the bluest of blue eyes. She was a little doll of an actress, quite unspoiled, whom he hoped to take back to Germany with him and develop into a star. But Yunghans nearly became a nervous wreck after that first singing rehearsal—because almost none of the Negroes in our group could sing.

Europeans, as well as Americans, seem to be vicitims of that old cliché that all Negroes just naturally sing—without effort. Other than two or three, the twenty-two of us who had come to Russia could hardly carry a tune. Being mostly Northerners, only a few of us had ever heard a spiritual outside a concert hall, or a work song other than "Water Boy" in a night club. I had traversed the South once, but many of our group had never crossed the Mason-Dixon line. They had but little feeling for folk rhythms, and no liking for the idiom. Being city people, college trained, they were too intellectual for such old-time songs, which to them smacked of bandannas and stereotypes. However, in order to become movie stars, they were willing to try to learn "All God's Chillun Got Shoes," "Didn't My Lord Deliver Daniel?" or the "Hammer Song." But if you can't carry a tune, and have no rhythmical sense for singing in the folk style either, you cannot learn to do so quickly. The discordant sounds that arose from that first rehearsal in Moscow failed to fool even a European. *These Negroes simply could not sing spirituals*—or anything else.

The woman who had performed with Ethel Barrymore saved the day for all of us. Sylvia had a good voice, and she knew many of the old songs, having once been a Baptist choir singer. So at the first rehearsal she sang all the songs in the script herself. To keep the young German director from being too depressed, she also gave an entire folk-song concert herself that afternoon in the big barren studio room. And she made many of the younger Negroes there, who had never before appreciated the beauty of the songs of their grandparents, suddenly aware of the power of "Nobody Knows De Trouble I've Seen," "Swing Low, Sweet Chariot," and "Go Down, Moses." But Sylvia was a moody woman. At later rehearsals, when she didn't feel like singing, she wouldn't. Besides, she said, the others threw her off key if they chimed in, and this upset her.

Sylvia was a large woman who had gone into the theater in the days of the shimmy-sha-wobble and the eagle-rock which she could dance with gusto. Sergei Eisentstein, after *Potemkin* at the height of his fame as a film director, gave a party for us shortly after our arrival in Moscow, and Sylvia sang. Late in the evening there was general dancing during which Sylvia tried to teach a staid old professor of semantics from the University of Moscow to shimmy. This dignified professor was a very stiff man and not really able to shake like jelly on a plate. But he liked Sylvia's warm teaching so well that he became her constant escort, squiring her to all the intellectual affairs of Moscow. And Sylvia became an American folk-song star on the Moscow radio—except that in doing spirituals they wouldn't let her sing "God," "Lord," or "Jesus" on the air.

At that time in Moscow, although some churches were open and one occasionally saw a cassocked priest on the street, there was an official anti-religious campaign under way. The radio belonged to the Soviet state, so religious songs were taboo on the air. An exception was made, however, of the spirituals—as examples of great Negro folk art —with the provision that when these songs were sung, the words *God, Lord, Christ,* or *Jesus* were not to be used.

When Sylvia announced that she had been signed to give a series of programs on the Moscow radio, all of us wondered how she would get around this edict, so we got into the habit of never missing one of her programs, just to see what surprises would pop out. Often for the Deity, Sylvia would substitute whatever word came into her head, usually something relating to religion, but sometimes not, if the Christian word in the text caught her unawares. For example, an old spiritual like "My Lord, What a Morning" might emerge simply as, "My

Soul, What a Morning." But one day, "My God is so high, you can't get over Him, you can't get under Him," came out as "Old mike is so high, I can't get over it, I can't get under it! Oh, this mike is so high! Hallellujah!"

One day Sylvia said, "Them Russians don't understand English, and I'm tired of faking. I'm gonna get God into my program today."

"How?" we asked.

"Just wait and see," she said.

All of us had our ears glued to the radio receivers in the Grand Hotel when Sylvia came on the air that night. She opened with, "Oh, rise and shine and give God the glory." Only what she actually sang was:

> Rise and shine
> And give Dog the glory! Glory!
> Rise and shine!
> Give Dog the glory . . .

"Ah-ha!" we said with glee when Sylvia got back to the hotel, "you didn't get away with it, did you?"

"What do you mean, I didn't get away with it?" cried Sylvia. "God was in my songs tonight."

"Where?" I asked.

"Where He ought to be," said Sylvia. "What is d-o-g but God spelled backwards?"

## THE MAMMY OF MOSCOW

AMONG the crowd of Russian actors and writers who greeted us at the station when we arrived in Moscow, there were also four Negroes: a very African-looking boy named Bob, a singer called Madam Arle-Titz, a young man named Robinson who was a technician, and Emma Harris. Of the four, Emma is the one nobody can forget. She was a "character." Everybody in Moscow knew Emma, and Emma knew everybody. Stalin, I am sure, was aware of her presence in the capital. Emma was perhaps sixty, very dark, very talkative and very much alive.

She had been an actress, and wherever she was, she had the ability to hold center stage. As our train came slowly to a stop in Moscow that morning, the first person we heard on the platform was Emma.

"Bless God! Lord! I'm sure glad to see some Negroes!" she cried. "Welcome! Welcome! Welcome!"

It seemed she had been wanting to see a sizable number of Negroes for a long, long time. Emma was from Dixie, and she had been in Moscow almost forty years. Since I am always hankering to see more and more Negroes myself, right off I took a liking to Emma.

All of us on the train were glad to see her. Emma made us feel at home. For the next few weeks, while we waited for the studio to start filming, "Let's go see Emma," was the phrase heard most often among us. When we didn't go to see Emma, Emma came to see us. She was a frequent visitor at the Grand Hotel. Official guides were assigned to our group by the theatrical unions and our film studio— but what the guides did not show us, Emma could, including the after-hour spots of Moscow. As old as she was, she liked to stay up all night, and she had incredible energy. Yet, in the middle of the capital of the Workers' Republics, Emma did not work. And, although freedom of speech was felt to be lacking in the USSR, Emma said anything she wanted to say. It was Emma who first told us the joke about the man who saw a swimmer drowning in the Moscow River. The man jumped in and pulled the wretch out. When the rescued one was revived, the man asked, "Who is it that I have saved?"

The rescued answered, "Stalin."

Whereupon, the man cried, "Oh, my God, how unfortunate!" and jumped into the river himself.

Emma had little use for the Soviet system as compared to Tzarist days. Nevertheless, she was a featured speaker at all of the big Scottsboro rallies then being held in Moscow on behalf of the unfortunate boys under sentence of death in faraway Alabama. Emma could make a fiery speech in Russian, denouncing American lynch law, then come off the platform and sigh, "I wish I was back home."

Emma said she was from Kentucky, but her last stopping place in the United States had been Brooklyn. She had come to Europe at the turn of the century with a theatrical troupe. In Russia she had attracted the attention of a Grand Duke, and there Emma had remained all these years, growing, as she claimed, ever more homesick for Dixie. Naturally, when the Tzar fell, the Duke fell, too. Emma was left with a mansion in Moscow. The Soviets cut up her mansion into a dozen apartments, but permitted her a sizable flat on the first floor, where she lived quite comfortably. Emma said she made her living as a translator, but I never observed her at work, never found her without the time to cook a feast, serve a drink, or talk. She had some of the best food in Moscow. Her table was the only one in Russia on which I ever saw an apple pie or, in a private home, a whole roast turkey. Yet she had only an ordinary citizen's ration card. But Emma knew all about black markets—and speak-easies. In a city where almost nothing was open after midnight, Emma could always find a place to buy a drink. One night she took me, at two A.M., to a cellar den, where vodka and brandy were only a little more expensive than at regulation cafés during legal hours. And the customers in the sub-rosa joint looked just like speak-easy patrons around the world. They all knew Emma and she knew them and, before dawn came, everybody got slightly bleary-eyed.

"I'm like a cat with nine lives, honey," Emma said. "I always land on my feet—been doing it all my life wherever I am. These Bolsheviks ain't gonna kill me."

At the enormous Scottsboro benfits, indoors or out, Emma would be introduced to a cheering audience as "our own beloved Negro comrade, Emma, who before she came to the Soviet motherland, knew the stinging lash of race hatred in her native America." Emma must have been in her early teens when she joined up with a show to leave Dixie. But she could denounce race prejudice in no uncertain terms, in long sentences, in fluent Russian, without taking a breath. At the end of her speech, she would hail the workers of the world, the Soviet Union, and Stalin, in traditional form, eyes blazing in her dark face, and walk off the platform to bravos. Had she been in a play, she would have taken a half-dozen bows after each speech.

"They ought to turn them colored boys loose," she would say, for Emma was truly moved at the plight of the youngsters in Kilby Prison. Her Scottsboro speeches came from the heart. But she had not been home for so long herself that she had lost all personal consciousness of color. When some of the members of our movie group told her that, were she to return to the land of color lines, she would not like it, she did not believe us. She honestly wanted to come back to America. "Things ain't what they used to be here since these soviet-skis come in," she said. "Why, I used to have me six servants and a boot boy. Now, best I can do is one old baba older'n me, part time."

It was Emma who first told us that summer that there was a famine in the Ukraine where, she said, the peasants had refused to harvest the grain. Living in the Grand Hotel and eating well, or accepting Emma's black-market hospitality, I never would have known there was hunger a few hundred miles South of Moscow. But Emma said, "Why down around Kharkov, people's so hungry they are slicing hams off each other's butts and eating them. That's no lie! A Russian I know just come from there; he told me folks is turned into cannibals."

Emma lived near one of the large Moscow railroad stations, so she met friends coming and going. She first told us about the many railroad wrecks that later that year were openly played up in the Soviet papers as an urgent problem to be remedied. Emma would say, "Man, last night there was a wreck right in the depot—one train going out, another coming in, both on the same track. These thick-headed comrades don't know how to run no trains. Bang! Fifty people smashed-up-kilt in the railroad yard. Ambulances been going by my door all night long."

Not a word of these frequent catastrophies would appear as news in the Moscow papers. But sometimes journalists in a position to know confirmed Emma's tales. Since the Soviet papers concerned themselves mostly with details of the Five Year Plan or decrees on collective farming, Emma would often say, "I ain't read about a good murder in no paper here in years. And these train wrecks you never read about, but they sure upset my nerves. Don't you think we need a little of this here Georgia brandy?"

The Georgia she referred to being in the Caucasus, not Dixie, Emma would pull out a bottle, almost always of a quality that few in Moscow could afford. Perhaps it was a gift from some foreign diplomat, she might explain casually, or from an American newspaperman with access to the valuta shops. Emma was a great favorite with the American colony in Moscow—of the right more than the left. The white Southerners especially loved her. Affectionately—and not at all derisively from their viewpoint—they called her "the Mammy of Moscow." Often to her they brought their excess food rations for a private feast, with the result that Emma's pantry was always full. She knew many styles of cuisine, having traveled all over Europe in her dancing days, and so could make anything from corn pudding to Hungarian goulash. But for her Southern friends Emma would cook corn bread and greens, spoon bread, also barbecued spareribs, if she could find any.

Emma had been in Russia long enough to know how to find almost anything. What she could not purchase in the regular food stores (which had little), she could locate on the open market, or else beg or borrow from some embassy, ballet dancer, or privileged foreign resident. Her friends were many, and her guests of varied sorts and character. For the dyed-in-the-wool leftist among the Americans in Moscow, Emma was too much of a "mammy," although they tolerated her. But the Russians of all classes seemed to accept her wholeheartedly. And the nonpolitical foreigners loved her. She was always a good hostess, jolly and full of humor—train wrecks or not. Certainly Emma added a big dash of color all her own to the grayness of Moscow.

## NEGROES IN THE USSR

OTHER than the colored students said to be in residence at the Lenin School (the official Communist Party School for foreign students which visitors never saw), there were in 1932 to my knowledge, not more than a half-dozen American Negroes in Moscow, with the exception of our movie group. Paul Robeson came later in concert, also Marian Anderson, and I believe Roland Hayes. Some years before, long before my arrival, the Jamaican poet Claude McKay had turned anti-Soviet and had gone to live in France, so his name was hardly mentioned when I was in Russia and his books were no longer on sale. What few Negroes there were in Moscow, of course, were conspicuous wherever they went, attracting friendly curiosity if very dark, and sometimes startling a peasant fresh from the country who had never seen a black face before.

The slender spectacled brownskin young technician named Robinson was well liked and was elected by his fellow factory workers to the Moscow City Soviet. Robinson invited me to a performance of *Eugene Onegin* at the Bolshoi Opera House, to which tickets were very hard to get. Being a worker in heavy industry, he could secure priority seats, so as his guest I sat in the orchestra of one of the great theaters of the world and saw a lavish production based on Pushkin's famous poem.

Pushkin, a descendant of "the Negro of Peter the Great," is adored in Russia and his mulatto heritage was constantly played up in the press when I was there. His *Onegin* and *Boris Goudunov* are standard in all Soviet schools. In the very heart of Moscow where the main trolley lines meet, there is a statue of Pushkin.

The professional actors in our group were by no means the first colored Thespians to visit Russia. Ida Forsyne had danced the cakewalk in Moscow at the turn of the century, and Abbie Mitchell and Georgette Harvey had had great popularity in St. Petersburg in Tzarist days. As far back as 1858, as the Moor in Shakespear's *Othello*, the New York Negro actor, Ira Aldridge, had created a sensation.

Russia, both before and after the Revolution, had a fondness for Negro artists, but after the Soviets came to power, not very many had been there. The reception accorded us twenty-two Negroes who came to make a movie—and whom the Muscovites took to be artists—could not have been more cordial had we been a Theatre Guild company starring the Lunts. The newspapers hailed our arrival with front-page stories and pictures. We were interviewed by press and radio. The leading theaters extended us invitations to dress rehearsals and performances. Bids to concerts, cultural events, receptions and parties were more than we could accept.

Although Negroes of African descent in Russia are few, there are millions of Asiatic peoples in the Soviet Union, so brownskins in Moscow were no rarity when we arrived to make our film. But, while we were there, the twenty-two colored folks from Harlem were lionized no end and at cultural gatherings we were always introduced as "representatives of the great Negro people."

Conscious of being wholeheartedly admired, we solemnly decided at one of our first group meetings in the Grand Hotel shortly after our arrival ,that we must all do our best to "uphold the honor of our race" while in Russia, and behave ourselves at all times in public. We did pretty well, I think; but occasionally somebody kicked over a bucket, to the embarrassment of most of the others. Then the leader would call a group meeting, speeches would be made, and the culprit chided for "disgracing the race"—usually by being a little too drunk at the Metropol bar. But occasionally something of more serious nature happened.

About a month after our arrival one of the girls in our group attempted suicide in a very unorthodox manner. Affairs of the heart having become complicated, as she later explained from a hospital bed, she came home one night to the Grand Hotel and put two bottles on her night table. One was a bottle of red wine, the other was a bottle of potassium formaldehyde, also red. She then put on her best lace nightgown, got into her enormous canopied bed and pondered whether to drink the wine and get drunk, or drink the potassium formaldehyde and die. When she thought of her beloved from Harlem with the Russian girl who had taken her place, she reached out and got the poisoned solution, turned the bottle up to her lips and drank. Fortunately, when it began to burn her stomach, she screamed, not once but half a dozen times. In fact, she screamed so loud that everybody in the hotel came running to see what was the matter. She was taken to the hospital and saved. A few days later she was back rehearsing spirituals with us. But the other girls declared that she, a Negro, had "disgraced the race," creating all that excitement in the Grand Hotel.

## WHITE SANDS OF ODESSA

PERHAPS if we had been hard at work making a film, the near tragedy of the suicide attempt might not have occurred. But by then we had seen most of the sights of Moscow, so there was little left to do except to go to shows, parties, Emma's house, or the Metropol Bar.

Folks were becoming bored. Few took the trouble to try to learn Russian, although a teacher was available. The days were long, and at night public places closed down too early to exhaust the energies of a group of lively Harlemites. One of the boys took up with a female truck driver, very buxom, hale, hearty and wholesome. But the others kidded him so about going with a truck driver that he ceased being seen with her near the Grand Hotel. Another of our intended actors somehow got his dates crossed for, at exactly the same moment one evening, two Soviet girls, not acquainted with each other, showed up at the hotel and asked to see him. The desk clerk rang his room, but before the fellow answered, the girls had begun to pull each other's hair out. When the young man arrived on the scene, he did his best to stop them, but the episode of hair-pulling spread all over Moscow. This deplorable incident, too, was considered at a group meeting as a "disgrace to the race."

"We need to be at work," our leader said. "Singing spirituals every other day is not enough. Idleness is demoralizing!"

Vainly he tried to get from the studio some schedule as to when actual filming would begin, but without success. I, as a writer, could get no information either beyond, "We're still considering the problems of the scenario."

Meanwhile, the director of the film, Yunghans, busied himself with the producing staff in casting the white roles. Only one white role was of any real importance to the plot, that of the labor organizer who endangered his life by attempting to organize Negroes and whites together in the South. For the part of this labor leader, an American dancer, John Bovington, had been chosen. When Mr. Bovington showed up at the studio, we did not think he looked like a labor organizer. He was of the school of modern interpretive dancing where every gesture has a meaning, a flow, a nuance. Our film was to be done in a naturalistic, not a stylized manner, so we were a bit puzzled at this selection for a worker's role.

After rehearsal, at supper with Yunghans and his charming blue-eyed wife, Yunghans asked, "Vot ist matter? Bovington nich look like American worker?"

I explained that American labor organizers, in the public mind, at least, were rough-and-tumble guys, not esthetic looking. Yunghans argued that he had been politically informed by Meschrabpom that progressive American organizers were very intelligent. I granted that they might be intelligent. But since in our film the man was to be portrayed organizing the steel industry, a tough field, he at least should look a little like a worker, and not walk like a dancer.

As Yunghans' wife made coffee after dinner, he and I went to sit on the balcony of their tall apartment house, the lights of Moscow in the darkness below. The young German was very distressed. After months of waiting to begin his first major picture, here he was with actors who had never acted, Negroes who could not sing, no scenario —and for his leading man, his worker-hero-labor organizer, a dancer! So much time being wasted, so slow, these Russians, so much red tape! In broken English, poor French and voluble German, Karl poured out his troubles on my shoulder. At the studio he was afraid to complain too loudly, to make too much fuss, because when he married one of Russia's prettiest young actresses, he had been promised permission to take her back to Germany with him. He was afraid this permission might not be forthcoming if he got in bad with the Soviet film-makers. But what can a man do? You can't make a film from nothing—and with nobody. Such stupidities drive an artist crazy.

In English, scanty French and bad German, I sympathized with Karl. But I also said quite plainly that I did not believe either of us would ever see a film called *Black and White*. Then, almost immediately I was sorry I'd said it. I could see that if the picture were not made, Yunghans would be even more disappointed than the young Negroes who had come all the way from Harlem to work in it. After all, film-making was his profession. He was young and ambitious. This was to have been his great opportunity. To the twenty-two of us from Harlem, it was partly a lark, a summer jaunt, plus a brief escape from the color lines back home. Only two or three of the Negroes were thinking seriously of a career in films. Most of them intended to get their Master's degrees in college and go into a profession. But Yunghans had come to Moscow to make a great picture. Now, with an absurd scenario, tone-deaf Negroes, and for a labor organizer, a dancer! His voice shook as he spoke of it. His world was going to pieces. I was glad when his wife came out on the balcony with the coffee, for I have never known what to do in the presence of heartbreak.

A few days later an order came from the Meschrabpom Studio that all twenty-two of us were to be transported that weekend to Odessa. We were told that portions of our picture would be filmed shortly on the Black Sea where the cotton fields of the South could be simulated. At the prospect of a change, we were all delighted. We proceeded to pack with alacrity, but we did not leave on schedule. Several days passed before the matter of tickets and train accommodations were worked out by the studio. Meanwhile some of us, at the invitation of the American journalist, Anna Louise Strong, attended a dance recital by John Bovington. Its main feature was a dance composition called *The Ascent of Man* which pictured Primeval Man emerging from the primal ooze to become MAN, with capital letters, in all his physical glory. This dance had originally been done naked. Moscow, although permitting nude bathing in the Park of Rest and Culture, did not condone nudity on the stage. So the night I saw him perform, Primeval Man possessed a loin cloth.

Circulating among the Americans in Moscow there were a number of amusing stories about John Bovington, who, like Isadora Duncan, had come to Russia seeking artistic freedom, only to find that he would be required to put on clothes when dancing. And he was a *nature* dancer, not a ballet dancer. He believed in the natural grace of the human body, not its distortion by toe-stands or the acrobatics of the entrechat. One of the stories about him was that he lived entirely on raw vegetables, fruits and nuts. He and his wife, Jeannie, were among the early American nudists. Another story about them was to the effect that once, in California, they had been invited to dance at an afternoon tea given by Charles Erskine Scott Wood and his wife, Sara Bard Field, at Los Gatos. Pedalling down from San Francisco to present *The Ascent of Man*, imagining themselves Adam and Eve in primal guise, within the gates of the estate, the Bovingtons dismounted from their bikes, removed their clothing, and proceeded to ride up to the door of Los Gatos unencumbered by raiment. The astonished butler, struck dumb, was unable to question their entry. Sara Bard Field and the Colonel, though surprised, did not bat an eye. The Bovingtons were presented to the guests as young dancers who would show how flesh emerged from the slime to become MAN and WOMAN.

A space was cleared before the stone fireplace and the dance began flat on the floor. But just as man wriggled upward to the point where he walked on his hands, and was about to become half human, somebody laughed. At this affront, Bovington leaped like Tarzan to the mantelpiece and sat there, glaring at the offender. People thought this a part of the dance at first, as both he and his wife froze into postures of contemplation. Finally, when nothing more happened, someone asked if the program was over, and if they might all have a drink. No answer on Bovington's part. He simply sat like Rodin's Thinker on the shelf above the fireplace. It took a great deal of persuasion on Colonel Wood's part to persuade the dancers to continue *The Ascent of Man*.

When I met John Bovington in Moscow, his wife, Jeannie, had divorced him to marry the famous Russian playwright, Afinogeniev. Without her lovely presence, *The Ascent of Man* was not as thrilling as I imagine it had once been. Nevertheless, Bovington still gave an impressive performance alone. When we met at the studio, it turned out he had never seen the scenario of the picture he was to make. No one *had* seen the scenario other than Karl Yunghans, myself, the studio executives, and, I presume, the Comintern. My copy had been taken from me for revisions. As to whether the script would be entirely rewritten or not, no official would commit himself. My guess was that the whole matter was undergoing political consideration at the Comintern, and that nothing creatively was being done on it.

When the members of our group asked me what was happening, all I could say was, "Certain changes still have to be made in the script."

"They certainly take their time," was the opinion of the Negroes, "but we should worry."

All of us were being paid regularly, wined and dined overmuch and had the whole theater world of Moscow for our enjoyment. Nevertheless, we were glad to board a train for the Black Sea. On the way south, stopping at Kiev, we heard there was a Negro resident, so we immediately expressed our desire to meet him. Since we were only there overnight, it took quite a lot of doing on the part of our translator-guides to locate him. But finally he was found and brought to our hotel late in the evening to meet us. I have never seen a more astonished human being, for this Negro in Kiev had probably never seen a black face before, other than his own in the mirror. At the sight of twenty-two Negroes all at once, he was struck dumb. His language was Ukranian, not Russian, and he was probably of Abkhasian descent from the small colony of former Turkish slaves on the Black Sea. Somehow, during the turbulent years of the Revolution he had gotten tossed onto the streets of Kiev where eventually he became a fireman, riding a big truck through the streets of the city whenever a blaze broke out. He looked to be about thirty, tall, dark and rather handsome, but not at all talkative. In fact, he looked as if he were afraid of us and as soon as he politely could, the Negro excused himself and disappeared.

In Odessa we were housed in a charming hotel near the sea, where an electric fountain fell in vari-colored spray at dinner in an open-air patio. Odessa was a de luxe Soviet resort for higher-echelon workers, and its hotels were very beautiful. I had never stayed in such hotels in my own country since, as a rule, Negroes were not then permitted to do so. Besides, I had never had enough money for such fine living in America.

At that time Piscator was working on a picture laid in Holland, and a whole Dutch village had been built for him on a plateau just outside Odessa. And not far from our hotel were the famous white steps to the sea where *Potemkin* had been filmed. The water front that served as background for portions of this famous film was within walking distance. And there were wonderful beaches all about. There were no signs of any sets constructed as yet for our film, and neither the director nor any of the studio executives had come to the Black Sea with us. We were completely on our own, and did as we pleased, so most of the day we spent in the warm sun at the beaches with crowds of Russians, all in their best bathing suits, since at Odessa it was not considered chic to bathe nude as did the Muscovites on the Moscow River.

By this time, the influence of our group leadership was at a low ebb. The Negro in charge had so often tried to present an optimistic picture as to the date for the making of our film, but weeks had gone by and as yet nothing encouraging had happened. The group had begun to split up into cliques and factions. One faction had begun to feel that the Soviets were deliberately giving them the run-around. So why go out of their way to please the Russians anyhow? As to bathing nude in Odessa, why not? With such wide and wonderful beaches, one faction reasoned, nude bathing made much more sense there than it did on the crowded banks of the Moscow River, where a person might dive under the water only to come up accidentally among the opposite sex a few feet away. The result of this reasoning was that, in spite of the pleas of our group leader, that summer thousands of astonished citizens from all over the Soviet Union, dressed in their best bathing suits, would suddenly see streaking down the Odessa sands a dark amazon pursued by two or three of the darkest tallest and most giraffe-like males they had ever seen—all as naked as birds and as frolicsome as Virginia hounds, diving like porpoises into the surf, or playing leapfrog nude all over the place.

## THE BITTER END

AS guest of the Theatrical Trade Unions we were invited on a pleasure cruise of the Black Sea, a gay and pleasant trip around the Crimean Peninsula to Sebastapol, Yalta, Gagri, Sotchi, Sukhum, and down the coast almost to Turkey. One of the members of our group had been left behind in Moscow, hospitalized with a minor ailment, so he was not with us on the cruise nor had he reached Odessa when on our return we went back to the hotel where the illuminated fountain played. More days of sunshine and sea bathing followed, but still there was no word of a filming schedule. Then suddenly one morning our entire group was rounded up posthaste for an urgent meeting. Our missing member had just arrived from Moscow with important news. When we were all assembled, the young man arose gravely, faced us for a moment in silence, then solemnly announced, "Comrades, we've been screwed!"

From his pocket he pulled a recent copy of the *Paris Herald Tribune* with a despatch to the effect that our film had been canceled. "And they didn't even have the courtesy to tell us," he cried. "I got up out of my sickbed and went to the studio to check this—*Black and White* is abandoned."

The story had been given to the newspapers a week before any of the cast learned about it. Later the studio claimed that since we were on a cruise, we could not be reached when the decision was made. The day after we got the news, one of the Meschrabpom executives arrived in Odessa to inform us officially that there would be no picture, but that we would be paid in full for the duration of our contracts, and that transportation via London, Paris, or Berlin, back to the United States would be available whenever we wished to depart. Relative to the future we were offered three choices: exit visas at any time, an extended tour of the Soviet Union before leaving, or work in the Soviet Union for any who desired to remain permanently. All of us were invited to stay in Russia as long as we wished.

No Negroes went bathing on the Odessa beaches that day. Instead, hell broke loose. Hysterics took place. Some of the girls really wanted desperately to be movie actresses. Others in the group claimed the *whole* Negro race had been betrayed by Stalin. Some said the insidious hand of American race prejudice had a part in it all—that Jim Crow's dark shadow had fallen on Moscow, and that Wall Street and the Kremlin now conspired together never to let the world see in films what it was like to be a downtrodden Negro in America. From morn to midnight factional group meetings were interrupted only long enough to eat. Almost everyone had a different opinion. There was a general agreement on only one thing—that we should return to Moscow immediately for a showdown with the film company. As soon as accommodations could be arranged, we entrained for the capital, leaving the white sands of Odessa behind us.

We got back to Moscow to find the city filled with late summer visitors, and all the hotels crowded to capacity. A great many English and American tourists were there spending foreign money, so they were given preference as to rooms. There was no space at the Grand Hotel. Finally Meschrabpom was able to get us accommodations at a small hostel directly in front of the main gate of the Kremlin. It was called the Mininskaya. Distinctly third rate, it had no dining room, and no private baths. Very minor officials from the provinces seemed to constitute its guests. But its location was fascinating, just a few hundred yards down the hill from St. Basil's Church, between the Moscow River and Lenin's Tomb, and right across the street from the big gate through which the sleek cars of Voroshilov and Stalin sped past the Kremlin walls. I liked the Mininskaya better than I did the Grand. It seemed much more like an integral part of Russia to me.

Violent dissensions split our group asunder. Tempers flared. Some contended that all of us were merely being used as pawns in a game of international politics. Because Washington's recognition of Russia was rumored in the offing, not only our film, some said, but the cause of Negro rights was being sacrificed to curry American favor. Two members of our group claimed that Colonel Raymond Robbins had urged them weeks ago, over drinks in the Metropol Bar, to withdraw from the cast of a motion picture which, in the colonel's opinion, would be a black mark against the United States. Colonel Robbins was said to have been sent to Russia as a negotiator concerning future diplomatic relations between the two countries.

Certainly newspapers all over the world reported the canceled *Black and White*. The New York *Herald Tribune* story read in part:

## NEGROES ADRIFT IN "UNCLE TOM'S" RUSSIAN CABIN
### *Harlem Expeditionary Unit Is Stranded in Moscow*

Moscow, Aug. 11—A sensation has been caused in the American colony here by the sudden collapse of the Meschrabpom project to produce a motion picture depicting "the exploitation of the Negro in America from the days of slavery to the present." As a result of this collapse the future of twenty-two American Negroes, including Langston Hughes, novelist and poet, who was brought here from New York two months ago to play the principal role in the film, is uncertain. . . . The correspondent understands that the Soviet authorities suppressed the film for fear that its appearance would prejudice American opinion against the Soviet Union.

Since the occupation of Manchuria by Japan the Soviet authorities more than ever have been eager for a re-approachment with the United States as a means, among other things, of strengthening the position of the USSR in the Far East.

Another American newspaper said:

. . . It was persistently rumored among Americans in Moscow that the film would never be produced. It was known that many influential Americans were actively working against the project. Foremost among these was Colonel Hugh Cooper, builder of the recently constructed Dnieperstroi Dam, the largest engineering feat of its kind in the world. Cooper is reputed to be the one foreigner who has free access to the offices of Joseph Stalin. . . . Upon hearing of the project, he hastened to Moscow for a conference with Stalin. Finding the Soviet Dictator out of the city, the engineer secured an interview with V. M. Molotov, chairman of the Council of People's Commissars. Those Russians and Americans close to the source of information in Moscow insist that the film was ordered off within twenty-four hours after this interview.

Some of the newspapers at home certainly made the physical situation of our group in Moscow seem much worse than it really was. One representative of a leading American news service cabled to New York—and the world—stories to the effect that all of us were stranded, starving in Moscow, unfed, unpaid and destitute. He knew better, for he saw some of us spending money daily at the Metropol Bar or lunching in its expensive dining room. But the papers for which he wrote were anti-Negro and anti-Soviet, so when we showed him the clippings after they reached us by air, he simply grinned. It was the first time I realized that a big-name correspondent would deliberately lie to conform to an editorial policy. We were neither stranded, unpaid, nor destitute and he knew it. But the result of his stories was a flood of frantic cables from relatives in America, worried about our fate.

The Meschrabpom officials finally informed the group officially that the scenario was inadequate. They said it was unfortunately not worthy of the kind of picture they had hoped to make. They also indicated politely that the Negro actors were not *quite* what they had expected, either—which did not soothe tempers any. But most of our group brushed these explanations off simply as false excuses to cancel the film. About half of our group leaned strongly to the contention that its cancellation was a betrayal of the Negro in exchange for diplomatic relations with Washington. I stated in a group meeting that, in any case, no decent film could have been made from the scenario, and had we made that particular film, all of us would have been ashamed of it in the end. Whereupon, one of the members of the group arose to call me a *Communist* Uncle Tom. He solemnly stated that my books in the United States had never amounted to much, so for that reason I had come to the Soviet Union to build a new literary career. And he closed his speech by terming me an opportunistic son-of-a-bitch. I arose to call him a similar name—so the meeting broke up in general vituperations. But later we laughed about it, made up, and from then on everybody jokingly called all of our meetings "son-of-a-bitch meetings."

As to what to do about the situation—since it seemed impossible to gain immediate access to Stalin as some wished—we argued loud and long in the Mininskaya Hotel. Sometimes during our discussion, across the street beyond the Kremlin walls, we would hear Stalin's guards at rifle practice.

Someone would say, "Hear that? They just shot another Russian."

Somebody else would joke, "Shsss-ss-s! I found a dictaphone behind the radiator this morning. Do you want to be liquidated?"

After several days it was agreed by unanimous vote that we would present our case to the Comintern, which was said to be, next to the Kremlin itself, the last word on international affairs. So a delegation including myself, was chosen to go to the Comintern. There we were received by several old Bolsheviks sitting at a long table in a gloomy room. Some of our delegation arose and denounced Meschrabpom, Communism and "the Soviet betrayal of the Negro race" in no uncertain terms. I took the position that it was regrettable no film was to be produced, but since the script had been so mistakenly conceived, it seemed to me wise to make none. However, I hoped that at some future date a picture dramatizing race relations sympathetically—in a way which, up to that time, Hollywood had not chosen to do—might be brought to completion. Gravely, we were thanked for our statements, and told that the Comintern would take the whole matter under immediate consideration and give it the most serious attention. So far as I know, however, no such picture as *Black and White* has yet been made in the USSR—or anywhere else in the world. The problems of organized labor and race in the Deep South are still to be brought to the screen.

# 4

# SOUTH TO
# SAMARKAND

MOST of my life from childhood on has been spent moving, traveling, changing places, knowing people in one school, in one town or in one group, or on one ship a little while, but soon never seeing most of them again. So it happened between me and the twenty-one other would-be movie-makers. When our contracts with Meschrabpom Films were terminated, we scattered to the four winds. Some returned to the United States almost at once. Others lingered in Berlin or Paris, taking advantage of their trip to become acquainted with various parts of Europe. Some stayed in Moscow until the November seventh celebrations. Three of the members of our group remained in Russia permanently—the actor, Wayland Rudd; the artist, Lloyd Patterson; and the former postal clerk from Minneapolis, Homer Smith. All three, so I was informed, eventually learned to speak Russian well and took an active part in the life of the Soviet capital.

Wayland Rudd appeared in the leading Moscow theaters as well as in motion pictures, and during World War II he performed for the Soviet troops at the various fronts. Lloyd Patterson, a graduate of Hampton in Virginia, married a young Russian who was a scene designer and together they created the sets for a number of Soviet plays. They had two beautiful children who, when brown youngsters were needed for plays or films, were often given such roles. But in the early 'forties Patterson died and was buried in Moscow. Homer Smith

supervised the installation of the first special-delivery service in the
Russian post offices, and helped modernize their postal-money-order
system along American lines. At the same time he acted as Moscow
correspondent for various American Negro newspapers and, during
the war, went to Ethiopia in that capacity. Smith also married a Russian woman. So, of the twenty-two of us, three adopted the soil of the
Soviets as a permanent homeland. And one, of West Indian nationality, was denied entry on his return to New York; so, as a result of
his movie ambitions, he was forced to return to his native island in
lieu of the residence he had hoped to establish in the United States.
Eighteen, however, eventually came back to the U. S. A. I remained
abroad for more than a year as a writer and journalist. Others stayed
in Europe even longer.

When the theatrical sections of the Soviet Trade Unions offered
us a tour to any section of the Soviet Union we might be interested
in seeing, some of our group—those who felt most deeply that we had
been betrayed—indignantly rejected the invitation. Others felt they
had seen enough of the USSR, so were more anxious to go to Paris.
But about half accepted the travel invitation before applying for exit
visas. It did not take us long to agree among ourselves that the portions of the Soviet Union we would most like to see were those regions
where the majority of the colored citizens lived, namely Turkmenistan
in Soviet Central Asia. This gave our trade-union hosts pause because,
at that time, this part of the Soviet Union was forbidden territory to
foreigners. Only a very few selected journalists, and no tourists, were
permitted there. It was said to be a land still in flux, where Soviet
patterns were as yet none too firmly fixed, therefore it was not open
to general inspection. But we stuck to our expressed desire to see it,
and I applied for a press permit not only to tour, but to remain in
Central Asia long enough to write about it for publications in
America.

The official *Guide Book for the Soviet Union* which I had purchased in Moscow clearly stated in italicized letters: *A permit granted
by the Consulate of the USSR to visit the Soviet Union is not valid
for the territory of Turkmenistan. Foreigners who intend to visit
Turkmenistan must have a special permit.*

Fortunately one of the prettiest girls in our motion-picture brigade had attracted the eye of the Soviet head of foreign press relations for the Kremlin, Constantine Oumansky, then a debonair young Muscovite. Since he spoke English and was friendly and cosmopolitan in manner, some of us came to know him quite well. The beautiful girl herself was frequently squired about Moscow to supper or the ballet by Comrade Oumansky, who later became the Russian ambassador to the United States, and some years thereafter was killed in a plane crash in Mexico. It was through Oumansky that I got my press card for Soviet Asia and, I think, due to his influence that the rest (including the girl he liked) were enabled to tour the regions beyond the Urals and travel almost to the Chinese border. So, with two representatives of the trade-unions, an executive of Meschrabpom Films, and our translators, about a dozen of us entrained for the long five-day trip to Tashkent, the regional capital of Soviet Central Asia. Loaded down with cheeses, sausages, teapots and enormous loaves of black bread, we departed. The Moscow-Tashkent trains were not de luxe express trains, and we were warned that the trip might not be so comfortable a one as a tour somewhere within European Russia. But I did not find the trip nearly so unpleasant as many I had made on Jim Crow trains at home, where I could not eat in the diner and was segregated in a single coach.

On the Moscow-Tashkent express, we had the run of the train, soon knew everybody and everybody knew us, so we had a lot of fun. Russian travelers, men and women, are great joke tellers. They spend hours telling witty stories, mostly smutty, and some downright obscene. Their jokes often put translators at a loss to convey the point in decent English. The first day everybody talked politely about such things as the Five Year Plan, Voroshilov's horse, or the new ballet at the Bolshoi. The next day folks inquired about conditions in "starving America" where, they had heard, the depression had reduced everyone to skin and bones. But the third day as the train rocked along into Asia such tame subjects had worn thin. By then, too, mandolins and guitars, balalaikas and accordions had set everyone to dancing in the aisles, and friendships had become more intimate across political and national lines. Russians are great folk singers, handclappers and dancers. Unfortunately, we were unable to meet our fellow travelers song for song. But I had brought along my victrola with Louis Armstrong and Ethel Waters, so I contributed some lusty canned music to the long ride through the Ural Mountains and the Kizyl Kum Desert.

With our new and interesting companions, the days on the road passed quickly. First, the rich farm lands of the Black Earth region slid by our windows with stations where buxom peasant women from the kolhozes sold chickens and cheese and eggs; then the Volga at sunset, famous old river of song and story; later, Orenburg where Asia begins and where we saw camels in the streets; then the vast reaches of the Kirghiz steppes and the bright tip of the Ural Sea like silver in the sun.

On the day we passed through the Kazakstan Desert, the fortieth anniversary of Gorky's literary life was being celebrated throughout the Soviet Union. The passengers and the crew of our train organized a meeting. At a little station where the train stopped in the late afternoon, we went onto the platform where short speeches were made in honor of Gorky and his work. Even in the heart of the desert, Russia's most famous living writer was not forgotten. Nomad Kazaks, the men in great coats of skins, the women in white headdresses, mingled with the passengers. A young student poet spoke; then a representative of the train crew; and someone from the station staff. My speech in English was translated first into Russian, and then into the Kazak tongue. Before we climbed back into our coaches, a telegram to Gorky was signed by all the passengers.

On that five-day trip I drank tea constantly. At every stop men and women would leap off the train and run with a teapot to the hot water faucet protruding from the wall of every station. Then they would jump back on the train and brew tea. So, singing, joke telling, dancing and tea drinking, we gradually emerged from the desert one afternoon to speed through a fertile oasis of water and greenery, cotton growing, trees in fruit, then crowds of yellow-brown Uzbeks in brightly flowered robes, waving from village stations. At evening we came to Tashkent, the regional center of Soviet Asia. As we pulled into the depot, there stood a young Negro resplendent in a stiff white shirt and black tuxedo.

Having since been around the world, I have learned that there is at least one Negro everywhere. In the crowd of Asiatic writers, artists and theater people who came to meet us at the station, stood Bernard

Powers, a graduate of the Department of Engineering at Howard University in Washington. Powers said he hadn't had a chance to put on his tuxedo for months, so he'd gotten all dressed up to meet us. Sweaty, dusty and tired from our long train ride, we were a bit embarrassed, not only at the elegant young man but also at all the exotically clothed Uzbeks, Turkomens and Tartars in their national gowns and veils, who crowded about us with gifts of fruit and flowers. In the night air there was the smell of the Orient—a kind of mixture of musk, melons and dust that seemed everywhere a part of the East. This smell, the tiny flares that in the early darkness augmented the street lights, and here and there the sound of a muted lute, were my initial impressions of Tashkent as we drove to a party.

Ten days had been allotted to the Central Asiatic portion of our trip. Then, leaving me behind to write, the group intended to go across the Caspian Sea to Azerbaidzhan to visit Tiflis, Rostov-on-the-Don, Dneiproistroi Dam, and Kharkov, then back to Moscow. Our Central Asian itinerary included the ancient cities of Samarkand, Bokhara, Ashkhabad and the Asiatic port of Krasnovodsk where the boats sailed for Baku.

At Tashkent we were luncheon guests of the Women's Club. Then the President of the Uzbek Republic, Achum Babief, and the Vice President, a former veiled woman, Jahan Abinova, received us at tea in the offices of their modern new government building. For three days, everywhere we went, delegations greeted us with speeches in Russian, Uzbek, Tartar or Turkomen. Between the sight-seeing and the speeches—Soviet speeches are often very serious and very long—by nightfall we were worn out. After the free and easy life we'd led in Moscow and Odessa, unregimented all summer long, the earnest and intense hospitality extended us in Tashkent with its day-long schedule of planned activities was almost too much to take. All of us were glad to get on the train and move on to Samarkand. But that fabulous old city was almost as full of Soviet socialist zeal as Tashkent had been. The famous Mosque of Bibi Khanum and a few other lovely sights were granted us. But most of our time was taken by a visit to the University, an inspection of the first medical school in Central Asia, then under construction, and by trade-union teas where statistics galore were relayed from one language to another, and expectantly aimed

at our nonabsorbent heads by enthusiastic Communists. Before the
week was up most of the members were weary of welcoming commit-
tees, weary of speeches, and weary of Central Asia, even if it was full
of colored Orientals.

The native officials everywhere tried too hard to convince us of
the progress made under the new regime. Perhaps they were afraid we
might think that not much had happened in Central Asia. A great
deal had happened, as I was to learn in a more leisurely fashion later.
But thousands of women were still in harems in spite of the new
decrees, and veiled from head to foot in public. Muezzins still called
to prayer from tall towers. Bazaars were still filthy. The streets were
dusty and it was very hot. For us, this intensified bird's eye view plus
a ton of statistics made our tour seem much like trying to do the
Metropolitan Museum in half an hour—leaving a daze in the mind and
a haze before the eyes. By the time we reached Bokhara, the Negroes
in our group were ready to go back to Moscow, or anywhere else outside of Central Asia.

"One more speech *triple* translated, and one more statistic on
anything will kill me," declared the pretty girl whose influence had
gotten us entry into this forbidden territory. "No wonder they refuse
to let tourists come to Turkmenistan!"

The last stop on our Asiatic schedule was to have been Ashkah-
bad where we were to have spent two days. Then the group was to
leave me there. With the help of our guides and translators, I expected
in two days to be safely settled in a hotel with contacts made for a
more extensive exploration of the region. In a city where the prevail-
ing language was Turkoman, of which I had never heard a word, I
would need the help of a translator at first to get my bearings. But
now most of the members of our group expressed a desire to eliminate
Ashkabad. I asked if they would stop with me for just a day, but a
group meeting to consider this was held on the train between Bokhara and Ashkabad, and everyone—but myself—voted to cut Ashkabad
out. Enough was enough, they said, of dust and sun, statistics and
speeches. Furthermore, they tried to persuade me to give up my idea
of remaining in Soviet Asia. For them a week had proved sufficient.
With Tiflis and Moscow (where the Metropol Bar had ice-cooled

drinks) in the offing, why linger in a dusty, sun-struck desert like Turkmenistan? Come on back to comfort, they argued.

I seldom become angry. When I do, I usually don't say a word. I just get sick inside. So after the group decision, I got sick and couldn't (or wouldn't) eat the luncheon of bread and cheese, fruit and wine that the others shared as the old train rocked and rolled across the Kara Kum Desert. The least my companions might do, I thought, was to stop overnight in Ashkabad—so that the translators and trade-union officials might help me get settled.

Come to think of it, maybe the Russian trade-union officials and the Meschrabpom representative on the train didn't think well of my staying in Central Asia, either. Maybe they had influenced the group's vote in the hope that I would not insist on getting off there without guidance and remaining to look too closely at this rugged part of the USSR, so far from Moscow. Certainly they hinted strongly that other portions of the Soviet Union which I had not yet visited—the Volga River region, for example—might be of more interest for writing. The Russians made no effort to persuade my companions to change their decision and get off the train with me for a look at Ashkhabad which, said the guide book, was in one of the oldest sections in the world, washed by the mighty tides of history. Old or not, nobody wanted to see it. And none of them did, for suddenly, almost without warning, the train came to a stop in the middle of a sandy plain, and there on a sign above a little wooden station was the word: ASHKHABAD.

Surprised at being at the station so suddenly, and angry with the others anyhow, I jumped off the train without handshakes or farewells. A couple of fellows were decent enough to toss my bags down. With a hoot, the train pulled away, gathering speed across the sands, leaving me alone. Dark heads from open windows cried, "Goodbye! So long!" But I did not say a word. Instead, I turned the other way and walked toward the station. As the last coach rattled by, to myself I said, "To hell with all of you! I hope I never see any of you again."

Then I looked around and did not see a human soul. The platform was utterly deserted. There was no town anywhere in sight. The city was miles away. I had been told that in Asia in Tzarist days, the Russians did not build colonial railroads for the convenience of travelers. They were military highways. Across this desert the tracks had been laid in a straight line between one garrison center and another, regardless of how far off the lines the towns might be. To the eye of passengers, ASHKHABAD was only a wooden depot in a dusty desert. Today it seemed deserted.

But presently an old Turkoman in a shoddy black robe and a moth-eaten turban appeared to pick up a mailbag that had been dropped from the train. He said not a word as he shuffled around a corner of the depot, then back out of sight. I quickly walked in that direction to see where he had gone. But his tiny one-horse cart with the bag bouncing around inside was already off in a cloud of dust down a long straight desert road that seemed to lead only to a curved and very distant horizon. I went inside the station and found behind the wicket a man who seemed to be the station master. He spoke Russian. I showed him my foreign press card. He asked me if I were German.

I said, "No, niet."

"French?"

"No," I said, "Amerikanski."

He replied in Russian that he would phone a man who spoke French, the editor of the newspaper. The telephone on the wall was like those I remembered as a child in Kansas before the First World War. He cranked it with a little crank, then he spoke with someone —evidently far beyond the curve of the dusty horizon. Then he said to me, "Sit down. He will come soon, perhaps."

I knew that to a Russian soon might mean anytime between morning and night, so I went down the track in the blazing sun and gathered up my baggage, bringing it piece by piece into the station— first my heavy bags, then the smaller bag and a lunch box, then my typewriter, my victrola and the record box. The records seemed heavier than usual, and I had no help to carry any of these things. All of my friends (or rather former friends) had gone speeding over the horizon toward the Caspian, heading for the gardens of Tiflis, then Moscow, Berlin, Paris and New York—while here I was in the middle of the Turkmenian desert with nobody to help me even carry a bag. It took three trips before I had all my luggage inside the station. A scorching wind filled the air with dust and sand. I was wet with sweat and sticky with dirt. But I was not sorry for myself, nor did I feel sad. I was just mad as I looked down the long empty track.

"You don't need to stop with me in Ashkhabad, you low-life Negroes! You dirty Russians! Double-crossing movie-makers! You trade-union Communists! I'll get along! I damn sure bet you I'll get along! Right here in the middle of this Godforsaken desert, I'll make it!"

As I dropped my last piece of luggage on the depot floor, the station master offered me a cigarette. I took it. Together we lit up. He must have noticed the frown on my face.

"*Nichevo,*" he said with a grin.

*Nichevo* can mean a hundred different things in Russian, depending on the inflection. In this case, there in the middle of the desert, I gathered that it meant, "So . . . Well? . . . What's the difference? . . . Anyhow, to hell with it!"

"*Nichevo,*" I grinned back at him.

We both laughed.

## ASHKHABAD ADVENTURE

AFTER a while, through the dusty haze of the afternoon, I saw approaching away off on the rim of the horizon, a cloud of dust. Then with—through—and out of the dust came a battered old car. From the car jumped a European in shirt sleeves, "Bonjour, comrade." He was the editor. Helping me pile my bags into the back of the car, we headed for Ashkhabad, a dust-laden city of some forty thousand Turkomans.

On the way I told the editor about myself and our movie of which he had heard nothing. The foreign papers had carried the news of its cancellation, but not the Soviet press. I told the man I wanted to stay in Ashkhabad awhile, get acquainted with the people, and write, and that I hoped I would find a Turkoman-Russian-English translator. He said he thought there was a man in town who spoke English, a teacher; he would locate him and send him to me. Meanwhile, he must find me a place to stay—and, more important, a place to eat. He telephoned the OGPU, which, everywhere I went, I learned was to be my greatest source of help. When the editor hung up his phone, we went out to the car again and I was driven to a small Soviet guesthouse not far from the public square of the city. I was told that I could eat at the OGPU restaurant and that someone would come for me in time for dinner. Then the newspaper man left me to relax and wash up.

Water was out in the yard somewhere, and one fetched it in a big old-fashioned white pitcher that sat in a china washbowl on a stand in the corner. The toilets were far out in the back yard and they were full of stinging white lime, strong enough to make one's eyes water. The guesthouse was very quiet when I arrived, and it remained that way most of the time. At first nobody in Ashkhabad seemed to be doing anything. In contrast to Tashkent and Samarkand, it was a sleepy old town. The big billboards of Stalin and Lenin in the park were veiled with dust. When I looked out of the guesthouse door that afternoon, all I saw passing in the street was a lethargic donkey with a pile of faggots on its back, whacked occasionally on reluctant haunches by a sleepy-looking little Turkoman boy. So I went inside, cranked my victrola and put on a good loud Louis Armstrong record which lit up the house with trumpet lightning. As the record ran down, I must have dozed off across the bed.

The next thing I knew, there was a vigorous rap and, without ceremony, in came a bright-eyed, grinning Oriental youth in a spick-and-span Red Army uniform, smartly cut, his boots gleaming. Caught half napping, before I could rise from across the bed, he had reached out his hand. A stream of musical inflections filled my ears—but I had not the least idea what he was saying. The language was one I had never heard. I took for granted, however, that he had come to take me to dinner, so I got up, ran a comb through my hair, and put on my jacket. He motioned that it wasn't time to eat yet, so I motioned him to sit down. Since he kept right on talking in his musical tongue without a word of Russian mixed in, I began to talk in English. Thus we carried on a conversation in which neither understood the other.

I would have thought understanding under such conditions impossible, but I learned differently. Later, when the teacher came to call on me, it turned out that he spoke *not* English but Flemish. There was at that time no one in Ashkhabad who spoke English—not a human soul. My Red Army friend came from the high Pamirs away up near the Sinkiang border, and spoke only his own strange language. He was a captain of the border guard, and looked like a Chinese Negro, very brown, but with Oriental eyes. He was my friend for weeks, in fact my boon buddy, yet I never knew a word he said. However, when the ear gives up and intuition takes over, some sort of understanding develops instinctively.

That evening when it came time to go to dinner, he talked all the way. The OGPU restaurant was a big, bright, spotlessly clean place. It seemed to be air-cooled, so pleasant was it in contrast to the hot, dusty streets. There were white table cloths. Dinner, Russian style, was good, and the room was filled mostly with Russians. More than half wore Red Army uniforms. I supposed all of the men were of the Russian Intelligence Service. The few whom I met were cordial, welcomed me to Ashkhabad, and said they hoped I would find it interesting. In the days that followed, I developed a speaking acquaintance with several, but never came to know any well, other than my Mongol-looking friend of the unknown tongue.

He was a very outgoing fellow, this captain, lots of fun, intensely active, crazy about my Ooo-wee Harm-Strung records (as he termed Satchmo), a stout vodka drinker, good at wine, a woman chaser and an acrobat. He invited me to the circus, and afterward came back to my room and did half of the flips and flops that the circus folks did. Another thing that intrigued me about this hard-as-nails little soldier was that at dinner, when apricots were served, he ate not only the boiled fruit, but cracked open all the seeds with his teeth, and ate them, too. He ate the seeds of everything, from melons to peaches and plums. I never did get his name straight, but it sounded like Yeah Tlang, or Yaddle-oang, or Ya-Gekiang. He said it so fast and matter-of-factly, as if I must be familiar with it, that when I slowed him down, it didn't sound the same at all. As nearly as I could gather, it had two and a half or three syllables. I finally settled for a nickname of my own coining, *Yeah Man*, and he called me *Yang Zoon* which seemed to be the best he could do with Langston. Yeah Man was a bright fellow, though I think he was allergic to languages. But after a while each understood everything the other said—or implied—without strain, and with laughter.

Yeah Man's Russian was far worse than mine when he would try to speak it at all. And only a woman could persuade him to try. Yeah Man had been in Ashkhabad about a month and he already knew half the women in town, married and unmarried, Russian, Turkoman, Uzbek and Tartar. He seldom slept in his barracks. Yet most of the women never knew a word that he said. When I met him, he was smitten with one of the wire-walking girls in the little circus that had somehow gotten away out in that desert. He brought her around to my room one night to hear my Ooo-wee Harm-Strung discs. When he called her a few sweet things in very comical Russian, she almost lost her balance, since she wasn't on a wire, just on his lap.

Yeah Man was not what one would call a gentleman in so far as women went. To kiss and tell was the least of it. He loved to describe his conquests in full, by gestures when words failed, with a play-by-play description of what happened the night before. He graciously told me that, should I ever come to visit him in his high mountain pass, one of his wives would be mine. (It seems he had several wives.) Thinking this strange, I read up on the high Pamirs in an old English history of Tzarist Asia that I found in the Ashkhabad library and, sure enough, it said there was a tribe on the Singkiang frontier whose hospitality was not complete until the host had offered each guest a wife for the night. Had I been able to jokingly convey my meaning to Yeah Man, I would have asked, "Is that sovietski?" But it would have been just a joke—for I knew that many things were still happening in Soviet Asia that were not what the Soviet idealists wished. So I simply indicated that I would be delighted to accept one of his wives were I ever to visit him. Then he proceeded to outline to me the sizes and shapes of the women in his harem.

Some guy, that Yeah Man! We saw the circus together five or six times that fall, and we went calling on various girls with gifts of bread or brandy. Sometimes girls came with us to the guesthouse to dance to my records. The days went by swiftly; October came—and I still hadn't the first note on the Turkoman cotton quotas or anything else of significance for the articles I intended to write. My conscience began to get the better of me. So one night I dismissed Yeah Man after our OGPU dinner, said good night loudly and indicated I was going home to sleep—eyes closed, palm to cheek—since by gestures I didn't know how to indicate home *to work*. At any rate, that cocky captain went his way, no doubt a-courting, and I returned to my abode alone intending to do a little writing. I opened my typewriter, putting a record on the machine meanwhile, and started searching around in my bag for some typing paper. But I have found the world over that, just when a writer *finally* gets in the mood to write, something happens. I had decided after the disc ran out, not to play another record, when a knock came on my door. Thinking Yeah Man probably had come around again in spite of my rather positive good night, I yelled without moving from my typewriter, "Come on in."

The door opened and an intense-looking young white man, in European clothing, with a sharp face and rather oily dark hair stepped in.

"Excuse me," I said in Russian as I jumped up, "I thought you were someone else. I don't believe I know your name."

"Arthur Koestler," he said in English.

"Where from?" I asked, since I'd never heard of him before.

"Berlin," he said. "I heard music playing and thought I'd knock. I just got here today."

"Well, sit down," I said. "I'm sorry I haven't got a thing to drink."

"I'm not drinking," he said, "but I like jazz."

So jazz it was—and that was the end of writing for the evening. I played half of my records. As I played, I learned that he had been to the North Pole with the Graf Zeppelin as a reporter for the giant Ullstein chain of German publications. Now he had come to the USSR to do a series of articles on socialist achievements. When I told him I was a writer, too, he asked what material I had gathered in Ashkhabad. I was ashamed to tell him, "Nothing." He had many questions about the city, but I was of little help.

"No matter," he said, "we'll start digging up facts together tomorrow. A writer must write."

So it was Koestler, really, who started me to work in Ashkhabad. He wasn't happy unless he was doing something useful—if happy then.

Even listening to music, Koestler would be thinking about work. But he spoke English—and I was glad to find somebody in the Kara Kum Desert who did. Together for weeks we tracked down what was happening in Soviet Asia.

Perhaps it was because of music that my room became a kind of social center. Everywhere, around the world, folks are attracted by American jazz. A good old Dixieland stomp can break down almost any language barriers, and there is something about Louis Armstrong's horn that creates spontaneous friendships. Among those who often dropped by my room, was the head of the Turkoman Writers Union, a frail parchment-colored little poet, Kikilov. Since his first name sounded like a cross between Cherie and Charlie, I settled for Charlie. Kikilov looked like a quizzical canary, or an esthetic Charlie Chan. His complexion was about that of a canary bird's feathers, and he had a sweet but doubting smile as if the world were "too much with him, late and soon." He seemed to me to be the Asiatic equivalent of the Russian word *nichevo* at the negative end of its scale. He had a very bad cough most of the time. He looked consumptive. My notes say he was born in the desert near Merv.

Once Arthur Koestler got to Ashkhabad that old-hand journalist began taking down everything, including the names of everyone he met, so that is when my note taking began, too. Shamed into action, I bought myself a half dozen of the only kind of notebooks available in Ashkhabad, oilcloth-covered with lined yellowish paper. Squired by Kikolov, Koestler asked for and was granted a series of meetings with various Turkmenian and Russian government officials and factory heads. And we were invited—often practically dragged (for even Koestler, the energetic, sometimes wearied)—to most of the public meetings. Through it all I dutifully took notes. Koestler was a great one for making contacts and, being a Communist Party member, very conscientious about uncovering all the facts at hand regarding what the Communists had done in Turkmenistan. But he did not seem to like the people much, and he did not like Ashkhabad at all, nor the dusty, uncomfortable guesthouse, nor the toilets full of lime. He had a German sense of sanitation, and neither Russians nor Turkomans were very hygienic. In fact, Koestler complained that Russian and Asiatic dirt together made a pretty thick layer. And every time he came back to our hotel he would wash. I had not known him long before I heard him say what I was often to hear him repeat, "If the Revolution had only occurred in Germany, at least it would have been a clean one."

Koestler was particularly perturbed at the unsanitary tea-drinking customs of Central Asia. At first I was a bit taken aback, too, at the general use of the common tea bowl passed from hand to hand, but I soon got over such squeamishness. However, I never really liked to drink after Charlie Kikilov. That pleasant but wizened little Turko-man had a hacking cough and a frequently running nose. But, as my official host, he always sat next to me at every gathering. And at every gathering, tea was served in little porcelain bowls. Kikilov would pass the bowl to me first. I would drink and pass it back. Then the man on the other side would pass his bowl. This interchanging of bowls was a part of the ritual of friendship. Convinced that Kikilov had tuberculosis, I became resigned to catching that disease. Koestler, however, was not reconciled to any such fate. He would curse in German, English, French and Hungarian every time he was subjected to the ritual of circulating tea bowls.

"Slobbering in each other's bowls," said Koestler, "a bloody disgusting filthy habit!"

I simply went ahead and drank and re-drank with the others, and forgot about it. But I must say that on days when Kikilov's cough seemed worse, I might busy myself more in his presence with taking notes than in drinking tea.

My notebook shows that Koestler, Kikilov and I attended quite a few tea conferences at various City Soviets, Trade Union Councils, factories and schools, and that a great many words and figures were translated by Kikilov from Turkoman into Russian to Koestler, and by Koestler from Russian into English to me. Together we attended the Turkoman National Theatre, inspected the new cotton mill, took notes on the Botanical Cultures Institute where native plants were for the first time being studied and a new food for camels developed. We dined at a landscaped workers' village on the edge of the desert, then visited a school for future railroad workers, where Asiatic boys learned all about engines and block signals, which rather puzzled me since not more than one train a day in each direction crossed the desert. "But more will come," the students said. "New railroads will be built in Turkmenia."

Another school, already three years old, which looked toward the future, was the film-workers' institute, where practice films were made under Russian directors. Illiterate actors from the nomad tribes of the desert were being taught to read and write at the same time as they were being taught to act, to operate movie cameras, and to develop films. There were among the students, one patriarchal old man with a splendid white beard, and a brown young girl with a desert tribal mark on her head. This interested me enormously because here were colored people being taught by white men, Russians, about the making of films from the ground up—the building of sets, the preparation of scenarios, acting, camera work—and I could not help but think how impregnable Hollywood had been to Negroes, and how all over America the union of motion-picture operators did not permit Negroes to operate projection machines, not even in theaters in Negro neighborhoods. Negro-owned establishments had to employ white projectionists. When I told this to Koestler, he said he could hardly believe it. But I was trying to make him understand why I observed the changes in Soviet Asia with Negro eyes. To Koestler, Turkmenistan was simply a primitive land moving into twentieth-century civilization. To me it was a colored land moving into orbits hitherto reserved for whites.

## DARKNESS BEFORE NOON

THE Atta Kurdov trial in Ashkhabad, which involved a group of Turkmenians accused of crimes against the state, was the first of the purge trials which Koestler saw in the USSR. I had been to the Atta Kurdov trial before Koestler came to town, and I'd found it boring—even to the accused and to the judge—all of whom seemed half asleep in the dusty chambers. But the day I called Koestler's attention to the trial, he hauled Kikilov in with him to take a look. I sat in the public square where formerly no colored folks were allowed, and waited for them to come out. Koestler, however, was so fascinated by this sleepy-eyed trial in which everyone looked half hypnotized, that he stayed until court closed. He seemed very much upset when he came back to the guesthouse. I guess that was the beginning of Darkness at Noon.

To me, Atta Kurdov, sitting on trial, looked like a portly bull-necked Chicago ward boss connected with the numbers rackets, so I pre-judged him guilty as soon as I knew he was the defendant. Had he looked woebegone and frail, like little Charlie Kikilov, I would probably have gone to court every day, since emotionally, I would have been on his side. But I did not care much about Atta Kurdov because I didn't like his looks. My notes are scanty:

TRIAL ATTA KURDOV: Communist (formerly White Guard) who went into Party and became President of City Soviet. Had many relatives he favored. Allowed his friends to come into district kolkhozes and exploit others. Letters from peasants to him complaining about conditions were torn up. Charges were brought against him at a Party meeting but he was defended by the head Workers and Peasants Inspector whom he had promoted to this office. Meeting ended in a resolution demanding removal and trial of the Inspector, as well as Atta Kurdov. Twenty-eight persons arrested, all of his clan. Their defense is that indictment is Russian chauvinism directed against the Turkomans.

Koestler took down a good deal of the testimony during the hours he spent in court, and he went to the Party offices later to get further data on the charges. I said, "Atta Kurdov looks guilty to me, of what I don't know, but he just *looks* like a rogue." But Koestler did not think much of my reasoning and said so quite seriously. I knew mine was not proper reasoning either and had nothing to do with due process of law. But when I saw that it upset him, I repeated that night just for fun, "Well, anyhow Atta Kurdov does look like a rascal."

Koestler went to his room and I didn't see him any more until the next day, although I thought he might come back to listen to some jazz or to share a hunk of camel sausages with me around midnight. But he didn't come back. The trial disturbed him.

## ONCE THE GARDEN OF EDEN

KOESTLER was a restless young man. After ten days or so of continual activity in Ashkhabad, he was ready to move on. By the end of October, I, too, was ready to leave Ashkhabad mainly because it was getting cold, and there were no signs of heat, nor any way to make heat in our guesthouse. It was my intention to retrace my steps by way of Bokhara and Samarkand to Tashkent. Koestler was headed in the same direction, so we decided to travel together. I don't remember now whose idea it might have been that a Writers Brigade be formed in Ashkhabad to visit a series of collective farms before we left that Republic. But that is what happened. Headed by Charlie Kikilov, and including Kolya Shagurin, the four of us were cleared through the Writers Union for a trip to the ancient city of Merv—where almost no one ever went—and to a group of collective farms in that region. The oasis of Merv, Kolya said, had been the cradle of civilization, the place where the world began, and the site of the original Garden of Eden. The women there, he declared, were still beautiful.

On the long desert train ride to Merv, Koestler and Kolya did most of the talking, in Russian. Kikilov's Russian was limited so, when not translating, he did not strain himself to converse. I had learned hardly a word of Turkoman, so Kikilov and I, who sat together on the train, just ate or slept most of the way to Merv, sharing a tea bowl whenever we woke up and found hot water available. Kolya was amusing looking, but not very amusing. He was somewhat earnest and I thought dull, except for the tattoos on various parts of his body, including a nude lady on his arm who did odd movements when he flexed his muscle. This never ceased to entertain him. He would always laugh at his cootch dancer's sly undulations. Then his blue eyes would twinkle behind his glasses and his tobacco-stained teeth would show in his big mouth. It must have taken considerable time to learn to twitch his muscle this way.

But Kolya had more useful tricks up his sleeve, too. He had once been a sailor in the Soviet merchant marine. I think maybe he had been a bezprizorni before that—one of those ever-resourceful wandering boys of the road. Kolya was like Emma in Moscow—he usually got what he wanted when he wanted it anywhere he might happen to be. He possessed only an ordinary food ration card—not a special foreign writer's *propusk*—yet he often managed to get extra pounds of bread or cheese. He knew how to climb over, crawl under, or walk through red tape, so he was a handy fellow to have around. Besides he spoke Ukranian, Russian and some Turkoman, and he had a great deal more energy than the ailing Kikilov. Kolya and Koestler were about the same age, I think, twenty-six or twenty-seven. I was a little older. And nobody knows how old Kikilov was. He might have been thirty-five or fifty-five. Sometimes he looked very old, and at other times more weary than aged. He had a shy smile and a sensitive nature. Perhaps he composed good poetry—I have always wondered—when he didn't have to rhyme the Five Year Plan.

When we got off the train at night near Merv, it was in the desert cold that seems so chilling. My teeth chattered. Merv, at least the part of it that had been a Tzarist garrison town in the old days, was as drab and ugly a city as I have ever seen, and even more dust-covered than Ashkhabad. The two-story hotel looked like a fourth-rate flop house in a slum. Like all hotels in the Soviet Union, it was crowded. There was only one room available. That had one big bed and one little bed. To Charlie Kikilov it seemed courteous that the guests from Europe and America have the big bed and he take the cotlike small one. So Kolya, Koestler and I slept in the one big bed. At least, we were warm—and so tired from our long ride that we all went to sleep at once. I perhaps would never have awakened had I not heard Koestler stirring around the next morning. Then I heard Kolya laughing, his white arm sticking straight up in the air from under the covers and his shake dancer shaking. No matter how drab a town might be, Kolya always had her with him.

Koestler was most unhappy that morning. There was dust all over everything and a film of dust on the water in the pitcher. The washbowl itself was grimy. The whole ugly barren room reminded me of cheap Negro hotels in the South where such hotels are the only ones in which colored travelers can stay. Here I was not segregated, but it was certainly dirty.

"This filthy hole!" said Koestler. "It will take more than a revolution to clean up this dive. I can't wash in this stinking water. It's been here a week."

Kikilov roused himself and went with Koestler to find some fresh water. Kolya got up and dressed without bothering to wash at all. I stayed in bed and waited to see if anyone said anything about breakfast. In that part of the world, as in most of the Soviet Union, you couldn't just drop into a restaurant and order a meal. Since we had gotten into Merv so late, no one had contacted the local branch of the Writers Union (if there was one) or the Communist Party headquarters which would look after Koestler—and, I hoped, the rest of us. Kikilov, as host, once he saw Koestler engaged briskly in washing his face and neck, departed to make arrangements for food. He was some time coming back, but when he did, a car came with him and we were taken to a co-operative dining room to eat enormous chunks of black bread with cups—this time—not bowls of black tea.

Our Writers Brigade stayed in and about Merv for several days, so I tore up an old shirt and took a scrap of my precious American-made soap and gave our room a good cleaning, washing out the pitcher and bowl, dusting everywhere, and polishing up the brass on the enormous bed. Koestler thought some mysterious attendant had gotten ashamed of the appearance of the room and had cleaned it. I never saw a maid or any other servant around that hotel in Merv, just a rather surly desk clerk of indeterminate nationality. But I knew that when people are sensitive to dirt, it can make them miserable indeed. Koestler seemed unhappy enough of the time without having to bear the burden of a filthy room for a week or more, so for his sake, I cleaned it.

I have known a great many writers in my time, and some of them were very much like Koestler—always something not quite right in the world around them. Even on the brightest days, no matter where they are. Richard Wright seemed like that in Chicago. Wallace Thurman in the Harlem of the 'twenties, Myron Brinig in California, and Ralph Ellison in New York—all friends of mine whom I liked for one quality or another, and certainly for their talent—seemed unhappy fellows, too. No matter where, under what conditions, or when, something was always wrong. There are many emotional hypochondriacs on earth, unhappy when *not unhappy*, sad *when not expounding on their sadness*. Yet I have always been drawn to such personalities because I often feel very sad inside myself, too, though not inclined to show it. Koestler wore his sadness on his sleeve.

My feeling was that not even Merv could be as bad as it seemed to us the first few hours after our arrival. And, sure enough, our expedition to the collective farm turned out to be, at least for me, a thrilling experience. I heard some wonderful music—Turkmenian flamenco.

The trip to the Kolhoz Aitakov in a battered and steaming old car was hot, dusty and long, for we left town in a dust storm. There were only twelve cars in Merv, and the car in which we went across the desert must have been, I think, the *oldest* of the twelve. It shook, it rattled, it rolled, it smoked, it steamed, it gave off heat like an oven, and it stank. It was built for five people and there were six of us in it. It caused me to swear that I would never travel any place again. Yet, when we reached the cotton farm which was situated in an area, such as I'd always imagined an oasis should be, all green and leafy, I was suddenly happy, gazing at a whole new world of fascinating people. Perhaps this *had been* the Garden of Eden. Here were handsome women with the tallest hats I had yet seen, enormous bright hollow cones, some fully three feet high, covered with gay silks in odd patterns, bangles and coins adorning the tall crowns. The men, too, had on great high hats of shaggy Karacul, black wild-looking headgear. And some had fierce-looking mustaches like Oriental brigands out of the Arabian Nights.

There were wide fields where the cotton grew waist high in bolls of bursting white at the Kolhoz Aitakov. Through one field moved a group of women picking cotton and stuffing it into their skirts or bosoms. Their foreman, Medshur Baba, was brought to meet us. I took a picture of him and his helper, a younger Turkoman, quite chocolate of skin, who looked as if he might have come from Harlem. That afternoon I also took snapshots of Koestler picking cotton, or lying on the ground taking notes. Kikilov, when not called upon to translate, just sat in the shade. And Kolya followed the women down the cotton rows. The women didn't pay any attention to Kolya or myself either, it being immodest in Central Asia for a woman to look at a strange man. Not even when Kolya bared his muscles to show his tattoo did they pay him any mind. He was very disappointed.

## TURKMENIAN FLAMENCO

ARTHUR KOESTLER asked me one day why in Moscow I did not join the Communist Party. I told him that what I had heard concerning the Party indicated that it was based on strict discipline and the acceptance of directives that I, as a writer, did not wish to accept. I did not believe political directives could be successfully applied to creative writing. They might well apply to the preparation of tracts and pamphlets, yes, but not to poetry or fiction, which to be valid, I felt, had to express as truthfully as possible the *individual* emotions and reactions of the writer, rather than mass directives issued to achieve practical and often temporary political objectives. Koestler agreed with me that it was very difficult to write both politically and individually at the same time, especially when the political lines were applied from above by bureaucrats who had no appreciation of creative impulses. But he said that, at certain historical periods, collective social aims might be worthy of transcending individual desires. However, Koestler did not press the point nor try to change my position.

In Turkmenistan, outside of official conferences and statistical sessions, Communism was hardly mentioned. I don't believe I ever heard Yeah Man say the word *communism*, although I am sure he was a loyal Red Army officer who enjoyed the achievements of the Revolution. In Moscow, where we twenty-two Negroes had been hailed so widely and where propaganda relative to the Negro's hard lot in America was played up, almost everyone took for granted that all Negroes were, or eventually would be Communist Party members, so it was seldom discussed with us there either. But good Muscovite Party members were usually amazed when they found out that only one of our number claimed Party membership.

Once I gave as my reason for not joining the Party the fact that jazz was officially taboo in Russia, being played only at the declassé Metropol hotel, and very badly there.

"But jazz is decadent bourgeois music," I was told, for that is what the Soviet press had hammered into Russian heads.

"It's my music," I said, "and I wouldn't give up jazz for a world revolution."

The Russians looked at me as if I were a decadent bourgeois writer and let it go at that. But they liked my jazz records as much as I did, and never left the room when I played them.

While I was in Moscow my third book of poems, *The Dream Keeper*, was published in the United States. When copies reached me,

I gave one to Ivy Litvinoff, the cultivated English woman who was most gracious to members of our movie group, and whose husband later became Soviet Ambassador to Washington. Mrs. Litvinoff said that she liked my poems, all save those in the religious group. When I informed her that they were based on the old folk forms of the spirituals, she said that such poems had no place in the class struggle and were not worthy of a Party member. When I told her I was not a Party member, she asked why, and I gave her the same reasons I gave Koestler. She said gently that she felt I should be a Party member, that the Party needed me. But, oddly enough, I heard later that she herself was not a Communist, although her husband stood high in Party councils. At any rate, Ivy Litvinoff was not dogmatic, and did not run my spirituals through so harsh a wringer as some of the American Communists did.

The party given for our Writers Brigade on the Kolhoz Aitakov had nothing to do with the Communist Party, so far as I could tell. The Kolhoz had only ten Communist Party members. There were forty or fifty men at least at our party, and that many more milling around outside after the room was filled. I supposed only eight of the ten Communists were there, since two members on the farm were women, and there were no women present that evening. Turkoman women did not share the social life of the men.

After supper the party folks started arriving, mostly on foot, but some galloping up on stunted Asiatic ponies, and some riding high on camels. Most of the Turkomans were big fellows, and their tall shaggy Karacul hats made them look enormous. In soft boots and padded robes and baggy trousers, that night they looked to me for all the world like figures out of Omar Khayyám's poems or the *Arabian Nights*. There were fierce old fellows with black mustaches, stout pin-cushion farmers in two or three padded gowns, Mongol-like youths with slanted eyes, and paler lads who looked like Persian figures on old vases or drawings on parchment scrolls. A couple of shepherd boys came garbed exactly as if they had stepped out of the Book of Moses. Their black Karacul hats alone saved them being Sunday-school characters of my Protestant youth, perhaps bearing the Lamb of God.

Balls of melons hung from the rafters in groups like yellow balloons and gave the room a sweet smell. But as the place filled up,

clouds of smoke from the odd-smelling mahorka tobacco, which the
men smoked wrapped in newspaper cones, gave off a ranker olfactory
atmosphere, mixed with the scent of sheepskin and camelskin and
sand and padded robes. Windows and doors were tightly closed for
after sundown it got cold outside. Everyone sat on well-worn but beautiful old Bokhara rugs that Park Avenue might envy, drinking tea
from bowls that went from mouth to mouth, around and around in
the customary ritual. Koestler got away off on the edge of the crowd
so that he would not be in the main circle of tea bowl passing, and
thus could avoid drinking from bowls that dozens of strange mustaches had touched. I had given up on this problem weeks before, so
I sat in the middle and drank from everybody's bowl. But fortunately
Kikilov with his cough went to squat beside Koestler and share his
bowl.

The men all sat on the floor. There was very little walking around,
and no cocktails, wine, or hard liquors, just tea. Although I didn't
understand a word of anything, I observed that as the tea bowls went
around and around, the party was becoming more lively. Groups of
men began laughing and joking together, and others shouted over a
forest of heads to friends across the room. In all this hubbub, it was
impossible to get from Kikilov via Koestler any accurate idea of what
anyone might be saying, so I gave up trying, and started talking in
English plus signs to those around me, which amused them no end.
I would say to a fellow who handed me a tea bowl, "Man, why didn't
you bring your girl friend?" And outline with my hands the shape of
a woman. Whereupon, he would answer God only knows what, but I
would laugh, and everybody would laugh. Somebody would roll me a
mahorka cone, and around would come another tea bowl. The next
day when I ran into some of these fellows digging irrigation ditches,
they greeted me like an old buddy. We had made friends.

There was a roaring fire outside on the ground and over it hung
a copper pot big enough to hold a giant genie. It was full of boiling
water from which the smaller teapots were continually replenished.
There seemed to be a party going on in the yard, too. It was alive with
shadow shapes in the chilly night. After a while some fellows arrived
with long-necked two-string lutes, and a shout went up. These were
the bakhshis, favored singers of the region, who had come from an-

other oasis to entertain us. And in a few minutes they had my hair standing on my head. Spanish gypsy music at its wildest never surpassed theirs.

Twang went one of the shaggy-hatted men on his lute, then sang softly in a semi-recitative a few short phrases, whereupon he threw back his head and, without warning, uttered one of the loudest, longest, most spine-chilling cries I ever heard. This was followed by a song that must have been about the end of time, for surely nothing else could inspire such a wail or such a song. Succeeding verses were interspersed with lesser wails from time to time as someone else in the crowd would utter a similar musical howl. I never heard madder music anywhere, utterly weird and bloodcurdling, a kind of cross between the Chinese scale at its strangest and gypsy flamenco at its wildest. To start a song the leader might make an odd clucking sound in his throat a few times, pluck a string, rock, hum, cluck again, then finally in a high monotone, begin a line. Sometimes two men sang together, sometimes they took turns, sometimes one or two fellows sitting cross-legged facing each other on the floor contributed a verse or punctuated a song with a single long cry. But most of the singing was solo, with high drawn-out earsplitting wails to accentuate the interlude.

I could have listened all night to this singing, but in due time food arrived, and the music gave over to feasting. Just before the food was brought in, a number of men left. Perhaps they had not contributed to the feast, or maybe there was not enough to go around.

We had not had much to eat on that farm all day, mostly camel stew and melon. But now in our honor, tonight they had slaughtered a sheep and made piles of hot unleavened bread in flat round discs. I was hungry, so when two men brought in a huge copper drum filled with steaming mutton swimming in juice, I was happy. Another kettle followed of the same fare, and in two groups, we gathered around them on the floor. Pleasant heat and a fine aroma arose from the pots. Into each a single large wooden spoon was dipped, filled with broth, and offered to Koestler and me first, then a spoonful each to Kolya and Kikilov. This was the first course, each man taking his turn at a spoonful of soup right out of the kettles. There were fifteen or twenty men and only two spoons. Turkoman hospitality, even to spoons, is based on sharing.

By now the food kettles had cooled enough for our hosts to reach in with bare fingers and pick up chunks of meat and tear them into smaller bits which they dropped back into the soup. This was so that we might more easily dine from these common bowls without having to pull the meat apart ourselves. Politely, the Turkomans motioned for Koestler and me to help ourselves, so we put our hands into the warm liquid and fished around until we found a nice piece of mutton, pulled it out and ate it. Then everyone else dived in, too, and sometimes there were several hands in a pot at once until all of that sheep was gone. Then we soaked the bread in the juice until the juice was gone, too. Full and happy, about three o'clock in the morning, I rolled up in a rug and went to sleep.

## KOESTLER WASHES HIS HANDS

THE day before Koestler and I left Merv I shall never forget. It was spent in going to and coming from a distant outpost of hell—a place called Permetyab. Just to get to Permetyab would try the soul of the devil himself. Why we went, I will never know. Kolya had better sense. He did not accompany us, having gotten acquainted with a lanky Turkmenian girl and gone into hiding. We never saw Kolya any more. Kikilov, claiming he had to get back to Ashkhabad, did not go to Permetyab either. Only Koestler and I and a tall Russian Communist Party official traveled across the broiling Kara Kum in the direction of the Afghan border to an ungodly spot fifty miles from civilization.

We were going to visit a collective farm established for Baluchis, peasants who came over the borders from Afghanistan and India, so we were told, fleeing oppression of the native princes and the English to seek sanctuary on Soviet soil. Naturally, for refugee guests of the Soviets, I had expected to see something even more pleasant than Kolhoz Aitakov, and perhaps more exotic, too. So I put a fresh roll of film in my camera at dawn that morning and set out through a dusty haze into the desert. On the way, however, I got my first shock.

As we bumped along the sand outside Merv our guide and driver said, "At Permetyab, we shall not stay overnight. It's dangerous."

The Baluchis, he explained, were from the wildest tribes in the Afghan mountains and they might take a notion to kill us. In the night, in the dark, he said, they could easily toss our bodies into the desert where sand drifts would cover us and nobody would ever find us again. At first I thought the man was joking, but he did not smile. When I saw the people at Permetyab, I realized that he might very well be concerned for our safety and his own, too.

Evidently it was not this Russian Party official's desire that we take this trip. The directive must have come from higher up the political ladder. Why such an excursion was suggested to Koestler and me is still a mystery. Probably no one would ever have heard of Permetyab had not we been driven there. Its existence seemed unknown to most of the people of Merv. The desert trip itself was torment, and when we got to Permetyab it was nothing but a treeless village of fifteen or twenty mud huts and sheepskin tents blistering in the sun—the most Godforsaken place I have ever seen, the dirtiest, and the hottest.

In our ancient Ford struggling across the roadless desert, we negotiated gulches without bridges by making detours for miles until we came to a place a car could negotiate. Sometimes we used the planks we had tied to the top of the car to make a hazardous bridge, the two planks placed like rails the same width apart as the car wheels. Then Koestler and I got out to walk or wade across the gulch while the Russian very slowly and carefully drove the car over. Then we picked up our plank bridge and tied it atop the Ford again. Twice a tire was punctured by desert thistles. Several times we were stuck in the sand and had to push and shovel our way out under the broiling sun. I said to myself, "If I ever get back to Merv and on to Moscow, thence to Harlem, *home I will stay forever.*" Koestler was even more disgusted than I that we had elected to take this particular trip.

"In Germany," Koestler said, "strangers would be told what they'd be getting into before commencing anything like this. What a hell of a part of the world to have a revolution!" With this I agreed.

Sometimes we would pass on the barren sands a collection of nomad tents called *yurts* or *kibitkas*, with a few Arab-looking men about, in the company of dirty children and half-veiled harem women, who would run and hide. Sometimes a gust of wind would pelt the car with sand and fill our eyes with it, too. But we could not close the car windows unless we wished to roast in its ovenlike interior. The Russian, who was born in that part of the world, did not seem to mind the sand, the punctures, and the hazards of the route. He was more concerned about the welcome we might get at the end of our journey.

"But," he said, "there's a rather pretty Russian gal out there."

"What?" exclaimed Koestler.

"A Ministry of Health nurse in charge of the clinic," said the Russian. "She's been there a year, with two more to go."

I knew that in the Soviet Union, medical students, nurses, engineers, and other trained personnel agreed that after their training was completed, they would serve a period of three years in any region of the USSR where their services might be needed, before settling down in a location of their own choice. This was their ardent and (I presume enforced) contribution to the building of socialism. So here, in the heart of this desert near the most primitive part of the Afghan border, we would find a lone Russian girl.

"What a book she could write," I thought to myself.

Koestler and I agreed that we would interview this Soviet pioneer of progress. But where was Permetyab? At that moment all around us was nothing but the burning desert—not a tree, not a house, only sand to the sun-hazed horizon. We had drunk up half our tepid water and poured almost all the rest into the steaming radiator. Still we seemed to be in the heart of nowhere.

"Suppose the car were to break down! What would we do?" I thought. "Die here in the sun for the buzzards to pick our bones?" But I did not even see a buzzard in the fiery sky. Permetyab must be, I concluded, across the borders of life, somewhere in Hades.

It was well after noon when we got to our destination, our throats dry with sand and the hard bread we had eaten on the way. The heat was such that I felt the film in my camera probably had melted. My clothing was soaked with sweat. Yet when we reached Permetyab the air seemed chilly, for a mean sharp little wind was blowing across the dunes. My eyes were red with sun and sand and my mouth full of grit. My legs were stiff and the soles of my feet burned. My head ached. Koestler had lapsed into complete silence as the Russian drove doggedly on. But the moment we got to Permetyab my European friend took out his notebook and began writing. I admired Koestler.

The village of Permetyab consisted of more sheepskin yurts than houses. What houses there were had only one or two rooms, walled with sunbaked bricks of thistle and mud. The floors were dirt. Mangy dogs bounded forward with hyenalike snarls as our car drew up, then slunk away whining as if used to severe beatings if they lingered too near a human being. Dirty old sultans (or so I was inclined to imagine each elderly Oriental male), smoking water pipes, sat in some of the tent openings. The women, like dogs, immediately scurried out of sight, as if they too were used to being beaten. A few half-naked children peeked at us. Almost everybody was barefooted, their clothing ragged, their turbans filthy. These were the most depressed people I had yet seen in the Soviet Union. If this were freedom for them compared to Afghanistan or northern India, what could their life have been across those borders? Their language not even our native-born Russian guide understood, but he located someone who could translate for him into Turkmenian from the Baluchi, or whatever they spoke. So the few notes I took were fourth hand—from Baluchi to Turkoman to Russian to Koestler to English to me. I soon gave up trying to understand anything and contented myself with visual impressions. These fierce-looking men did not object to photographs, so I opened my camera and took a few. A one-eyed man lent me a turban that I put on my head to pose, but Koestler, for fear of vermin, refused to don such headgear, so in their midst I photographed him looking quite European. Eventually they invited us into one of the huts and squatted down on the floor for the ritual of the tea bowls. There were three or four bowls, which about twenty men shared. The water had been scooped up from a filthy irrigation canal, and there was mud in the bottom of each bowl after the tea was drunk.

"Koestler," I said, "we are all going to die of cholera germs."

"I wouldn't be surprised," said Koestler, although he had scarcely touched his lips to any of the bowls. Not even the Russian drank much of this tea. Shortly he commanded the translator to get into the car, and we drove away in the direction of the kolkhoz. Why the farm center and village were not in the same spot, I never knew. It was two or three miles to the cotton collective, which semed a more lively center than the village, with a sprawling mud-brick structure which was the administrative center, the school, nursery and clinic all in one. There we had luncheon of canned meat, bread hard as stone, melons and tea. And there we met the Russian woman doctor-nurse, who was young, and not bad-looking. She was the only European in this fantastic desert community, inhabited by evil-appearing sore-covered, dirty people. I looked at this young white missionary on the dark frontiers of progress with wonder and admiration, and I asked Koestler to translate into Russian my compliments, "How brave you are!"

The little woman—brisk yet feminine in appearance—smiled at me and said, "Spaceba," thank you. Then she told us about her work. She said, "Childbirth is a problem. Since the women have no say about anything here, some of these men still buy their wives in spite of Soviet decrees. There are men who will not permit me to attend their wives when a baby is coming. They believe an axe or a sabre under the mat on which the woman lies aids childbirth, or firing off guns over the mother speeds delivery. Some of the women bite off the umbilical cord themselves, as their mothers and grandmothers did before them. Since water is scarce in this desert land, it's an old custom to wash a newborn child in sand. I have trouble with babies' eyes festering. Sometimes children lose their sight. But I have been at Permetyab long enough now for some of the women (and men, too) to see how the babies I've been allowed to deliver thrive and are healthier than most of the others—so, in time, in time, I hope. . . . It takes time."

The conference with the doctor-nurse took place just after luncheon. The food we had eaten had been handled by Baluchis whose hands were none too clean and some of whom had runny eyes and scabby faces. They had cut our melons with the same dirty knives with which they cut tobacco. We had drunk from their grimy bowls. So when the nurse at the clinic told us that all of the health problems there were aggravated by the fact that ninety per cent of the population of Permetyab had syphilis, Koestler almost keeled over. I was a bit upset myself.

"I try to save the children from it," she said. "But then they have other venereal diseases, too, just as bad."

"Syphilis!" Koestler exploded looking at me. "Ninety per cent syphilitic! Why didn't they tell us what we were running into?"

When, about midnight, Koestler and I were dropped at our hotel in Merv, where now we had a whole room to ourselves and a bed each since Kikilov and Kolya had gone, I was so tired and so cold that I got into bed quickly. But in the chill night air, Koestler began to wash his face and hands, his mouth and teeth—not once, but three or four times—emptying the water after each washing, until he had used up the whole pitcher. Then he went to the outside faucet, got more water and washed his body, then rinsed it in a second bowl. Finally, he washed his hands again. Syphilis, dirt, Permetyab, the frontiers of revolution, ugh!

Perhaps from the chill of his unheated bath, or the cold night air, or the memory of that desert day, Koestler shuddered as he emptied his last bowl of water and finally went to bed.

## HIGH HOLY BOKHARA

WHEN Koestler and I reached Bokhara in early November, we went to the same hotel where I had stayed when I came through with the movie group, and where I thought the desk clerk might remember me. He acted as if he had never seen me before, and said with a shrug that anyhow all the rooms were taken. Finally, after much showing of documents, he muttered that a room was scheduled to be empty at noon and Koestler and I might have it. Meanwhile, the two of us left our baggage with him and went looking for something to eat.

When we came back, the clerk said the room was empty and to go upstairs and down the hall and we would find it. There were no bellmen or porters, so with Koestler's help—for he was traveling light —we lugged my bags, my typewriter, my victrola, and my box of records up the stairs and found the room. The door was open and a barefoot Tartar maid was sloshing all over the stone floor with a big mop. We could not immediately occupy the room, nor even get in without wetting our feet. So we decided to go back into the street again. We asked the maid if she would please transfer our baggage from the hall into the room when she had finished. She said, "Niet," no, and went on mopping. Koestler exploded.

"Why?"

"Because I am a maid," she said, "and my work is not that of a porter to move luggage."

"What a hell of a place to have a revolution," said Koestler, or words to that effect.

Afraid to leave our belongings unprotected in the hall, we waited until she had finished cleaning. After fifteen or twenty minutes without a word, the maid passed us and went downstairs. Her attitude I often encountered later in other portions of the Soviet Union. One did what one was supposed to do, no more—and that was that—no matter what inconvenience to others such rigid interpretation of workers' rights involved.

At least, our room was fairly clean and cool, and the hotel, although very plainly furnished, was a palace after the dirty hostel in Merv. And for me it was a relief not to be running on schedule for a while, not to have to go anywhere or see anything. A few days of just not having to do anything was all I wanted.

"Don't tell anybody I'm here," I requested of Koestler, for I knew he would be on the quest of notes again immediately, since he had never been in Bokhara. He promised he would leave me out of his expedition for a while, and he did. That afternoon I took a nap while he went to a union hall. My first night in Bokhara I went alone to see a movie, several reels of a popular Soviet serial called *Miss Comrade Mend*. (The comrade being a woman, the word in Russian had a feminine ending which we do not have in English, so in translation, I suppose, it would have to be *Miss Comrade*.) The theater was filled with turbaned males, smoking what smelled like hashish. The episodes on the screen were long and tedious. But I had rather have been at the cinema than listening to the production plans of the Bokhara Rug Artel. After the movie I found a winehouse and had a few drinks, then went for a long walk alone in the starlight through the silent streets of the Old Town, out to the very edge of the city where a group of camel drivers were loading their beasts for a pre-dawn start into the desert. The camels snarled and, as they shook their long necks, their bells tinkled in the darkness. The drivers cursed and groaned and strained at the sacks of grain being secured on the backs of the smelly old animals. As I watched, nobody said anything to me.

When I got back to the hotel, it was after midnight. Koestler was worried. He thought maybe I'd gotten lost. He did not think much of my wandering around alone in the streets of a dark Oriental town, especially when I couldn't speak a word of its native language. Suppose I did get lost, how could I ask my way back to the hotel?

"Nichevo," I said, grinning. "What kind of notes did you get today?"

He showed me. Always, if he had any notes I wanted, Koestler would share them with me—which saved me a good deal of work. In Bokhara I did not try to keep up with Koestler during the week that followed. I mostly wandered around by myself. I watched the Oriental auctioneers in the bazaars calling for bids on quilted robes, silken shawls, embroidered eating cloths in bright reds and greens, hand-wrought jewelry, brass pitchers, bowls, and long-stemmed water pipes, tin trunks, bunches of carrots, onions, peppers, caps, hats and cloth for turbans, almost anything. I was told the auctioneers got five per cent of the sales, the remainder going to the owners who instead of doing the merchandising themselves, stood by and watched while their goods were sold.

I wandered again, as I had done on my first trip to the city, through the rooms of the palace of the former Emir, partially destroyed by the Basmachi counter-revolutionaries who did not wish it to fall into Communist hands. It was enormous, built in 1912, and not especially beautiful. There were panels of mirrors, glossy mosaics or gilt everywhere, and in the Emir's bedroom was an enormous brass bed that might have been made in Grand Rapids.

The harem quarters, where the Emir kept his many wives, were like dog kennels, separated from the palace proper, a series of rooms around connecting courtyards. Nearby was the Emir's Rest House with a balcony facing the private pool in which, at his command, his dozens of wives bathed nude before him. He had so many wives that he did not know them all by name. But when he fled to Afghanistan before the approaching Communists, he left most of the women behind to take with him, instead, his harem of boys, for male harems were not uncommon among emirs in those days.

Bokhara of the Many Mosques, more than three hundred—Bokhara the Mullah Ridden—as the Communists termed it, had been a great Moslem city with hundreds of muezzins calling to prayer in the name of Allah! One of Asia's most religious cities—High Holy Divinely Descended Bokhara. At the same time, the histories say, it had been as corrupt as Chicago and more dangerous. Its Raiz, or official Protector of Religion, once walked the streets with a whip quizzing people as to the tenets of their faith. Woe betide those who did not answer to his satisfaction! Between tithes to the mullahs, taxes and semiserfdom, the masses lived in abject poverty. Infant mortality was appalling. The streets swarmed with beggars. The Emir was one of the most despotic of monarchs anywhere on earth, and his tax collectors reputedly the cruelest in all Asia. Yet, instead of money, they would sometimes accept little daughters of the poor for their harems. And in these things the Tzars protected them.

When our movie group, a few weeks before, had visited Bokhara's Museum of the Revolution, the handsome old Uzbek in charge had told us a great deal about the last Emir, and showed us the whips, torture irons and chains with which this despot punished his prisoners in underground dungeons. Then the venerable curator showed us a photograph of himself—his back raw from the whip marks of the Emir's jailers—taken just after he was charged with revolutionary activities and ordered beaten to death. A secret sympathizer among the Emir's henchmen saved his life. But beneath his quilted robe the scars of his beating (in the form of great welts across his body) he still bore. This old man's name was Haji Mir Baba Murcin—*Haji* meaning one who had been to Mecca. On my return to Bokhara with Koestler, I took him to meet Haji, and they spent several hours together. Koestler took down his story and devoted a chapter to him in *The Invisible Writing*, for the old man had many memories. Haji Mir Baba had been to Moscow in the early days of the Soviets, and there he had met Lenin. When Lenin asked him how he had happened to become a

Communist, Haji turned around, slipped out of the upper part of his robe so that his back was bare, and Lenin saw his scars.

## SYNAGOGUES AND PENCILS

ARTHUR KOESTLER'S father was a Hungarian Jew in Budapest, and young Koestler in his teens went to Palestine. Among my classmates at Central High School in Cleveland had been many sons and daughters of orthodox Jewish families, and I had gone a few times to their synagogues. Once I went to a mass prayer meeting for the victims of a Polish pogrom, where the old people stood beating their heads against the walls of the auditorium. When I came to the Soviet Union, I sometimes saw on the streets of Communist cities, orthodox Jews with curled sideburns, black hats and long ankle-length form-fitting black coats. In Bokhara I saw such Jews, too, and I became interested in learning how they fared in this sovietized city of the Orient. With Koestler's help, in the old Jewish quarter of the town, I gathered a book full of notes.

Jews, of whom there were about ten thousand in Bokhara, could now live anywhere they wished, but formerly under the Emir they had been segregated in a ghetto section. One of the peculiar regulations of the city formerly was that the doors of Jewish homes had to be *less* tall than the men who lived within, so that Jews were forced to stoop when they entered their houses. No Jewish windows could open on the street. Jews were permitted to have no schools, and they took no part in the official life of the state. The men all had to wear a special kind of belt designating them as Hebrews, and they were permitted to ride only on donkeys, not horses. Those Jews who disobeyed the Emir's rules might legally receive up to fifty lashes on the bare buttocks, and the Bokhara tax collectors preyed upon the Jews even more heavily than they did on others.

With the coming of the Soviets to Turkmenia, all forms of minority discriminations were abolished, so when I reached Bokhara, there were Jews in the City Soviet. Jewish, Uzbek and Russian children all went to the same schools. A large number of the teachers were Jewish. Attached to the *Bokhara Proletarian*, a daily paper, was a young native-born Jew who spoke both Russian and Uzbek. This young Jew had become a Communist Party member.

I am afraid I found myself then taking much the same position toward Asiatic Jews in relation to Party membership as many Russians in Moscow took toward Negroes in that regard. Since Communism had brought about such a change for the better in the status of Jews, abolishing the old stigmas formerly applied to them, why were not all Jews Communist Party members? The young reporter explained to me that many of the older Jews resented the Party's anti-religious tenets, which included attacks in the press upon not only mullahs, but rabbis as well. These old people, this young man said, put religion above social, political, or industrial progress. They clung to the Ark of the Covenant and still wanted their synagogues where, said this young Jew who no longer ate kosher food, "Life is a wail and an outworn prayer."

There was a synagogue just around the corner from the hotel where Koestler and I were staying. It was a beautiful building, a hundred or more years old, in a winding lane shaded by plane trees. Its interior was hung with tapestries and rich rugs in the Oriental manner. On its wooden columns were typical Bokharian designs. The day I visited the synagogue there were some very old men with beards, dressed in patriarchal robes. They kept their skull caps on in the temple, and their caps were black, not varicolored and embroidered as were the *tibitekas* of the Uzbeks. These were hospitable old gentlemen who took great pride in showing Koestler and me about the building and the rooms of the Hebrew School. They showed me the high prayer seat in the temple to which a man had to be lifted. And they unrolled from gorgeous ancient leather holders the heavy parchment scrolls. Their altars of stone engraved in Hebrew they said were over three hundred years old. It was quiet and peaceful in this old synagogue, and I went back there more than once during my days in Bokhara. But I saw other former synagogues, which had been turned into storage houses, offices, or trade-union centers, and where, over the Star of David had been superimposed the Hammer and Sickle.

After about a week in Bokhara, Koestler became restless and wanted to move on to Samarkand and Tashkent. Because I liked Bokhara, I decided to linger awhile, promising to meet him in Tashkent before the end of the month. So we parted company. But before Koestler left Bokhara an incident occurred that is still vivid in my mind, I suppose because of the human qualities involved—possibly, too, because it had a direct connection with note-taking. It concerned my last American pencil.

Certain items such as soap, toilet paper, silk stockings and lead pencils were very scarce in the Soviet Union. It was impossible to buy a good lead pencil. I had brought with me to the USSR a big box of pencils, nice long yellow pencils with erasers. Soviet pencils had no erasers, and were of such soft lead that the points wore down no sooner than you had written a few lines. Resharpened, it soon wore down again, so you had to keep sharpening Soviet pencils after every fifty words or so that were written. You had to carry a penknife for just this purpose. Soviet pencils were a nuisance. But, by the time I had gotten to Bokhara, I had used up all my American pencils but one.

The afternoon before Koestler was to leave for Samarkand, the young Jewish newspaperman dropped in. As he sat in our room talking his eye lit on my pencil lying beside the typewriter. He said, "I would love to have a souvenir from your faraway country, America. Could I perhaps have this pencil?"

"Oh, why, of course," I said, not thinking at the moment how valuable that pencil was to me. "Please accept it."

"I will give you my pencil," said the young man, "and I will keep yours forever as a souvenir from your country. Thank you very much!"

When the young man had gone and I started typing, I picked up the pencil he had left on the table to make an erasure, but it had no eraser. This irritated me a bit. Later when I started to write with his Soviet pencil, after a few words the lead wore down so quickly that I really became upset. Here I was without a single decent pencil in the middle of Asia where there were only Russian pencils like the one I had in my hand.

"Gee, Koestler," I said, "I wish I hadn't given that fellow my last good pencil."

"Your last pencil!" Koestler exclaimed. "Why did you give it to him?"

"Because he wanted a souvenir from America," I said. "But I'd much rather have given him a shirt."

"Nothing's more valuable to a writer than the tools of his trade," said Koestler. "That fellow's a newspaperman. Souvenir from America —so much camouflage! He knows Soviet pencils are no good. He tricked you. That Jew!" Koestler said, "I'm ashamed! Ashamed! Langston, I'll get your pencil back for you."

"Oh, no, man!" I said. "Let him have it for a keepsake."

"Keepsake, bah!" cried Koestler in a rage. "Can you write with the pencil he left you? No! He didn't want a souvenir, I tell you—he wanted your pencil!" With that Koester grabbed his coat—he never went out improperly garbed—and stormed off to retrieve my pencil.

I was embarrassed. I had not intended to make an issue of it—a mere pencil. In high school with hundreds of Jewish youngsters I had learned how sensitive some Jewish people can be when another does something considered shameful—just as many Negroes feel keenly any sort of behavior which they think "disgraces the race." But I had not thought of Jewishness at all when I mentioned wishing I had back my pencil. Yet, as soon as I saw Koestler's face, and heard him explode, "That Jew!" I felt that he thought one of his own had misbehaved, so he set out to do something about it. It took Koestler two or three hours to find the young reporter. But when he returned he had my pencil.

## DESERT CARAVANSERAI

LEFT in Bokhara without a translator, I managed to get along. My small Russian vocabulary stood me in good stead and I don't recall speaking a word of English with anyone there after Koestler left. No longer note-taking, I spent my time soaking in the atmosphere, or just sitting across the street from my hotel in a latticework of sun and shade on the edge of the enormous square cistern dating from the days of antiquity. Watching the turbaned old camel drivers in their padded robes and the young sovietized citizens in Russian blouses and embroidered caps passing up and down the narrow street through the

Old Gate of the city to or from the Citadel and the Tower of Death, I mused upon the turbulent history of ancient Bokhara, a city so old that it is said to have been mentioned in Chinese manuscripts as far back as 200 B.C. I was intrigued by the harem wives in long horsehair veils, like walking bundles, who passed completely hidden from all eyes, still slaves to the old customs. But sometimes sitting on one of the slightly raised platforms of a new trade-union teahouse in the late afternoon, squatting on an old soft well-worn Bokhara rug with a pot of green tea before me, I watched a modern Bokhara woman who had escaped from a harem, burned her veil, and gotten herself a job as cashier there. She was now taking in cash and coupons for tea and cakes, as the camels of old Asia and the new motor buses of the Soviets passed in the busy streets outside. Each day when Rakhat Razik finished her work, she got on one of the new motor buses and went her way, free to go and come as she wished.

For almost a month I lingered in Bokhara. On the day of my departure from the old town that I had grown to love, I took a motor-bus to the railroad several miles away, arriving there about sunset. The first thing I learned, as I lugged my bags and baggage to the station platform, was that the train for Tashkent was late. The bulletin board said five hours late. That should make its arrival about eleven P.M. But by midnight no train had come, and nobody knew when it would come. The stationmaster stopped chalking up anything on the board. The station was packed and jammed with men, women and children, for it had turned quite cold. There was not even standing room within. There were no empty benches anywhere to sit on, inside or out, and it was too cold to sit on the ground. I had been on my feet for hours and was very sleepy and very tired. Far down the road through the pitch-black dark, I could see the dim flicker of the lights of a *chaikhanna*, so I decided to head for that distant tea house, leaving my luggage in the hands of fate.

As I approached the *chaikhanna*, there were no signs of life. It was bitter cold and so dark that, as I turned off the dusty road, I could not see the single stone step that tripped me at the entrance to the building. I stumbled toward a crack of light and fell against a heavy door that opened as my body struck it. A blast of fetid air rolled out—but at least the air was warm. The big murky room was filled with men sleeping on the floor and on shelves, huddled together in the light of two or three flares that fluttered and smoked. Smoke or no smoke, I was glad to see light and people again!

I could not find a clear space anywhere so finally I went down like a stone wedged in between two sleepers I had never seen. But it was good to sleep.

The next thing I knew, a man was walking on my head. I blinked as a rain of sand from some soft anonymous boot obscured whoever I might have seen as I looked up. The room had begun to move and stir. Then I smelled tea, so I sat up. Near at hand a little bowl gleamed hot and white. It steamed. At the end of the room, pale through the open door were stars. Folks stretched, talked, moved, went in and out. I heard the sound of camel bells. Gusts of clean cold air cut the smoke. It was dawn in the East. Dawn in Middle Asia!

A hand with a bowl of tea swung toward me in a matter-of-fact way. I drank and passed the bowl on to a shadow of a fellow in the murk next to me. He drank, too, and the bowl moved around from hand to hand and then returned to the pot to be refilled. Life came back to us all, warm and conscious. Turbans were rewound, lost *tibetekas* recovered, belts and sashes tied, noses blown, as everybody began to move. I got to my feet, stretched, and went to the door. It was almost day with the desert a mulatto-brown under the last stars wan in the fresh blue sky.

I looked down the road—and suddenly remembered that nobody had known last night when the Tashkent train might come. Panic-stricken, I began to run. Had it come—and gone? Left me? And were my bags still piled in the corner of the platform alive with people— but no train? Nevertheless, I hurried.

My bags were there, a baby asleep on top of them, golden like a little Buddha. The waiting room was still packed with people, for the sun was not yet high enough to warm the world without. I went back to the platform and looked around. Under the eaves of the station, there was a big sign in two languages, Uzbek and Russian:

BOKHARA, UZBEKISTAN, USSR

A smaller notice chalked on a blackboard below now simply said:

TRAIN LATE

There was no expected time indicated for its arrival. The station-master had evidently given up.

I looked up and down the track gleaming long and lonesome in the morning sun. No sign of a train. If that baby Buddha wasn't sleeping on my suitcases, I'd open one and see what small and meager lunch the Bokhara hotel wrapped up for me last night. It couldn't be much, for food was scarce in Central Asia. The wise thing to do would be to control my appetite until I got on the train. There probably would be no dining car and, since it took all day to reach Tashkent, I would be very hungry later. Restless, I got up and walked to the edge of the platform.

"*Drasvoti, tovarish,*" I said to a young Uzbek in half-European, half-native clothing—an English-type coat, a tibeteka cap of bright embroidery, and soft heel-less boots. "Good morning."

He answered in a glow of guitarlike syllables that certainly weren't Russian. I grinned and shook my head. We began with signs. Hand to belly: *hungry.* Fingers pointing down the track with a frown: *disgust, train late.* Hands across brow, then pretending to fan: *hot, sun getting hotter.* He pointed at my face, then at his: *Brown, same color.* But myself, *ni Uzbek.*

"*Russki?*" he asked.

"*Niet,*" I said. "No. Me, Americanski."

He shrugged. More guitarlike syllables. I thought I might as well speak English since it really didn't matter. Neither of us understood a word, but it was fun to talk. So I said, "American going to Tashkent. Then, by and by, next week, next month, I'll go to Moscow. Then home to America. I'm a writer. I write articles and books. What do you do? *Konsomol?*"

"*Da,*" said the youth, affirming that he was a Young Communist. He knew two Russian words anyhow. Then back into his own tongue, *king-ting-a-ling-ummm-ding,* which is about the sound of the Uzbek language—a kind of musically tinkling tenor speech, as decorative to hear as Persian script is to see.

It is constantly amazing to me how much one can understand of a language of which one knows not a word. Before the train came I had somehow gathered that my Uzbek friend lived near Bokhara, that he had never been even to Tashkent, let alone Moscow, that he was going to be a student of medicine in the newly formed medical school at Samarkand, and that he was learning (or rather intended to learn) Russian and German. In the Uzbek tongue there were no modern medical works as yet.

When the train came, with the customary courtesy of most young Soviet citizens, Asiatic or European, the Uzbek student helped me with my baggage, pushing and scrambling in the thick crush to board an ancient coach and find a seat before all were taken. Then he stood on the seat he had secured in the middle of the car and waved and shouted until I saw him. There was but one place. He insisted on giving it to me. I refused in every language I knew, then took it, thanked him and offered him half of my lunch, which turned out to be a single large but very hard sandwich of cementlike sausage in brick-bat bread. The Uzbek boy imitated a dog with a bone, squatting in the aisle. Everybody laughed. A Russian in the coach, a Red Army man, joined us in the aisle, miraculously producing a pot of tea which we shared, so our luncheon became a jolly affair.

Nobody on the trip had a balalaika or accordion, nevertheless, after a while the Russians began to sing and clapped their hands and probably would have danced but the coach was too crowded with people sitting on the floor in the aisles and everywhere. The student got off at Samarkand. So did the Red Army man. I slept the rest of the way into Tashkent.

It was dark when I reached this largest and most important town in Soviet Central Asia, the regional capital of all that section of the world, where there are streetcars, bright lights, European shops, theaters and even night clubs. I went directly, bags and baggage, to the largest hotel where I found Arthur Koestler. The hotel was filled, so I could not get a room there, nor find anything to eat. But Koestler had a lot of bread, cheese, and camel salami, which he graciously offiered for supper. He spread a newspaper on the bed and shared his food with me. It was my second cold lunch of the day—if the half sandwich on the train could be called lunch. I was hungry, but in a nauseating sort of way. My head ached. I forced the dry food down my dusty throat. Koestler had no tea.

"Tea's hard to find," he said, "and there's no sugar in town. A train wreck held up the shipment."

As we ate, I asked Koestler how he found Tashkent.

"Dirty and ugly and dusty," he said, head down over our meal. "This disgusting part of the world! In Germany at least we'd have a clean revolution. Besides, people are starving here. There's famine. Folks are living on grapes and melons."

"Tashkent can't be as bad as Permetyab," I said. He smiled wryly.

"At least I didn't see a prison out there in the desert." Suddenly Koestler looked up and stared at me intently. "Here in Tashkent the jails are full of people, the Atta Kurdovs of Asia."

"Don't you think that some of them belong in jail?"

"Not so many," said Koestler. "Not all—maybe none."

I had shared with Koestler the Atta Kurdov trials at Ashkhabad, then Permetyab in the desert, and now Tashkent—traveling with him through the heart of Asia along the old caravan trails at the crossroads of the East. Were I a socio-literary historian, I might hazard a guess that here in 1932 were Koestler's crossroads, too—his turning point from left to right that was to culminate a few years later in his bitter attacks on communism.

Shortly after I reached Tashkent, Koestler left for Moscow. I never saw him again until he had become world famous.

## LITTLE OLD LADY

WHEN I left Koestler's hotel, the next one I tried took me in, but all they had was one large and very expensive room filled with heavy furniture, including a canopied bed from the days of the Tzar. I registered and went to bed. My bones ached. The cold, the hard benches of the train, the previous night passed on the dirt floor of the caravanserai, no decent food, all caused me to feel sick, very sick, inside and out.

In the morning I woke up even sicker. I couldn't eat, nor was I able to go anywhere, except to get my papers okayed—which was absolutely necessary in order to receive a food card in case I ever should want to eat again. I also managed to see, as I had promised to do on my return to Tashkent, the State Publishers about a book of mine,

*The Weary Blues*, then being translated into Uzbek—a book of poems about Negro life in America. The Uzbeks were interested in this because, under the Tzar, they remembered they had been treated by the Russians as Negroes are treated in Mississippi. Before the Soviet revolution in Tashkent, there had even been a Jim Crow section for Asiatics on streetcars. The old partitions were still there now, but segregation itself had gone since the Uzbeks control the affairs of their autonomous republic.

The State Publishers of Uzbekistan gave me a check for six thousand rubles as an advance on my book, enough money to buy thirty camels. Had I not been ill, I would have been jubilant—so many rubles and a book of mine coming out that would be read in Samarkand, Bokhara, Kokand and Fergana, after I had gone back to Harlem. But my head was splitting that morning, my tongue was coated with camel sausage, and my stomach felt like lead.

At the hotel, a group of Tashkent writers awaited me. But when they saw how ill I was, they busied themselves to see that I was looked after. So that I would not be alone, it was arranged that I move upstairs and share an apartment with a young man who, it turned out, was the Physical Culture Director for the city of Tashkent. His name was Yusef Nishanov (the *ov* being a Russian termination which the younger Uzbeks were adding to their names as they began to speak Russian). Yusef was a muscularly handsome youth with skin as brown as my own and very black hair, crew-cut, heavy and shiny as silk. His eyes were jolly, his smile broad and bright, and his disposition sunny. Nichan knew about a hundred words of Russian—our only language in common. But he could tell that I needed a doctor, so he sent for one.

All the tallow in all the cold mutton I had eaten during my past weeks in the desert, all the fat of all the camel's meat, and all the sand, silt and dirt of the irrigation ditch water I had drunk on barren collective farms and silk artels between Merv and Tashkent, all the hard sausage and rocklike bread of which I had partaken, plus Koestler's salami of the night before, seemed to have rolled into a single cement boulder in my belly, weighing me down flat on my back in a strange bed in a strange room with a strange Uzbek boy bending over me asking, in a language that sounded like guitars, "What hurts?

What is the matter? Where did I feel sick? How come? *Sto ta koy?*"

About sunset a doctor came. I never knew what nationality that doctor was—a Tartar perhaps—but I pointed at my head, at my stomach, and groaned. He tapped me a bit, took my temperature, held my pulse, and left a prescription which my host took to a pharmacist to be filled. Shortly Nichan returned with a big bottle of bright green liquid with a flaky white sediment at the bottom. I took a dose, and in a few minutes I almost died. So I took another dose. Then all I had ever eaten in all my life came up. As the night wore on, the more I took of the medicine, the worse I got. The next morning I resolved to meet my Maker—for no sicker could a mortal be, and live.

About noon a group of Uzbek writers came to visit. When they saw me, they were frightened. I could hardly raise my head. They immediately sent for the most famous doctor in Middle Asia, the personal physician to the President of Uzbekistan. He was a Russian of the old school, educated in Berlin. In bits of German, French and Russian I explained my case, showed him the bottle of green liquid, and told him how, a few minutes after each dose, I had thought it was the end. He looked at the bottle.

"Is there anything the matter with your heart?" he asked.

"*Nein*," I answered.

"No wonder you are sick," the doctor stated holding up the bottle. "This is arsenic—for the heart."

The big stone in my stomach turned completely over. I groaned, "Will I live?"

"*Nichevo*," he said, in such a way that I couldn't tell if he meant, "So what? It's nothing that you're going to die." Or, "It's nothing to worry about that you've taken arsenic." Or, simply, that nothing was nothing.

"Well," I said, "*Nichevo*, too!"

I threw the arsenic out the window. But a new problem intrigued me—to find the required diet. The doctor had prescribed a list of rare, delicious and delicate dishes—nourishing soups, fowl, and wonderful custards—but practically none of them, nor the ingredients for creating them, were to be had in the state food shops or at the meager bazaars of Tashkent. I consulted with Nichan. Chicken, Nichan said, could be gotten from the farmers—but at banquet prices. Besides, who would cook it? That was another puzzle—there being no dining room in the hotel. But Nichan set about solving things for me. A day or two later he brought into the room a little old Russian lady who looked like Ouspenskaya. She said she would cook my chickens. And she lived right there in the hotel where I was.

Her name I have forgotten, but I remember that since she did not like to be called *tovarish* (*no* comrade, she) we always called her *grasdani*, citizen. I arranged to give her a certain sum of money every week for chickens, plus a modest salary agreed upon. To her I turned over my convalescence. Grasdani took excellent care of me. She even made pancakes for breakfast—thin Russian blintzes with sour cream.

She was a kind, sad, wisp of an old lady—a remnant of the upper classes—who had been living in that same hotel since the days of the Tzar. The Soviets let her stay, permitting her a small apartment where she had her own cooking facilities. She had been a woman of means once. Now—well, she said, it would be a pleasure to nurse me and help me back to health, a mere courtesy that any Russian would pay a stranger ill in a foreign land. But, regretfully, as things were, she would have to accept the payment I offered her. The sum I suggested (for at first she was mute on the subject) she cut by half. Too much, she said. So, for what seemed to me woefully little remuneration, she prepared my meals, nursed me back to health, and talked to me by the hour in a flow of Russian, which I began to understand more and more. She aided me greatly in acquiring a better working knowledge of the language of the Muscovites while living in the land of the Uzbeks.

The burden of her conversation (and Grasdani made no bones about it) was that she had grave doubts concerning a regime that permitted wild and unwashed nomads, just out of the desert, to live in a hotel such as this one where once barons, diplomats, colonels, majors and rich merchants from Moscow used to stay. Now the rooms were all cluttered up with Tajik commissars, Tartars, young Kazak Communists, Russian mechanics sent to teach the natives how to service tractors, and former camel drivers from yurts in the desert now delegated to the Regional Soviets to make laws.

The old lady snorted and gave vent to her favorite verbal illustration of the general hopelessness of all this. "They don't even know," she said, "how to use the toilet. They throw tin cans in it, these *tovarishi*, then pull the chain!" She looked at me lying in bed and added her final coup. "Ever since the Soviets came to power, the plumbing has been out of order."

After that, or a similar statement almost daily, she would gather up the luncheon dishes with such force that, had they not been solid Soviet-made cement china, they surely would have broken. Then the old lady would stalk indignantly down the hall with my tray, leaving the fragrant scent of chicken broth and sour cream trailing after her. I knew that every day a line of such old Russian ladies stood outside the OGPU prison in Tashkent with baskets of food for relatives within—political prisoners who had not yet reconciled themselves to the new regime and who fought it verbally or physically, dangerously and violently. In my heart I was sorry for these irreconcilables (just as my slave grandparents must have been sorry for certain of the gentler aristocrats of the South when the Yankees came). Yet, as the little old lady went muttering down the hall, I could not help thinking, "She has had her day." Something hard and young in me could not not help thinking, now had come the hour of those from the desert, who once had to work seven years for the beys in order to afford a wrinkled worn-out old wife that some richer man had first enjoyed, in the days when women were bought and sold like cattle. Today women are free, and men, too, for now has come the time of those who formerly had to till the overlord's vast acres in return for the use of just a little water to irrigate a single barren acre of their own. The overlords have fled, along with the Emirs, the Khans and the Tzarist officers. Now it is the turn of those who in former days had to beg of the Cossacks, "Please, master! No more lashes, please! White master, no more! Please!" Of course, in those days the Uzbeks had had no toilets.

As dusk approached, that vast hotel room where I lay would fill with the shadows of Cossacks and soldiers, adventurers and barons, tax collectors and colonial officers from St. Petersburg, who once ruled Turkestan for the Little White Father—spice dealers and silk stealers from the North who supported the despotic Emirs—the men who had once wined, dined, danced with, and courted this little old lady who now brought my dinner and remained to talk with me as I ate, mourning the passing of the Romanoffs, the old culture and the days of no tin cans in the toilets.

But as the afternoon faded into darkness, Nichan, the Uzbek, would come bursting in full of news of the great Sports Festival he was arranging where Asiatic peasant boys and girls who, a few years ago, never knew what it was to play, would exhibit their youth and strength in the new stadium at Fergana. "And here, next month," Nichan said in a mixture of his wild musical language, "Fut-bal! Here in Tashkent. Fut-bal! You go. Get up, *tovarish*, get well, we see fut-bal!"

Ten years ago Nichan himself had been a homeless orphan, an Oriental besprizorni, dirty, ignorant, scab-covered, wandering the caravan trails of Central Asia. The Soviet government had corralled him into one of their schools and had found him eager and alert, with qualities of leadership. Now, Nichan was in charge of the athletic activities of thousands of boys and girls who, like himself, until recently had never had a chance.

But my sad kind little old lady, who had had her day, resented these things, and was very critical of young Uzbeks like Nichan. Change is seldom enjoyed by the aging, whether they be individuals or nations. However, for her sake( as well as mine), I took it upon myself to explain to Nichan the general incompatibility of tin cans and modern plumbing. Since Grasdani perhaps still had a number of years to live under the new system, I wanted her to be as happy as she could and to get along with these nomads from the desert. Certain things we enjoyed in common. For instance all of us, the old lady, Nichan and I liked blintzes with sour cream. It was our good fortune, as part of my diet, to have them every day. So sometimes the three of us dined amiably together.

## HOOLIGANS OF THE ROAD

NICHAN, my host, the former homeless boy, was now living in what had been a private banquet room for the entertainment of Tzarist officers in the old days. It was a large corner room on the second floor at the front of the hotel with tall French windows opening onto a long balcony. The room was called an "apartment" now because a portion of it, about a fourth, had been boarded off with a partition slightly taller than a man. This made a small bedroom in which, on two narrow cots at opposite sides, Nichan and I slept. In the main room there was a large leather sofa which often served as a bed, too, for Nichan had many friends, visiting athletes from other parts of Uzbekistan, Tajikistan and even the Pamirs, or Red Army men in Tashkent on leave, or various cousins and peasant relatives from the country oases. Sometimes two or three pallets would be spread on the floor, which was agreeable to the Uzbeks, as they were not used to beds, anyhow.

In the center of the room when I moved in, there was a sculptor's stand and a big box of damp clay. On the stand an athletic figure, a third life size, had begun to emerge under the skillful hands of Nina Zaratelli, a Georgian sculptress, who was modeling Nichan from life, to be enlarged into a gigantic figure of *Uzbek Youth* to adorn the entrance of the new stadium being built in Tashkent. Nina Zaratelli modeled two or three times a week, depending on when she could catch Nichan long enough to persuade him to pose.

So, with a statue being made in our room and student-artists often gathered to watch this process, visiting athletes dashing in with soccer balls, tall Red Army men pulling off stiff boots to rest their feet, country cousins unrolling bundles of bedding for a nap in a corner, and the little old lady coming in and out to look after me—with all this going on every day, the room in which I lay ill was not unlike Grand Central Station in New York at rush hour. Conversations in Uzbek, Tajik, Russian, Georgian and Tartar flowed around me continually. At times bedlam could hardly have been more linguistic than this room in the former Tzarist—but now Soviet—hotel in Tashkent.

It was very cold in Tashkent by the end of November, although Muscovites considered the climate of Central Asia almost tropical. But to me the temperature was much like that of the wind-swept plains of the Kansas of my youth. By the end of November there was snow on the ground. Russian sleds with horses and bells sped through the streets past slow humping camels whose breath rose like clouds of steam to float above the burdens on their backs. In Nichan's room the air was often like ice. Even ill and covered up in bed as I was, I got cold, for the hotel had no central heating, fuel was scarce, and our room was vast. Built in the wall was a ceiling-high porcelain stove, white and beautiful, but quite empty of fire. This stove had a narrow little door and thick inner walls of brick. The few times that we had fuel—sent by the Writers Union during the first week of my illness, I watched the process for heating this stove. I was appalled because, it seemed, the *height* of warmth to a citizen of Tashkent was to get a little glow inside the stove, then shut the door tight and let the thick brick walls get barely warmed through. This in turn slightly took the chill off the room, but gave out no real heat at all. In fact, you could still see your breath in the air. I began to study how to remedy the situation.

Coal was not to be had. Wood, in a largely desert country, was very expensive. It was then that I learned that, even in the Socialist Soviet Union, money in large amounts is a blessing. For what seemed to the other residents of the hotel a prohibitive sum, it was possible for me to buy from private dealers a whole camel load of wood—two or three loads if I wanted to pay the price. Fortunately, I had just received the rubles for my book, so I paid out a large handful of them to a camel driver who unloaded from his beast in the snow in front of the hotel a big pile of wood. An Uzbek porter stacked it on our front balcony for me. Promptly I filled the big old white porcelain stove *full* of wood and lit it. The door of the stove I left open like a fireplace—so the heat rolled out! It was very jolly. Everybody loved it. Result: Nichan and I had more company than ever. So, with a roaring fire, pretty Nina Zaratelli modeling in the center of the room, the nice old Russian lady serving chicken and blintzes, my Harlem victrola playing Bessie Smith, Louis Armstrong and Ethel Waters—plus Uzbek athletes demonstrating handsprings, and Red Army men, local authors and native university students, both girls and boys, paying calls—my convalescence was anything but dull.

To further enliven my recuperation, there came two besprizorni, dirty little white-skinned wanderers in oversized men's coats down to their heels, whom I discovered looking up at my balcony one day when I went out to get an armload of wood.

"*Kleb*," one of them said, "bread," motioning toward his mouth.

So I threw down the bread left from my luncheon, and also the wing of a chicken. Every day after that, for a month or more, the two boys came back about the same time to stand across the street looking up at the balcony until I appeared. They never came into the hotel, and as soon as I tossed them some food, they disappeared. I never knew their names, but they were not Asiatics. When they took off their caps to catch whatever I had saved to throw them, their matted hair was ash blond. They spoke Russian, or at least they said *bread* and *thank you* in Russian.

Besprizorni were wandering delinquents, a problem to the Soviet authorities and a source of amusement and irritation to ordinary citizens. These were the homeless children of the Revolution, children of passing armies, death, broken homes and maladjustment, who refused to stay in the schools assigned to them. If there were old people like Grasdani, who could not adjust to Soviet society, there were young ones, too, who could not—or would not. My roommate, Nichan, had adjusted brilliantly after his years of wandering, and had become an inspiring and useful citizen under state guidance, helping others along the path of progress. But many young vagabonds had refused to accept—or accepted only temporarily—the aid of institutions established for them. These determined little hooligans were making a last stand for freedom.

I first became aware of the besprizorni in Moscow, where I was warned that such homeless boys might pick my pockets in the tram-cars. Nothing of the sort happened, but I was wary of tattered teen-agers who came too near. It was not until I got to the Black Sea that I had a chance to become acquainted with such youngsters. The first one I knew was only a child. He turned up at sea on the excursion boat bearing our movie group toward Yalta. Laden with summer travelers from all parts of the Soviet Union the ship softly undulated through the smooth water off the Crimean coast. I was seated on the boat deck sharing bread and chocolate with a girl from Harlem when suddenly, from beneath the bench, up popped a besprizorni—ragged, dirty, hard and wizened, yet with a smile like a million rubles—this small jack-in-a-box of humanity. He might have been ten years old, he might have been fifteen. There were several years difference between his head and his body. He looked like a little old wise man in the face.

"*Drasvouti*," I said, meaning good morning but perhaps pronouncing it so badly he thought I was speaking a foreign language.

"*Kleb?*" he asked.

The girl beside me held out a piece of bread. The besprizorni took it, went behind a rope hamper as a dog might do, ate it, then looked at us and smiled.

"Ask him what his name is," we said to a Red Army man standing near the ship's rail, who knew a little English.

"*Kola*," said the besprizorni in answer to a stream of Russian from the man in uniform. (Kola means Nick in our language—short for Nickolai.)

The Red Army man asked Kola where he was going, and the boy replied casually, "For a trip."

The military youth laughed, and he and Kola began to banter each other in a flow of Russian. Other passengers gathered around laughing and questioning. The little old boy in rags was holding high court on the boat deck when a sailor came up the stairs. Behind the rope hamper fled the besprizorni, but the sailor saw him and laughed. The group of grownups scattered, smiling. By and by, Kola's hatless head peered over the top of the hamper, bobbing up and down. The coast was clear. The little stowaway came out. We fed him more bread and chooclate, and talked with him in our limited Russian.

These vagabond boys were one of the major problems of the Soviet government, roaming across the Union, making a desperate stand to continue the wild life to which, as children in the tempestuous years following the Revolution, many had become accustomed. These youths roamed in bands, begging, stealing, sleeping in doorways, holes and corners, and riding the rods or stowing away on boats when they tired of a place.

For these pitiful and half-savage children of upheaval, there were many communes. In these school-homes, the wild boys of the road were taught to read and write, and trained in trades, citizenship, music and dancing. From such homes, I was told, they might run away if they chose, then come back, and no questions were asked. So long used to their precarious freedom, Soviet psychologists knew that, even when well housed, these boys must still *feel* free. Therefore the door was open for them to go back to the highway if they chose. And some did. Some got tired of comfort and regularity. Some wanted the sting of road dust in their eyes again, or to feel the cinders from an engine blowing in their faces as they hopped a boxcar. Some loved the thrill of purse snatching in theater crowds. But, like Gypsies, the besprizorni, in spite of their tendencies toward gangsterism, had acquired in the eyes of the people a sort of romantic aura. Of these young hooligans, as the Russians termed them, many strange and amusing tales were told.

One of my interpreters told me of her mother's experience with some besprizorni in the early 1920s. Everyday, one cold winter, a little group used to come to the window for bread that the old woman would place on the sill. But the boys would never come in. Nor would they come too near the house if the door were open, for fear of being captured. They slept in a railway station. Their clothes were rags and tatters. By winter's end, this kindhearted grandmother was able to make friends with the leader, a boy of fourteen. One day she persuaded him to come into the house to warm himself and drink a cup of hot tea. Gradually the youth began to trust her. But in the spring, when it was becoming warm enough to ride the rails again, they came one morning to say goodbye. Shyly, the boys presented the old woman who had been kind to them with a beautiful traveling bag that they said they had stolen from a foreign lady at the station.

Some of the besprizorni had a highly developed technique for extracting what they wanted from an unwary passer-by, even in broad daylight. One of their famous and frightful tricks was the Saliva Threat —which usually brought results. It was commonly believed that all the besprizorni were diseased and that the scabs and sores that filth produced on their bodies were indications of the worst venereal infections. The besprizorni knew almost everybody believed this, so they capitalized on it. A ragged little boy would suddenly walk up to a man in a crowded street and hiss into his horrified ear, "Gimme five rubles —or I'll spit in your face! I'm full o' disease." The boy, being a crack shot at spitting, usually got the five rubles.

In Moscow, a band of homeless girls were said to have broken into a large department store late at night and arrayed themselves in the choicest garments to be found. Then they began to eat cheese and drink vodka in the food department. It was so nice and warm in the store that they lay down to rest awhile but, due to the potency of the vodka and the heaviness of the cheese, they slept until the astonished manager came to open the store in the morning. Then their wanderings were arbitrarily curtailed by the police.

When the Torgsin stores were first opened (shops where one might trade only in gold, silver, or foreign currency) a young besprizorni is said to have appeared one morning with a human head full of gold teeth. This legend is indicative of the kind of colorful tales to which the besprizorni lent themselves. Some of the stories had a Robin Hood-like quality. Often the vagabond boys were said to give their bread, gotten by begging, to professional beggars, saying, "We can steal ours. You only know how to beg." And to people who had been kind to them, they would often say, "Can we swipe something for you?"

Once in Moscow I saw a half-grown besprizorni caught stealing from the counter of a little shop. A huge piece of cheese was removed from the boy's shirt front. Two good citizens held him while a third went for the militia. (The police in Russia are never called *police*. There is too much Tzarist terror about the word *police*, so they are called *militia*.) A young militiaman arrived, not much bigger than the teenage boy he was to arrest. The besprizorni refused to go with the militiaman. Such scenes were fairly frequent in the Moscow streets— the arrested refusing to be arrested, with long and lengthy arguments ensuing, since in the Soviet Union the ordinary militia used no clubs, believe it or not, nor were they allowed to beat prisoners (at least, not in public). Today the little cop argued with the boy. The citizens in the shop argued with him. A sort of forum was held.

"After all, my lad, you took the cheese," they said, "you should go and be punished."

"Yes," agreed the militiaman, "come on."

Suddenly the boy's knees got so purposely weak he could no longer stand. He wilted to the floor. The little cop tried to pick him up. The boy would not rise. Finally, in desperation, the young militiaman asked for the help of the citizens in taking his prisoner to the station house. The boy wriggled, screamed and cried. The policeman took a foot, a clerk took the other foot, two men took an arm each, and thus they carried him off to explain to the judge.

"It must be spring," a man in the crowd said. "The besprizorni are on the road again."

On the station steps in Tashkent, in the summer, as our movie group was leaving, I saw an amusing little hooligan of not more than twelve, doing antics to attract the attention of travelers. With our interpreter, we stopped and asked the boy jokingly what train he was waiting for.

He said, "The train to Moscow."

"Have you got your ticket?" we asked.

"Sure, ten of 'em," he said, and held up his hands, indicating that he intended to hang on to the blinds.

Our interpreter, interested in the boy, asked him how he—obviously a Russian child—happened to be way down there in Asia.

The little boy proceeded to give a long, witty tale of his exploits, mentioning a dozen cities he had visited, and ending up by saying that he had been taking a ride on the Caspian Sea in a steamboat when the mate got orders to push him off. He ran and hid in a big barrel of pickles behind the galley door, intending to stay there until the port was passed. The heat of the galley and the fumes of the brine got the best of him. When the cook, reaching into the barrel for pickles for supper, pulled him out, he himself was nearly pickled.

We laughed. A girl in our group gave him a chocolate bar—a rarity in Asia. He regarded it with a quizzical expression, and remarked that he wished it were a chicken leg.

"Our train is leaving," we said, hearing the bell. "Goodbye."

Some of the girls patted the pert little youngster on the head—to his disgust. He ducked. As a more manly gesture of friendship, I held out my hand. He eyed it solemnly.

"If you give me a ruble," he said, "I'll shake it."

"Don't be a hooligan," scolded our interpreter, frowning at such impudence.

## TARTAR RENDEZVOUS

WHEN Nichan burst into the room, a dynamo of life always came with him. He was one of the most energetic of young men, happily occupied most of the time with sports, dancing, girls, or talking to his scores of friends in that *ting-a-ling-gong-ling* language of his. Yet Nichan never got on my nerves with too much energy as some people I've been around have done. In Asia, Nichan was in his way as amiable and as thoughtful a host as had been Mrs. Bethune in Florida, Amy Spingarn at Troutbeck, or Noel Sullivan in San Francisco.

As I got better, my appetite came back in leaps and bounds. Grasdani's boiled chicken and blintze-thin pancakes once or twice a day were not enough to fill me. I could almost relish camel sausage again. In the evenings Nichan would bring me a broken disc of Asiatic bread or some goat cheese from his worker-teacher-student restaurant. Then we would sit in front of the ceiling-tall open-door stove, drink tea, eat and talk until some of his student friends came bounding in to roughhouse the evening away. When the other young folks were gone Nichan would fall on his cot opposite mine and sleep like a log.

The big front room in the old Tzarist hotel in Tashkent was quiet all day when Nichan was out of town sometimes, no students about, no athletes bouncing soccer balls, no statue being modeled. Only Grasdani coming in with my meals, of which I now partook more and more heartily, leaving little to share with others. Sometimes the Negro engineer, Bernard Powers, might drop by for a chat. But in the gray quiet of those long lazy afternoons, I had time to remember many things and to think back over my past at leisure, from Topeka to Tashkent, Cleveland to the Congo, Mexico City to Moscow. In my first thirty years I'd been around quite a little, and I'd known a great many people in many towns. Now my best friend and boon buddy was a tousle-haired Uzbek named Yusef Nichan. Yusef had just borrowed a thousand rubles from me.

A delayed vacation period had been granted him, and a long-planned hunting trip to the foothills of the Pamirs was about to take place. But his monthly salary did not come through on schedule. Nichan held off his departure for a week or more, but still no money. His voucher was all tied up somewhere in red tape, going through channels—meanwhile, no cash. Finally, Nichan asked me abashedly if perhaps I would lend him a few hundred rubles. We agreed upon a thousand. During my illness he had been so attentive that this was a loan I was happy to grant. Nichan said his brother would repay me within a week or so, as he was giving this brother a properly stamped authorization to receive his salary for him when the delay got straightened out.

I had met Nichan's brother but once. He was an older fellow, hard, leather-tanned, tall and gaunt, whose work was the loading and stabling of camels at a caravan station on the edge of the city. This brother had never been educated, could not speak Russian, and lived and dressed as an ordinary Uzbek peasant in thick padded robes, whereas Nichan usually wore a European coat and trousers. Nichan was very fond of his brother—they had found each other after years of being apart, quite by accident coming face to face in the Tashkent bazaar. He particularly admired this brother since he was a worker—an honorable thing to be in the Soviet Union. But to me Nichan's brother, on first acquaintance, did not seem nearly as wholesome a citizen as Nichan—who had had, by a lucky turn of fate, many more advantages. However, I accepted Nichan's word that his brother would surely bring my money back to me. What happened is another story—indicative of the problems of transition in an old land faced with a new set of values.

Toward the end of November, Nichan went away to the Pamirs leaving me almost recovered from my illness. I was able to get about a bit and explore the town. During my convalescence, Nichan often had guests sleeping in his rooms overnight, sometimes for several days —visiting athletes from Fergana or Samarkand, or desert relatives occupying the couch, or spreading pallets on the floor of the big room, while Nichan and I kept our cots in the partitioned dormitory. Sometimes Nichan's cot opposite mine was empty since occasionally some amorous Uzbek girl—an emancipated sovietized girl, of course—shared the couch with him in front of the ceiling-high porcelain stove. Nichan and his girl would usually just lie there and talk quietly for a long time. But then, if I were still awake, beyond the partition I might hear in the middle of the night a terrific rolling and wrestling, scuffling, pushing, pulling, leaping and running about—which, when I first overheard such sounds, I thought must be indicative of rape. Later I heard that it was just the way Uzbeks make love.

My personal experience with the details of such love-making came about through the good offices of a dashing young Red Army man from Tajikistan. One day during Nichan's absence a tall fair-skinned Asiatic soldier showed up with a properly stamped propusk permitting him to share Nichan's room for a month, since it contained an empty bed. He had come to Tashkent to take a special course of some kind at the Red Army School, and so was out all day. This young Tadjik soldier did not even speak Uzbek, so there was scarcely a word we could say to each other, yet we got on very pleasantly. He slept in Nichan's cot opposite mine. Sometimes at night we would lie there talking—after a fashion—in the few Russian words that each of us knew. He was, among other subjects, taking a course in Russian. But even with my meager knowledge of that language, I could teach him something. Hajir, however, was interested in instructing me in certain other things he thought I ought to know. He wanted to take me to meet one of the local girls. He had shortly after his arrival become acquainted with two Tartar lassies who were, so he indicated, oh, boy! Wow! Ummm-mm-m! Arbors of delight! Tartar girls! Come see, we go now—tonight!

But I didn't take him up on his proposed introduction for several days. It was too cold and snowy outside for me to be going where I was sure there would be no heat, on the off-chance of a blind date with a girl I probably couldn't exchange a word with. I had no idea what language a Tartar spoke. Some nights Hajir did not come home at all. He stayed with his Tartar. But when I saw him, he would give me a graphic pantomimed description of the evening before. He aroused my curiosity to the point where I agreed to go with him to visit these girls from the Kyzle Kum desert. I gathered they were sisters or cousins and lived together.

"Kleb," said Hajir, "and something to drink," he pantomimed.

Bread and brandy, I gathered, were in order as gifts to the fair ones. So I took my foreign food coupons to the single big store in town—open only to executives, engineers and foreign workers—where a person might be reasonably sure of finding something to eat and drink for sale at most times. Tashkent shops were all "controlled," with ration books required, but most of them were also mostly empty. The famine of the Ukraine and Volga regions seemed to have penetrated into Asia. Citizens who did not eat in co-operative restaurants and had to buy in food shops were having a hard time filling out their menus. And there were no shops at all where a person could just walk in and buy something without coupons and stamps. My coupon book was almost intact, since, being flush with rubles during my illness, Grasdani had done most of my shopping on the open market or directly from peasants selling in the bazaars. This was expensive, few could afford it, and there was little offered save chicken, eggs, or wild game, even there. Now I had no objection to using up several of my extra ration coupons for bread and brandy for Hajir's enamorata and her Tartar sister, cousin, or friend. I was never quite sure what, if any, relationship existed between the girls.

On the night of our romantic hegira from my warm fireside, fresh snow had fallen over Tashkent, and all the somber old brown-gray buildings and mud-brick houses of the city were flecked with white. The streets were almost trackless, for few persons were abroad, even so early as nine in the evening. The camels all seemed to have laid down their burdens for the night. We waited a long time at a cold corner for an ancient streetcar to rattle by, almost empty of passengers. I did not know where we were going but, with a heavy loaf of black bread and big bottle of cognac, my friend and I were on our way. Hajir sat up very straight in his becoming heel-long Red Army greatcoat, with his polished leather belt and gleaming boots. He was a handsome young man, more Persian-looking than Mongol, with ivory skin, a lean, strong face and very black hair. He was at least six feet tall, perhaps more, wiry and tough, from the high mountains near the point where India almost touches the Soviet border. He was not as capable of communication as Yeah Man had been in Ashkhabad, so I did not learn much from him about life in the wild cold hills in the heart of Asia from which he came. But he called me *tovarich*—comrade—and behaved toward me as any good buddy in America might. Now we were headed for a festive evening with the Tartars.

As the old streetcar rattled along, my teeth chattered with cold. Tashkent is a big town, the streets are dark, and I had never been so far out on the edges of the city before. In time only a few bedraggled Uzbeks were left on the car. Where on earth were we going? We must have been riding for an hour. Finally the tramcar stopped and the turbaned motorman and everyone else got out. We were at the end of the line.

"Come on," Hajir said, or its equivalent. Rapidly he started off marching like a young general through the snow, carrying the big round loaf of bread, while I tagged along behind with the cognac. Now there were not even street lights or sidewalks, just rows of sleepy-looking mud houses in the snow. I finally decided we were heading for a yurt in the desert, a nomad tent fleetingly anchored in the remote wilderness. I'd heard that many Tartars were still nomads. The road was full of ruts and the snow had gotten into my shoetops, and even walking rapidly, I was cold. It was hard to keep up with the tall young army-trained Hajir. But I had no intention of being left behind in the darkness on that suburban road with no idea of how to get back home. Panting through the sticky snow, I kept up fairly well. Finally I saw, vaguely silhouetted against the night in the distance, what looked like three or four sawed-off American skyscrapers. A housing project! I'd heard there was a large workers' apartment village newly constructed on the edge of Tashkent. This, I took for granted, was it.

"Is that where those broads live?" I shouted at Hajir a dozen yards ahead of me. He must have understood my question for he answered, "Da," yes. Was I glad! One more mile and I would have dropped of cold, weariness, and breathlessness together. But Hajir in his greatcoat and boots did not mind the weather or the snow at all and, accustomed to maneuvers in the high atmosphere of the Pamirs, he would never get out of breath. Besides, he was heading for a familiar romance. I was headed for I knew not what. Maybe that girl's sister or cousin or friend was sixty-five years old. As a Tartar, I envisioned a wild-eyed woman from the steppes with sand in her hair and fingernail-claws. Who knows what? To brace myself, I opened the bottle of cognac and took a drink there in the road.

"Hey, fellow, have one," I said.

Hajir understood perfectly. He halted his pace for once, turned the bottle up and drank like a trooper. Then he pointed at a high window where a light was visible. The tall, barren, boxlike buildings had no elevators. We had to walk up several flights. Hajir took the steps two at a time, singing. When I got where he was going he was already there—in an apartment consisting of a single room with an alcove where there was a single bed. A vague aura of warmth came from a built-in wall stove, just enough to take the extreme chill off the air. Sitting by the stove were two drab red-haired women. On a cot against the wall was a sleeping child, a girl of maybe nine or ten. The women, since neither Hajir nor I understood Tartar, talked excitedly between themselves as they unwrapped the bread, opened the cognac, and poured us all drinks. The black bread they hacked off into thick hunks and ate like cake with the cognac. Hajir grabbed his girl as she stood cutting bread and gave her a bearlike squeeze that caused her to scream, "Ow!" He motioned for me to attack mine in the same manner, but the other woman was busy putting a knot of desert wood on the fire. With this warming procedure I did not wish to interfere as my feet were wet with snow and I was chilled to the bone.

I simply said, "More power to you, boy," and lifted my glass, grinning at Hajir and his Tartar mistress.

The girls were not good-looking. Hajir's sweetheart was the younger, a squat solidly build female in her twenties, I judged, with a round Mongoloid face and a bush of coarse auburn hair of a wiry nature. She was rather thick-lipped, heavy-lidded, and of a sullen cast. The other woman was skinny, big-eyed, and rather anemic, with reddish wiry hair, too. Both looked as if all the grime of the steppes of Asia had been imbedded in their hard, leathery skins. With poker faces, they wolfed down big chunks of black bread as if they had missed their supper that day. The cognac they hardly touched. Instead, Hajir emptied their glasses down his own singing throat.

When most of the bread was gone, he pointed toward me, the older woman, and toward the bed—then toward the door again, the bed, the door—then me. I shrugged, not knowing exactly what he meant in relation to the door. So he got up and took my arm and indicated that he wanted me to come outside. He led me down an ice-cold corridor to a big dormitory at the end of the building where there were perhaps twenty cots in rows. The room was both dark and empty. I learned later that most of the Soviet housing projects had such large dormitory rooms where residents might house relatives and guests when they came from a distance to visit, since the small apartments had no guest rooms. That night I gathered that Hajir was asking whether I wished to stay in the room where the stove was, or come with the skinny Tartar girl to this enormous empty icebox for the night.

I shook my head violently, "Nyet—no! I stay where the stove is."
I turned immediately and went back down the hall where the girls
were. By this time they had either eaten or hidden the remaining
hunk of bread, and had refilled our glasses with cognac.

Hajir grabbed his girl around the waist again and squeezed the
breath out of her. Then he took her by the hair, turned her around,
slapped her soundly on the buttocks, and pushed her with his knee
out into the cold hall as she screamed. He turned back for a final
swig of cognac, then departed for the Siberia of the dormitories. I was
left alone with the skinny redhead and the sleeping child. Not one
word did we know in common. Not a single sentence could we say
that either of us understood. But the Tartar pointed unsmilingly toward the alcove, took off her boots, turned out the light, and went
to bed, indicating to me to do the same. She had taken off nothing but
her boots—the soft high-topped Asiatic boots that most women in the
Tashkent area wore. Otherwise, she went to bed fully clothed, sweater,
skirts and all. This did not surprise me, as cold as it was. I took off a
minimum of outer garments and lay down beside her.

The skinny Tartar rolled to the far side of the bed with her back
toward me. After a while she moved a little closer, then closer still. I
put my arm around her. But when I tried to unbutton her sweater, she
struggled violently and pulled away. Puzzled, I desisted. In the silence
I heard the child stir on the cot near the stove. After a few moments,
the skinny one again got very close to me, and this time I managed to
unbutton one sweater button, when she brusquely removed my hand
and kicked. Thinking perhaps that she had only accepted me as a
house guest because of the other girl's interest in the Red Army man,
I gave up. I was embarrassed, too, by the presence of the child on the
cot. But as soon as I had turned over to go to sleep, she turned over
toward me for the first time, and put her arms around me. I kissed her,
whereupon, she sat bolt upright, vaulted over me, and jumped out of
bed.

When I made no move to pursue her, she came back, rolled over
beside me, and squeezed me with a grip of iron. But when I in turn
squeezed her, she gave me a push that almost sent me onto the floor.
Each attempt to undo a sweater button, of which there were at least
six or eight, set up the most determined resistance—kicking, pushing,

hunching—and a flood of what sounded like Tartar curses.

Finally, I said, "Oh, woman, I give up! I'm going to sleep." I rolled over on the far side of the bed this time, face to the wall and went to sleep. The next thing I knew, Hajir, and his girl were banging on the door. It was dawn. By eight Hajir had to be at his studies.

The Skinny One of the still unbuttoned sweater brewed some tea, which we all drank, spiking it with the residue of the cognac. The sleepy-eyed child on the cot woke up, blinked, then turned over and went to sleep again. I wished I could, too. But Hajir motioned for me to get dressed. He and his Tartar girl were grinning and frolicsome, and I gathered they had had a whopping good time in the enormous dormitory room. Tramping the long two or three miles to the car line, Hajir indicated to me that his night had been a night of delight— sleep, no, just love, no sleep.

"And you?" he pointed at me.

"Nyet," I said, "not me."

Hajir looked puzzled. We had no language in common for me to tell him how strangely that Tartar woman had behaved. All I could do was shake my head glumly and say no, nyet, nothing had happened. When we boarded the streetcar, we both lapsed into silence. Even at the end of the carline, in the morning, going into the city to work, the tram was almost full of Uzbeks in padded robes, Russians in fur caps, and an assortment of other Soviet nationalities in all sorts of headgear and clothing. After a few stops, the car became more tightly packed than a New York subway train at rush hour. Before we reached the heart of Tashkent, folks were hanging all over the car, inside and out, packed like sardines and clustered like bees. Hajir battled his way to the door somewhere near the site of his studies, and left me to return to our hotel alone. By now I knew the heart of the city fairly well, so I reached home safely, tired, sleepy, cold, and ill-humored. Why had he led me on such a wild-goose chase? Was it a gag? Or a ruse for the sake of the bread and brandy? At that moment my opinion of Hajir as a friend was very low.

That evening, fortunately, the American road engineer, Bernard Powers (he who had greeted the arrival of our movie group in Tashkent dressed in a tuxedo) happened to drop by my hotel. I told him of my experience of the night before. He laughed fit to kill, as did the various Uzbeks and Tadjiks gathered. Powers said that the same thing had happened to him the first time he had attempted to make love to an Asiatic gal.

"Man," Powers said, "these women never take off their clothes in this part of the world when they go to bed. It's bad manners or something. And they won't let a man take them off either, without a struggle. That's bad manners, too, not to resist. A man might think the girl is a prostitute. Women have to fight every button of the way. If they give up without a struggle, they aren't considered nice. But they don't really mean it when they kick you. A fellow is supposed to keep right on unbuttoning, and pulling, and hauling until he gets down to the last garment. Then he fights to get whatever that is off, if he can. In Tashkent even a prostitute doesn't take off her own clothes for a client. The man has to do it. It's a ritual, that's all. Next time you'll know."

I understood then why so much commotion went on with Nichan and his girls in the middle of the night. Nichan wasn't raping them. He was just trying to unbutton their sweaters or untie a sash.

When Powers, via a two-or three-way translation, later that evening, had made Hajir understand my lack of success with the Tartar lass who had eaten our bread, and when Hajir was told that women in America did not usually behave with such violent modesty once a man was permitted in the boudoir, Hajir indicated that he could have very little feeling or respect for a barefaced female who just *took her own clothes off* and got on into bed with a man, no matter how well she knew him. How shameless can a woman get? Hajir asked a Tadjik-Uzbek speaking friend in the room to explain to an Uzbek-Russian speaking friend to explain in Russian to Powers to explain to me in English that if he, Hajir, had known that I didn't know how to just kick back after unloosening each button—and to keep on kicking, tugging, pulling, and struggling until I got the girl's sweater off, then go through the same struggle with her blouse, then her skirt—he would have told me. Hajir couldn't imagine that men didn't undress women by force in America.

"So sorry nobody explained to our visiting comrade," said Hajir. "But tonight, we'll go back out there—now that my friend knows what to do. Come on, Langston, we go—right now!"

Still fresh as a daisy after an amorous night of no sleep and a long day in school, Hajir reached for his greatcoat, raring to wrestle a Tartar again.

## WEDDING IN TASHKENT

WHEN Nichan returned to Tashkent from his vacation in the Pamirs with a string of wild ducks about his neck, he asked me if his brother had brought back the money he had borrowed. When I said, no, that I had not seen hair nor hide of his brother during the month, I could see that Nichan was deeply hurt to think that his brother would behave in such a fashion. He might at least have come by to see me. Flinging his brace of wild ducks on the floor under the couch—in all their soft russet and gunmetal plumage with their limp dead heads— Nichan rushed out in search of the man who had failed to repay the loan for him. In vain I protested that I did not need the money then; I had not been worried about it at all. And I tried to convey to Nichan how glad I was to see him back. But I could tell that Nichan was angry and distressed. When I looked out the windows, I saw him disappearing rapidly down the street in the direction of the caravan stands at the far side of town.

After an hour or so Nichan came back, flung himself down on his bed, and began to cry. Frightened, I thought that perhaps his brother was dead—or, even worse, arrested by the OGPU for some political crime. But nothing of the sort had happend.

What made Nichan weep, I did not know. But I sensed it might be too personal a matter to discuss through an interpreter. Then, too, he might not wish anyone to know that he had borrowed money from me. At any rate, I did not fathom why this usually merry boy just back from duck hunting with a fine lot of fowl should be lying in the dusk crying. I left him alone and went down to the Engineers Club looking for Powers, who could speak both Uzbek and Russian. Powers was not there, but I left a message for him to come to see me after dinner. When I returned to the hotel, I found Nichan sitting gloomily in front of the porcelain stove.

"*Nichevo*," I said, "don't worry about it, fellow." But he was worried.

That evening when Powers came, I found out what it was that troubled Nichan. His brother had gotten married. But it was not that he had gotten married while Nichan was away, nor that he had not kept his promise to repay my money that distressed Nichan. It was that this brother had taken the money—the largest sum he had ever had in his life—and had *bought* a wife! Not wooed and won a woman, but *bought* one. It was this that hurt my roommate so deeply. *His* brother had gone to the black market, to the bootleggers in women, in defiance of not only the law but of all that Nichan respected and loved in the new society that had given him his code of values. In defiance of Soviet ethics, this brother had *bought* a wife. Still not able to take it so seriously as Nichan, at first I wanted to laugh, but I am glad I didn't.

Being curious to find out if she was beautiful, I asked, "What does she look like?"

"Like a camel," said Nichan.

"Where is she?"

"In his house," said Nichan, "in the back room—as they kept women in the old days. My brother is not sovietized, *ni sovietski*." The tears started to roll down his cheeks again.

Powers and I both did our best to comfort him, but the fact that *his* brother would do a thing like this, revert to the old customs, buy a woman—who herself must be *ni sovietski*, too, to permit it—made a most unhappy homecoming for this simple youth who wanted so much to be a part of the new world, not the old. Now his generally sunny face was clouded with hurt and disappointment and tears. I came near wanting to cry myself as I realized his feelings. Instead, I sent Powers with my ration book for a bottle of cognac. When he got back the Red Army man from Tajikistan came with him, and later in the evening other friends dropped in, so eventually Nichan stopped thinking about his brother, and smiled as he pulled his ducks out from under the couch and started telling us about his trip. The ducks, ten or twelve of them, he displayed proudly, and they were beautiful. Then he put them under the couch again.

By morning in the tightly closed room—for no one opens a window anywhere in the Soviet Union in winter—I could smell dead ducks, a smell at first not unlike that of a wet dog. Upon arising, I suggested to Nichan that he put the fowl out on the balcony in the snow where the stove wood was piled, but Nichan shook his head, no. The Tadjik soldier agreed with him, no. Leave the ducks where they were under the couch. So, not being in my own home, I complied with my host's desires, and the ducks remained on our living-room floor, a pile of limp heads, dark feet, and glossy softly colored feathers on heavy bodies.

Nichan disappeared early that morning. When I saw him again, he had five hundred rubles for me. Again I told him not to worry about the money, but he indicated he soon would have from his brother the remaining half due me. In the meanwhile, he called his brother a few choice names like *swolosh* in Russian, and a few bass-chord guitar sounds in Uzbek that I took for granted were as vulgar as *swolosh*, or worse. Now, on my part, it was safe the morning after to laugh about this brother who bought a wife who looked like a camel. Nichan laughed, too, as he pantomimed her stupid modesty, indicating how she had pulled a scarf about her face like a veil when he met her at his brother's house before the groom shooed her into the back room like a chicken—just as if there had never been a revolution!

"*Ni sovietski*, the two of them," Nichan said, indicating backwardness.

Meanwhile the ducks were smelling to high heaven. I pantomimed, when are you going to cook and eat them? Nichan shook his head, meaning I presumed, that he didn't know when. I motioned against to the balcony. More headshaking, no! And off he went to instruct young athletes in boxing and tumbling or fut-bal, and I didn't see him any more until that night. By that time, I had taken the ducks and piled them out on the balcony myself. Their gamy decomposition and dead eyes were upsetting my stomach, still a bit queasy from my recent illness. Besides, I thought they should be out in the cold rather than in our warm room. But as soon as Nichan missed them on his return, he cried, "*Gedieh?*" Where? I pointed to the balcony, and Nichan went right straight and got the fowls and brought them back, this time to put them under his own bed in the partitioned cubicle where we slept. I gave up.

"*Nichevo*," I said to myself. There was nothing else to say.

That night Nichan did some of the dances he had seen in the Pamirs, with the peculiar side-to-side glide and quick snake-like darting of the head, movements seen in Balinese and East Indian dancing, too. Nichan danced very gracefully with that minimum of gesture and movement characteristic of the Asiatic dance. Others in the room sang Uzbek songs, much softer and sweeter than the wild melodies I had heard in the Turkmenian oasis near Merv. In Uzbek singing there seemed to be no sudden heartbreaking flamenco cries such as the Turkomans emitted. All was gentler, sweeter and more civilized. The second evening of Nichan's homecoming would have been delightful had not the air been heavy with ducks under the bed.

But a few days later Nichan came bounding in to invite me to his brother's house for a feast. He dragged out from under the bed, thank God! the ducks—by now at their most gamy, smelling very high —and off he went with them slung around his neck.

"Cognac," he said pointing to me and then in the general direction of the food store. I knew he was asking if I would use my coupon book for drinks.

"Sure," I said, as he departed. He could have made use of my entire ration book had he wished, in return for removing those ducks. Nichan was a good fellow, anyway, and had never before asked me to get anything for him on my ration book. But now, I guessed, he and his brother had made up, so he was taking his ducks to prepare a belated wedding feast for this camel-loading relative with the camel-faced wife. I was curious to see the bride.

I never did see her. When Nichan returned and took me to his brother's house, the purchased female was in the back room attending pots and pans, and she was never asked out to meet the company. Obviously, Nichan's brother was entirely of the old school, not sovietized. All his guests were men, squatting on the floor around a big copper dish full of pilaf—not mutton this time, but wild duck pilaf— a great steaming mound of rice and raisins with bits of duck all through it—into which everybody dived with bare hands, washing it all down with bowls of tea that went around and around the circle of fellowship.

Many Moslems do not partake of strong drink—no true Moslem should—so at Nichan's brother's house the cognac did not disappear as rapidly as had the bottle which the Tadjik and I took to the Tartar girls. Only a few of the men drank at all, and they but little, so we had cognac left to take back with us to the hotel. Full of pilaf and tea, I went home early, leaving Nichan to enjoy the evening with his newly married brother and friends. Had it not been so cold sitting on the floor of his heatless home, I might have stayed to see what an ordinary Uzbek worker's party became as the evening grew late. No doubt there would be singing, and perhaps dancing. Having no heavy padded robes such as they wore, and unused to sitting cross-legged on the chilled floor so long, my limbs were stiff and my haunches frozen when I got up to leave, and my hands were coated with cold grease from the pilaf eaten with the fingers.

"Good night!" I bowed to Nichan's brother who had bought a wife with my money—in whom I still had a half interest of five hundred rubles, not as yet paid back. "Good night," I said. "May you have a happy marriage."

I wanted to add, "May Allah bless you both," which I think he might have liked, but I was afraid Nichan might feel I was making fun of his brother. I would not have been making fun of him—for the camels of this man's dreams, I suspected, still headed toward Mecca. Nichan's headed toward Moscow, yet they were brothers.

## LIGHT FOR ASIA

NOT all of those who were being made over for the better in Central Asia were Asiatics or former people of the poorer classes. My interpreter was of the once-aristocracy, and her parents were Russian. She was a rather prim middle-aged widow, very serious-minded, who looked like a New England school teacher in spite of her long fur-collared coat, Russian style, and Asiatic boots. Born in Tashkent, but educated in St. Petersburg, she had lived a life of genteel leisure, French novels and embroidery, before the revolution. Now she went to work every morning as a translator-aide to a German engineer. She seemed happy, having found a life of usefulness under the Soviets. As an expert translator working on highly technical material with foreign engineers or scientists, German or American usually, she lived for months at a time at some of the most important construction works— dams, mining, irrigation or electrical projects in the desert—and was familiar with all the ambitious new building being done or in the planning stages throughout Central Asia.

Assigned to me by the Writers Union, her services were of great help, evenings or on her free days, in gathering information and interviewing people for my articles. Never in her conversations or in her translations did she intrude—as some interpreters were not averse to doing—sly insinuations against the Soviet power, nor show scorn for the native peoples who now ran the city of her birth, Tashkent, where formerly Uzbeks had no power. Her speech and her work indicated only respect for the struggling new society and a deep personal interest in its development.

"My child will grow up under this modern, dynamic, forward-looking kind of life," she said. "It is better than the old. Now children learn to be interested in the whole world, too, from Scottsboro to China."

Certainly children in Uzbekistan seemed to me to know more of world politics than American children. They would stand on strong little legs, independent and confident, and comment on subjects as big as war, colonies, lynchings and world revolution—things many a New York child had not even heard of before adolescence, if then. The schools of Central Asia were filled to overflowing. And thousands of sturdy Asiatic young men and women in their early twenties were in positions of trust as representatives of the people. Kurbanov, chairman of the City Soviet of Bokhara was then only twenty-eight years old. Fifteen years before, he had been a herdboy in the mountains, who couldn't read or write his name.

But, other than Nichan, of all the new citizens I met in Central Asia that winter, I think I shall remember best a simple teenage worker at Chirchikstroy, the site of a new dam under construction. I am not even sure of the youngster's name. I think he said Tajaiv. I didn't take notes, and I wasn't speaking with him long. But the glow in his face, the pride in his voice, as he told me about the construction of his barracks, the very first building on the dam site, sticks in my head to this moment.

About an hour's ride from Tashkent, I had driven out with my interpreter and the manager of construction to the site of the great dam that was to be the enormous Chirchikstroy Electrical and Chemical Development. It was only just beginning then. Until that very month they had not even had a barracks for the laborers on the site, only tents. So the young men working on excavations said, "We will build our own barracks." In their spare time, they did. That is why I went motoring through the snowy dusk along a rough country road across the steppes, to attend the opening of these barracks.

Tajaiv, the brownskin Uzbek lad, didn't welcome me at the door or anything like that. Nor did he speak on the program, and nobody introduced him to me. He was not one of the official committee. But once inside the big warm wooden barracks with its many cots in a row like a Red Army dormitory—red banners and ribbons of red and blue crepe paper hanging from the rafters in honor of the occasion— it wasn't long before I saw Tajaiv. He wasn't a big fellow. He was shorter than the other young workers about the room, but he had on an udarnik's badge, and a very clean shirt, and he wore a big smile. Just a hard little Uzbek boy of perhaps sixteen or seventeen, a young-ster who had probably never seen a bed of roses—but tonight he was happy. He felt himself to be one of my hosts, so he came over near the stove to greet me. And my translator told me what he said.

"Look what we have built," he cried, "the first barracks at Chir-chikstroy. Here all of us will live while the dam is made. Before we built this, there was nothing on this land. Nothing at all. This is the first building—our work! We made it after hours in our spare time as a contribution from the youngest workers here, like me. We are not skilled—but we could build this. And next year when the dam is built, we will have light."

His dark, round, young face was aglow with this achievement— this crude wooden barracks—and with the much bigger achievement to follow, Chirchikstroy, meaning light and power and chemicals for all that section of a once-backward Asia. Tajaiv would build it—his hard young hands with their power to transform the future of this wilderness. He would build his dam to light *his* Asia.

The ceremonies began and, beneath the dim oil lanterns, there were speeches of which I understood almost nothing. Everyone talked too rapidly for my translator to be of much help. But I gathered that the gist of the speeches was that Chirchikstroy would make such a light that it would blaze across all the borders of the East and shine not only on Uzbek lands alone, but far over the Pamirs into Afghanistan, India and China. Tajaiv sat beside me, his eyes glowing with pride in what he, a simple Uzbek youth, was helping to create. Although I only met him once, I accepted him as my host for the whole of the Soviet Union. Ten years before, a brown young Uzbek like Tajaiv would have had to ride in the back of the streetcars in Tashkent, for previous to the revolution in Asia there had been Jim Crow streetcars in Uzbekistan. The old partitions that once separated natives from Europeans, colored from white, were still there when I arrived—I saw them. But now anyone sat anywhere in the Tashkent trams. In ten short years, Jim Crow was gone on trams, trains, or anywhere else in Central Asia. Russians and Uzbeks, Ukranians and Tartars, Europeans and natives, white or colored, all went to the same schools, sat on the same benches, ate in the same co-operatives, worked in the same shops or factories, and fussed and fumed at the same problems. Gains and defeats were shared alike. In Tashkent, whenever I got on a street car and saw the old partitions, I could not help but remember Atlanta, Birmingham and Houston in my own country where, when I got on a tram or a bus or a train, I had to sit in the COLORED section. The natives of Tashkent, about my own shade of brown, once had to sit in a COLORED section, too. But not any more. So I was happy for them. How had this change been brought about in so short a time? At the City Soviet I asked Kurbanov about it. He said, "Those who don't like it are almost all in jail—or dead."

By dead, I knew he meant liquidated. Koestler and Grasdani both had told me that the jails of Tashkent were full of political prisoners. I, myself, had seen the long lines of relatives outside the OGPU prison, waiting with food for their loved ones on visiting days.

Perhaps, as Grasdani claimed, many there were unjustly imprisoned. But some behind bars, I felt sure, were those who had not wished to see the Jim Crow signs go down—both whites and Asiatics who would prefer that the old freewheeling days of plunder and power came back, when the strongest lived in luxury and devil take the hindmost, when a rich man might have a hundred wives and a poor man no wife at all, when a kid like Tajaiv could never dream of the building of a dam to light his world. Life in Tashkent was far from comfortable and perfect, and the nearest approximation to comfort was only in the upper-echelon hotels or the homes of the very top commissars, engineers, writers, or dancers. But I could not bring myself to believe, as Grasdani did, that life was not better for most people now than it had been in the days of the Volga boatmen, the Asiatic serfs and the Jim Crow signs.

To me as a writer, it was especially interesting to observe how art of all sorts—writing, painting, the theatre—was being utilized as a weapon against the evils of the past. To be sure art, put to such use, often degenerated into propaganda. But even propaganda in talented hands took on dramatic dimensions. In Tashkent, talented Russian directors were using all the folk elements of Uzbek music, poetry and dance in aiding to create an Uzbek national theatre where there had been none before. About these new theatres in Tashkent, Samarkand, Bokhara and Fergana, I heard a great deal from the leading native dramatist, Ismailov, who told me, "We try to use the theatre to teach people how beautiful life can be if we destroy the old ugly selfish customs of the past. And we try to show our varied nationalities how to get along together, Turkoman with Uzbek, Tadjik with Tartar, and Russian with Asiatic. I try to say in my plays that we must all be comrades."

Only a few nights before this talk with Ismailov, I had sat in a motion-picture theatre with Nichan looking at a powerful new Soviet talking film, *My Motherland*, the story of a clash on the Siberian border between the Red Army and Manchurian troops over the Chinese Eastern Railway. This picture, I was told, due to the complex international situation, would not be released for foreign showings—a pity, since it was a most beautiful film with a powerful musical score played by the Leningrad Symphony. In the early portion of the picture there was a scene that especially impressed me with the Soviet way of teaching friendship between peoples of varying colors and races.

It is night. Snow. Across the Siberian border the soldier-provocateurs of Manchuria are firing into the Soviet defenses where Red Army men stand guard. The scene changes to the inside of the Soviet barracks. Officers and men are shown fraternizing together, laughing, shaving, playing cards. Suddenly the door opens and a man from the front is carried in dead. His body is placed in a bunk and the sheet drawn over him. A young Russian soldier, fists doubled, rises from his card game and begins to curse those slant-eyed bastards who have killed his comrade. Quietly, an officer goes toward the body, draws back the sheet so that the Russian boy may see the still, brown face there, and says simply, "Our comrade's eyes are slant eyes, too."

## DIXIE CHRISTMAS USSR

IN the autumn, if you step off any train almost anywhere in the fertile parts of Central Asia, you step into a cotton field, or into a city or town whose streets are filled with evidence of cotton nearby. The natives call it "white gold." On all the dusty roads, camels, carts and trucks, loaded with the soft fiber, head toward the gins and warehouses. Outside the towns, ofttimes as far as the eye can see, the white bolls lift their precious heads. The same thing is true of the southern part of the United States. In Georgia, Mississippi and Alabama, you ride for hundreds of miles through fields of cotton, bursting white in the sun. Except that on our roads there are no camels. Mules and wagons bear the burdens. And Negroes do most of the work. When I was in the South, I had wanted to visit a big cotton plantation.

"It's a little dangerous," my friends said. "White folks don't like strange Northern Negroes around. You can't do it."

But I finally managed to do it. During the December holidays in Alabama, I went with the head of a section of the Red Cross—a Negro section, of course—to distribute fruit to the poor—the poor meaning in this case the black workers on a rich plantation.

We set out in a rickety Ford and drove for miles through brown fields where the cotton had been picked. We came to a gate in a strong wire fence. This passed, some distance further on, we came to another fence. And then, far back from the dirt road, huddled together beneath the trees, we came upon the cabins of the Negro workers—a dozen cheerless one-room shacks. A group of ragged children came running out to meet us. The Negro with the Red Cross button descended from the car and spoke to them in a Sunday-school manner. He asked them if they had been good, and if they had gotten any presents for the holidays. Yes, the children said, they had been good, but they hadn't gotten any presents. They reached out eager little hands for the apples and oranges of official charity.

We went into several of the huts. While the Red Cross man talked about the Lord, I asked a few questions. I asked a very old man if the cotton had been sold. He answered listlessly, "I don't know. The boss took it. And even if it is been sold, it don't make me no difference. I never see none of the money." He shrugged his shoulders and sucked at his pipe. A woman I spoke to said she hadn't been to town for four years. Yet the town was less than fifteen miles away.

"It's hard to get off," she said, "and I never has nothing to spend."

She gave her dreary testimony without emotion. The colored Red Cross man assured her that God would help her and that she shouldn't worry as long as she could work and had credit at the commissary store.

A broken-down bed, a stove, and a few chairs were all she had in her house. Her children were among those stretching out their arms to us for fruit. Yet the man who owned this big plantation lived in a great house with white pillars. His children went to private schools in the North, I was told, and his oldest girl traveled abroad. Black hands working in white cotton created the wealth that built his fine house and supported his children in their travels. A woman who couldn't travel fifteen miles to town was helping to send somebody else's child on a trip to Paris.

Economists call it the share-crop system. The plantation owner advances every month a little corn meal and salt meat, calico and candy from the commissary, gives seed and a cabin. These advances are charged to the black peasant's account. At the end of the year when the cotton is picked, the plantation owner takes the whole crop and often tells the worker his share is not large enough to cover the rent of the cabin, the cost of the seed, and the price of the corn meal and fat meat. "You owe me," says the planter. So the Negro is automatically in debt, and must work another year to pay the landlord.

In Soviet Central Asia I visited several cotton kolkhozes. I filled two notebooks with figures and data: the number of hectares under cultivation, the yield per hectare, the percentages fulfilled according to the plan—some not always good—and method of irrigation. I stayed for two days at the mechanization station for farm machinery near Tashkent. I saw the Cotton College. I visited the big building of the Cotton Trust at Tashkent. I studied charts. I looked at statistics. The figures I've forgotten. But I shall always remember what the natives themselves told me: "Before, there were no schools for Uzbek children—now there are. Before, we lived in debt and fear—now we are free. Before, women were bought and sold—now no more. Before, the land and the water belonged to the beys—today they are ours—and we share the cotton."

One of the Negroes at a Soviet collective forty miles from Tashkent where the seed-selection station and cotton experimental laboratories were located, came into Tashkent to invite Bernard Powers and me to spend Christmas with them in the country. The Christmas before I had spent in Alabama. Now I found myself halfway across the world in Uzbekistan—but again I would be passing the holidays with my own people. There were about a dozen American Negroes attached to this cotton experimental farm, most of them from the South. Some were agricultural chemists, graduates of Tuskeegee or Hampton, others were from Northern colleges, and some were just plain cotton farmers from Dixie, whose job it was in Soviet Asia to help introduce American methods of cultivating cotton. Some worked in laboratories at the collective, testing the quality of seeds and the strength of cotton fibers, and some worked in the fields just as they had done at home. It was an oddly assorted group of educated and uneducated Negroes a long way from Dixie—and most of them not liking it very well. Conditions on the Soviet collective, while a great change for the better for the Uzbeks, were for Negroes from America more primitive than most of them had known at home, especially for the younger college people who, when they got dressed up for Christmas in the middle of Central Asia, still looked exactly like American undergraduates.

When I got out to the cotton collective, I could understand why, though well paid, they were not happy. In the first place, the trip there was physically worse than any Jim Crow train trip I ever made in the United States. And, due to the almost continual snows that autumn, I found the whole collective farm one vast swamp of Asiatic mud in which a man sank almost to his ankles. The houses were comfortable, but there were no fireplaces, no gas stoves, no radio programs, and no juke boxes or movies anywhere within driving distance. Only a few Negroes had learned to speak Uzbek or Russian, so they were largely dependent upon themselves for social life in that far-off oasis. But despite their problems they were not a gloomy group, and Christmas with them was a very jolly period for me—once I got there. But getting there was another story which, in comparison, made my trip with Koestler through the burning desert to Permetyab a pleasure jaunt.

Just as the trip to Permetyab had been blistering hot, so the trip to the cotton collective was freezing cold. When I arrived, I felt like an icicle. It took me all night to thaw out. But perhaps it was my own fault. If I had arranged the trip through official channels like the Writers Union, I might have traveled differently. But Powers and I both thought that since it was only forty miles by train, we would just go down to the station, buy our tickets and go. I should have known better. Nothing is ever that simple in the USSR.

It was very cold in Tashkent when Powers and I left in a horse-drawn sleigh for the station. At the station in the late afternoon we found an enormous crowd of robe-padded Uzbeks, jamming the entrances and filling the snow-covered sidewalks outside. I had never seen such a mass of travelers. The lines at the ticket windows contained hundreds of persons in each queue. And, no doubt because we were so nearly the color of the Uzbeks themselves, nobody took us for strangers and urged us to the front lines as folks in Russia might have done. As our train was scheduled to leave shortly, Powers decided to use his foreign worker's card and go directly to the stationmaster's office for tickets rather than wait in line. This worked. The stationmaster purchased our tickets for us quickly, and we passed onto the train platform. This long platform, like the station, was crowded to capacity, and the trains standing on the tracks were jammed to the doors.

When we located our train, it was even more jammed than any of the others. Besides the coaches were antiques, with each coach having open platforms at both ends. Even these platforms were already filled with people. Powers and I went from coach to coach until we found a platform where we could at least mount the steps to stand in the cold outside the coach. Luckily we had gotten on when we did, for within a few minutes, even the steps of our car was packed with Uzbeks, clinging to the rails. The train was late starting. Just before the tiny little engine gave a few hoots and pulled out of the railroad yards, it began to snow in large soft flakes.

Facetiously, I said, "It's going to be a very white Christmas this year."

"We are going to be white in a minute," said Powers, standing between a dozen closely packed Uzbeks on the open platform of the train.

Already the soot-blackened railway yards were newly whitened by fresh snow, soft, wet clinging flakes that had covered the shoulders of my coat and the brim of my hat before the train started. When we got under way, the speed of the train caused the snow to hit us all on the platform with great force and to stick to us more persistently than ever. Within a few miles everybody was covered with snow—Powers, the Uzbeks, and I. But at first I was not cold, wedged in between many padded robes as I stood there in the open. Shortly, however, the open platforms between the coaches were whipped by snow and wind as the train gathered speed. The damp snow on my hat brim and on my shoulders crusted over and froze into crinkly sheets of thin ice. The snow that stuck to my face made it a white mask, as were all the other faces around me.

So close together were we that it was difficult to turn around to put my back to the wind. And when I did achieve a turn, the wind drove stinging bits of snow down my neck. The wind from the Pamirs seemed to delight in assailing our little train driving into the storm.

And the snow that had looked so white and lovely when it first began to fall, turned into a stinging terror for us on the moving platform. The usually voluble Uzbeks were silent, huddling together like sheep. Powers had turned into a snowman now. Around our feet and between our legs, the chill wind rushed. The wind blew up between the cracks in the floor and whistled between the couplings. I became so cold I could hardly move when the train came to its first stop, ten or fifteen miles outside Tashkent. If it had been anything other than a stationless whistle stop, I would have gotten off and sought shelter until I could return to Tashkent. As it was, almost no one got off, so none of us on the platform could squeeze into the sardine-packed coach.

After one or two more rural stops, I managed to push, half-frozen, into the car, which was without heat but steamy with human breath and vile with the stench of camel drivers, peasants and bazaar merchants, with all the sacks, bundles and baskets of onions and melons they had piled beneath the seats in the aisles and on the shelves overhead. Another stop and a few more Uzbeks pushed and shoved to get out. A blast of ice cold air came in as the door opened. The storm had turned into a real blizzard now, and the remaining poor souls who fell into the coach from the platform where they had been riding, were like human sticks of ice. The melted snow on my clothing enveloped me in a chilly dampness. I was sure I would catch pneumonia, but Powers looked so miserable wedged in between the Uzbeks and the door that I did not tell him my unhappy thoughts.

When, at dusk, the train finally slowed down at the place where we were to spend Christmas—*it did not even stop*. It just whistled so that those who intended to descend there might jump off into the blizzard. This collective had no village attached, I learned later, so trains did not really stop there. As a convenience, they did slow down. Powers and I jumped off into the snow and immediately we sunk into a mixture of slush and mud almost to our ankles.

I said to myself, "If I ever get back to Tashkent after this, I will go right straight—by plane, if possible—home to the U.S.A. Never another foot of travel in the USSR!"

Colonel Young's son from Wilberforce, Ohio, with Golden, and a young chemist named Roan met Powers and me at the railroad. It was only a short walk to their quarters. But as we slithered through the sticky snow and pulled our feet from the sucking mud at each step, I am afraid I failed to hide very well my lack of joy at seeing at last a large group of fellow American Negroes away out in Asia.

Christmas Eve in Uzbekistan—and I was most miserable! But inside Golden's neat white-painted cottage, it was jolly and warm. Three or four jovial colored wives, who had come from Dixie to this, greeted us, and poured drinks, and let us smell the delicious aroma of the supper cooking in the kitchen. But nothing cheered me up, or thawed me out for hours, and I am afraid I did not act civilly. Never being much of a cardplayer, except at poker when I was in the Merchant Marine, I refused to join in the whist game that was proposed before dinner. I just sat glumly by the fire, nursed my cognac, and wished I was home in the U.S.A. Powers, who had come through that chilling train ride with me, thawed out before supper and was grinning like a Cheshire cat, joking with the other men's wives. Laughing and joking, folks were getting in the mood for Christmas. Every so often someone poured me another drink, and left me in the corner with my thoughts. But after a supper of stewed rabbit, hot bread and buttered squash, I felt better. And when midnight came and it was Christmas, in spite of the fact that I never could carry a tune, I sang "Silent Night" with the others.

Christmas Day was wonderful. We even had pumpkin pie for dessert, and the tables were loaded down with all the American-style dishes that those clever Negro wives could concoct away over there in Uzbekistan. That morning I didn't feel homesick at all when I got up and found a stocking full of halva, cashew and pistachio nuts hanging on the head of my bed. They were delightfully amiable hosts, these cotton-collective Negroes from America in the middle of a mud-cake oasis frosted with snow.

I never left the house the whole holiday, but when I looked out the windows Christmas morning I saw padding around the stables in the snow some tall brown Uzbeks who looked like the pictures on my Sunday-school cards in Kansas when I was a child. In their robes these Uzbeks looked just like Bible characters, and I imagined in their stable a Manger and a Child.

## FLOWERS TO THE FAIR

NINA ZARATELLI moulded a head of the Negro engineer, Bernard Powers, and made a bas-relief of me, while she was working on the big model of Nichan in our room. This was eventually to be cast in bronze many times larger than life, for the new athletic stadium in Tashkent. Nina Zaratelli was a very pretty woman, a Georgian, given to dressing in simple black, over which she slipped a white smock when she came to our hotel to work in clay. She had been commissioned by the Uzbek government and brought from Tiflis just to make the statue of Nichan, which was to be a symbol of the new Uzbek youth. Nichan was a worthy model, and a handsome one, too, very muscular, alive and laughing. All of Nichan's friends enjoyed watching Nina Zaratelli work with Nichan posing, trying to keep still long enough for her to capture a likeness. The clay in which the sculptress worked was, curiously, almost the exact color of Nichan himself. And the statue she was making, before I left for Moscow, had begun to look a great deal like the boy, and to have in it something of his outer grace and inner strength.

Nina Zaratelli was a cultured woman who spoke beautiful French, and it was in French that she generally conversed with me. I told her about Paris and New York, and she told me about Tiflis and Leningrad. And sometimes, as she worked, I played her my jazz records.

As a farewell prior to my departure for Moscow, Nina Zaratelli and a few of her friends gave a small dinner party at a little restaurant in Tashkent where I had never been. It was the only restaurant in the city, I understood, where one could just walk in and order a meal without a food card of any kind, so naturally it was very expensive. Contrary to Soviet custom, one tipped the waiters there and the page boy, too. It was, so far as I ever knew, the only equivalent in all of Central Asia of the Metropol Café in Moscow. Powers had been there a few times with some of his engineer friends, so he had told me, "It's the kind of place where I can wear a tuxedo." Certainly, its very presence in poorly and monotonously fed Tashkent amazed me. And it confirmed something I had long suspected from observation, not only in the Soviet Union but around the world—even in places where there is almost nothing, the rich, the beautiful, the talented, or the very clever can always get something; in fact, the *best* of whatever there is. From Topeka to Tashkent, San Francisco to Samarkand, I had learned that some can always get cream while most drink milk, some have wine while others hardly have water. The system under which the successful live—left or right, capitalist or communist—did not seem to make much difference to that group of people, in every city around the globe, who managed by hook or crook to live well. Be it Asia, Europe, or America, these folks had theirs. Not always were they the rich folks, either—sometimes merely the beautiful, the talented, or the clever.

In this small, secluded restaurant in Tashkent, there were thick steaks the like of which I had not dreamed existed in all Soviet Asia. But they cost a week's wages of even a very highly skilled worker. Workers did not eat there very often, if at all, I gathered. After dinner one could have Benedictine in a small individual bottle, priced about the same as a steak. Naturally, workers did not drink there, either. None of the Uzbeks I met in Tashkent had ever mentioned the place to me. Of course, they could go—but other than top officials, dancing stars and factory managers, how many had the money to go? Even I, with still a large packet of literary rubles in my suitcase, could not have afforded to dine there often. I am rather glad it was not until near the end of my stay that I knew the café existed for, with the ever-growing appetite I had developed after my illness, I might have spent most of my rubles on steaks and had but little left for my return to Moscow.

In a quiet street lined with trees, in a charming little bandbox of an old Russian house, nestled this small restaurant. Its main room was like a large living room, containing perhaps a dozen tables with very white tablecloths, gleaming cut-glass carafes, and heavy crested silver. Tapestries hung on the walls, and on a platform against one of the tapestries a trio, consisting of a piano, violin and cello, played popular French and American melodies. Most of the tables were taken when we arrived, filled with people who must have had pockets full of rubles —speculators on the open market, or authors, foreign specialists or visiting commissars, and perhaps a few skilled technicians, who had saved a long time for a single big evening of good food and vintage wines. I noticed that those who had finished their dinners were being served coffee—real coffee in individual glass urns, black and bubbling, steaming over fat lighted candles in copper holders. The red-coated waiters moved leisurely and courteously, and the whole atmosphere was that of the better restaurants of Paris or San Francisco. It must have been an old restaurant that had kept its European staff from pre-revolutionary days, I thought. But the mystery of its why and how I never solved.

Our little party that night was quietly gay, but most of us concentrated on the food rather than conversation. Some had shaslik on skewers, but I had a big steak with rice, a custard for dessert, and a Benedictine with the coffee. I was intrigued by the trio of odd musicians who after the Russian hit, "Dark Eyes," suddenly burst into "The Sheik of Araby." The violinst, who was the leader and gave the signal for beginning each piece, had on what he must have considered a very swanky jacket. It was electric blue, double-breasted and extremely tight, fitting him like a picture on a wall, with pockets slanted. He swayed a great deal as he played. A huge and quite fierce-looking woman tackled the cello. She was larger than the little Louis XV chair on which she sat. Her hair was a fuzzy helmet on her head, and she was no longer young. Nina Zaratelli, lovely in black velvet, whispered to me across the table, that this woman used to be a concert artist and had played in Tiflis and Moscow before the revolution. Now she sat sawing sternly through "The Sheik of Araby" in Tashkent, followed by what I could have sworn was "Tea for Two." "Probably," I thought to myself, "she's politically suspect, exiled to this far-off Asiatic city a long way from Moscow and Leningrad. Otherwise, why would she be here in this tiny restaurant? She plays beautifully."

When, after midnight, a lull came in the popular tunes, and the swaying violinist in the tight coat left the stand, bobbing and bowing as he went out, the big fierce woman at the cello and the wizened old man at the piano, the two of them alone, began to play Schubert's "Serenade." Then the woman's face sweetened just a little and the music became a rose of loveliness that warmed the whole room with its fragrance. Nina Zaratelli, who dreamed someday of going to Paris where there were many such cafés, listened to the music as though it were being played for her alone.

## FAREWELL TO SAMARKAND

SAMARKAND! Green-curled Samarkand! City of Tamerlane, the Earth Shaker; before that city of Ghengis Khan, leader of the Mongols; and before that the sporting ground of Alexander the Great, who murdered within its gates his old friend, Clitus, when both were drunk with wine three thousand years ago. Samarkand, flourishing center of Arabic culture in the twelfth century; seat of the ancient observatory of Ulug Beg; golden name to the Venetian merchants in those Middle Ages of silks from Cathay and spices from Samarkand; lovely song-city of the Oriental poets; city of the turquoise domes—Samarkand! Green-curled Samarkand.

Today the old Samarkand is there for all who wish to see it in its crumbling splendor. The new Samarkand is a silk factory and a Communist University, a hydro-electric station and a Medical School. According to the Soviet Guide Book, it is also a commercial distribution point for "huge provisions of dried fruit, grapes, rice, raw hides and wine." Its main street is now called Karl Marx Street.

Because of the great difficulties involved in the liberation of Uzbek women from the harem and the veil, when I was in Samarkand a special effort was being made to supply women with the means of economic independence. The silk industry was utilized for this purpose. Since time immemorial Uzbek women had raised silkworms. As a rule, in the past, their husbands always took the profits. Now, however, cocoons were being purchased directly from the women themselves. And since silk is their especial province, new mills were being built for the training and employment of women. At the Deliverance of Women Mills which I visited, there were twelve hundred female workers, and not one was veiled.

When the mill first opened, it was difficult to get women to work at all—shy and timid as they were, afraid of their male relatives, afraid of machines, smothered by veils and burdened down by traditions of the past. Now the mill operated three shifts a day, seven hours each. The women workers were not only learning the regularity and exactness of factory work—something entirely new to the timeless Orient—but there was a factory school where women were taught to read and write. On a hill across a stream from the factory, there was a kindergarten for the children of employed mothers, a diet kitchen and a room to which nursing mothers came every three hours to care for their babies. Nearby were the new dormitory homes, in which men and women of various nationalities—Uzbek, Tartar, Tajik, Jewish, and Russian—lived. Some of the residents ate Oriental fashion on the floor. Others dined from European chairs and tables.

Formerly, in colonial days when the factories in Samarkand were owned by Russians, most of the foremen and technicians were Russian, just as in America most skilled workers and executives are white. Under the new set up three technical schools for the training of Uzbek workers had been opened. There had been only five thousand industrial workers in Samarkand. Within less than ten years that number had been increased by twenty. Electrification had much to do with Samarkand's increased industrial activity. Once in darkness, under the Soviets the entire city had become electrically lighted and its factories supplied with power.

During my stay in Samarkand, at the office of the Chairman of the City Soviet, I received a great deal of statistical information about the city and its problems. One of its problems, as in most Mid-Asian cities, had been that of water. In a land where wells sometimes have to be 170 feet deep before water is struck, people became accustomed to drinking from rivers, irrigation ditches, and whatever other convenient source they can find, without regard to sanitation. Now the city of Samarkand had sunk five artesian wells. Spring water from the nearby hills was also piped in, with the result that there had been a considerable decrease in typhoid and the various intestinal diseases common to the East. Yet some citizens still drank from gutters. The City Soviet wanted to make this a crime, punishable by arrest.

As to crime, for a city of many dim and winding streets, I was told that there were few murders, although pickpockets and petty thieves were plentiful. These were said to be a holdover from old times when, as a big trading and caravan center, Samarkand was exceedingly dangerous. Begging, however, that scourge of the Orient, had almost disappeared. With work for all, the building of homes for the aged and the infirm, and the creation in Samarkand of six communes for homeless children, the old familiar cry of the East, "Alms, alms, for the love of Allah," was seldom heard, except from a few holy beggars whose religion demanded that they live by charity.

The whirling dervishes—whose fanatic rites once greatly excited a portion of the populace, and who in wild frenzy would slash their flesh into strips in public—had been forbidden to dance. Some, however, were still said to hold secret rites. Calmer Mohammedan sects gathered at the few mosques still open, but among them not many young men were seen. The young men of Samarkand were almost all going to school rather than to mosques.

To the Soviet colleges at Samarkand all Soviet Asia sent students. The classrooms I visited were crowded with both men and women, but many more men than women since Moslem families were slow to allow girls to be educated. Textbooks to meet the various language problems were a problem. The advanced courses had to be given in Russian, for as yet no books were available in Uzbek, Tartar, or Tadjik, so Russian was a required language. English and German were also taught, but at that time, so it seemed to me, greater stress was being put on German. Being a writer, I was naturally interested to find if there were classes in literature, and I was assured that there were. I was told that three times a week there was a class in the European and American novel. Out of curiosity I made it a point to visit this class, where I found about a dozen young Asiatics engaged in a study of Gorki, whose works were put aside temporarily to listen to me read some poems of mine in English and to permit the students to ask me questions.

I was amazed at being asked by one student who looked as if, only the day before, he might have emerged from a yurt—a nomad's felt tent—if I knew Sink-Lair Loo-ees. During his literature course he had read *Elmer Gantry*, which was then very popular in Samarkand, translated into the alphabet of the Uzbek language.

Samarkand campuses seemed to me not unlike our own in many respects, except that the average age of students was higher—usually twenty-two to twenty-five years upon entering college. Another difference was that most Samarkand students were members of trade unions, many of them having been sent to college by their unions. Examinations and tests were given, much as in American colleges, and for graduation, a thesis was required. Students were graded: *Fine, Good, Satisfactory,* and *Not Satisfactory.* Students did social work in connection with their studies, spreading their knowledge in the evenings and on free days to the teahouses, factories, workers' clubs and collective farms, thus acting as shock troops in the government's liquidation-of-illiteracy campaign. If a man's Red Army duty came during his college period, he was released from service until his studies were finished. And in the Red Army, college graduates served a shorter term than those who had not had advanced study.

My last evening in Samarkand, I went on foot alone at sunset to Tamerlane's Tomb. The gates were locked, but I looked into the charming courtyard that I had often visited before. Birds were nesting in the trees and a little grey lizard scurried across the ground. The setting sun gleamed warmly on the lovely old tiles, and on the great patches of sun-dried brick where the tiles had fallen away. Near the walls, beneath the mulberry trees, a little stream of water gurgled. Across the stream a child ran after a bantam chicken to put it to roost. In the courtyards round about, people were lighting fires and cooking.

As I walked back toward the center of the town, darkness began to fall, but the street lights were not yet turned on. In the dusk, little pools of light marked an occasional teahouse, where men gathered in the cool of evening. In front of one of these teahouses, in a dark grove of trees, I heard music—the high string lutes of the East. I went into this grove of darkness, where the glow of charcoal fires made the only light. I mounted one of the outdoor platforms, sat cross-legged on a rug, and called, "*Chai,*" the Russian word for tea. But before the attendant reached me, several bowls of tea were offered me in the half-darkness, and soon I was a part of a group of young Uzbeks sitting on the platform. As everywhere in the Soviet Union, so here in Samarkand, a stranger was immediately the target of a hundred questions.

I said several times that I was an *Amerikanetz,* and that I lived *delico, delico,* far, far away. Their limited knowledge of Russians was on a par with mine, so I was not embarrased. Some of the young workers did not speak Russian at all, so everything I tried to say was echoed again in Uzbek for those who didn't understand.

"*Eee kok Amerika?*" they said, meaning, "How is it in your home?"

"Cris-ses," I said, putting the accent, Russian way, on the second syllable. "*Bolshoy cri-ses!*"

"*Eee kok technika?*" For all the world has heard of American machines and technical knowledge, and some collective farms near Samarkand used Chicago tractors.

"Fine," I said, "very good," not knowing how to explain to them that partially due to our *technika*—the advance of machine production without a corresponding advance in the distribution of goods—our crisis had come about with its resultant unemployment.

"*Eee kok Moscu?*"

"Big city," I said, "Moscow *horoshi* big city!"

"*Eee kok . . .,*" somebody else began. But I motioned that I wished to hear—if they would let me—the music being played on a nearby platform. "*Musika, musika,*" I kept saying until finally the barrage of questions stopped, and the thin wail of the strings held sway, delicate and strange to Western ears. Meanwhile, the tea bowls went from mouth to mouth in simple comradeship and complete lack of sanitation. When I rose from the rug to leave, it was quite dark and I was still a long way from my hotel.

"I'm going to my *gostinitza*," I said, meaning hotel.

Immediately the platform filled with voices again. Several men jumped to their feet and tied their robes about them with big square silken sashes. Some paid for the tea, refusing to allow me to share the bill.

"Goodbye," I said, but the men had no intention of permitting me to leave alone. Remembering what I had been told of thieves in Samarkand, I wondered if these new-found friends of mine were robbers, or perhaps even bandits from the desert. It was very dark now, and the spaces from street light to street light, I noticed, were tremendous. I started rapidly toward the hotel when my companions pulled me in the opposite direction, talking volubly the while in Uzbek and Russian.

"*Autobus*," they were saying, I finally gathered from a shower of words.

"*Niet*," I said, "thank you," knowing from past experience how infrequently the buses ran, and being already late for dinner at the hotel where I was to meet my translator. But the men insisted, "*Autobus!*"

Finally I went with them. They took me a few blocks away to a big garage that housed the municipal buses, and there they proudly pointed, "*Amerikanetz!* See!" They wanted to show me that their buses were from my country. They went inside and spoke to a driver, and in a very short time one of the big buses rolled out. I was helped in and, as the only passenger, driven to the very door of my hotel—as a gesture of hospitality toward a stranger.

An hour later during dinner, in came several young Uzbeks and made straight for my table. I recognized them as my friends of the teahouse, now freshly scrubbed and all dressed up. Their padded robes and little round embroidered caps seemed more than ever Oriental in the brightly lighted café of the European hotel.

"They come," my translator explained as the fellows stood around our table, "to see if you were brought back safely, and to ask you to visit them at their club tonight, and to come tomorrow to their homes and share their pilaf."

I said that unfortunately I was leaving that night to return to Tashkent.

"They want you," said the translator, "to accept the hospitality of the Uzbek workers. They want you to stay a long time in Samarkand, so that when you go back to America, you will remember their city with pleasure."

"Only with pleasure could I remember Samarkand," I said. But it was time to start for the station then to take the late train to Tashkent, and finally go on to Moscow, and in a few months home to America, for as Omar had written:

> The bird of time
> Has but a little way to flutter—
> And the bird is on the wing. . . .

Regretfully I held out my hand to the friendly Uzbeks who had come to offer me their hospitality. They shook it in my foreign fashion. Then they bowed, both hands folded over the heart in their own way of saying farewell.

# 5

# SPRING BESIDE
# THE KREMLIN

### ZERO WEATHER, ZERO HOUR

THE train from Tashkent got to Moscow in the middle of the night, several hours late, on one of the coldest nights of the year, more than twenty below zero. There were only a few sleepy porters about and it took a long time to get all my belongings in a taxi, but at least I had no heavy records or victrola to lug. Fortunately the porter got me a taxi instead of an open *drosky* or a sleigh. I told the driver to take me to the Grand Hotel where I had asked the Writers Union in Tashkent to wire for a reservation. At the Grand the desk clerk, who recognized me, said that they had gotten no message concerning a reservation and anyway, unfortunately, were entirely filled. He suggested I try another hotel on Twerskaya. That hotel was filled, too. In desperation I decided to try the deluxe Metropol. It, too, was full.

Taxis were then very expensive in Moscow. It was getting later and later and colder and colder. The streets of the city were utterly deserted, and highways, buildings, earth and sky were white with snow. It looked as if it had been snowing all winter, and it was still snowing, delicate isinglass flakes. I decided to try the one other hotel I knew, a lush *valuta* (foreign money) hotel serving first-class tourists—although I did not intend to spend my remaining American dollars to stay there. I thought I might persuade them to permit me a night in exchange for rubles. No luck. The clerk was adamant. Twenty dollars a day, gold currency, or nothing. Meanwhile, my bags were still in the taxi outside. I said I had no foreign money. The clerk said simply, "*Nichevo!* Then try the new Moscow."

That was the big hotel across the Moscow River from the Kremlin where I knew many foreigners stayed at ruble rates—especially technicians waiting to go to their assignments in various parts of the country. But it was generally overcrowded. I asked if he would phone and see if there was a room available. He did so, and said they had rooms. I returned to my by-now-impatient taxi driver, and we went speeding off again over the hard-packed snow, through Red Square in the darkness, past Lenin's Tomb with its immobile sentinels, past the Kremlin gates with the old Mininskaya opposite, where I had lived in the summer, and over the river to the doors of the New Moscow Hotel. The clerk inside said yes, he could give me a room. So I went out and asked the taxi man to bring in my luggage.

While the desk clerk was examining my papers and permitting me to register, the driver made three or four trips to the car for my baggage. He had just gotten it all inside the lobby when the desk clerk uttered a loud cry. From among the mass of my papers, he had just gotten down to my travel permit.

"This," he cried, "has run out!"

"What?" I said, recalling that the permit had been good for six months. I had been away from Moscow just about that long, and I had neglected to have it renewed in Central Asia.

"It expired the day before yesterday," said the desk clerk. With that he pushed all my papers back to me and crossed my name off the register.

"I can't sleep in the streets tonight," I said.

"Nichevo," shrugged the clerk, closing the guestbook with a bang.

"I'll have it renewed the first thing in the morning," I said.

"But you *cannot* stay here," said the clerk. "Without a valid permit, you cannot stay in any hotel." He called the taxi man to remove my baggage. The man reached for a valise.

I said, "Put my things down. I'm going to stay here."

The desk clerk said, "Take his things out. He will not stay here."

As the taxi man started toward the door with an armload of luggage, I cried in the strongest Russian I knew, "Stop! or I'll call the OGPU."

It worked. The man dropped my bags as if he had been shot. Then I began to argue with the desk clerk again, but to no avail. He would not let me have a room. Twenty below zero outside, and I had no place to lay my head. I made, as the French say, a *scandale*. I threatened, I begged, I shouted. I called it a disgrace that a foreign visitor should be so treated in the Soviet Union. But I got no room. Meanwhile the taxi driver began to talk in a Moscow argot of which I understood nothing, but I gathered that he wanted to be paid and to leave, for which I could not blame him. I paid him his enormous price, and tipped him besides. As the desk clerk still demanded that he should take me and my luggage with him, the taxi man disappeared in a hurry and all we heard was his motor speeding across the bridge.

I looked at the irate clerk and did not say another word. Leaving my bags piled against the wall where they were, I curled up in one of the big lobby chairs, hat and coat on, and slept until dawn. In the morning I went into the restaurant and had breakfast. And after breakfast I went to the Writers Union to see about getting my travel permit renewed.

At the Writers Union I found Walt Carmon, the amiable American editor of the English-language edition of *International Literature*. Walt immediately started the wheels turning for me to get my permit renewed—but with all the red tape involved in the renewal and stamping of papers in Russia, he and I both knew that this might take three or four days or even a week. Meanwhile, where could I sleep? Walt solved that problem by inviting me to stay with him and his wife, Rose, in their single room in a new housing project far across Moscow. I had no alternative but to accept their kindness. Intending to remain with them only for a night or so, I stayed a month.

During that month most of my waking hours were taken up with papers—a new food card, a new residence permit, a new travel permit, a new press card. Six months in Asia, and all my permissions had expired, or were on the verge of expiring. Without the proper papers in the Soviet Union one could not leave, but one could not stay either. Then, to my consternation, I discovered that even my American passport was about to run out. As yet we had no diplomatic representation at Moscow, so I would have to go to Riga to have it renewed. Meanwhile, I sat in Moscow with nearly a half-suitcase full of rubles that had almost no value without the proper papers. It took a food card to get food, a residence permit to get a hotel room, and a travel permit to travel. And when I found out that my American passport was about to become invalid, that was my zero hour.

## BREAD, RED TAPE AND POETS

BY the time I had gotten my residence and travel permits renewed, there were no rooms available at the New Moscow Hotel where the Writers Union had put in for a reservation for me, so I simply stayed on with Walt and Rose Carmon, those two genial souls who had a single room with a family from Brooklyn in a new Soviet apartment house. It was a fourth-floor four-room apartment, large for Moscow— and the last word, in that it had a bathroom. It was occupied by an American Jewish family, the man some sort of technical adviser, the woman just a housewife. Their daughter and son-in-law, Jack Chen, lived with them. The Carmons were roomers—and I was like the man who came to dinner, a guest who simply stayed and stayed, and slept on a cot in one corner of their room. During my month there, there were seven of us in this apartment consisting of three bedrooms, a kitchen-dining room, and a bath. We were crowded, but warm. And we pooled our food rations.

Sometimes I would go with Rose Carmon by streetcar, the long way into the heart of the city where our foreign food store was located, and help her bring back supplies. This particular store always had ample food, but little variety. Fortunately, I liked red caviar which was, I believe, ration-free and inexpensive, and available by the tubful. Bread was strictly rationed down to the last tenth of an ounce, and carefully weighed, chopped off at any angle and given without a wrapper. To the store one carried one's own baskets and papers to wrap up things. The Russian clerks were great choppers, cutting meat or fish at any point to make it the proper weight which a person's ration coupons—or combined coupons—called for. I remember once, Rose and I saw the butcher stalls piled with ducks and decided to combine our ration coupons and have a duck for dinner. But her coupons, mine, and Walt's, were not quite enough for a whole duck. Wham went the cleaver wacking off about a third of the duck wherever the blade landed without regard for joints or anything else. We came home with a one-legged, half-backed fowl cut on the bias.

I remember once I passed the foreign food store alone and thought I would take home a loaf of French bread, which I spied available that day, sold by the loaf rather than the pound as was Russian bread. It was snowing outside and I had no basket with me into which to put the bread, not even a brief case. After going through the complicated process of pricing the bread, ascertaining if my coupons would cover it, then going to the cashier, paying for it, getting a ticket entitling me to have it, and finally returning to the bakery counter for it, the clerk handed me the bread without any wrapping. I asked if, please, I could have a piece of paper.

She said, "Niet."

I said, "Puchimo?" Why?

She said they did not give paper with bread. Paper came only with sugar, caviar and things of that nature that had to be wrapped.

"But it's snowing outside," I said, "and the bread will get wet."

"Nichevo," said the clerk and walked away.

Indignantly, I took my bread and went looking for the manager. Upstairs in an office I found that august bureaucrat and went through the same arguments, getting only a "No paper for bread" answer.

I said, "I will sit right here in your office until I get some sort of wrapping for this bread." So I sat down.

"Pydion," said the manager finally, after busying himself with papers for half an hour and seeing that I would not leave, "Come on." I followed him back downstairs and was given a few inches of brown paper, enough at least to cover the middle of the loaf.

But it was mere child's play getting a piece of paper to wrap bread as compared with getting the proper papers to be entitled to have bread, or a room, or to travel, or to collect money after one had earned it as a free-lance writer. I did a number of articles on my trip to Central Asia for Izvestia, International Literature, and other Moscow publications. The prices paid were good, equivalent in rubles to the better newspapers or magazines in the United States. But the order for one's money had to be signed by the editor first, then the business manager, and perhaps even the political editor. Then this order had to be taken to the controller or bursar where the cash was. But first just try to catch the editor! "He's off on a lecture tour of the Ukraine," or "He's busy getting the paper to press." When finally the editor is captured and he has signed the slip, the manager's secretary says, "Sorry, but today is the manager's free day." Although it might be Monday, Tuesday, Wednesday or any other work day, there was never any telling whose free day was when—since Moscow then had no such things as Saturdays or Sundays off, as we have in America. Any day might be somebody's free day in any office or plant. This was most confusing to a foreigner. But one would come back the next day and perhaps manage to get the manager's signature. But that day might be the free day for the paymaster. Of these customs I complained loudly at the Writers Union, but they could be of no help. Literary agents were unknown in Moscow, and publications had no system of mailing checks or money directly to writers. Each writer had to attend to the collection of his own fees. One of Moscow's most successful short-story writers once told me that he had three secretaries—one to do his typing and two to collect his money. But I, who had no secretaries, had to do all this myself. It took a great deal of time and patience, but eventually I would emerge from a publishing office with a whole bundle of rubles, paid at last. I made more from writing in Moscow in terms of buying power than I have ever earned within the same period anywhere else. I made enough to travel all over the Soviet Union, to come home via Japan and China, and to live (except for the interlude with the Carmons) at what were equivalent to eight- or ten-dollar-a-day hotels in America. Writing in the USSR was one of the better-paid professions. But it often took more time to collect for an article than it did to write the article itself.

Karl Radek was my editor at *Izvestia*. He was a genial debonair little man, rather like Lincoln Steffens in California. Radek's office was a busy office, so he never had much time for conversation. I did not get to know him well. But I was sorry to learn after my return to America that he had been purged. Perhaps he was a little too witty for the rigid red tape of revolution. He once made me laugh about the difficulties writers had getting through this red tape to collect their fees. Radek said, "That's why we pay bad writers so well, Hughes, to make it worth their while to stop writing to collect."

Among the other famous literary personalities whom I met in Moscow, were the playwright, Sergei Tretiakov, whose *Roar China* was produced in New York by the Theatre Guild, and the popular lyric poet, Boris Pasternak. Everyone in Moscow seemed to think that Pasternak might fall into political disgrace at any time, but he was still going strong the last I heard. It seemed that Pasternak would not, or could not, write political poetry. He simply wrote beautifully about trees in autumn, birds and fields and flowers. One poem about a sweetheart went:

> From that day, from your head to your feet,
> I carried you with me and knew you by heart—
> As a provincial actor knows a play of Shakespeare's.
> I took you about with me in the city and repeated you.

Unfortunately, Pasternak did not produce a lyric line about the Five Year Plan, nor such Edgar Guest type of proletarian rhymes as did Demian Biedni, then the most widely printed of Communist versifiers. Yet Pasternak's poetry was very popular not only among Soviet intellectuals and students, but with ordinary people as well. I found him a gentle, likable man, cultured in appearance and shy with strangers.

Sergei Tretiakov and his wife, on the other hand, were dynamic, talkative people and outgoing hosts, with a spick-and-span apartment, modern and bright. Tretiakov himself was very political minded, interested and excited about the Scottsboro Case and the problems of American and African Negroes in general and, of course, the problems of colonial Asia where he had been. He made me a present of an enormous poster, showing a gigantic Chinese coolie breaking his chains, and he gave me a copy of *Roar China* inscribed in English. When I left for the Far East, he and his wife came to see me off at the station.

Another Russian writer, critic and lyric poet, Julian Annisimov, translated a number of my poems into Russian, and introduced me to a very bright young woman, Lydia Filatova, his protegee, who wrote brilliant critical articles. Filatova spoke English very well, and helped

me to translate for American readers some of the poems about Negroes by the great Vladimir Mayakovsky who committed suicide in
1930, but whose work was still much talked of in Moscow. Mayakovsky was the mad surrealist poet of the revolution, writing strange
but intriguing slogans for May Day Parades, fantastic poetic ads for
Soviet shoeshops, and rhymes in favor of hygiene, such as:

> Let a little more culture,
> Workers, take place!
> Don't spit on the floor—
> Spit in a vase.

## THEATER OF THE WHIRLING SEATS

WHEN I did secure a room in the New Moscow Hotel, just across
the bridge from the Kremlin, it was a very nice room, not large but
quite comfortable. Downstairs there was a good dining hall with a
Gypsy orchestra and a very pretty Gypsy girl singing. I soon got acquainted with the Gypsies, and, in the spring, was invited out to the
girl's home one afternoon. She lived with relatives, some of whom
were musicians and other ordinary workers. They offered me kasha
and cabbage soup, a little more highly seasoned than the Russians
made it, and they had a pitcher of kvass to drink—a sort of foamy
malty drink popular in Russia, but which I never liked very much. The
pretty Gypsy girl told me they had been living there for four years,
since it was very hard for Gypsies to travel much any more. I told her
it seemed hard for anyone in the USSR. I asked her relatives how they
liked the new Soviet life. They said, "Nichevo."

There was an attractive Gypsy Club in Moscow, and a Tsigane
Theater, performing a wild and picturesque version of Carmen. But
the Gypsies who played and sang in the New Moscow Hotel were
neither wild nor particularly exotic. They sawed away at their fiddles
in "smokings"—as the Europeans call tuxedoes—and the girl wore a
silver-spangled evening gown much as any cabaret singer might wear
anywhere. Only occasionally, quite late at night, did their music sound
lonely and wild and rebellious.

Muscovites are great playgoers, packing not only Russian-language theaters, but the various national playhouses as well—Ukranian, Jewish, Gypsy—and offering the hospitality of their stages to visiting groups. When the Rustavoli Players from the Georgian State Theater at Tiflis came to town with their whirling sword dances and half-floating, half-gliding women, not a seat could be had for days in advance. And at the International Olympiad of Workers' Theaters, the Mongolian musicians and actors excited great interest. They had traveled to the Soviet capital from Ulan Bator in Outer Mongolia, bringing their silken costumes and exotic instruments with them via the Trans-Siberian Railway. When the curtains of Moscow's vast Music Hall parted to the low monotone of Chinese pipes and fiddles, the slant-eyed actors were welcomed with a prolonged roar of applause.

Only Stanislavsky's great Moscow Art Theater, and its smaller affiliate, the Maly, housed productions untouched by Soviet ideology —famous old productions like The Cherry Orchard, The Three Sisters, The Lower Depths, or The Inspector General. Other theaters might tamper with these plays, to slant them or bring them up to date in stunning new productions, but the Moscow Art Theater had a large and faithful public for its established classics unchanged, and its seats were booked months ahead. It was interesting to me to compare the the various ways in which a single play, like Gogol's The Inspector General, might be performed. With Meyerhold's constructivist sets, it certainly came out differently than under Stanislavsky's carefully realistic treatment. But the theater that fascinated me most of all was Oklopkov's Krasni Presnia, the most advanced in production styles of any playhouse I have ever seen. Arena staging was the least novel of its innovations. For each production the entire seating and platform arrangements of the theater were changed, and the whole auditorium was always used as a playing area, front, back and aisles. Sometimes a conventional stage was utilized, too, with perhaps a runway from the stage up to the balcony. Sometimes there were runways along the side walls all the way to the lobby. And one amazing production was so designed that important things were happening all over the place, so the spectators sat in swivel chairs, whirling around at will to catch whatever interested them most.

From the young Oklopkov and the older Meyerhold, both of

whom were kind enough to talk with me and to invite me to attend rehearsals, I acquired a number of interesting ways of staging plays, some of which I later utilized in directing my own Negro history play, *Don't You Want To Be Free?*, done in Harlem without a stage, curtains, or sets. I used two raised half-circles connected by a narrow runway against a side wall. The actors changed costumes behind an upright piano in the middle. This play of mine, before arena staging became popular in New York, intrigued Negro audiences for more than a year, chalking up a record run in Harlem of 135 performances.

The Meyerhold and Oklopkov theaters were a little special, even for Moscow. Much more popular with the general public and the run-of-the-mill intellectuals were the Vakhtangov and the Kamery Theaters, whose innovations were not as radical, but whose productions were expertly done and quite beautiful. The Vakhtangov's dynamic production of *Hamlet*, in which Shakespeare's hero became a man of action, entering on a dashing white horse, provoked much discussion in Moscow and was a great hit. Tairov's Kamery was then the *theatre du snobisme* in the Soviet capital, Moscow's smartest playhouse, given to the presentation of foreign dramas like those of Georg Kaiser and Eugene O'Neill. It was at the Kamery that I saw the scenery constricting, in and out, in *All God's Chillun Got Wings*, like the throbbing brain of its poor Negro with his intermarriage problem.

Soviet ideology did not favor picturing colored people in subservient or clownish roles on the stage, for which I was grateful. One of the most popular of the plays at the Moscow Children's Theater concerned a handsome little Negro boy, presented most sympathetically, I was told. But I could never get in to see this play, so crowded was the theater, and adults were admitted only when accompanying children.

Most of the plays I attended were so vividly done that I could usually follow the action without the aid of an interpreter. Nor did one need a translator to enjoy the wonderful indoor circus. But at those few playhouses devoted to vaudeville and the music-hall skits, where the songs were topical and the comedy in Moscow argot and highly political, satirizing *kulaks* and profiteers and lazy workers, I could understand but little. The music-hall productions were shoddy, and not at all on a par with the serious dramatic or operatic theaters.

In contrast to motion-picture houses, all of the dramatic theaters in Moscow, even in subzero weather, were well heated. The motion-picture theaters, except for a few expensive first-run houses, were ice cold. To go to the movies, one put on more clothing than to go into the street. At the cinema, it was often difficult to see the screen for waves of white vapor rising from the mouths and noses of the spectators like a mist. Lacking heat, these houses also lacked ventilation. Every crack was kept tightly closed against the weather. Full of seldom-bathed comrades, the motion-picture theaters in Moscow smelled like very pungent kennels. I seldom went to the movies that winter.

## MOSCOW ROMANCE

AT one of the Meyerhold's rehearsals I met an actress, a sort of apprentice actress, playing bouncing country peasants, awkward maids, and other small bit parts verging toward comedy. She had a buxom body, a round smiling face, Slavic—not beautiful, not ugly—and was very healthy-looking. But she had a one-track mind. Without advance warning, Natasha simply came to my room in the New Moscow Hotel one night when I was out—and was in bed when I got back.

I had met her after my return from Central Asia. It was late when the rehearsal was over and not a *droski*, taxi, bus, or tramcar was in sight. The Moscow streets were silent and eerie white under the snow. I asked Natasha if she would like me to walk her home. She said, "Please." So I did. She lived near the Chinese Wall of the Old City, across the river not far from my hotel. She was very talkative, spoke French well, and kept up a running conversation as our feet went crunch, crunch, crunch through the dry snow. Natasha was amusing, and flirtatious.

She said, "Take off your glove." I did. She took off one of hers, and took my hand, and laughed. She said, "See your dark hand and my white one together—pretty, no? *Comme c'est beau!*"

"They're different," I said.

"Oh, I love the Negroes," she cried in French, "and I have not

known one before, only seen them in theater, in cinema. But I love
the Negroes."

At home in America, Negroes are immediately suspicious of persons who protest too much their love of colored people. But I knew
she was not being condescending. Still I saw no need for her to stretch
the point.

"*Bien*," I said, "that's nice of you. I love the Russians, too."

She squeezed my hand, and that was about the end of it that
evening. I said good night at her door, went down along the river and
across the bridge to my hotel. But the very next time I went to Meyerhold's theater one afternoon when a new set of spirals and bridges
were being built on the stage, there she was. Lloyd Patterson, the
Negro artist of our movie group, had asked me to meet him there and
watch how a constructivist set was put together. His wife, whom he
had married while I was away in Asia, was with him. I introduced
them to Natasha. This time when I took Natasha home, she asked me
to come in and meet her husband. He was a quiet pince-nezed old
gentleman about twice her age, half bald, scholarly and blanched, and
somewhat absent-minded in manner.

"He works all the time," Natasha said, "studies formulas, charts,
I don't know what." It seemed he was attached to a scientific institute, and took his position very seriously. He seldom went out. He
had but little interest in the arts, but he was pleasant enough that
afternoon as the three of us had tea. There was a real old-fashioned
brass samovar in the living room, but there was no fuel to heat it.
However, to show me how it worked, tea was brewed in the kitchen,
then poured in the samovar. With the tea in tall glasses, bits of hard
candy were served instead of sugar. You put a piece of candy between
your teeth and drank the steaming tea over the candy. An American
has to get used to hot tea in a hot glass plus candy between the teeth.
My struggle tickled Natasha. She laughed and laughed. Her husband
smiled and let his eyes stray to a treatise he seemed to have been reading before I came.

"Go ahead, read," said Natasha. "We'll forgive you." So the old
man drank tea and read and jotted pencil notes on the edge of the
pamphlet.

Natasha asked me to take her to a party later in the week, a small party of theatrical friends, mostly bit players. The party turned out to be far out on the edge of Moscow in a suburb of large old-fashioned wooden houses and log *dachas* among the pine trees and chalky white birches, ghostly in the snow. We rode to the end of a car line, then walked perhaps a quarter of a mile to a two-room apartment in one of the big old wooden houses. The party was lively, prankish, with folks reciting poetry, doing impersonations and showing off, rather like a bohemian party anywhere, except that tea and vodka were the main refreshments, rather than whiskey.

I do not know how the various tipsy guests got home, but I remember Natasha saying quite late, after all the others had departed, "I'm sure the last streetcar has gone."

"Oh, yes," said our hosts, a young married couple, "but don't worry. You can spend the night with us."

It was miles back to the heart of the city. There was no telephone. And even if one could call a cab from the Metropol in Moscow, they were known not to arrive for hours, if at all. I pulled back a window curtain. Outside, not a soul stirred. It was zero cold, white and still in the moonlight, with the tall fir trees and the wooden houses like a picture post card of what I'd imagined Old Russia to be.

The married couple made up a cot in what appeared to be a combination kitchen-dining-room-library. They also spread a pallet on the floor. The cot was for Natasha and the pallet for me—both in the same room. In Russian trains, men and women, utter strangers to each other, slept in the same compartments. With the Russian housing shortage, I knew that even former husbands and wives who had gotten divorced, but could find no places to move apart, sometimes occupied the same room for months, until one found a vacancy elsewhere. That night Natasha insisted in both French and Russian that I, being a guest and a foreigner—*Negrochanski*—take the cot. But I would not, of course, be so ungallant. While she was still talking with her friends, I went ahead to bed on the pallet. But that room was quite cold, and the scanty covering was very thin. At the end of a carline again! I thought of my Tartar rendezvous in Tashkent and how cold it had been there, and I resolved *never* to go to the end of another streetcar line at night anywhere in the USSR.

Shortly Natasha came to bed on the cot across from my pallet.

With my face to my wall, I pretended to be asleep, but she knew I wasn't.

"So little blankets," she murmured. "*Mon dieu!* I'm cold. *Cheri,* I shiver!"

"Me, too," I said.

With so little cover between us, in order to keep warm, our hosts must have known that we would have to sleep together.

## IRRITATED AND SALIVATED

EVEN in the dead of winter the New Moscow Hotel was full of foreigners, mostly non-Communists and nonpolitical foreigners, technicians waiting to go to the Ukranian factories, or engineers expecting assignments to the Urals or wherever impending dams or other projects were about to be erected. Everybody quickly got acquainted in the lobby or in the dining room. It was a friendly place with quite a deal of visiting back and forth in the rooms and between floors. There was the usual hum of anti-Soviet talk, common to irritated foreigners as frustration with red tape and disillusionment with "the system," the delays, the hotel and the food set in. In the dining room there was plenty of food, such as it was, but little variety and the same unvarying menus of greasy rich sturgeon, cutlets—a kind of chopped meat shaped like a pork shop; *kasha,* a sort of cereal; cabbage, both red and green; and that horrible warm calves'-foot-jelly-like dessert, *kisel.* Red caviar saved my life. I could eat it morning, noon and night. Besides, once I have enough to eat, no matter what, food does not worry me much. Although Soviet hotel menus were a bore, I could put up with them.

But some folks complained continually about the food. Some complained even more about the crowded streetcars that would curve around the corner below the New Moscow with people swinging from the doors and windows, and on which a hotel guest could seldom get a foothold. Others lamented the scarcity of taxis, the high tariff of *droskies,* and the noncommittal attitudes of clerks and public servants, and how hard it was even to buy a stamp in the post office. Although I wasn't a Russian, in the face of such continual complaining, I often felt like saying, "Why don't you go back where you came from?" Some people did go back. Others—most others, in fact—stuck it out until they got where they had been contracted to go, although sometimes it appeared that they were just being paid to sit in the New Moscow Hotel—as our movie group had sat in the Grand—and do nothing but wait and wait. Russian delays were often long and intolerable. One Englishman had been in the hotel all winter, waiting to be sent to a plant that finally he heard the Russians as yet had not even begun to build. One day he took up with a girl from Pittsburgh who had just come to the Soviet Union to have a child.

Very pregnant, she arrived with the first group of American tourists that spring. They were booked for a ten-day tour of Moscow, Kiev, Kharkov and Leningrad. But when this young woman got to Moscow, she stayed. Not having in advance a contract to work, and not being a diplomat on a mission, she could get into the country only as a tourist. So, she had bought a one-way ticket from New York to Paris, and there booked a ten-day tourist trip to Russia, keeping secret her intention to stay. She was a starry-eyed idealist, who had heard that in the Soviet Union there was no stigma attached to an illegitimate child. At home in Pittsburgh she had become pregnant by a man who was already married, so she had come to the Soviet Union to have her baby in a land where illegitimacy did not matter, where all children were equal, and women were free. She planted herself in the New Moscow Hotel on a three-day permit, intending to remain until she became a mother.

For three days she saw all the sights of Moscow and then, when her group moved on to Leningrad, the hotel naturally asked for her room. In fact, the management thought she had departed with the group. When it was discovered that she had not, a great furor ensued. Where were her papers permitting her to stay? The extension of her visa? Her residence permit? Her police permit? Her card for food? "What! Nothing?" She would have to go! The British engineer found her in the lobby, surrounded by bags, pregnant as could be, and dissolved in tears. The kindhearted engineer took pity on her and, over the hotel's violent objections, invited her to share his room until things could be straightened out. It seemed that she really had neither papers nor any more money—but she was carrying a child she determined would be born free of stigma—in a land where all children are equal, she cried, and there is no illegitimacy.

The British engineer felt this to be an admirable sentiment. But the hotel's Soviet executives simply said, "*Nichevo!* So what? Why aren't things as she wishes in America? It's not our responsibility where her child is born. She has no permit to stay here. Her three-day tourist card is finished. Her room is already taken by someone else, and booked through the entire summer. She has no food card for this dining room. She *cannot* stay at the New Moscow Hotel."

Since I was the nearest American neighbor to the British engineer, just down the hall from his room, he knocked on my door to inform me that he had an hysterical American lady from Pittsburgh in his diggings. Would I kindly come and talk to her? I found a tall, simply dressed, nice, middle-class American girl sitting beside his luke-warm radiator weeping quietly, her unopened bags on the floor by the door. She said she thought everybody in Russia would understand her problem. But nobody did.

I said I understood, and the Englishman declared he did, too. But, when she had calmed down, we tried to explain to her how difficult it was to do anything in the USSR without the proper papers. Money really did not help much—even if one had money—without a half-dozen permits. True, at the Metropol anyone could eat in rubles or dollars, but at terrific prices. And, with foreign money, a person might be able to live fairly well by buying at the Torgsin shops which accepted only gold-back currency of other lands, no rubles being tenable as exchange.

The girl said, "But I haven't got *any* money, only a few dollars left. And I have no ticket back—and even if I did, *I wouldn't go home.* I'm going to stay here, I *have* to stay here, where my child can be born with no mark upon it, no stigma. My baby! I *have* to stay here —the only country I know in the world where people don't care if a woman isn't married when she has a child. Don't the Russians understand?"

"We'll have to try to find one who understands," I said.

"I understand," said the Englishman, and he put the tired, distraught girl to bed. He slept on the floor.

The next day I told Walt and Rose Carmon about her, and they suggested that she go to see Anna Louise Strong and the folks at the *Moscow Daily News*, the English-language paper edited by the once famous Borodin. Nobody, left or right, in Moscow's American colony thought much of the *Moscow Daily News*. Always a day or two behind the Russian press with news, it was usually filled only with stock propaganda editorials, dull industrial reports, and sloganlike headlines. But any American with a problem was always dumped in the lap of the *Moscow Daily News*. It was a kind of Travelers' Aid Bureau, or so used by American residents in Moscow to get rid of fellow countrymen in trouble. I must say, the harassed staff of that harassed paper arose to each occasion as best it could. In this case, they actually found a room for the girl.

The poor Englishman had been threatened with eviction from the New Moscow Hotel for housing a foreigner without papers. But he withstood the management nobly and sheltered her for two or three nights until she got located. The room found for the girl was on the far outskirts of Moscow, in a muddy, sidewalkless suburb, miles from the only store where English was spoken and where this girl might trade if she ever got a food card. Somehow a temporary permit allowing her to remain in Moscow for a month had been secured— but nothing else. The Englishman pressed upon her a few pounds. I gave her a roll of rubles, and we saw her safely into a *drosky* and off to her abode, smiling happily.

Two days later she was back in the lobby of the New Moscow Hotel, bags and baggage. Cold and rainy that spring, and sometimes still snowing, the suburban streets were ankle-deep in mud. The American girl could hardly get out her door without sinking into a kind of swamp. The nearest car line or bus was a mile away from the house. The house itself was damp, penetratingly cold, dank with mildew and cobwebs, with a fire nowhere but in the kitchen stove—and then only at meal times. The Russian family with whom she lived were ordinary, kindly people who understood not a word of English, nor did the girl from Pittsburgh speak a single phrase of Russian, although she had studied the vocabulary in the little *Russian While You Travel* booklet, mispronouncing everything miserably. There was no bathroom in the house, and the toilet was far out in the yard through puddles of water in a morass of black sticky mud. But the last straw was that the walls of the house were full of bedbugs. When the poor girl finally managed to get back to the New Moscow Hotel, she had been bitten all over by vermin, chilled to the bone, and had caught a miserable cold.

The genteel Englishman took her into his room again. But by now the girl was really ill, and so upset that she could not eat. Her generous Russian landlady's cabbage soup, shared from a common bowl into which all dipped their spoons, had not agreed with her. The thought of cabbage nauseated her. That first night back in the hotel the girl ran a fever. The next morning the Englishman went for a doctor, and I stayed with the sick woman while he was out. Still talkative, even though ill, she told me in detail of her love for the man in Pittsburgh, who already had a home, a wife and three children, and whose home she respected—but whose child she nevertheless wanted to have.

When the doctor came, he felt her pulse, took her temperature and left a prescription. The Englishman went to have it filled. When he returned, he brought a small bottle of gray-black pills and an armful of large tins of fruit juices. Such orange and grapefruit juices were a luxury which could only be purchased in foreign money at the Torgsin stores. His guest was proving quite an expense to the poor British engineer, but he was most decent about it all and tended her like a nurse. He gave her the medicine and after she felt better, all day long he fed her on canned fruit juice.

That night the Englishman knocked rapidly on my door quite late. He was greatly agitated. "The American," he said, "I don't know what is the matter. Please come quickly!"

I found the usually voluble girl silent, unable to say a word. Sitting bolt upright in her bed, her tongue was swollen so that it almost filled her mouth. Slobbering, she could not speak. At that time, in the after-midnight hours, we knew of no way of getting a doctor, nor was the desk clerk of any help. But when I saw the empty tins of fruit juices in the wastebasket and saw the gray-black tablets beside the bed, and uncorked the bottle and smelled the tablets, I guessed what the matter was. I remembered such pills from my childhood in Kansas, popular there with the old people as a laxative—but always accompanied with the dire warning to anyone who took them, never to drink acids or citrus juices afterwards on pain of becoming salivated.

The tablets in the bottle which the Russian doctor had prescribed for the girl were calomel tablets. On top of the calomel, the Englishman had given her canned citrus juices all day. She was salivated. When you get salivated your tongue swells up, my grandmother always told me. This speechless American's tongue was swollen as thick as a sausage—*salivated!* I could diagnose that.

But the next day she could talk again. And when she could talk, *she did!* A week in Moscow was just about enough— in fact, dear God, too much! "I have never gone through such horror," she cried. Now she had begun to fear for the safety of her coming child. Better to be born with a stigma than not to be born at all! The cables got busy, money came from home, and the girl bought a ticket back to the U.S.A., where at least you don't need a permit to get a hotel room. She was hoping to get home before her baby came.

## ILLUSION AND DISILLUSION

LOOKING a long-held ideal in the face is about like looking a gift horse in the mouth. The poor old ideal, beaten and battered by reality, its gloss gone and its veneer cracked, often does not appear as pretty in actuality as it seemed in dreams. Glimpsing the ideal in naked reality may be much like seeing your favorite movie star in broad daylight without make-up. What the girl from Pittsburgh had dreamed the USSR might be, and *what it was,* were two entirely different things. But the case of the salivated girl, although the most extreme and to me the saddest, was by no means the only case I witnessed of dire disillusionment with the Soviets and all their works that year in the corridors of the New Moscow Hotel. There came to the Soviet capital many varied types of people from around the world. Among the ships that passed in the Moscow night (I know it's a cliché, but ships *do* pass in the night)—among the ships that passed in the Soviet night, while I was there, I shall probably remember longest the pregnant girl from Pittsburgh.

But I won't forget the poet, Norman Macleod, either. I had known Norman in New York, and so was glad to see him when he showed up in Moscow, accompanied by a little girl from Greenwich Village who had come to design bath towels for a Soviet trust. Norman had a sorry tale to tell. It seemed that he had gotten high on white wine in Paris and had been arrested by the French police for singing the *Internationale* in a loud voice on the Grand Boulevards. Then, hardly had he gotten to Moscow than he had gotten high on vodka, and was arrested there on the main street because he could find no men's room and did not know how to ask for one. Having to relieve himself of excess liquid on a public corner near the post office, he did so. Two militiamen politely requested that he come with them to jail. So within two weeks he had known two police stations in two different countries. But Macleod took it all in stride and was laughing when I saw him in the New Moscow Hotel.

Other passers-by during my months in Moscow included John Hope, the venerable Negro President of Atlanta University, who treated me to a wonderful *valuta* luncheon at the National Hotel where he was stopping. Earl Browder showed up one day and gave a talk at the Writers Union on the relations between literature and the class struggle. And from somewhere there arrived a Negro dancing boy named Banks, who occasionally hit a few steps in front of the very bad jazz band at the Metropol Café. Banks was not a very good dancer and the band was no inspiration to him.

In Moscow, too, that year my paths crossed the paths of such worldlings as the French poet and novelist, Louis Aragon, and his lovely writer-wife, Elsa Triolet; the Chinese poet, Emi Sao; the Japanese theater director, Seki Sano; the hard-drinking British poet, Charles Ashleigh; the brilliant but dogmatic Negro lawyer, William Patterson, making speeches on Scottsboro; and dozens of English and American tourists coming and going, most of them sympathetic liberals friendly to "the Soviet experiment"—but many of them unsympathetic when they departed, and others entirely shorn of any illusions they might have had as to man's ability to make himself over into a new unselfish image through communism.

I think most idealists expected too much of Russia in too short a

time. The Soviet Union was then only fifteen years old. I kept thinking of what someone once said about the freed Negroes in America,
"Don't try to measure the progress of the Negro by how far he has
gone but rather by the distance from which he had to come." Maybe
my having gone to Central Asia gave me a broader viewpoint on Soviet
achievements. In Turkestan the new setup was only eight years old,
dating from 1924—yet there they had already come from almost complete illiteracy to schools for *all* the children, from ancient feudal serfdom to wages and work for all, from veils and harems and marriage
marts to women treated like human beings and not chattels, and from
Jim Crow cars to a complete lack of segregation—all in less than a
decade.

Maybe the fact that I was colored, too, made a difference. All the
tourists I saw in the Soviet Union except John Hope were white. Most
of the other travelers, such as the technicians and writers I saw there,
were white, too. Some things irritated these people much more than
they did me. Just as the dirt in Central Asia upset Koestler, so it
upset me. Dirt without Jim Crow was bad—but dirt *with Jim Crow,*
*for me,* would have been infinitely worse. In the old days, Koestler and
I could not have stayed in the same hotels together in Turkestan, nor
ridden in the same railway compartments. My segregated compartment would have been dirtier. As a white man before the revolution,
Koestler could have ridden first-class—but not I. Koestler perhaps
could not understand why I did not complain as often as he did, nor
why I was not quite so impatient with the maid who refused to set our
bags over the doorsill in Bokhara. Koestler had never lived as a Negro
anywhere. Even with dirt, there was freedom for a Turkoman now to
sit in Ashkabad's dusty park and not see the old signs FOR EUROPEANS
ONLY that formerly kept him out. Even with eternal grime and continued famines, racial freedom was sweeter than the lack of it. To
Grasdani, such freedom in Asia meant only tin cans in the toilets and
dark guests in the best hotels. But to Nichan it was education and
football and *his* brown statue over a new stadium.

If, rather than a Negro, I had been a Russian of the old school
like Grasdani, or a famous Berlin journalist like Koestler, or a comfortable white American tourist affording twenty dollars a day for a

room, or a highly skilled foreign engineer impatient with lesser skilled men and bungling red tape, or a pregnant woman with romantic illusions, maybe I would have become quickly disillusioned, too, and found nothing good to say about a backward people who had come so far—to so little.

As to the purge trials, the liquidations, the arrests and censorship, deplorable as these things were, I felt about them in relation to their continual denunciation in the European and American press, much as Frederick Douglass felt before the Civil War when he read in the slave-holding papers that the abolitionists were anarchists, villains, devils and atheists. Douglass said he had the impression that "Abolition—whatever else it might be—was not unfriendly to the slave."

After all, I suppose, how anything is seen depends on whose eyes look at it.

## D. H. LAWRENCE BETWEEN US

THE first evening that I came back to my room in the hotel and found Natasha in bed, I said, "But, listen, Natasha, you've got a husband. Q'est ce que tu fais, alors?"

"My husband has long been sleeping," she said. "He will not wake up till six or seven in the morning."

"But staying out this way, don't you care anything about him?"

"I like him, yes—but I like you, too," said Natasha. And that was that, alors!

She was fun and as wholesome in body as an apple. But she got in the habit of coming to the hotel more and more often, which eventually began to be annoying. On the other hand, she was most helpful sometimes in indicating to me ways of getting around, over, or through the unwinding of the vast amount of red tape involved in my getting out to Latvia to have my American passport renewed, then in getting all the dozens of papers and permissions needed to go eastward around the world, home via the Pacific. I had decided that, with all my surplus rubles, I might as well circle the globe. One could buy with rubles a rail ticket all the way from Moscow to Shanghai via Peking. To see the ancient city of Peking I had never even dreamed, but now I could, if the Russians would let me cross Siberia. Meschrabpom Films had arranged for all of us to go home via Europe. Siberia was not in the Meschrabpom plans, and the film company seemed quite unprepared to aid me in making my exit from Russia by way of the Far East. The Writers Union was not very helpful, either. In the end Constantine Oumansky and Natasha were the most helpful of all. But as to Natasha, I still didn't want an almost nightly guest, the reason being that I had begun writing again, and I always do my best writing at night—alone.

The circumstances of my beginning to write were curious. Shortly after I moved into the New Moscow Hotel, I met there Marie Seaton from London. She was doing a study of Russian motion pictures, and gathering data on Sergei Eisenstein and his work, which she later used in her biography of him. Marie Seaton had with her a paper-bound copy of D. H. Lawrence's short stories, *The Lovely Lady* which she lent me. I had never read anything of Lawrence's before, and was particularly taken with the title story, and with "The Rocking Horse Winner." Both tales made my hair stand on end. The possessive, terrifying elderly woman in "The Lovely Lady" seemed in some ways so much like my former Park Avenue patron that I could hardly bear to read the story, yet I could not put the book down, although it brought cold sweat and goose-pimples to my body. A night or two after I had read the Lawrence stories, I sat down to write an *Izvestia* article on Tashkent when, instead, I began to write a short story. I had been saying to myself all day, "If D. H. Lawrence can write such psychologically powerful accounts of folks in England, that send shivers up and down my spine, maybe I could write stories like his about folks in America. I wonder."

It had never occurred to me to try to write short stories before, other than the enforced compositions of college English. But in wondering, I began to think about some of the people in my own life, and some of the tales I had heard from others, that affected me in the same hair-raising manner as did the characters and situations in D. H. Lawrence's two stories concerning possessive people like the lovely lady and neglective people like the parents of the "Rocking Horse Winner." I began to turn over in my mind a story that a young lawyer in California, Loren Miller, had told me. He said that in one of the small towns in Kansas where he had lived during his childhood, there had been a very pretty colored girl who, as she grew up, attracted the amorous eye of the town's only Negro doctor, the town's only Negro undertaker, and the town's Negro minister. All three of these men enjoyed her favors. The girl became pregnant. But by whom? At any rate, the doctor performed an abortion on her and she died. The undertaker who had courted her took charge of her body. The minister preached her funeral. Since all the colored people of the town knew that each one of these men had been intimate with the girl, they wondered what would happen at her funeral. All three men were present, but nothing happened. She was just buried.

When I sat down at my well-traveled typewriter and began to write my first short story, "Cora Unashamed," the material of the factual narrative I'd heard from Loren Miller changed into fiction. The Negro girl became a white girl of middle-class family, whose parents did not want her to fall in love with an immigrant Greek boy whose father ran an ice-cream stand. My story consisted of what happened when this girl's mother forced her to have an abortion, the girl died, and the Negro cook spoke her piece concerning love and morals at the funeral. None of the situations in my story were as in the real one, but its inspiration came from Loren Miller's tale.

It was Marie Seaton's loan of D. H. Lawrence that started me off writing short stories in Moscow. I had had no thought of doing so. But I am glad it happened that way because I sent my first three stories from Russia to an agent in New York, and by the time I got back to America he had sold all three, one to *The American Mercury*, one to *Scribner's Fiction Parade*, and one to *Esquire*. The money came in handy. And once started, I wrote almost nothing but short stories.

When in Moscow I started writing intensively, I really did not want to be bothered with an almost nightly female visitor. On the other hand, I hated to be rude to Natasha and say, "Go home." But another and more possessive "Lovely Lady" from D. H. Lawrence's stories had come between us.

## MAKING RUSSIANS DO RIGHT

WHEN I went to Latvia to get my passport renewed, this procedure at the American Consulate in Riga took only a few minutes, in contrast to the great length of time required to get almost any paper stamped in the Soviet Union. I stayed only overnight in Riga, not wishing to spend any more of my precious *valuta* than necessary. Possessing less than a hundred dollars in American money, I wanted to save that for China and Japan. Fortunately, one could buy in Moscow a round-trip ticket to Riga with rubles, and my only expense in Latvia was a hotel room and an enormous dinner. When I saw the great varieties of food on the hotel menu there, I could not restrain myself. I went from soup to nuts.

When I got back to Moscow I had a very busy spring, writing at night and chasing down permits for my trip to the Far East by day. I had definitely determined not to leave Moscow until I received permission to board the Trans-Siberian for Manchuria and China. Meanwhile the Japanese had bombed Chapai, the Chinese section of Shanghai, again, and had stepped up their military operations in Manchuria. In May, the American journalist, Agnes Smedley, arrived in Moscow from China with stories of grave trouble in the Far East. The Soviet Foreign Office continued to withhold permission for me to exit by way of Siberia. Nevertheless, I went ahead with my plans, badgering Constantine Oumansky at the Foreign Press Bureau, and worrying the Writers Union and Meschrabpom to help me. At last my exit visa came through.

My next problem was to get a compartment on the Trans-Siberian Express. That train, of all the trains in the Soviet Union, was the most difficult to get on. It was booked up for weeks, sometimes months, ahead. Diplomats and Red Army men were given priority, and an ordinary citizen might be bounced off even after he had gotten a place. As soon as I received my proper documents, I applied for a berth leaving Moscow as soon as possible. It was three months before I finally got on the train.

Meanwhile, I struggled with Intourist, the agency through which foreigners bought tickets in Moscow. The courtesies of Muscovites to me as an American visitor, and especially as a Negro, I shall never forget. But those who composed the staff of Intourist were far from courteous. The bureaucratic males and females behind the counter there—whom I hope have all since been purged—were as rude and inefficient as any clerks I have ever encountered—ruder, in fact, since they knew that no foreigner could travel anywhere in the Soviet Union, or leave Moscow, except by and through their dispensation. Before I went to Riga I had traveled always under the wing of Meschrabpom or the Writers Union, who attended to tickets for me. But when I went to Intourist alone to purchase a ticket to Latvia, my troubles began. First you applied for the ticket, and left your various papers. Then when you went back to see if the ticket was ready, as likely as not the person who had taken the application would be having his free day and so was not on duty. No one else knew anything about a Riga ticket. You went back again later in the week and yes, the ticket would be validated, but the man investigating your papers has his free day today. Come back tomorrow. Finally, the papers and the ticket are validated and handed to you over the counter. But the ticket is to Warsaw instead of Riga!

I have seen foreign tourists go utterly to pieces in the Intourist office merely trying to get a *wagon-lit* to Leningrad or make a slight change in a sight-seeing itinerary.

The Intourist clerks would usually begin by saying, "No, it's not possible," to whatever request one might make. Then, when pressed, they would say, "We'll see." When you went back a few days later, they were still "seeing" in a lackadaisical manner. This would go on until a scene—as the French say, a *scandale*—erupted on your side of the counter. Scandals did not phase Intourist. Their clerks remained unruffled. The officials then would become even more noncommital, more disinterested, and ruder than ever. Old residents of the American colony in Moscow said they thought Intourist must be entirely composed of saboteurs placed there by counter-revolutionists especially to wreck whatever good will travelers might have acquired toward the Soviet Union. To make an enemy of me, at any rate, seemed to be the determined aim and objective of Intourist each time I had occasion to deal with it.

Other state employees could be difficult, too. One night, in my room in the New Moscow hotel, a water pipe beneath my washbowl sprung a leak and a steady stream of water started shooting out, wetting my bathroom floor and the rug in the bedroom thoroughly before I noticed it. I immediately phoned down to the desk and reported the leak. Then I took the biggest vase in the room and started catching the water and pouring it into the toilet bowl near the leaking pipe. This went on for fifteen or twenty minutes, and no one came to attend to the leak. I phoned again. The clerk said blandly that there was nobody on duty but himself and he could not leave the desk. I explained that the water would, if not stopped, flood the whole room and seep through to the floor below.

He said, "But what can I do about it?"

I said, "Call a plumber."

He said, "But there is no plumber until morning."

I said, "As a Soviet citizen, do you intend to let this hotel become flooded with water and the rugs and ceilings be ruined by an all night leak?"

I could not see him, but I am sure he simply shrugged as he answered, "I can do nothing."

I said on the phone, "But, comrade, I can't stand beside the leak with a vase and catch the water all night. At least, send a tin pan or a bucket up here, please."

Another half hour went by and no pan or bucket arrived, nothing. Finally, I employed my constant ace in the hole. I went to the phone and said in my most deliberate Russian, "Listen, I am a foreigner and a guest in your country. Yet I care more about Soviet property than you do. I cannot bear to see this floor flooded and the plaster below ruined because you will do nothing. If you do not have someone up here to stop this leak in the next few minutes *I am going to call the OGPU.*"

It worked. In no time at all the hotel engineer arrived with a helper and soldering tools, and in a few moments the leak was stopped.

When I told Emma about it the next day, that long-time colored resident of Moscow said, "That's the way Stalin stopped them train wrecks in the station yard last fall. He just called the OGPU—and when they got through shootin' engine drivers, there was no more wrecks. You have to get hard with these Russians, to make 'em do right."

## MAY DAY IN MOSCOW

"ONI SEDIT—he sits," was the expression used by Russians to describe incarceration by the Political Police, the OGPU. I did not know anyone in the USSR who "sat" during my year there, except a student poet in Moscow. He came to see me once or twice early in the spring to read me some of his poems in schoolboy English. When I did not see him for a month or two, I asked where he was, and was told, "Oni sedit."

"Why?" I said.

But the answer was not clear. Bourgeois family background seemed to have something to do with it. A few years after my departure from Central Asia, Faisulla Khodjaiev, President of the Council of Peoples Commissars in Uzbekistan, whom I met in Tashkent, was arrested and tried as a traitor accused of negotiating with the British across the Afghan border. My Moscow editor, Karl Radek, disappeared in a later purge. And Sergei Tretiakov of Roar China was shot in 1938, "liquidated" as they say in Russia. In the USSR politicians were often not simply removed from office, they were removed from this world.

I attended a few sessions of the public trial in Moscow that spring of six British engineers accused of spying and sabotage. The director and five English employes of the Metropolitan-Vickers Electrical Company had been lodged in Lubianka Prison. Twelve Russians in the company were also arrested by the OGPU. One of the English engineers confessed on the stand to the charges against him, as did each of the twelve Russians. Another of the Britons signed a confession of guilt before the trial, but repudiated it. With Vishinsky as the prosecutor, however, both he and the director were sentenced to prison—as were all of the Russians. American and British spectators were amazed at the complete and detailed testimony against themselves which the Russian prisoners gave without cajoling. It was interesting to witness in action that famous and perplexing pattern of self-confession that was to become a feature of many subsequent purge trials.

Spring was soft and beautiful in Moscow. There were hundreds of tulips in the Park of Rest and Culture, and a blue haze over the distant Lenin Hills; and on the trees around the Kremlin Wall new young leaves appeared, delicate and green; the great chunks of ice floating down the Moscow River became smaller and smaller until finally the river was just a ribbon of brown. Red Square, which I crossed every day to get to my hotel from the center of the city, was swept by teasingly warm-now-cold breezes. St. Basil's Cathedral with its Oriental pineapple domes looked like a gaily painted toy church in its triangle of streets below Lenin's Tomb. That terraced tomb was like a child's block of red and violet porphyry against the Kremlin Wall with its fir tree sentinels and its soldier sentinels, too—an immobile Red Army private with a Red Star on his cap at each side of the entrance. Several times in passing I went inside the tomb, down the narrow stairs, past Lenin's body, then up and out into the spring sunlight again. All day, winter and summer, there was a long line of men, women and children, waiting to file past the bier of the greatest of the Soviet revolutionists.

On May Day, I saw those who had inherited Lenin's authority take their places on the terrace of his tomb to review the mammoth parade that would pass. The Writers Union had gotten me a coveted place in the Red Square not a hundred yards from the tomb, in the special stands reserved for diplomats and distinguished foreign visitors. This I had not expected when I asked if I might see the parade from Red Square, which required a very special OGPU pass. If this permission were granted me at all, I thought I would be on the far side of the Square, not on the side with Stalin. But perhaps my being the only Negro writer in Moscow secured so favorable a location for me.

At any rate, when the parade began, there I was not a hundred yards from Stalin, Molotov, Voroshilov, Kalinin, Litvinov, and the other leaders of the Kremlin. Once in the Square, however, one could not leave until the parade ended, and it lasted almost six hours. For hours and hours, sometimes in three or four massed columns at once, through the Red Square, poured the special crack units of the Red Army, the Red Cavalry, and Red Fleet; and the colorful delegations from all the varied Workers Republics of the Soviet Union in their regional costumes; the athletic delegations, the youth delegations, the shock workers groups, the school children. And when this part of the parade was over—after which guests could leave if they wished—but I didn't—came the thousands and thousands of just plain workers marching past in a great solid fifty-or-more-to-a-row mass of men and women with their banners, WORKERS OF THE WORLD UNITE! . . . HAIL TO THE SOVIET UNION! . . . HAIL THE PROLETARIAT OF ALL LANDS!

Overhead planes zoomed, in the streets bands played, flags flew. Sometimes that great rumbling cheer of the Red Army men began in the front ranks of a unit of troops and gathered volume as succeeding ranks joined in for blocks, until the whole of Moscow seemed filled with a mighty masculine rolling baritone, a human rumble of mounting rhythm and power like nothing else I have ever heard.

Americans who had been in residence in Moscow for several years and had seen a number of November Seventh and May Day celebrations, told me that almost always something went wrong right in front of Stalin. The year before I was there, they said that the largest of the Soviet jumbo tanks, one of the showpieces of the parade, conked out in front of Lenin's tomb. The roaring armored tank came speeding into the Red Square with a great rumbling clatter, gun turrets swirling—then sputtered, backfired, gasped and stalled, dead in front of Stalin! The rest of the parade had to circle around the moribund tank, stuck there until a number of little tanks pulled it away. Emma said she was sure the captain of this tank "*sedit*" the rest of his life.

The May Day on which I saw the parade, a similar thing happened to another piece of military equipment. All the papers had been heralding the new streamlined Soviet fieldpieces the Red Cavalry would display—long sleek guns that could shoot a great distance. When the Parade Marshall wished especially to accent something in the line of march, the rest of the parade would be temporarily halted at the entrance to the Square. This time, while the remaining units were held back, proudly into the Square, drawn by four beautiful white horses, with an arrow-straight driver mounted on the swivel gun carriage, came the longest, sleekest, steel-grey cannon I have ever seen, that looked as though it could shoot at lightning speed for miles. The driver sat up straighter than ever as his handsome piece of field artillery approached the dictators of the Soviet Union. Nearing Lenin's tomb, even the horses seemed to sense that they were passing Stalin, Kalinin and Molitov, for they pulled steadily and proudly ahead to cross the Square. But without the gun! Just in front of the great dignitaries, the gun became detached from the gun carriage on which the driver was riding, and the nose of the artillery piece on its two detached wheels swooped down to the cobblestones. The proud soldier drove on unawares, leaving his deserted fieldpiece behind him in the middle of the Square. The groans of consternation and the cries of the crowd, the soldier thought were cheers, as out of Red Square he disappeared, never looking back—with no gun at all following him.

"*Oni sedit*," Emma said when she heard about it. "He's in jail for sure."

From within the Kremlin gates, horses came shortly to drag the sleek left-lonesome cannon away in disgrace as the rest of the parade swirled around it. The incident tickled most Muscovites. Whether Stalin was amused or not, I don't know.

But I rather expect the masters of the Kremlin laughed at these contretemps, too, for most Russians seemed to have a great sense of humor. Certainly, they told an infinite number of jokes and humorous anecdotes on themselves and the Soviet state. Russian Jews then had a number of jokes about Trotsky which would sound, were a non-Jew to tell them, not only anti-Soviet but anti-Semitic as well. And concerning the masters of the Kremlin on the Red Square reviewing stand at May Day atop Lenin's tomb, there was a macabre saying that went, "The men who look at parades from Lenin's tomb, when they go to be buried themselves, will have a fine funeral with a motor hearse and miles of limousines; lesser bureaucrats will just have a horse-drawn hearse and their mourners will march on foot behind the coffin; but if you're an ordinary worker—you walk to the cemetery and bury yourself."

Soviet citizens, like American Negroes, often had a rather grim sense of humor. I remember in a colored paper once, after the Detroit race riots, there was a cartoon showing a little white boy displaying to another little boy the hunting trophies on the wall of his father's den. There hung the head of an elk, a bear, a lion, a buffalo and a deer. Among these handsome trophies was the head of a Negro. Said the little boy, "My father got that one in Detroit."

There was an anecdote going around Moscow the spring I was there about an official delegation sent by the Kremlin to a distant mountain village in the Caucausus where no part of the Five Year Plan had been fulfilled and where nothing worked. The delegation from Moscow was to try to win the villagers over to socialism by peaceful methods. When the commissars arrived, the villagers greeted them with open arms and said, "We want to show you that you are wrong if you say that we have nothing here that works. Come with us to the public square!" They led the commissars to the village green and when they were standing in front of an old war trophy of the Crimean War—a cannon in the middle of the square—the villagers said, "See, this works!" *Bang!* They blew the commissars off the face of the earth! When word got back to the Kremlin, Stalin said, "Those stupid jackasses should have been liquidated!" So the village was given the Order of the Red Banner.

Concerning the editorial blessings showered by *Pravda* and *Izvestia* on the shock brigade workers who overfulfilled their Five Year quotas, they said the Kremlin had a slogan, "Never shock a shock worker by shocking him into a promotion where he won't need to work so shocking hard." But the play on words in the original Russian, I gathered, was even more satirical. The double edge of wit is dulled in another language where overtones are not the same. But one of the slogans which Soviet citizens declared the Church had adopted in Russia, is just as ironic in English: "*Work for God with Bolshevik Tempo.*"

Then there was the one about the Muscovite who stepped on his own foot in a crowded street car and said, "Pardon me!"

Concerning the difficulty of getting seats for Chekov's plays at the Moscow Art Theater, since priority was given to the men and women in heavy industries, there was a current saying among the intelligentsia to the effect that, "Only workers can get seats to see intellectuals suffer."

One of my favorite laughs concerned a writer who went to a big department store that rainy spring to buy a pair of rubbers. He picked out the rubbers from the sample styles and sizes on the counter, went through all the complicated routine of going to the cashier, having his coupon torn out of his book and paying for the purchase, then taking his sales slip back to the counter where he was given an already wrapped package containing his rubbers. But when he got home with them, they were for two *left* feet.

Screamed the writer, "We've gone too far left now!"

## NATASHA'S BIG SCENE

DURING May Day week the servants in the New Moscow Hotel had a party, and I was invited. It was given by the maids, porters and cleaning women. I did not see there any of the other guests in the hotel, so I think I was the only resident invited. This I took as an amiable compliment. I once had been a hotel worker, too. So I felt related to the servants of the New Moscow Hotel and, although I had not told them about my work in the past, they must have felt related to me, so they invited me to their party.

It was held in the workers' quarters in the basement of the hotel, where crepe paper had been strung up for the occasion, and a table spread with cheese, black bread, vodka and kvass. There was a balalaika player, accordions, and dancing. Those on duty took time out to come to the party in their working clothes or uniforms, stamp out a few dance steps, then go back to work. As the evening wore on and the music got livelier and livelier, two or three buxom Russian girls from the country took to the floor, started clapping hands and singing old folks songs, and taking turns jogging out a rapid country jig all by themselves. Then maybe one would choose a man to jig until he became breathless facing her in a kind of rapid heel clicking songdance.

Farmer boy, better grab me, hey!
Before I fly like a pigeon—
Fly like a pigeon—
Fly like a pigeon away . . .

seemed to be the refrain of one of the songs a girl panted out as she danced. But it was this girl who grabbed the most men to dance with her. When she grabbed me, I jigged awhile, too, as everybody egged me on until I was out of breath.

The Russians have enormous energy for singing and dancing, and they must have kept this up until dawn in the basement of the New Moscow. But about two in the morning, I went upstairs to bed—and there was Natasha come to call. When I told Natasha I'd danced with the peasant servants from the country, she said, "Beaux gens, no? Such nice people, fine girls!" She was sincere. Although she herself had been born and educated in Moscow, in the theater she played peasant parts. She just liked peasants—and Negroes.

I never knew why the desk clerk or the floormaid let Natasha into my room when I was away. They never let anyone else in, and what Natasha told them, I don't know. I suppose she was like me—if she decided to get somewhere, or go someplace, she went. I have discovered in life that there are ways of getting almost anywhere you want to go, if you *really* want to go. You might have to squeeze through a knothole, humble yourself, or drink muddy tea from consumptive bowls or eat camel sausage, pass for Mexican, or take that *last* chance, but—well, if you really want to get there, that's the way it is. If you want to see the world, or eat steaks in fine restaurants with white tablecloths, write honest books, or get in to see your sweetheart, you do such things by taking a chance. Of course, a boom may fall and break your neck at any moment, your books may be barred from libraries, or the camel sausage may lead to a prescription of arsenic. It's a chance you take.

I'd told Natasha when I first met her that I was on my way home to America. She had told me that she had a husband. Nevertheless, as long as I remained in Moscow, she came to the hotel to see me. But the last time she visited the New Moscow, a few days before I departed, Natasha staged a big scene, created it and played it herself, and held the center of the stage for hours. She ran the gamut.

Hardly had she come into my room that night than she said, "I have told my husband all."

For lack of a better rejoinder, I said, "All of what?"

"About us," Natasha said.

"Why?" I demanded.

"Because I love my husband and want to be honest with him."

"Because you must want to hurt him," I said.

"No, *mais non*, because I love you *most*—and want you to stay here. I can get divorced."

"I don't think you're sensible," I said. "I'm going home."

"No! Please! No! You can write scenarios, work with Meyerhold, lecture at the university." Then she began to cry.

Six months anywhere is enough to create complications, I thought to myself, especially with women.

"If you have to go," she said, "then take me with you."

"Natasha, I can't take you with me to America."

There were enough troubles just trying to earn a living in the land of Jim Crow without having a white wife on my hands. My father had married a German woman in Mexico, but I had no idea of marrying a Russian in Moscow unless I were intending to stay in the Soviet Union. And to take one back to America with me!

"But I don't really want to go to America," Natasha wailed. "*I just want you to stay here.*"

There were, I knew, many girls in the Soviet Union who did their best to marry a foreigner, hoping in that way to be able to visit abroad or, in some cases, to escape a political system they did not relish. Russian women in Tashkent were always chasing Powers with that intent in mind. But Natasha seemed to possess a deep attachment for her own land and to have only admiration for the Soviet system. She was just in love, that's all, she said.

"I have to go home," I said. "This is not my country, and I *have* to go home."

"If you loved me you'd stay," wailed Natasha. "But you don't love me. *C'est moi qui t'aime. Je t'aime! Je t'aime!* But you don't love me. No, you don't! You don't! You don't. . . ."

Her lamentations filled the room, filled the hotel, filled the night. Accustomed to robust, though small, parts in large theaters, she had a good strong voice. She shook the New Moscow Hotel in English, French and Russian. Finally when her breath and her emotions were exhausted, she departed without so much as a kiss.

## HECTIC FINALE

MY last weeks in Moscow were hectic ones—trying to get a ticket to the Far East, trying to collect the remaining monies due me in various editorial offices, and rounding up final visas and permissions to get off. Besides all this, I was getting letters from home that my stepfather had wandered off again and my mother and teen-age brother were in dire need. I cabled my publishers in New York to turn over to my mother whatever royalties I might have coming. This was the money I had intended to use in China and Japan. But I determined to go to the Orient anyway—with less than a hundred American dollars in my billfold. At least I could use rubles as far as Peking. But just before I was to leave, I read where the Japanese had cut the Chinese Eastern Railway line at the Siberian border. Said the *Moscow Daily News* of June second:

> The keys of the switches of the line connecting the railways were seized from the chief of Pogranichnaya Station. The line was blocked and a barrier erected at the head to obstruct the movement of trains.

The next day I was informed at Intourist that I could no longer obtain a through ticket to any point in China. Intourist now had a directive permitting them to sell tickets only on the Russian Trans-Siberian itself, with no connections via the Chinese Eastern. I was told I might, of course, go to China by way of Japan, and that I could buy a ticket in rubles to Vladivostok, thence by boat to a Japanese port. Beyond that I would have to pay my transportation in dollars. My dream of seeing Peking vanished. Now a whole new series of ticket reservations had to be made. It had taken three months to achieve the point where I could leave Moscow for China—now the Japanese had cut the railroad! So I started the nerve-wracking ordeal of trying to get, instead of a ticket to Peking and Shanghai, one to Vladivostok, plus difficult Foreign Office permissions to pass through that highly guarded military port. I must say, in this effort, Oumansky was of great help. Both the permissions and the tickets were finally secured from Moscow to Japan.

Meanwhile, I got a severe toothache. Almost everywhere I have ever been in the world, I've had to go to a dentist. In Calabar, on the African coast, I once had a tooth pulled by a French dentist who said he was Gauguin's cousin, but who had no anesthesia in his office, so he simply called a little barefooted African boy to hold a glass of water, grabbed his pliers, and pulled. In Haiti, I had a tooth filled by a dentist who neglected to treat the nerve. In the middle of the night the filling started hitting the nerve like a trip hammer. I went to sit on his doorstep until daylight when he woke up and pulled the tooth out. Now in Moscow an old cavity began to hurt like fury. I went to the Writers Union and asked them to recommend a dentist. They gave me a slip and sent me to a neat office near the Pushkin Statue. The dentist filled my tooth immediately and requested that I come back the next day to polish the filling. I asked him how much would it be. He looked at me in astonishment and said, "Nothing. You brought your Writers Union slip."

I was amazed. It was the first time anywhere a dentist had not charged me a small fortune. So, in the Soviet Union, a writer, or any worker, could have his dental work done for nothing! This I have never forgotten. Elsewhere I have sometimes had to go without a much-needed new suit to have my teeth fixed. Moscow dental customs, the unveiling of the harem women in Turkestan, and the disappearance of the color line throughout Soviet Asia, are the three achievements I remember best of the whole USSR. A free dental filling seemed to me a minor miracle.

But then many things were happening in the Soviet Union that I had never seen happen elsewhere. For example, there had just been held in Moscow the First Conference of Prostitutes-Become-Workers. This unusual gathering gave out statistics which state that just before the Tzar fell, there were forty thousand prostitutes in St. Petersburg and almost as many in Moscow. But now in Moscow there were only about four hundred. As far as I could tell these four hundred were invisible. The old organized vice rings of pimps, procurers and brothel keepers had entirely disappeared, along with the infamous Yellow Ticket, the card that prostitutes once carried. That ticket, so this conference of reformed women said, had now been turned into a Trade Union Card for most of the women of sin, since all who wished had jobs, and a special effort was being made by the government to rehabilitate those who needed medical or social aid.

In Moscow, I had met only one woman whom I thought might formerly have been a prostitute. I had night-lifed in many seaports as a sailor, and I recognized her as the type of higher-priced, delicately perfumed, well-dressed but demurely bold hustler to be found in the politer bars from Hamburg to Naples, Le Havre to Havana. This woman in Moscow had been the recent mistress of a tough American old-line labor organizer turned Communist. But now that he had gone back home, she was looking for another lover. Meanwhile, having a good clerical job, she no longer needed to sell her favors, but was free to give them away generously to any man who caught her fancy. Of course, she would accept gifts—soap, stockings, foreign lipstick—since such items of decent quality were almost impossible to purchase. But she herself was not now for sale as I believe she once had been. Every morning she went to work, and her little boy was a sturdy Young Pioneer, not neglected as he might have been in the old days when his mother had to haunt the bars all night in search of a livelihood.

One of my problems upon leaving Moscow was what to do with all the stuff I had accumulated—gifts from one end of the country to the other, books, and manuscripts of poems—since in continuing around the world, I wanted to travel light. All of my books by Negro writers I gave to the Foreign Library in Moscow. I gave to various friends my excess gifts. The remains of my soap and toilet paper I gave to particularly favored friends like the Carmons, Emma and Natasha before she staged her big scene. My camera I gave to the schoolboy son of the woman I thought had led a sinful life. It had given me good service and I had taken dozens of excellent pictures of Koestler, Nichan, Powers, Nina Zaratelli and the workers and peasants of Central Asia. I kept my typewriter, however, and a copy of Thomas Mann's *The Magic Mountain* to read across Siberia. But the Russians are a sweet gift-giving people, and I hadn't counted on the numerous farewell presents they were going to give me before I went away. It turned out in the end that I got on the train as loaded down as ever.

A few nights before I left Moscow, Fred and Ethel Ellis gave a farewell party for me. The Ellises were perhaps the most popular young American couple in Moscow then, liked by both left- and right-wingers among the American colony in the city. Living in the heart of the capital as they did, folks were always in and out of their big hotel room. Fred was, I believe, a cartoonist for the Moscow paper, *Trud*, an organ of the Central Trade Unions, and also, I think, sent drawings to the New York *Daily Worker*. Ethel, as I recall, did nothing except take care of her family. Fred was a sleepy-looking, amiable fellow, and Ethel a lively, sparkling little woman. Energetically she rounded up all my friends, the Carmons, and the Chens, Emma, the American journalists, the last three Negroes of the movie group—Rudd, Patterson, and Smith—and Natasha, and gave me a lively send-off indeed. It was marred only by some woman resident of the hotel knocking on the door at two A.M. and gasping in various languages, "Help! I've got a fishbone in my throat."

Everybody stopped talking and dancing to get the fishbone out of the strange woman's throat. Then the fun continued. Natasha was in a not very festive humor, so she left without saying goodbye before the party was over. Charlie Ashleigh—whom everybody called poor Charlie (he was going to the dogs)—became very intoxicated and passed out, occupying the Ellis boy's bed. This created a situation because, when about three A.M. Emma announced that she could no longer stay on her feet, either, the Ellises said, "Emma could stay here, but we can't get Charlie up. Somebody will have to take Emma home. There's no place for her to sleep."

Since Emma was colored and I was colored, and there were no other colored people left at the party, my race pride demanded that I take Emma home. (I did not want her to "disgrace the race.") She lived miles across Moscow over by the station! She was then about sixty years old, stout and heavy on her legs. Emma did manage, however, to get down the stairs with my support and navigate a block or two as we sought in vain a passing bus. But at the sudden sight of a *droski*, Emma cried, "I can't make! I can't, Langston," and started to sink downward. It cost me eighty rubles to take Emma home in a cab. But, as we jogged along, the cool spring air quickly revived her and she started telling me the latest Moscow gossip. She also asked me to give her regards to Harlem when I got home.

## TRANS-SIBERIAN EXPRESS

ON those days when the Trans-Siberian Express leaves Moscow for the Far East, the atmosphere at the station is almost like that of a New York pier when a big liner is sailing. Crowds come to see friends off, to jam the coaches, to laugh and talk and weep. And when the train, finally emptied of visitors, pulls away, cheers, cries and screams follow it from the station. Hats and handkerchiefs are waved. Some people run all the way to the end of the platform trying to keep up with the moving windows in which their relatives or friends are framed as the coaches gather speed. Then the station is gone. Moscow is retreating. The gray houses, tall apartments, Kremlin towers and the bulbs of the Greek Orthodox Churches recede back, back, backwards to give way to wooden houses and mud streets, rustic suburbs, then patches of open country, log *dachas*, farms, forests of birch and pine, and open fields. Then the coaches are quiet, except for the clicking of rails, as the passengers sink into their compartments and catch their breath.

That is the way it was on the day I started home in the spring of 1933 by way of the Orient. Twenty or thirty people had come to see me off—Russians and Negroes, actors and writers and representatives of Meschrabpom, Lydia Filatova and the two film translators, Doris Nemirova and Lydia Mirseva, who had gone through the movie days with me; Muscovites and Americans all waving as the long train pulled away from the Moscow station and I hung out the window waving back. When at last I sank down in the seat I found myself sharing with a lone Red Army man, I took a deep breath, happy at last to be headed home. I lay back comfortably in a corner to relax, for I was very tired. I was glad the Red Army man sharing the compartment with me was tired, too, and a little drunk from the vodka he and his friends had been drinking to their parting. He was more sleepy than talkative. Before the train got outside the city, this soldier had settled into his corner and gone to sleep. I sat looking out the window, thinking how wonderful it was to be going to Japan, China, then home, and how one phase of my existence had ended and a new one would be beginning. At least, I thought one phase had ended. But I was wrong. Just as the train began to speed through the spring-time peace and quiet of the green fields in the late afternoon sunlight, the door of my compartment burst open—and there stood Natasha.

"Where did you come from?" was all I could say.

She burst out laughing, and laughed for a very long time. Then she came in, threw her arms around me and said, "I am going to Vladivostok with you."

"Great day in the morning!" I must have looked very distressed. She said, "Don't you want me to go?"

I said, "It will cost you a fortune."

She laughed, "I don't care. I've taken all the money I've saved. Since I can't go to America with you, I'm going right to the boat— right to the edge of my own land, to the Pacific—as far as I can go with you." I was so astonished that I guess I didn't say anything encouraging because Natasha began to look hurt. Then she repeated, "Don't you want me to go?"

I said, "I don't think you should. What about your husband?"

She repeated, "Don't you want me to go?"

I said, "No, I don't believe you should go." Thinking all the while of ten days of Natasha, the whole way to Siberia! Great day, no! All the peace and happiness and freedom of the first half hour of that train ride gone!

"Then you don't want me to go with you," Natasha said, and she began to cry. Big tears rolled down her cheeks, then sobs came. Another scene! She put her head in my lap and wept aloud. But the Red Army man in his corner slept on. And the fresh green forests and the wide green fields kept gliding backwards outside the window. About that time the train porter knocked on the compartment door and said the dining car was open.

"Natasha, don't cry. Sit up," I pleaded. "Come on, let's go in the diner and get some tea."

Russians under almost any circumstances, I had learned, will drink tea. Natasha stopped crying, wiped her eyes, stood up and began to powder her face in the mirror.

"We can't talk in here, anyhow," I said, "we'll wake up that army officer."

"I don't want to talk any more," she choked. "You don't want me to go with you."

But when the tea came, she did talk. We sat there at the table for two or three hours as the train rolled ahead in the twilight. She ate a little dinner. And at some tiny village station where the engine stopped for water about nine o'clock, she got off in the darkness to return to Moscow.

I had missed Natasha in the crowd at the station, among all the other friends who came to see me leave. But I did not miss her badly enough to wish that she were on the train with me. Yet, when she got off alone in the dark, I felt unkind, ungallant, embarrassed and unhappy. Natasha probably had to sit in that dreary little wayside depot all night waiting for a train back to the capital, I thought, and maybe when the train came, it would be crowded and she could not get on it. I felt very sad, very bad—yet very glad she didn't go any further.

## TEN DAYS TO VLADIVOSTOK

NATASHA left behind her on the train a little box of gifts, including a beautiful old Russian cashmere shawl for my mother. And at the bottom of her box was a little red-covered notebook, all of its pages blank except the last one. On this page she had written, "Consolez-vous—s'il y a un peche, c'est mon peche." Then in the very corner, quite small: "Aimez moi."

I didn't feel very happy as I put the little notebook back in the box, so I picked up The Magic Mountain and started to read. But before I had read a page, I went to sleep.

The next morning we were rolling through the Black Earth regions of rich farm lands. We crossed the Volga, then over the Ural

Mountains into Asia. At stations on the vast steppes, peasant women in white headcloths sold fermented mare's milk, sour pickles and hot cabbage rolls. Cities passed like Ekaterinburg and Tiumen on the Tura River, and Omsk where the Fifth Time Zone begins, Tartarskaya and Novosibirsk where the new Turksik Railroad from Tashkent meets the Trans-Siberian. Then came Krassnoyarsk founded in 1628, and Irkutsk, a center for furs and gold near Lake Baikal whose cold blue waters shimmered in the Siberian sun. Here began the Soviet Far East sparsely populated by Russians, Ukranians, Koreans and Chinese, but teeming with reindeer, elk, wolves, foxes, ermine, sable and otter. Then came Khabarosk on the Amur River, and finally Vladivostok on the Bay of the Golden Horn, the terminus of the longest railroad in the world, The Trans-Siberian, fifty-five hundred miles in length.

On my train, but not traveling first class, I found the actors of the Buryat-Mongolian musical troup that had so delighted Moscow theater audiences that spring. They knew almost no Russian, so we could not talk together, but I drank tea with them a few times on the way to the Mongolian border where they were to take buses, or maybe camels, to get home. All through Siberia I saw camels outside the stations, and also those long-maned, funny, stumpy little Siberian ponies—very strong and swift, I was told. I saw few automobiles. People rode ponies or camels. These ships of the desert, whom I'd thought of as being incapable of standing Siberian winters, would rise from their wobbly knees in the railroad yards loaded down with lumber or zinc pipes, and hump themselves over the horizon to distant constructions rising in the steppes. I wondered what the camel population of the Soviet Union was. Including Turkestan, it must run into the millions.

As far as I could learn, the most distinguished passenger on my train was a Hollander, Professor Dr. J. Rahder, a famous authority on obscure Oriental languages, their history, roots and derivations. Dr. Rahder was heading for Mongolia to do further work there on the verb-endings of some language of which I had never even heard. He had forgotten all his baggage except his brief case—completely forgotten it in changing trains in Warsaw—and so had nothing with him but paper and pencils, not even a change of clothing for the trip across the Soviet Union. But in Poland he had bought two enormous wicker baskets full of oranges and lemons and a case of bottled water, and on the trip drank nothing but this water and fruit juices, for fear that even Russian tea might be germ-laden. Dr. Rahder, a big fleshy man, was in a merry mood and did not seem to mind the loss of his bags. He was looking forward with excitement to once more delving into a comparatively unknown and scarcely annotated language.

It seems that from the university at Leyden, Rahder went every summer to the Far East for purposes of study. He had crossed on the Trans-Siberian a dozen or more times, so the trip was no novelty to him. On the train he occupied himself correcting a draft of his annotated translation of the *Gukansho* written about 1220 by the Buddhist abbot, Fujiwara Jien. This, he said, was one of the earliest attempts in the East to interpret and *comment* upon, not merely to *record*, the past. It was a sort of philosophy of history as derived from the then-known records of India, China and Japan. A few years later Rahder's translation of Jien was published in English in several sections in *Acta Orientalia* and reprints were sent to me, as he had promised they would be. Professor Dr. J. Rahder might forget his clothes but no small detail of his work; not even a casual promise to send the *Gukansho* to a stranger he met on the Trans-Siberian, was forgotten.

Many of the people on the train got off before it came to Irkutsk. There Rahder and the Buryat-Mongolian actors of Ulan-Bator left us, as did a young Russian who had gone to Moscow to get married and was taking his bride back to a forest reserve for sables in the Barguzinian Taiga far across Lake Baikal. Several of the coaches of the train had been dropped and, by the time we got Khabarovsk on the Amur River where Japanese speedboats lurked, my coach was almost empty. There were very few passengers left on the train when we got to Vladivostok, the end of the line.

A gray fortress of a town edging the water at the foot of a series of scraggly hills, Vladivostok, dismal, damp, depressing and dirty, looked like the last outpost of a shabby frontier. The hotel was unattractive and the tariff very high. Dinner consisted of plain boiled potatoes, red cabbage, tea and the toughest steak I've ever tried to chew—but at least I could stick a fork in the gravy. There seemed to be in town almost nothing to see worth the trouble. Since much of the area was marked off limits to the casual stroller, I contented myself walking mostly up and down Lenin Street, where I saw newspapers in Japanese and Chinese on the kiosks, and Chinese lychee nuts on street-corner stands. In the cobbled roadway of a main street near the curb a man who looked as if he might be Chinese lay quite stiff and dead. No one seemed to pay him any mind. People simply walked around his body as they passed.

I was glad the next day to get on the boat sailing for Korea and Japan. In Vladivostok I had been unable to find anything amusing to do with the bulging pocket full of rubles I had left. Since rubles would be of no value in any other country in the world, I finally gave them all to the maid at the hotel.

# 6

# COLOR AROUND
# THE GLOBE

**MYSELF AND TWO AUSTRALIANS**

THERE was on the boat to Japan an Australian shopkeeper and his sister making a trip around the world. They were pleasant middle-class people, and the only persons on board who spoke English. The chubby Japanese captain had us at his table for meals, but he knew only a half-dozen English words, and his Russian was almost inunderstandable, so conversation was limited. Yet the captain seemed to like us, and he invited the Australian male and myself to visit his favorite Geisha house with him in Kyoto where he lived. Naturally, we accepted the invitation.

We stopped for a day at Seishin in Korea, a pretty little town surrounded by hills sloping down to the water. There I saw quaint old sages in tall white hats like single-deck pagodas, made of what looked like silk, with very high crowns and round white brims, with a white cord hanging beneath their chins. A little Korean boy in a European jacket and knickers guided the Australian and me about and offered to take us to a house of prostitution, but we didn't want to go. We walked all over Seishin instead and up into the hills. Two men the little boy said were Japanese (he knew simple English words like "American," "Russian," "Japanese" and "money") followed us everywhere we went, even up the steep hillsides, and did not try to hide themselves, but were always a dozen or so yards behind. They never spoke to us as they trailed us all day. At the dockside we paid off our little boy and waved goodbye to the men, who looked as blank as ever, as if they did not see us wave.

The next day we crossed the Sea of Japan to steam through a series of the prettiest, greenest, hilly little islands I have ever seen, with pagodalike red-roofed temples high among the fir trees. It was summer, warm and bright and sunny, and the sea blue-white with tiny little wavelets breaking on its surface, so I didn't read Thomas Mann, but instead leaned on the rail and looked at the sea. Late one afternoon we were at Tsuruga on the western coast of Honsu, Japan's main island.

We were driven to a charming inn where guests took off their shoes at the door, but where there was one wing with European furnishings, chairs and beds on legs for Occidental travelers. Since the Australians and I both wished to save money, we two men took a room together with two beds, and his sister took a single room. There was a bath house somewhere in the backyard, with a big wooden tub in the center, which a little Japanese maid filled. She came back with buckets of fresh water while you were bathing and stood there until you had finished, when she offered to dry you off with an enormous towel.

In the afternoon the police visited us, sitting cross-legged on the floor in the Japanese living room where there were no chairs, so we sat cross-legged too, as they inspected our papers and asked us why we had been in Russia, how long, and for what good reason. They were very polite and did not linger, but as one questioned us the other took down everything we said. After that we had a very attractively served dinner of fish and rice and bits of meat in bean curds and vegetables and tea. The next day we caught the train for Kyoto and by late afternoon we were in the oldest and most beautiful of Japanese cities. There our boat captain came promptly in the evening to the Kyoto Hotel as he had promised, to take us to see the night life of the town, beginning with the geishas.

The Australian thought the geishas were prostitutes. But I assured him that I had heard they definitely were not, and should not be treated as such. I did not want my companion to commit a faux pas and embarras me. He didn't. Both of us sat through several hours at the geisha house in squat-legged silence, as the Japanese captain seemed to glow with enjoyment. Three very delicate and prettily kimonoed little girls were shooed gracefully into our large, airy private room which was covered with mats on the floor. Tea things were brought, and the girls played three-stringed *samisens* and zitherlike instruments. On their knees, they poured tea charmingly. Then they talked with the captain, and chattered and smiled shyly at us, and played and sang in high whining tones with lacey little runs and ripples, looking down most of the time at their instruments while the chubby old captain nodded and smiled at the Australian and myself. There was nothing at all sensuous or wild or even mildly flirtatious about the evening. It was quite charming and quiet and—for the two of us from America and Australia—most conducive to sleep after the first half hour. But the captain and the girls were too polite to appear to notice if we nodded over our tea.

It was perhaps eleven o'clock before the captain indicated that we should go. The brightly lighted streets of Kyoto looked like a child's dream of a marionette theater fair—very clean, very pretty, and very impersonal—and *Japanese* rather than really Oriental—none of Samarkand's turquoise tiles, minarets, or the smell of musk and melons and dirt. This time the captain walked jauntily ahead of us on the narrow sidewalks, and I could tell by the way he walked that he was taking us to a bordello.

"At last!" said the Australian.

Here there were a dozen brightly kimonoed girls, each with an elaborate, towering hair-do, full of colored pins and combs. Each had her own little wooden headrest for working purposes, so that her intricately dressed hair would not touch the mat on which she lay. Customers were not to touch their hair, either, so these little ladies, who knew quite a bit of English, warned us. I learned that hairdressing in Japan took most of the day, and good hairdressers charged well for their attention. The captain seemed to know all the girls, and proceeded to indicate to us which ones might give an Englishman or an American the best service. The girls themselves were not forward in the manner of many Western prostitutes. They simply fluttered around swaying like trees and waving silken fans, until someone in the room chose one of them. Then she picked up her wooden headrest and disappeared behind a sliding screen.

There were a few gay young blades sitting around on mats with the girls drinking saki, black kimonoed youths who looked as if they might be students, plus one or two middle-aged men less robust than our captain, quietly squatting in a corner eying the possibilities. Everything was very subdued and dignified, as if a joint Y.M.-Y.W.C.A. committee meeting were about to be held. The night life of Kyoto was certainly not rowdy—or else the captain was putting his best foot forward for the sake of foreign guests. But, to cap the evening, he insisted on treating each of us to a girl at his expense.

Kyoto, founded in the year 794, was for a thousand years the capital of the Japanese Empire. So I saw the Park of the Old Imperial Palace and, with the Australian and his sister, I tramped up Tea Pot Lane to the Falling Water Shrine. The parks and temples of Kyoto are visually charming, but somehow to me the city seemed as impersonal as a Technicolor movie.

The next day I saw Fujiyama from the windows of as modern an observation car as I've ever ridden in. On the swift express to Tokyo there was an hour-long view of various aspects of its lovely white crest floating above the clouds. Before reaching Tokyo, I had made up my mind—come what may, and even if I went broke doing it—to stay at the much-talked-of Imperial Hotel built by Frank Lloyd Wright. But my Australian friends preferred a less expensive place.

"The Imperial Hotel," I said to the taxi driver, outside the Tokyo station. So the Australians and I parted company there, and I have never seen them since. They were a couple of amiable ships that passed my way—and went theirs—pleasantly.

## TEA IN JAPAN

AT the Imperial Hotel I was given a cream and beige room with deep rugs, a wide soft bed and a big bath. It was on the first floor just off the lobby and, at the rate of exchange then, did not cost very much. It was good to rest in a clean attractive place and not have to do anything, not take a note on any subject, nor look at any factories or temples. The first few days in Tokyo I did nothing except what I wanted to do—which was nothing. Then I went to the Tsukiji Theater.

When I asked the desk clerk how to get to the Tsukiji, he said, "But, sir, why do you want to go there? What you must see is the Kabuki."

I replied that I intended to see the Kabuki. But I also wanted to see the Tsukiji where *Porgy* had been performed, and other foreign plays. I did not realize that the Tsukiji was under a political cloud. But I learned later that the whole cast of one of its plays had been imprisoned, and that it was considered a center of left-wing activities, pacifist, and opposed to the current Japanese invasion of China. The clerk told me how to get to the Tsukiji, but he no doubt also told the police where I was going.

I saw a play by a contemporary Japanese writer about a strike of fishermen in feudal days—one of the few Tsukiji plays not modern in setting. But it was performed in the naturalistic manner of the West, not stylized as traditional Japanese plays are. I thought it an excellent production, very well acted in conventional proscenium style, but nowhere nearly as exciting as Meyerhold or Tairov or Oplopkov in Moscow. The reception the cast gave me, however, was exciting. From Moscow, Seki Sano, a former director of the Tsukiji Theater, had written that I was on my way to Japan, so when I went backstage after a performance, the actors greeted me with open arms. It was as if Eugene O'Neill or George Bernard Shaw had walked into the theater. As soon as I rather timidly announced myself to the first actor I saw in make-up backstage, he gave the alarm, and all the other actors and technicians poured onto the stage. Although only a few spoke English, I was warmly welcomed as the first Negro writer to visit their theater, and everybody wanted to drag me off someplace for food and drink. But not knowing who any of them were, nor even how most of them looked without make-up, I decided to accept their hospitality another day. So after talking with them for half an hour, I returned to my hotel. But before I left, I found out that the man who, all during the performance, had sat at a lighted desk at the back of the theater, with a script of the play before him, was not a prompter or a director. He was a police censor. If the actors varied one word from the approved script, he had the right to ring down the curtain for the evening.

The next day several Japanese writers and actors, artists and news-papermen came to see me at the Imperial Hotel. From then on for the next two weeks my time was not my own. I was interviewed, photographed, shown the town, the temples, the theaters, the parks, the university; wined, dined and entertained most interestingly but energetically, but finally to the point where I wished I'd remained anonymous a little longer. It would have been so agreeable, after my busy Moscow days, just to loaf awhile. But Japanese hospitality was most gracious. And it was, of course, interesting to me to see how Tokyo's people lived and worked, though my contacts were limited largely to the arts. Some of my poems already had been translated and published in a Japanese literary magazine and my picture had ap-peared on the cover—a drawing made from a photograph—in which I appeared quite Japanese, with my eyes slanting a bit. The translations of my Harlem blues poems, so I was told, were quite well done and attracted considerable attention in Tokyo. Blues were not unknown in Japan. "The St. Louis Blues," W. C. Handy's classic, was very popu-lar. The words had been translated into Japanese—"I hate to see de evenin' sun go down,"—and records of it were whirling on Tokyo jukeboxes. The Tokyo jazz bands, with a number of Filipino musi-cians in them, played good jazz.

Meanwhile, the Pan Pacific Club, composed of both Japanese and foreigners, invited me to their monthly luncheon, and asked me to make a speech. A baron in a cutaway coat came in person to invite me, having learned of my presence from the press. I accepted and found myself sitting on the dais next to the wife of one of our Ameri-can consular officials. She was a white woman from St. Louis, a town where color lines were strict and where, only a few years before, I had been refused a soft drink at the soda fountain in the train sheds of the Union Station. When I lectured there, no place downtown would serve a Negro food. I did not have very pleasant memories of race relations in St. Louis, so I thought I would use those memories as the theme for my luncheon talk that day. The consular wife preceded me in addressing the gathering, and told of her delight over the Japanese tea ceremony in what seemed to me a rather patronizing manner—as if she were amazed that the Japanese possessed such graces— exclaiming how wonderful it was for an American to know that they could so tastefully arrange flowers and pour tea. I was a little embarrassed at her talk and the provincialism behind it. But, of course, I did not say so when I rose to speak.

I complimented her on her subject as I reminded our largely Japanese audience that American freedom had begun at a tea party, the Boston Tea Party. Then I proceeded to say that I found it quite wonderful to be sitting beside a fellow American in Tokyo at a public luncheon because in St. Louis, her home, it would hardly be possible for white and colored people such as myself on the one hand, and herself on the other, to dine together at any of the leading clubs or hotels. This I found to be one of the charms of Japan which I, as an American wished to mention as an additional tribute to the beautiful compliment my colleague had paid the tea ceremony. I then complimented the Japanese people on being the only noncolonial nation in the Far East, having their own independent sovereign government. I hoped, however, that they would not make the old mistakes of the West and, like England, France, Italy and Germany, attempt to take over other people's lands or make colonials of others.

"How wonderful," I said, "it would be if all the colonies and color lines in the world were wiped out. Meanwhile, I am glad that Japan is able to enjoy her ceremonial tea without the unwelcome intrusion of the imperialist powers of the West who brought the color line to Africa and Asia."

Most of the people in the room were colored, so they applauded me for a long time after I sat down. Meanwhile, the American lady on my left whispered, "You did not speak very well of your country."

"I love my country, but you and I both know what St. Louis is like," I said. "We couldn't even drink tea together in a public place there."

When the luncheon was over the lady left without bidding me goodbye. I was sorry I'd mentioned tea. I wonder if she really thought I wanted to drink tea with her. I hope she didn't misunderstand. I was simply trying to drive home in terms of the Japanese tea ceremony —designed to illustrate the beauty of friendship—an impersonal point about provincialism in St. Louis.

## WATERMELON FROM THE YANGTZE

I FOUND the Kabuki Theater in Tokyo quite wonderful. An enormous state theater, the most famous theater in the Orient, its seats were expensive and usually sold out well in advance. It was my good fortune to go as the guest of a Japanese professor of English literature, and his wife, who knew some of the actors. The actors in the theater, in traditional Oriental fashion, were all men, some of them very famous and very old, but still playing the parts of young girls. Age and sex did not seem to matter to Japanese audiences as Kabuki acting was largely stylized, not naturalistic. One of the male stars whom I saw perform had a double chin, but he was playing a youthful princess.

The platform of the Kabuki is much longer and wider than the stages of American or European theaters. It is rather like a very long panel, and its sets, like Japanese prints, are stunning indeed. There was a runway from the balcony to the stage down which in one scene a Shogun rode a dashing horse onto the stage. The drama which I saw began at four o'clock in the afternoon and ran a very long time, with the addition of two other plays with *kiyomoto* music, as afterpieces. Since performances lasted for hours, the hippodromelike building housing the Kabuki had at least a dozen restaurants and tearooms on various levels. Patrons could put in an order before an act, and return to dine at the next intermission. There was an eel room, a European room, a Chinese restaurant, a buckwheat dining room, and several cafés with distinct styles of cooking and serving—the *sushi*, *benmatsu* and *shiruko*. There were fruit nooks, tea parlors, tobacco stands and smoking rooms, a barbershop, a photographer's studio, a playroom for children, and an emergency room with a nurse in attendance. I have never anywhere in the world seen so well-equipped a theater.

In Shanghai, a few weeks later, I found no such playhouses as the Kabuki with high social, artistic and governmental status. But I saw some exciting performances in China with ancient warriors fighting across the stage in slow-motion pantomime, and dragonesque actors lifting brocaded legs to deliver shrill soliloquies on one foot.

Speeches were punctuated by cymbals and clanging gongs. It was summer, so boys went up and down the aisles tossing hot towels to patrons to wipe their sweating faces. Chinese theaters were very noisy. But sometimes the whole audience would be quiet, listening to a brief bit of famous thousand-year-old poetry, but eating sunflower seed and calling for hot towels again as soon as the Chinese "to be or not to be" was over.

I reached the international city of Shanghai in July, with the sun beating down on the Bund, the harbor full of Chinese junks, foreign liners and warships from all over the world. It was hot as blazes. I didn't know a soul in the city. But hardly had I climbed into a rickshaw than I saw riding in another along the Bund a Negro who looked exactly like a Harlemite. I stood up in my rickshaw and yelled, "Hey, man!"

He stood up in his rickshaw and yelled, "What ya sayin'?" We passed each other in the crowded street, and I never saw him again.

The rickshaw man took me to a little Chinese-owned but European-style hotel in the International Settlement not far from the post office. There the rates were reasonable and the room clean. But the hotel had no restaurant, and I had been warned about both color lines in public places and unclean food in Shanghai. But when I stepped from the door of my hotel into the busy street in the late afternoon, I saw a vendor selling the reddest of red-hearted watermelons I've ever seen. They were on an uncovered cart in the hot dusty street and the vendor was shooing flies away with a paper fan. I bought a piece of his melon and it was delicious, so I ate another piece. Later, I learned that I should never eat watermelon in Shanghai, nor any fresh fruits or green salads that were not first washed in some sort of antiseptic solution. Careless eating could be very dangerous, foreigners said, since the Chinese used human manure for fertilizer. As to watermelon, well, they threw stillborn babies by the hundreds into the Yangtze River every year, I was told. It was down this death-polluted river that junks brought the red-hearted watermelons to Shanghai. Unscrupulous vendors, in order to make their melons bring higher prices on the Shanghai market, where they were sold by the pound, put the melons into rope nets and sunk them in the filthy waters of the Yangtze, dragging them behind their boats for miles on the way to the market, so that the melons would soak up this water and thus weigh more. This I found hard to believe—so I kept right on eating watermelon the whole time I was in Shanghai. Even if they were dirty, they were sweet. The Chinese had been eating watermelon for centuries—and millions were living!

## INCREDIBLE SHANGHAI

THE American and English journalists in Shanghai told me some hair-raising stories about that multi-racial city, stories that would put Chicago at its wildest to shame. The most appalling things they told me—which I, of course, had no way of verifying and so do not repeat here as gospel truth—concerned the traffic in narcotics said to be flowing through Shanghai. From the interior of China by junk, on foot, or by rail, came the cans or cakes of jellied opium—from which are derived morphine and heroin. Each province through which the Shanghai-bound opium passed levied a tax, and each war lord took his cut or else confiscated the opium for himself. In Shanghai, the diplomats of a certain great European nation allowed this opium—called black gold—to be stored in their section of the International Settlements until it was shipped abroad by the Green Gang, the political racketeer combination which controlled the dope trade.

A fantastic story concerning foreign diplomats and the narcotics trade was current in Shanghai when I was there. It was said that a certain consular official, whose presence had proven unsatisfactory to the Green Gang, had been removed by his government and was about to sail for home. Some big Chinese exporters prepared a farewell banquet in his honor, attended by a number of the leading European diplomatic and consular officials in the city. At this feast the departing European ate well, drank a great deal of champagne, and was roundly toasted. But when at midnight he staggered on the liner that was to take him home to Europe, he died before the ship had cleared Chinese waters—poisoned as a warning to his successor not to be un-co-operative with the narcotics trade that was bringing millions to the men who had prepared this bon voyage party. The details of the man's death never reached the press.

Meanwhile, the Japanese were muscling in ever more aggressively on Shanghai's various rackets, legitimate and illegitimate, and everyone was aware of their presence, although officially in the city itself they had not yet taken over. Newsmen declared that one reason Japan was pushing its invasion of China so intently was to get a cut on the monopoly which the Europeans then held in the Chinese dope trade. This view was enlarged upon by a *San Francisco Chronicle* correspondent who wrote: "Manchukuo, the new colony Japan has seized from China, is turning into a huge dope factory. They are making this year in that province alone 1,430 pounds of heroin, the most dangerous of all habit-forming drugs, and there is no legitimate use for heroin in the practice of honest medicine anywhere in the world." That summer, walking on the Bund, I wondered when I saw great ships leaving the port of Shanghai with their hulls high in the water for lack of cargo, what they could be carrying to make their trips worth while.

Certainly, without trying, even I could see, as might any visitor, that this free port and its various International Settlements were wide open to all sorts of vices and corruptions. In the garish amusement parks and on the sultry streets of Shanghai wrinkled old amahs offered little girls of ten or twelve—or little boys, too, for that matter—for rental or sale for sexual purposes. Children were prostituted quite openly. Adult prostitution was, of course, everywhere on the streets, in houses, bars, parks, in the public baths. Women of all nationalities from White Russians to Japanese, French, English, or Chinese, were easily available. Adult beggars in Shanghai deformed themselves, the better to excite pity. And at the Whangpoo docks emaciated women lifted up babies with running sores on their faces, appealing to tourists on the cruise boats to toss down a few pennies. These children, I was told, were often *rented* babies on whose faces at night their owners put spiders and other vermin so that they would be ready to farm out at a fee the next morning to professional beggars. Kidnaping was common in Shanghai—of adults, not children. Well-to-do Chinese merchants, so newsman Harold Isaacs told me, would be seized by gangsters in the very middle of Foochow Road, dragged into cars, and

taken away to be held for ransom. That is why many Chinese businessmen employed bodyguards. It was not uncommon to see a fat sleek
Chinese trailed by a big White Russian with a couple of guns in his
hip pockets, guarding his employer.

Yet in Shanghai there were all sorts of police and the Kuomin-
tang had its dreaded secret agents, the Blue Shirts. In the British area
there were tall, bearded Sikhs from India. The French had imported
hundreds of swarthy little Annamites to direct traffic and patrol their
concession streets for them. The Japanese had their own unofficial
police. And there were American Marines about. Soldiers of various
nations were everywhere. In 1933, Shanghai was like an armed camp.
Chapai, a vast Chinese section of the town had been bombed by the
Japanese, and it was there that I first saw ruined buildings that were
destroyed by air raids. The rickshaw boys ran faster in Shanghai
than they did anywhere else in the Orient. If they didn't run fast, a
Chinese war lord or banker might kick them soundly on dismounting
from a rickshaw, and then not pay the fare. The Germans or the
English or the French did not usually kick coolies, but were known
to slap them at will. And the police, to keep traffic moving, might at
any time whack a rickshaw boy soundly across the rump with a bamboo cane. But few residents of the city seemed disturbed by brutality
or death. The year before, according to the official figures of the
Shanghai Municipal Council, thirty thousand dead bodies of the poor
and homeless had been picked up in the streets. Cruelty and violence,
corruption and graft were written all over the face of Shanghai the
summer I was there. Even in changing money, or receiving change
after buying something, I was warned to look carefully at each bill
and test each coin to be sure it was not counterfeit. Even then, almost
every day I would end up with money that nobody would accept.

While I was in Shanghai, a meeting of students at the Chinese
Y. M. C. A. on Szechuen Road was invaded by the British Sikh police
and broken up for harboring "radicals." At this Chinese Y. M. C. A.
I might have rented a room—but I could not stay at the "white"
Y. M. C. A. in another section of the city. There only white Ameri-
cans or Europeans could secure accommodations. And none of the
leading hotels in the International Settlement accepted Asiatic or
Negro guests. The British and French clubs, of course, excluded

Orientals. I was constantly amazed in Shanghai at the impudence of white foreigners in drawing a color line against the Chinese *in China itself.*

But fortunately, as everywhere in the world, there were white people in China who did not approve of color lines. Such people included the two gentle American women on the staff of the Shanghai Y. W. C. A. who took me one day to see the child workers in a large textile factory. The American women told me that many peasant children were sold ("*indentured*" would perhaps be a politer word) to factories as soon as they were tall enough to stand at a machine. Starving parents, in return for a small amount of money, allowed labor contractors to take their sons and daughters away to work in such factories for a period of as much as ten years. The children slept in the factory dormitories. They worked twelve hours a day and often they died before they ever got home again.

This I found hard to believe of a modern city in the twentieth-century world. But, with these two Christian white women from the United States, this is what I saw: a big grey barracklike building with a guard at the gate; inside was an enormous room where various types of machines were running without safety guards of any kind; and at these machines were some two hundred children, boys and girls, about ten to sixteen years of age, some very small and some adolescent, busily working in a very inadequate light. Several men and women overseers with bamboo sticks in their hands moved up and down the aisles of the machines. There were only Chinese in the room. One of the women overseers led us around the plant. The child workers hardly looked up as we passed, and no child smiled. Some of the older girls knew the white women who came once a week to teach them games and hygiene, but the girls did not more than speak shyly, then turn back to their work. We saw the dormitories, one for boys and one for girls, where they slept on wooden shelves in long narrow cheerless rooms. These youngsters spent the whole of their youth here like prisoners—their only crime the misfortune of having been born.

Incredible Shanghai! While the raw materials of the narcotics trade flowed over the Bund to the Western world, child slaves were sold to factories, and students imprisoned for harboring "dangerous thoughts" against Chiang Kai-Shek; on Nanking Road, Bubbling

Well Road and the other brilliantly lighted streets, at evening, in the cafés and gambling houses mah-jongg chips rattled like locust pods in a high wind. In luxurious bath houses, singing crickets in cages and musical frogs croaked for the amusement of the bathers. Jazz bands played in fine cafés and clubs, and thousand-year-old operas were performed by brocaded actors in noisy theaters. While barbed-wire barricades went up at the gates and Japanese patrols in ever increasing numbers stalked the city, the foreign newspapermen predicted, "It won't be long until the Japs take over." So it was in Shanghai the summer that I was there.

## JAZZ IN CHINA

DESPITE warnings by Occidentals not to go outside the International Settlements alone at night nor wander too far even by day into the Chinese districts of Shanghai, I did so many times just to see what would happen. Nothing happened. I had been told, too, not to trust rickshaw boys outside the Settlement boundaries—they might lead the unwary stranger into traps. None did. The rickshaw men waited patiently for me if I chose to descend from their cabs and walk around in the teeming odd-smelling exotic streets or go into the shops. So I came to the conclusion that perhaps these well-meant warnings given me might have some validity for white foreigners—not much liked by the Shanghai masses in spite of years of missionary charities. To the Willow Pattern Teahouse or the Dragon Flower Pagoda or the Butterfly Bazaar, or anywhere else I wanted to go outside the barbed-wire fences and patrolled gates of the International sectors, I went; into Nantao, Chapai or Hongkew any time, day or evening with or without a rickshaw, and nothing unpleasant happened to me—just as I never had ill effects from eating Shanghai watermelon. On the whole, I found the Chinese in Shanghai a very jolly people, much like colored folks at home. To tell the truth, I was more afraid of going into the world-famous Cathay Hotel than I was of going into any public place in the Chinese quarters. Colored people were not welcomed at the

Cathay. But beyond the gates of the International Settlement, color was no barrier. I could go anywhere.

Shanghai was an enormous city of almost four million people, so I never saw the whole of it. But I did see a great deal of it, from the Bund to Bubbling Well Road and the race tracks and outlying districts, the theaters, amusement parks, and the Canidrome Gardens, where the best American jazz band in the Orient was playing. Headed by the pianist, Teddy Weatherford, this group of Negro musicians at the Canidrome were known from Calcutta and Bombay through the Malay States to Manila, Hong Kong and Port Arthur. They were very popular in Shanghai, which seemed to have a weakness for American Negro performers. The sparkling Nora Holt had just completed a long engagement at the Little Club shortly before I arrived, singing and playing at the piano her intriguing versions of French and American songs. The young radio singer, Midge Williams, and her dancing brothers had been in China that spring, too. Other performers that Shanghai loved were Valaida Snow, a kind of Josephine Bakeresque artist of stunning gowns and varied songs. Bob Hill's band, Jack Carter's band and Buck Clayton's trumpet thrilled the International Settlements. But these people came, performed and departed. Teddy Weatherford, however, had become a sort of permanent institution in the Orient, covering the circuit from the Winter Garden at the Grand Hotel in Calcutta and back again to Shanghai almost every year, stopping at Singapore for side trips into the Malay jungles to play for parties and dances at remote British clubs on rubber plantations in the up-country.

Once, Teddy told me, he was returning by car to Singapore when he thought he ran over a fallen tree trunk across the road. It turned out to be an enormous serpent that his car left writhing in death behind him. "Man, if that there boa had ever wrapped his self around my car, I wouldn't be hittin' these ivories and eating with chop sticks no more!"

Teddy could play some wonderful blues when he wanted to, but he had to be in the mood. He had played at the old Sunset in Chicago in the days when Louis Armstrong first came North from New Orleans, and he had played with Sidney Bechet, Noble Sissie and

Eddie South, and had been all over Europe as well as Australia. But now the Far East was his personal stomping ground. Stiff-necked Britishers and Old China hands from Bombay to the Yellow Sea swore by his music. It was the best! A big, genial, dark man, something of a clown, Teddy could walk into almost any public place in the Orient and folks would break into applause.

The night that he came and got me in his car to go out to the Canidrome Gardens to hear his band, I soon found myself sitting under paper lanterns in a softly lighted outdoor pavilion at a table with a white American woman named Irene West. She was an old trouper of the vaudeville stage, now turned manager, and in Shanghai she had under her wing a team of Negro dancing boys billed as the Mackey Twins, featured in the Canidrome show. But they were a headache to Miss West.

"These boys," she said to me, "I don't know what I'm gonna do with 'em. Them—and Shanghai together—is about to drive me nuts!"

While Teddy Weatherford's Band, on the bandstand, was playing genteel pop tunes for dancing and white Shanghai filled the waxed floor, Irene West told me of her problems as the manager of two chocolate colts whom she termed "the finest young dancing team in the business."

"I could take them to the top," she said, "the very top—if they would just behave themselves. Mr. Hughes, I wish you would talk to them."

It seems that the Mackey Twins were running wild in Shanghai. In their late adolescence, they were both feeling their oats—and sowing them. Between the White Russian women and the Japanese girls, the boys almost never got back to their hotel at night. They slept all day and evening. And when it was time to come to the Canidrome for the show it was hard to awaken them.

"I don't know what I'm gonna do with 'em," said Miss West. "I have to be their mother, their father and their manager."

She told me that the Mackey Twins were not twins. They were just two unrelated boys who had run away from home down South somewhere, hoboed their way to California, and first started shaking their feet in the Central Avenue honky-tonks in Los Angeles. Sebastian of the Culver City Cotton Club spotted them and put them into his show with Louis Armstrong's Band. Later they won a Charleston contest at the Golden Gate Theater in San Francisco, and somebody took them to Reno to appear in a club there. These lively lads then in their early teens made a big hit. When Irene West was putting together a colored show to play Honolulu, she heard of the boys, engaged them, and they had been with her ever since, continuing from Hawaii to the Orient when the rest of their show went back to the States. Now, here they were in Shanghai, the neon-lighted Dragon City of the East. The twins were trying to take the dragon by its tail.

"Why, Mr. Hughes, do you know," said Miss West, "them boys have run themselves down so in Shanghai, I'm telling you, that when it comes time for them to go on the stage at night they're too tired to put their own jock straps on."

It seems, too, that they would often come rushing into the cabaret so near showtime that they hardly had a chance to get into their dancing costumes.

"They give me heart failure," said Miss West. "Now, suppose you come to our hotel tomorrow, and deliver them boys a good talking to, as one of their race."

"I wouldn't have the least idea what to say," I said.

"Tell them to behave themselves," said Miss West. "Wait till you watch them dance, and you'll see that they've got talent. Tell them it's a shame to waste their talent with these whores in Shanghai. Why, I can have 'em in the *Folies Bergères* in Paris and the Palladium in London next year—if they're still able to stand up by that time. Discipline, that's what they need, discipline. They got the ability—but sometimes I don't believe they got a bit of sense."

When the lights went down at the Canidrome and the show went on and the boys eventually danced into the spotlight, they were talented—two lanky, humorous-looking chocolate-brown youths with mischievous eyes, white teeth flashing in a wide smile every time they finished a complicated step. They could whirl their long legs around in the air and come down in perfect rhythm, their jazz tapping making merry percussion across the stage as they seemed to float like birds. They had the sort of infectious personalities that count in show business. When I met them backstage after the first show, I found them simply frolicsome, uneducated colored boys trying to get some fun out of life, in the theater or outside—but apparently putting as much vigor into fun as they did into dancing. But the fun, being mostly of an amorous nature, was more debilitating. That was what interfered with their art—living and loving, not wisely but too well.

Backstage I also met a two-hundred-pound Honolulu princess of the hula, a Eurasian crooner, and a couple of white American adagio dancers, who were very angry with each other that night. I watched the second show of the evening from backstage and, just before the dancers whirled gracefully out into the spotlighted platform, they exchanged epithets that should not be put into a book. The man called the lovely girl in swirling white tulle a name that implied she was a female dog. But just as the orchestra went into their most lyric sequence, she told him in his tight silk trousers and spangled bolero that he was a word which means a man who never had a father. Nevertheless, they both looked like dreams of divine happiness as they waltzed rapidly around the whole stage cursing under their breath. Then he picked her up smiling most charmingly in a mist of gauze and lifted her high above his head. As she came down she spat into his face in a vicious whisper, "You bastard."

I could hardly believe such handsome young white Americans used such vile language. But as they danced near the edge of the stage where I was standing in darkness and he flung the girl from him, then pulled her to him and spun her spiritedly around in the spotlight, I heard him say to her the equivalent of "Go rape yourself!"

Finally he lifted her up and marched toward the footlights, holding her like a goddess on a ship's prow before him, her arms outstretched with one foot gracefully over his head. At the end of their number, they smiled most sweetly at the audience and at each other, and bowed and bowed their smiling way into the wings. Off stage, instantly their faces went grim again, and they called each other a few very choice names before they danced smilingly back out for an encore.

Returning to the heart of Shanghai in Teddy's car at six in the morning, he explained, "Aw, man, 'dagio dancers is always fightin' with one another. Seems like fightin' goes with their kind of work. 'Dagio dancers is the toughest people in show business and the oneriest." Concerning the Mackey Twins, Weatherford said, "They got a fine manager, that Miss West really looks after them studs. She knows her business. That team can make money. Them Negroes better straighten up and fly right."

Back on the Bund in Teddy's car in the early dawn, the steaming city of Shanghai lay behind us, and the warships of the world were in the waters offshore. The tall, rectangular sails of big brown junks and the smaller sails of little Chinese houseboats and fishing boats rocked gently on the Whangpoo. Sitting beside the big, dark, hulking musician in the car, I thought how fascinating it must be to be a band leader like Weatherford, making music all around the world from Paris to the Orient, or dancers pantomiming grace and strength and beauty like the adagio dancers on the wide stage of the Canidrome Gardens—even if each figure did end in a cascade of curses. The audience did not know—just as the audience had no idea from their dancing that the dynamic Mackey Twins were going straight to the dogs in Shanghai. I had always been in love with show business. If I were a performer, I thought, and could play or sing or dance my way to Hong Kong and Singapore and Calcutta and Bombay, I would never go home at all. But I was not a performer, only a writer, so I had to think about heading for the U. S. A. It was too expensive for me to stay very long in that incredible city. As it was, I'd had to cable Blanche Knopf for an advance on royalties.

## BON VOYAGE CHICKEN

MADAME Sun Yat Sen, wife of the founder of the Chinese Republic and sister-in-law of Chiang Kai-Shek, invited me to dinner at her home in the French Concession. A daughter of the wealthy Soong family, she had been educated in the United States, and spoke beautiful English. Dinner that night was a traditional Chinese banquet with intriguing dishes from bird's nest soup to "thousand-year-old" eggs. I found Madame Sun as lovely to look at as her pictures, with jet-black hair, soft, luminous eyes and a complexion of delicate amber. She was a relaxing and delightful woman with whom to talk. She asked me for news of the Chen children in Moscow—Percy, Yolanda, Jack, and Si-Lan—sons and daughters of Eugene Chen, the former Trinidad merchant who had given his early savings to the founding of the Republic and had been Minister of Foreign Relations under Dr. Sun. Si-Lan Chen, the dancer, who lived in the de luxe Metropol, had been a winter's delight in Moscow, serving me tea and cakes in her lovely room overlooking the Bolshoi Square on snowy afternoons, and telling me dramatic tales of the Chinese Revolution and the family flight over the Gobi Desert into Turkestan when the counter-revolution took over.

When I arrived in Moscow a Chen family row was going on. The father, retired in Paris, sent his children's monthly allowance to the oldest son, Percy, as is the Chinese custom. Percy then was delegated to allot to his younger brother and sisters their just due. A great deal of disagreement with what this "just due" was occurred every month, so the three younger Chens were angry with Percy most of the time. Si-Lan, I found a delicate, flowerlike girl, beautiful in a reedy, golden-skinned sort of way, in her long, tight, high-necked Chinese dresses with a little slit at the side showing a very pretty leg. Si-Lan was the girl I was in love with that winter. But she was going away on a long tour of the Soviet Union to dance, and shortly before I left Moscow, she departed. Subsequently, Percy went to Hong Kong, and Jack, the artist, moved to London. Only Yolanda remained in Russia with her husband, a motion-picture camera man. The Chen children became scattered all around the world. The next time I saw Si-Lan she was married, living in Hollywood, and directing the dances for *Anna and the King of Siam.*

A group of Chinese journalists and writers gave a luncheon for me before I left Shanghai, and I met there the young man engaged in translating my novel, *Not Without Laughter,* into Chinese. And at a private gathering one evening I met the elderly Lu Hsin, then under a cloud for his "dangerous thoughts" but nevertheless one of the most revered writers and scholars in China. I went by train to Nanking to see Sun Yat Sen's Tomb in the Purple Mountains near the famous Ming lions, dragons and camels, overlooking the city. I wished very much to go to Peking, too, but it was not possible then due to the Japanese armies, who sometimes allowed trains to pass, and sometimes not. At least I got to see something of the interior and its farm lands, but since China is larger than all the countries of Europe together, I did not see much. When I got back to Shanghai, with my money running low, I began to think seriously of starting home, so I got a ticket on the *Taiyo Maru* sailing via Yokohama for San Francisco.

When Teddy Weatherford and the fellows in his band heard that I was leaving, they insisted on giving a farewell breakfast on the date of sailing. When I think about that breakfast, my heart almost stops beating. On account of it I came near being stranded, probably forever in the Orient, for after I had gotten my ticket I had almost no money left. My boat sailed at three in the afternoon. The fellows had been playing music all night long the night before. Two of the musicians and Teddy Weatherford came directly from the Canidrome Gardens to fetch me at my hotel about eight in the morning. I was still asleep, and had not as yet packed anything for my departure. But I dressed hastily and went with them, thinking I would pack on my return about noon. But I did not get back at noon.

It turned out that Teddy, when he stopped by for me, had not even bought the chickens for breakfast yet. And at the nearest bar before heading for market, the bandboys stopped to buy us all a drink. It was two hours before we got to market. The house of one of the musicians, where he lived with his Japanese girl friend and where the breakfast was to be held, was far out on the edge of Shanghai. It was eleven o'clock when we got there. Other musicians and their White Russian girls or Japanese wives were gathered by that time, having highballs and awaiting us. The one Negro woman in the group, wife of one of the bandboys from Harlem, said that fried chicken wouldn't amount to anything without hot biscuits, so she went into the kitchen to make some. Meanwhile, the chickens that had been purchased alive, had to be killed, cleaned, plucked and their pin feathers pulled out. It was already approaching noon!

"Teddy," I said, "I'll have to be going soon."

"Don't worry 'bout it," he waved. "We'll get you to the boat."

"But, man, I still have to pack my bags."

"Don't worry," said Teddy, "them girls'll have breakfast fried up here before you can shake a stick. You got to eat yet. You can't go without eating. This here bon voyage chicken is in your special honor."

By that time I could smell the chicken cooking in the kitchen where the colored wife was busy with the biscuits, and assorted Japanese and White Russian females were all cooking, too, drinking and chattering away like mad. Everyone was in high spirits, so it took quite a little time to get anything done. Anyhow, the chicken certainly did smell good! But I looked at the clock and both hands had passed high noon! On my ticket envelope it said in large letters to be on board ship at least an hour before sailing. That meant two o'clock. Here I was ten or twelve miles from the Bund, breakfastless, and with nothing packed at my hotel for my departure.

"Teddy, man, I'm gonna *have* to go."

"Asaki, how about that bird?" Teddy bawled. "Shenshi, Kiki, Tamara, what you-all doing out there? This man is hungry!"

The girls started setting tables—a big table and two or three smaller ones in the front rooms, as there were more than a dozen people.

Said Teddy, "If I had me a piano, I would beat out some blues." But there was no piano, so Teddy and the rest of the folks just kept on mixing highballs and *um-ummm-mm-m-ing* at the wonderful smells of the chicken frying in the kitchen—that seemed as if it never would get to the table.

"We're making gravy," shouted the colored girl. "What's hot biscuits without gravy?"

"Southern fried!" said Teddy. "Hot biscuits with gravy! Man, this here is a bon voyage for fair!"

"If I wait for breakfast now I'm afraid I won't get off," I said.

"Don't worry 'bout it," cried Teddy. "Just don't worry! Take it easy in this life and you'll get there."

But by now I was worried. It was almost one o'clock—and my hotel was at least an hour away through the crowded Shanghai streets, driving normally. "Man, I *got* to go." But that chicken smelled so good! And I could see that things in the kitchen indicated breakfast would be served soon. I was almost tempted to let the *Taiyo Maru* sail without me, and just stay in China.

Instead I went out in the kitchen myself and said to the colored wife, "Couldn't I just have a biscuit before I go?"

"Go?" she said. "All this chicken is for you—and you got to go! You reckon that boat leaves on time?"

"I'm afraid it does," I said. "Once Teddy starts eating, he'll never get up from the table to drive me to the dock. I think I'd better start now. I'll just take my chicken with me. But give me a biscuit to eat on the way."

That is what happened. As the big golden-brown platters of Southern fried, and the bowls of gravy, and the fluffy bowls of white rice, and the enormous pans of biscuits were coming to the table, borne by fluttering Japanese and Russian and Negro hands, at half past one there on the far edge of Shanghai, Teddy and I were climbing into his car, each of us with a sizzling drumstick and a buttered biscuit, on the way to my hotel miles off near the Bund. I never got to sit down at the bon voyage table, but the chicken and biscuit which the colored wife gave me, I ate on the way into town. Wonderful, that one piece of chicken!

With greasy hands I rushed up the stairs of the hotel and started throwing things into my bags. Teddy gathered up my typewriter, books and such items and took them down to the car, then came rocking jovially back to see if he could be of further help. It was then about two-thirty P.M. I still had to pay my bill! When I tumbled panting into the car with a string of ties and two pair of shoes in my hands, and we headed at top speed for the pier, I just barely caught the last lighter going out to the ship anchored offshore in the Whangpoo, flags flying and steam up for sailing. I left Teddy waving on the docks with the whole backdrop of Shanghai behind him.

## SPIES AND SPIDERS

THERE were not many passengers on the *Taiyo Maru* as we headed for the open sea. It was sticky hot and very calm. I slept the whole way to Kobe. There we had an entire day to go ashore while the boat loaded. I got in line for the routine inspection by the Japanese police and port officials. All of the intransit passengers simply showed their

documents and walked ashore. But when I reached the table where
the Japanese officials sat, they asked me to wait until everyone else
was cleared. Then one of the men said, "Why did you go to China?"

"As a tourist, sight-seeing."

He said, "Whom did you see in China?"

I said, "Why are you asking me these things? You asked no such
questions of anyone else. If I must be interrogated before I go ashore
for just a day, I'll stay on board."

"Very well, you may go ashore," the official said. I was permitted
to pass without another word.

In Kobe that morning it was my good fortune to run into two
American seamen from a freighter in the harbor. They had already
been there for several days and were happy to show me all the hot
spots of the town, from the water-front bars to the saki houses in
Motomachi. In the late afternoon we gathered into a taxicab three
vivacious reed-thin Japanese girls, with American-styled bobbed hair,
and we all sped to a noisy and very lively pavilion that seemed to be
a kind of combination dance hall, shooting gallery, bar and sea food
grill all under one roof. Anyway, it was fun. And when it came my
time in the cool of the evening to go back to the *Taiyo Maru*, the
seamen and the girls came with me as a farewell reception committee.

The next day in Yokohama, I was again the one passenger delayed in the line of those temporarily going ashore while the ship took
on cargo. This time the same preliminary. "What were you doing
in China, Mr. Hughes?"

"Sight-seeing."

"Then why," out of the clear blue sky, "did you go to see Madame
Sun Yat Sen?"

"Because she's a very famous woman and I wanted to meet her."

"Who else did you meet while you were in China?"

"I am en route to San Francisco on this boat," I said, "but I
understand passengers may go ashore here during the three-day layover.
If I am to be put through a series of personal questions that you do
not ask other passengers, I'll stay on board."

"You may go ashore," said the port official.

Since it was my intention to return to the Imperial Hotel in
Tokyo for my last few days on Japanese soil, I took with me a small

bag, leaving the rest of my luggage aboard ship. This bag contained mostly shirts and several dozen of letters, since I thought I might answer a few ashore, or at least send cards to folks at home postmarked Japan, as I had neglected to acknowledge any correspondence for weeks before I left Moscow. I was always behind with personal mail, but usually managed to attend promptly to business letters. From Yokohama I took the train to Tokyo and by nightfall found myself back in the same pleasant room I had had a month before at the Imperial, with the same water lilies floating on the pond in the courtyard outside my window.

By the time I had called a few friends—the Japanese professor and his wife who had invited me to the Kabuki, and a young architect who had studied in the United States—and taken a bath and changed clothing, it was after eight o'clock. When I went across the lobby to dinner, the headwaiter said that the big dining room was about to close, but that supper was being served in the roof garden where, also, there was an excellent movie being shown. The movie turned out to be *Mata Hari*, a spy picture, with Pola Negri and Ramon Navarro starred. I had met Ramon Navarro during my lecture tour in California, but had not seen a picture of his for a long time. Just as I was enjoying my supper and the picture, a pageboy tapped me on the shoulder politely and said I was wanted on the phone. A voice on the wire identified itself as that of a writer whom I had met previously in Tokyo, and informed me that several other Japanese writers and himself wished to honor me with a luncheon the next day so that they might see me again before I left for America. He said someone would call for me at the hotel shortly before noon to take me to the restaurant. I accepted with pleasure and went back to my table and the movie. By this time the intrigue on the screen was becoming critical, and Ramon Navarro was about to be locked in the arms of the spy, Mata Hari.

Another gentle tap on my shoulder. The pageboy again. This time he said there were some gentlemen downstairs in the lobby to see me. I asked him to request that they wait a few minutes; I would be down as soon as I had finished my supper. I really wanted to see how the picture about spies would turn out, but it delayed so long in reaching its climax that I had to leave before Pola Negri met her fate.

As I went down to the lobby, I wondered who my visitors could be. In the large busy room, I looked around but saw no one I remembered. Then I noticed two portly Japanese gentlemen in European clothes who rose from their chairs and bowed my way. In their midst was a much smaller man in a black and gray kimono. As I went toward them, one of the men extended his hand. Then he introduced the others as writers. The man in the kimono, he presented as Naoshi Takunaga, the famous author of *The Street Without Sun* that had been published in the United States. This writer, a pacifist, had recently been imprisoned, so I'd read in Shanghai, for contributing money to an anti-war organization. The first thing I said to him was, "But I thought you were in jail?"

One of the other men answered for him. "He was, but is now free, and wanted so much to meet you. Do you know Mike Gold?"

I said I'd read his *Jews Without Money*, but had never met him.

"Do you know John Dos Passos who edits the *New Masses?*"

"No, I'm sorry, I don't. But I've read him, too."

"How about Claude McKay in Russia?"

"I've never met him. McKay hasn't been in Russia for years, and I missed him when I was in Paris. He'd gone to the South of France."

"But you know Theodore Dreiser?"

"Great guns, no—that great writer! I wish I did know him."

In the back of my mind, it suddenly dawned on me that these men were not writers, they were policemen pretending to be writers—except perhaps the little man in the dark kimono who I sensed was a prisoner. I suddenly realized that they were questioning me about American left-wing writers. Never being good at concealing what I am thinking, I am sure this realization must have shown in my face at once, and all three of the men sitting there knew what I thought. The pale little writer in the kimono smiled wanly as if to indicate he was relieved that I had found out I was the center of a police trap. The Japanese gentlemen in European clothing, who looked like fat spiders, turned the conversation away from literary personalities. They asked me how I liked Shanghai, and did I not think Tokyo a more beautiful city. Certainly, they said, I was welcome back to Japan. The conversation dragged, and shortly they rose to go, with the kimonoed writer between them. As he left, I said to Tokunaga, "I hope everything comes out all right for you."

He answered in halting English, "I, too."

We all bowed and said goodbye. I went to my room and shortly to bed, wondering how *Mata Hari* ended on the screen. Pola Negri was such a beautiful spy!

## AMERICAN, GO HOME

THE next morning was a lovely day, bright and sunny outside my window. I slept late and had toast and coffee in my room. About eleven o'clock, as I was getting dressed for the luncheon, a knock came on my door. There stood a smartly uniformed young bellman who informed me that two gentlemen were awaiting me in the lobby.

"Oh," I said, "tell them I'll be right out as soon as I finish dressing. I wasn't expecting them this early."

Not wanting to keep my writer friends waiting, I hurried into my shirt, tie and jacket and went out to the lobby. But I did not see anyone I remembered meeting in Tokyo. Instead, two quite strange gentlemen approached me and bowed. Then one of them presented his card. It read:

I. Hikado
Tokyo Police Department

He said, "Our chief would like to meet you."

I said, "I would be happy to meet your chief, but I have a luncheon engagement shortly. Could I not meet him this afternoon?"

"You will be back in time for luncheon," said the man.

"In that case I'll meet your chief. Where is he?"

"At Metropolitan Police Headquarters," said the man, "if you will be so kind as to come with us."

"Let me leave word at the desk for my friends," I said.

I told the clerk I was going to meet the Chief of Police and to kindly tell my writer friends that I would be back shortly. The clerk said he would. I walked beside the lily pond, to a waiting chauffeur-driven car and off we went in the direction of the Imperial Palace. The Tokyo Police Headquarters was just across the moat from the Palace grounds. The building was quite imposing, large and modern, of several floors, and a bank of elevators with ornate bronze grilles. The long marble halls were spotlessly clean. And inside it was pleasantly cool after the brilliance of the summer sun. The men ushered me politely into an elevator in an "After you, my dear Gaston" fashion, and up we went to one of the upper floors. There I was shown into a small office and asked to have a seat. I looked out of the window and saw the traffic in the busy street below me, and the green and lovely trees swaying in the Palace gardens. Then three men came in, one in a kimono, the others in sack suits. They bowed, spoke politely, and we all sat down.

"We would just like to ask you a few questions," one of the men began in fairly good English.

"I hope you won't be long," I said, "as I have a luncheon engagement at noon."

"Yes, we know," said the man.

"Then I may get back to the hotel in time?"

"Of course," said the man pleasantly, "you are not under arrest. We just want to speak with you."

"O.K.," I said. "Let's go."

"Why did you come to Japan?"

"Because I've always wanted to see your beautiful country."

"Why did you come by way of Russia?"

I told him briefly about the abortive motion picture, that I had stayed on in the USSR as a writer, and had earned enough rubles to come home around the world.

"Why did you go to China?"

"Because I've always wanted to see China, too. Why not?"

"Russia is not friendly toward Japan, nor is China," said the man. "You can understand why we ask you about your being in those countries, and passing through Japan on the way from one to the other."

"I had intended to go directly from Moscow to Peking by rail, but your armies have cut the railroad," I said, "so I had to come to Japan first in order to get to China, as I'm sure you know."

"Yes," said the man, "and did you bring any communications from Russia to Japan?"

I laughed, "Of course not," I said.

"Nor take any from Tokyo to Shanghai?"

All this amused me. "You're talking like folks in the picture I saw last night," I laughed. "Do you think I'm a spy?"

"Of course not," said the man, "but we want to ask you a few more questions. Tell me, why did you go to see Madame Sun Yat Sen in Shanghai?"

"Because I was invited to dinner," I said.

"And what did you talk about?"

"My travels, her college days in America, books, theaters, whatever people talk about after dinner anywhere in the world."

"Nothing else?"

"Nothing folks might not talk about in Paris or New York. Why?" I asked.

I had noted that as soon as our interview began one of the men in European clothing started taking down all that was said. The man in the kimono just sat there silently.

"You know," said my interviewer, "that Madame Sun is opposed to Japan. Russia is opposed to Japan. Tell me, what do the Negroes in America think of Japan?"

"Some do not think anything at all. Some think Japan might be the savior of the darker peoples of the world. And others who have had some contacts with Japanese in the United States think quite otherwise, since they believe the Japanese there do not care to associate with Negroes. The Japanese in America don't suffer all the inconveniences we do, so I can understand why they might not want to be identified with us—and perhaps Jim Crowed as a result."

"Japan is trying to make Asia free of that Jim Crow you speak of, which the white nations have imported here. You said in your speech at the Pan Pacific Club last month that you were glad of Japan being able to drink tea without domination. Would that not be good for all the rest of Asia?"

"Of course, it would be good," I said. "Certainly! But for your country or any other Asiatic country to make colonies of other people's lands in Asia, that would not be good."

"You do not understand Japan," he said. And what had begun to be an interesting discussion changed again into a question period. "I must ask you why you went to the Tsukiji Theater in Tokyo?"

"Because I wanted to see Japan's most famous modern theater," I answered.

"The Kabuki is our most famous theater," he said.

"Classical, yes—I wanted to see it, too."

"You went to the Tsukiji first. How did you happen to have met Seki Sano?"

"At Meyerhold's Theater in Moscow."

"He did not give you letters to bring here?"

"He did not!"

"No one gave you messages to bring here?"

"You flatter me," I said, "if you think I am an international courier or something. I'm not. I'm just a writer. And some Japanese writers are waiting for me now at the Imperial Hotel to take me to luncheon. Is there anything else you need to ask me? Or may I go?"

"You may go," said the man. So I rose. They rose politely, too. We all bowed. I excused myself and said, "Goodbye, this has been very interesting." They bowed again.

I opened the door and went down the hall to the elevators. I had just pressed the buzzer when the two men who had come for me at the hotel that morning walked up. They said, "But, Mr. Hughes, you have not met our chief yet."

I said, "I have just finished talking with three men. One of them is not your chief?"

"Oh, no! You have not yet met our chief. He would like to meet you."

"But I am already late for luncheon. Could I not come back this afternoon and meet him?"

"Our chief would like to meet you now."

"Where is he?" I asked.

"Just at the other end of this corridor," I was told.

So I went to meet the chief in a huge office with an imposing desk at one end. Behind the desk sat a man in a military uniform. Up to this point no one had been rude or unpleasant. But this man behind the desk did not rise as I walked in, nor bow, nor offer to shake my hand. He simply said brusquely, "Sit down."

I said, "I'm late for luncheon, I'm afraid. So, if I may, I would prefer visiting with you sometimes in the afternoon."

He said in rather halting English, "I invite you to have lunch with us. We have nice tea garden on roof."

"But I've told your men I have a luncheon appointment," I insisted, "and these gentlemen informed me I would be back at my hotel in time for it. It is noon now."

"I invite you have lunch here," said the chief.

"Does that mean that I am not free to go? Am I under arrest?"

"Oh, no, nothing so. You not arrested. But you have lunch with us here."

"I do not wish to have luncheon here," I said, "and I will go now, if I may."

"You cannot go," said the chief.

"Then I consider myself under arrest, and I demand the right to call the American Consulate."

"You not arrest, no, and you no need call Consulate."

"You've just said I cannot leave. In that case, I am being detained against my will if I can't leave. I have the right to call my consul." I reached for the phone on the chief's desk. It was a bluff, of course. I did not know how to call the Consulate. But the chief snatched the phone from my hand.

"We will now go on roof for lunch," he said, already on his feet.

"I will not!" I said. "I will stay right here until you put me in touch with the Consulate."

I sat down. Briskly the chief walked from the room with the other two men behind him. They left me alone in an office several stories above the street, whose windows looked out across all of Tokyo. I sat there waiting to see what would happen. For about an hour nothing happened. It was after one o'clock when the door opened and my two guides of the morning appeared followed by a white-coated waiter with a large covered tray. He put the tray down on a table near the windows and placed a chair there for me.

"Your luncheon," announced one of the men. "So sorry it takes so long. The chief remembered perhaps you like bread, being an American. Our roof garden has no bread, only rice, so we have been across town to the Imperial Hotel to get American bread for you."

Sure enough, there were several slices of fresh white bread on the tray. The rest of the luncheon was American style also, as nearly as the Metropolitan Police Restaurant atop the Tokyo Headquarters could make it—steak, salad and a large bowl of rice, with a knife and a fork, not chopsticks, beside my plate. Angry now, I started not to eat anything. But the steak looked so good, and the salad so crisp and green, that, after the two men and the waiter left the room, I ate it all.

Finally the Chief of Police returned and with him were four other men, one of them a young officer in a smart uniform who spoke excellent English and had, I imagine, graduated from Stanford or Yale. He even seemed to know something about American literature. The chief informed me that he would be busy with other matters that afternoon, but if I would go with these gentlemen into another room, they would continue to speak with me. I said I considered myself under arrest and would first like to call my Consulate.

The chief said again that I was not under arrest, that I was free to go as soon as the others spoke with me, and therefore I did not need to get in touch with the Consulate.

"Then if I am free," I said, "let's finish up our conversation soon so I may go."

I was curious to know what more they might ask me, so I went with the four men into a library where books and legal cases lined the walls. There was a long table in the middle on which some of the men took notes and others spread out lists and documents. Our "conversation" lasted until late in the afternoon, beginning with exactly the same questions as I had been asked in the morning—I suppose to see whether or not I would answer the same way. One man, as before, took down everything. The bright young officer with the excellent English did the questioning.

When the simple questions were over and the man with the documents began to chime in with interrogations too, I realized that the Tokyo police had an almost complete dossier on everything I had done in both Tokyo and Shanghai. I was amazed as well as flattered that my activities had been so closely watched. The man with the documents would say, for example, "Now, when you went to Asakusa Park in Tokyo on the afternoon of July fourth with so-and-so (naming the Japanese writers or actors who had taken me there in honor of my own national holiday), what did you talk about with them?"

Or he might say, "In Shanghai last week when you dined at the Lotus Flower Café with two Chinese newspapermen known as Ah Wong and Lee Ching Way, did Ah Wong ask you about Si Bong Chai in Moscow?"

Most of the names presented by the man with the documents meant nothing to me. Even English names I forget easily, and being unfamiliar with the languages, Japanese and Chinese names I retained scarcely at all, unless they were famous names like Sun Yat Sen or Lu Hsin the writer. But most of the questions were simple—at least on the surface—and to them I could answer *yes*, or *no*, or *I don't know*, without hesitation. Only once or twice did the police choose to hammer away at the same question in various forms, or come back to it obliquely later on.

The whole procedure was most politely done with no one raising his voice, and no show of anger or impatience when my answers led nowhere. I quite honestly did not recognize most of the Japanese or Chinese names the man had on his lists. And in China, as I told him, most of the writers I had met were probably not using their own names anyway, for fear of the Blue Shirts and the Green Gang. And why were the Japanese police interested to find out what American writers I might know at home? They even asked me about Floyd Dell. At that time I had not met any of the really famous American leftist writers. Carl Van Vechten, Julia Peterkin, James Weldon Johnson, Paul Green and Mark Connelly hardly fell into that category. John Dos Passos was just a name to me.

"Why are you so interested in American writers?" I asked.

"We wish to know more about them," said the bright young officer—who probably had read more of their work than I had. Then, changing the subject, he said, "Negroes in America must know that Japan is the strongest of the nations in the East, do they not?"

"Of course," I said.

"And you," he said, "how do you feel about Japan."

For the young officer's benefit I repeated the gist of my Pan-

Pacific talk and reminded him that it had been reported in the Tokyo press almost in full—that to me it was wonderful Japan remained independent, drinking her tea without domination, but it would be an error were she to become a colonial power herself—an error and a sin, I felt.

"You refer now to our invasion of China?" asked the young man.

"Yes," I said. "From all I can see, the Chinese do not like to be invaded."

"Since in Shanghai you met Harold Isaacs, I know he gave you copies of the *China Forum*," said the young officer.

"Yes, he did. I'm saving them to read on the way across the ocean."

"That paper lies about Japan," the young man said. "You will not get the truth about Japan there. You should have visited North China, Mr. Hughes, and seen what Japan has done to improve the people."

"I would have gone through North China," I said, "if the railroad had not been cut."

"Did you discuss these things with Madame Sun Yat Sen?" the man with the documents broke in. "Did you speak about the situation in China with her?"

"If I did, what would she say to me that she had not already said in hundreds of speeches and articles? You know Madame Sun's attitude, I'm sure, as well as I. She's not in favor of Japan taking over China. Look," I said, "we've gone over this same ground more than once today, and you've asked me the same questions many times. I've answered you as best I can. What's the point now in repetition? If there's nothing new you want to ask me, I'm tired, it's getting late, and since your chief insisted I'm not under arrest, I will go back to my hotel, if I may."

"Of course you may. But, if you don't mind, just a moment, please."

The young officer stepped to an intercommunications phone and spoke rapidly in his own language. In a few minutes a very tall Japanese—the tallest I believe I have ever seen—came in and sat down and spoke with the others in his own tongue. Then the man with the documents said, "You will remember the writer who phoned you last night to invite you to luncheon? He tells us today that when you were last here, you took down some names. Another writer verifies this."

"*I took down some names?*" I repeated incredulously. Then I realized that they probably had arrested the whole luncheon party and had them in nearby rooms under questioning.

"At the house of a certain young architect, you took down many names," he continued.

Not knowing what he could mean, I shook my head.

"You do not remember? Well, when you return to your hotel, we ask permission to search your luggage."

"Certainly, come ahead," I said, "because I am going to my hotel now—unless you detain me further."

I stood up. The young officer said, "Just one more moment, Mr. Hughes. Please have a seat a moment more and listen carefully."

I sat down on the edge of my chair, a little weary now of the procedure.

"I must tell you before you go," said the young officer staring at me, "that you are *persona non grata* in Japan, and the police request that you please go home. Meanwhile do not speak with or communicate with any Japanese citizens in Tokyo. You will leave as soon as possible, and I inform you that you are *not* to return to Japan."

"I'm sure you know I'm booked on the *Taiyo Maru* leaving day after tomorrow. That's the first ship, so I can't leave any quicker. And since I don't travel around the world every year, I will hardly be coming back soon. At least, at the moment," I smiled, "I have no such plans."

As he rose, the young officer looked as if he wanted to give me a friendly half-smile, too, but five other men were in the room—so he simply bowed politely. I said good afternoon, and they all replied, some in English, some in Japanese, and I walked out. In the corridor my two companions of the morning were waiting.

"The car is downstairs," they said.

In the car were other detectives and the driver. Several came with me to the Imperial Hotel. There the detectives asked me to open my suitcase. They went through every item in it. They glanced at the contents of every letter—of which I had many, some six or eight months old—still unanswered. Seemingly they found nothing that really interested them in my bag until they came to a fan that had been presented to me by the cast at the Tsukiji Theater, a beautiful fluted Japanese fan of white parchment in a bamboo case. On this fan the cast had inscribed their names in lovely Japanese characters. At the young architect's house later other artists and writers had inked their names on this fan, too.

"Ah, ha!" said the detectives, "we were told you had taken down a list of names!"

Carefully one of them put my souvenir fan into his inner coat pocket. They had looked at everything, but took nothing else. Then they left. I wonder if they arrested all the people who autographed that fan for me. I never knew.

After the detectives departed, I started putting my belongings back into my bag. Hardly had they gone, however, when a knock came at the door. I opened it, and there stood about twenty Japanese almost filling the hallway. They were newspaper reporters. Among them was an American, Stanley Wood of the New York Times.

To the Japanese, I said immediately, "I am sorry, but I am forbidden to talk with you. The police have just ordered me not to speak with or communicate with any Japanese so long as I am in Tokyo. But, of course, if you want to take down what I say to the New York Times man, that's none of my business."

They all came in. I then proceeded to give out an indignant statement, which would have cost the Times reporter a mint of money in cables and used up two full columns in the paper had it been sent. But Mr. Wood listened to me patiently, and seemed as indignant as I was about the day-long questioning of the Tokyo police. It was he who told me that all the writers who turned up at the luncheon party for me had been arrested and that they were still under detention. As we talked the Japanese newspapermen stood about the room and made notes. I suppose some of them were secret-service men. But among them I recognized reporters who had interviewed me on my previous and less circumscribed visit to their city. I said that I considered my treatment as a tourist disgraceful, and that such behavior on the part of the Tokyo police indicated that Japan was headed down the same path as Hitler's Germany. I made quite a righteous speech. But inside myself, I really did not mind being put out of Japan since

I was headed home, anyhow. Why not go in a gale of excitement? Only I was sorry about the Japanese writers and the luncheon at which no one ate.

## IDENTICAL DESIRES

WHEN the newspaper reporters left, I washed up for dinner. As I stepped out of my room into the hall, the two Japanese who had escorted me to Police Headquarters and brought me back to the hotel, stepped up. They said, "Where are you going?"

I said, "To dinner."

They said, "We go with you."

I said, "Very well, but you'll have to pay your own bills."

I went across the lobby and into the dining room of the Imperial as they walked behind me. I did not invite them to sit at my table, so they sat at a nearby table and had beers while I ate dinner. As I was eating a pageboy brought a young American to me. The young man introduced himself as a graduate of Central High School in Cleveland where I had graduated. He said that he had seen in the press where I had returned to Tokyo. As an alumnus of Central he had come to meet me, and he was unaware as yet that I had been detained all day by the police. Immediately I told him what had happened, and that even then two plain-clothes men were watching us.

"Under such circumstances," I said, "perhaps you would not wish to sit down with me."

But the young man said foreigners were always watched in Japan. He stated that he knew well how the Japanese police behaved. I invited him to have a seat then, if he wished. But I again warned him that it might not be wise to stay. Nevertheless, he sat down and had coffee with me, and told me that he had been in Japan for two years, working as an industrial chemist. I told him my adventures for the day. Then we talked about Central High in Cleveland and some of our old teachers who were still there, particularly Ethel Weimer who had introduced so many young people to the beauties of modern poetry and who had encouraged my writing. When dinner was over, the young American left. With my two Japanese escorts, I returned to my room, bowing to them in the hall, and went to bed.

The next morning when I went out to breakfast, as I crossed the lobby, there they were again, so we bowed good morning. They did not go into the dining room with me this time, but waited in the lobby until I had finished breakfast. When I came out, they asked me what my plans were for the day. I said, for one thing, that I had to go to the bank to cash an international money order that had come from my publishers in New York.

One of the men said, "We would be happy to show you the nearest bank."

"Thank you," I said. "I know where it is."

But they walked with me, anyhow, like old friends, to the bank. Then we went to the big Mitsukoshi Department Store where I bought some toothpaste and other things I needed and a few souvenirs to take home. After that, I said, "I think I'll go to a movie."

"We also go," said the men.

"O.K.," I replied, "as long as you buy your own tickets."

They tagged along with me everywhere I went that day. In strange cities, I always like to walk as much as possible, the better to see the sights. That warm day, just out of cussedness, I tried my best to walk those men to death. When they suggested taking a cab, I said, "Oh, no, I'll be on a boat for two weeks. I need the exercise. Besides, I'm not going anywhere particularly, just walking to see the city."

"It's so hot," said one of the men, "let's stop have cool drink."

We all had refreshments. They were amiable fellows, but as the day wore on and evening came, they must have been very tired of walking. That night I thought I'd take in a Tokyo musical. My escorts came with me and seemed to enjoy the show immensely. Afterward they asked me if I would like to go to the red-light district. Not having accepted any of their offers of guidance all day, I refused to accept this one and said coolly, "No, thank you. I think I'll walk to the hotel and go to bed."

To tell the truth, I didn't want to walk myself. So I let them find a cab and we all rode in comfort to the hotel. At the head of my corridor they bade me good night and stood there until they saw me unlock my door and go into my room. I looked back down the hall at them and grinned. Evidently, there was no change of shifts for poor plain-clothes men. The same two, by now, had been on duty all day and half the night watching me.

But there they were the next morning bright and early in the lobby. When I stopped at the desk to inquire about the Tokyo-Yokohama boat train, my two escorts said they could secure a car for me at very little more than train fare, then we could all ride more comfortably. To this I agreed. After breakfast, they had a taxi waiting outside for the twenty-mile drive to the port. We left in ample time to make the boat. But, strangely enough, the same fatality happened to this taxi as had happened in Berlin when I was leaving the Soviet consulate for the boat train there. On the road through the Tokyo suburbs, the driver ran into a boy on a bicycle. The lad was sent sprawling into a ditch, badly frightened, but seemingly no bones were broken. His face and hands were bloodied by the rocks and gravel in the dry bed of the roadside canal, and his bicycle was pretty well smashed up from the sideswipe our car gave it.

This time I was delayed even longer than in Germany. We had to wait for the police to arrive, so I began to think I would miss the boat. Or if I made it, it would be again by the skin of my teeth. Four times on this trip of mine around the world, starting at Brooklyn, then Berlin, then Shanghai, now Tokyo, I had almost missed the boat! An hour before sailing time I was still fifteen miles from Yokohama watching a bleeding boy trying to keep from crying over his smashed bike while an excited driver and two plain-clothes men jabbered and gesticulated and traffic jammed the highway. But finally we reached the pier.

Again I was the last passenger to board the *Taiyo Maru* at Yokohama, just as I had been the last at Shanghai. The two detectives rushed me across the deck and accompanied me right to my cabin, where they requested that I stay until the ship cleared the harbor. On the way to the boat I had picked up a copy of the daily *Tokyo Japan Times and Mail* in which my deportation was headlined:

**NEGRO AUTHOR ASKED TO LEAVE JAPAN BY POLICE**

The paper carried a report of my questioning and the fact that I was sailing that day for home on the *Taiyo Maru*. It continued:

> Following Monday's all-day examination, the police were satisfied that the Negro was not a Communist, but ordered him to leave the country anyway. Discussing his experiences, Mr. Hughes said that his request that he be permitted to call up the American consul was refused. . . . Mr. Hughes declared he had no intention of remaining in this country a minute longer than he had to, and was taking the first ship away. In this respect his desires coincided with those of the police.

## HONOLULU LEIS

IN my cabin on the *Taiyo Maru* as the ship headed for the open sea, I examined the luggage I had left on board ship during my three days in Tokyo. The newspapers said it had been searched. I found nothing missing. The examiners had repacked everything carefully—in fact much better than I myself had packed the bags on leaving Shanghai. I lay back on my bunk and relaxed as the big old liner rolled out into the wide Pacific with me aboard on my way to American soil at last. The ship was not crowded, so I had a whole cabin to myself. I intended to sleep and read all the way to Honolulu.

I was behind on my reading of papers and magazines I had bought in China and Japan and had a big bundle of them piled in my cabin. One of the things that interested me in even the English language papers in Japan was how they played up crime among the Koreans living there. It seemed that the Korean subjects of Japan were in somewhat the same position as Negroes in the United States in relation to newspaper coverage. Seldom was anything good about Koreans mentioned, but if one committed a crime, it was headlined with a racial identification tag included. An item on the front page of one paper stated:

KOREAN WIRE THIEF CAUGHT

A Korean specializing in removing copper wire from electric power transmission systems was caught recently as he was attempting to make away with a section of wire 360 feet long. According to the police, he is Kyo Tohachi, 25, alias Hachiro Keneko, with no fixed address.

Small thefts like those of a bicycle or a watch were headlined:

### KOREAN STEALS WATCH

Another headline might read:

### KOREAN CAPTURED WITH BIKE

just as so many American papers headlined with a racial caption any news of Negro misdemeanors. A German-American, an Italian-American, a Jewish-American, or an Irish-American committing a crime was not so identified in the press with a racial tag. But just let a Negro-American run afoul of the law and the headline said:

### NEGRO ARRESTED FOR CRIME

The Koreans, being a subject people of the Japanese, received the same kind of press treatment in Tokyo. Both the Japanese and the Koreans were colored races, but I saw quite clearly that color made no difference in the use of race as a technique of hurting and humiliating a group not one's own. In Japan, Asiatics did so to Koreans. In America, whites did so to Negroes. In Shanghai, the Japanese were quicker to slap a Chinese coolie than the white colonial overlords. I, a colored man, had lately been all around the world, but only in Japan, a colored country, had I been subjected to police interrogation and told to go home and not return again. The word "Fascist" was just coming into general usage then. When I got to Honolulu, I said in a newspaper interview that in my opinion Japan was a Fascist country.

In Hawaii, I saw the dispatches that were cabled out of Tokyo by the American news services the day after my departure from Japan. The Associated Press item closed:

The police suspected Hughes of aiding the Japanese Communist movement which is being vigorously suppressed. This was not proved, but the police "suggested" that Hughes leave Japan immediately.

In Honolulu, I was shown, too, an alleged interview with me before I departed from Tokyo in which I was quoted by the *Tokyo Nichi Nichi* as saying that Japan was the destined savior of the darker races of the world, the leader of Asia, and a great stabilizing force in those areas of backward China where the armies of the Rising Sun were spreading culture. Apparently, what had happened after I sailed from Japan was that the Japanese police had composed and released to the press a purported "interview" with me in which words were put into my mouth affirming all the pro-war attitudes I had heard expressed at the Metropolitan Police Headquarters by my interrogators, but to which I did not subscribe. In the Japanese-language papers, I was pictured, on sailing, as praising Japan's imperialism to the highest. This fake interview seemed to me a most dastardly and contemptible thing to impose upon a visitor. Certainly I had given out no interviews nor seen any reporters before the *Taiyo Maru* sailed. Having been escorted directly into my cabin by plain-clothes men, I had not even uttered *Sayonara* in farewell to anyone, let alone praising Japan's leadership.

Since there were no amusing passengers on the *Taiyo Maru*, I read *The Magic Mountain*. It was my first crossing of the Pacific, and I found it much rougher than the Atlantic. For a week we wallowed, rolled and tossed in an unpleasantly restless sea. I was glad to spot Diamond Head rising out of the Pacific and the palms of Hawaii fringing Waikiki as we steamed into Honolulu. There were reporters at the pier. One redheaded newsman with a wry sense of humor said, "Mr. Hughes, I came to greet you—but there is the man who came to meet you."

He pointed at a tall young white fellow standing some distance away. I said, "Who is he?"

"The F. B. I.," said the reporter. "Nice guy. I'll introduce you." This he did. We shook hands and the F. B. I. man stood around while I repeated for Honolulu newsmen the details of my Tokyo police experience. These reporters showed me a dispatch which stated that another young American had just been requested to leave Japan. He turned out to be the young man from Cleveland who had taken coffee with me at the Imperial Hotel the night the plain-clothes men observed us from a nearby table.

I had heard of Hawaii's leading Negro, Nolle R. Smith, a member of the Island's Legislature. Teddy Weatherford in Shanghai told me to be sure to meet him. So from the pier I telephoned the Smith home. A gracious family, well-fixed, with a pretty bungalow and charming children, they received me hospitably, invited me to a delicious luncheon, then took me sight-seeing all over town—the University, the famous beach at Waikiki which I thought disappointingly small, the lovely Moanalua Gardens, and the view from Pali with almost the whole of Oahu below, then to Punchbowl Crater. In the city I saw the courtroom where the notorious Massey trials had been held of the Hawaiian beach boys accused of raping a white Naval wife. The Massey case had left a scar on the city's soul. But the Smiths reported many warm personal friendships across the various race and color lines in Honolulu. Certainly I liked the Smiths very much. When they said Aloha to me on the pier and hung leis about my neck as the *Taiyo Maru* sailed at sunset, I hoped I might someday return to Hawaii and see them again.

# 7
# WRITING FOR
# A LIVING

THAT sunny summer morning when the *Taiyo Maru* came through the Golden Gate with the green-brown hills of San Francisco and Marin County rising out of the water on either side of the Bay, I was glad to be in my own land again. The buildings were still standing, depression or no depression. There was the Coit Tower on Telegraph Hill and, in the distance on the other side of the Bay, the Campanile of the University at Berkeley. On the San Francisco side, from the rail of the steamer, I could spot the little cable cars climbing the steep hills, and atop Russian Hill I could pick out quite clearly the flower-covered house I knew on Hyde Street. I had written Noel Sullivan from Shanghai that I would arrive on the *Taiyo Maru*.

A long cream-colored car with a liveried chauffeur met me at the dock and drove me again to the old Robert Louis Stevenson mansion on Russian Hill where, after an absence of fifteen months, I was again a guest. It was in this house in San Francisco that I had packed my bags more than a year before for what turned out to be a trip around the world. On a terrace overlooking the bay luncheon was served—artichokes, abalone, a sparkling wine, strawberries and cream. As Noel Sullivan sat there listening to my recent adventures, saying little, but radiating kindness, good will and sympathy, I thought of a phrase in one of Walt Whitman's poems as applying to him, "I and mine . . . convince by our presence."

I told my host of my hopes to complete a series of short stories, so that with those I had already done I might soon have a book. Sullivan offered me his cottage at Carmel-By-the-Sea, which he said I might occupy for a year, with a houseboy in attendance. This generous offer I accepted gratefully. News of conditions in the East hardly encouraged my heading for a Harlem in the throes of the depression, especially since I wanted very much a chance to be quiet and write. Carmel would give me this chance. At the same time, from the sale of whatever stories I might place in magazines, I could send money home for my mother's needs. So, after a brief visit in San Francisco, I settled down at Carmel-By-the-Sea that fall and began to work.

But the prelude to work at Hyde Street was delightful for, as before when I had been there, fascinating guests were coming and going daily: Judith Anderson, Duke Ellington, Marie Welch, Roland Hayes, José Iturbi, the young William Saroyan, Kenneth Spencer, Krishnamurti, Elsie Arden, Dwight Fiske, Marian Anderson, bearded old Colonel Wood and soft-spoken Sara Bard Field, and the Irish Hebrew, Albert Bender. In permanent residence was a wonderful dog named Greta, a beautiful shepherd, companion to a mischievous dachshund, Joel; a majestic chow, Turandot, and a French bull called Ratus. In San Francisco I went to the dentist again. But this time, unlike Communist Moscow, for a single platinum filling the dentist charged me what amounted to the entire fee for one of my recently sold short stories. Anyway, safely housed on Russian Hill above the Golden Gate, it was fun to get back to Capitalism. And at Carmel, I was soon most comfortably situated in that seaside village that had once belonged almost entirely to artists and writers. For company, I borrowed Greta, the lovely shepherd dog. And there was a Filipino boy who kept the cottage clean and prepared meals. All day I could hear the surf, and when I looked out the cottage windows, I could see the sea. Sometimes friends or relatives of Noel Sullivan, driving up or down the coast, might occupy an extra bedroom overnight. But most of the time I was alone with nothing to keep me from working. Sometimes the writers, John Evans and Claire Spencer, came by. Once a friend brought Jimmy Cagney and his wife to call. Roland Hayes spent a few days with me when he gave a Carmel concert. And Jean Sablon stayed overnight on his way north to a singing engagement in San Francisco. Nora Holt, back from the Little Club in Shanghai, and

Wallace Thurman, the novelist of Harlem, then writing grade-B movie scripts under a white pen name in Hollywood, were once my weekend guests.

Sometimes the mysterious Garbo went into retreat at a little inn in the Carmel Highlands. Sometimes Jean Harlow was at the Del Monte Hotel, or Lady Diana Manners at Pebble Beach Lodge. Krishnamurti came for lectures. Almost all of Carmel's notable visitors would pay a call on the venerable Lincoln Steffens who lived not far from me. Robert Cantwell was then in consultation with Steffens concerning a biography of Filene, the merchant prince of Boston. Jo Davidson, the bearded sculptor, I met at the Steffens home, too, and Robert Montgomery. Dynamic young Mrs. Steffens, Ella Winter—whom her friends called Peter—then working on a book, would often welcome guests in an elegant house-coat of red velvet with a sable border, slipped on quickly over an old sweatshirt and blue jeans. Ella Winter had incredible energy, busy from morning till night, dividing her time between writing, gardening, her bright but ailing husband, their active young son, Pete, and a continual stream of visitors. Students from Stanford and other California colleges were always coming to quiz Steffens, who delighted to hold forth like a pert Socrates on sunny afternoons on his veranda. Steffy, Peter and Pete were among my best friends at Carmel.

Ella Winter, her friend, Marie Short, and I, with some other Carmel writers and artists, organized a big Scottsboro auction of original paintings and drawings which many of America's leading artists contributed. We had intended to hold the auction at Carmel, but so many pictures and sketches arrived in answer to our letters that we transferred the sale to San Francisco where, with James Cagney as auctioneer, a considerable sum was raised for the defense of the Scottsboro Boys. We also raised money for the relief of the migratory workers about whom John Steinbeck, then living in nearby Pacific Grove, wrote in *The Grapes of Wrath*. Sometimes I visited the migratory camps, filled with depression victims from other parts of the country. But most of the time, for days at a time, I did nothing but write. It was very quiet at *Ennesfree*, as the cottage where I lived was called, and I was alone, so I got a good deal done that winter.

Sometimes Lincoln Steffens and Ella would invite me to dinner, or Douglass and Marie Short would have me for a meal with them and their charming children. When Noel Sullivan came down from San Francisco, we might drive out the Highlands to visit the Martin Flavins or along the Seventeen Mile Drive to see the John O'Sheas and his paintings. If Edward Weston, the photographer, had a spur-of-the-moment party he might telephone me to come. But the artists and writers at Carmel were mostly a serious hard-working lot, and life was generally quiet. The town was still small with no sidewalks and no street lights, before the war changed it greatly, many new people came to live there, and new houses began to go up all around.

In the late afternoons I would often take a walk along the ocean with Greta. Sometimes I would stop to say hello to the Jeffers, Robin and Una, and their twin sons, Garth and Donan. Once when Mabel Dodge (Mrs. Tony Luhan) came over from Taos, Una Jeffers asked me to Tor House to meet her. Robinson Jeffers had built himself a stone house and a tower beside the sea, protected from the ocean road by a rocky overgrown slope and from the village by a thick grove of trees. Tor House had no electricity or gas, and its rough exterior belied the cozy fireplace comfort of the tiny rooms within. Una Jeffers, in contrast to the grave and taciturn Robin, was a dynamic, talkative and beautiful little woman, gracious to friends, but protecting her poet husband from strange intruders with a sharp tone—and a rifle, if need be. Old Carmelites say she once fired point-blank at some curious tourists who climbed over the rocks to the very windows of Tor House.

Una had quite positive political opinions, Republican and highly conservative as to national or international issues, but variable as to local problems. Once at a county election, she and Robin disagreed on a certain amendment being put to the voters. A great family argument ensued. On election day each went to the polls to vote his own opposite choice. When they got back to Tor House, Una said, "Robin, I have a confession to make. You know, you convinced me—and I voted your way."

Robin answered, "Why, Una dear, you had convinced me—so I voted yours!"

When I came to Carmel, there were only three colored families in the village, and a few others in nearby Monterey. Negro social life centered in the tiny house of Mrs. Willa White Black, the jolliest, stoutest woman on the Monterey Peninsula. She lived just behind the

Carmel School. Willa, as everyone in town called her, was a cook, and a wonderful one, on her job or off. So the memories of my first year at Carmel are filled with happy recollections of her shrimps and rice, red beans and ham, corn bread and greens—and the Thursday- and Saturday-night parties at her little house. Everybody, white and colored, loved Willa. Carmel was a happy and prejudice-free little town until Fort Ord opened and the army came to the Monterey Peninsula, bringing with it many Southerners, spreading to the village the problems of their color line.

My short stories written at Carmel all dealt with some nuance of the race problem. Most of them had their roots in actual situations which I had heard about or in which I had been myself involved. But none of them were literal transcriptions of actual happenings. All of the stories I wrote at Carmel were sold to magazines, and one of them, "A Good Job Gone," concerning miscegnation, created a furor in *Esquire*, hundreds of letters pouring in to the editor, some extremely heated. Fourteen of the stories appeared in my Knopf book, *The Ways of White Folks*. Others were published in a later collection, *Laughing to Keep from Crying*. That winter by the sea I also wrote a number of articles. One of them, concerning the liberation of women from the harems in Soviet Asia, brought from a big slick-paper maga- zine the highest fee I have ever received for a piece.

At Carmel I worked ten or twelve hours a day, and turned out at least one story or completed article every week, sometimes more. I needed to write prolifically. My mother wrote from Ohio that she was not very well and that my stepfather was God-knows-where. So it was a godsend to me that I could live rent-free at Carmel and send most of my earnings home. To Noel Sullivan I am indebted for the first long period in my life when I was able, unworried and unhurried, to stay quietly in one place and devote myself to writing.

## MAILBOX FOR THE DEAD

I WAS in Reno when my father died in Mexico City. Ernestine Black, a friend of Noel Sullivan's, had invited a group of folks for a late-summer weekend at her cabin on Lake Taho in the High Sierras where pallets were spread on sleeping verandas under the stars. I had always wanted to see Reno so, being near the California-Nevada border, I decided to go there. In Reno I stayed about a month and gathered the material for a story called "Slice Him Down" published in Esquire. Also in Reno the germ of the idea for one of my best stories, "On the Road," came to me. The background for both stories was the American depression, then in full sway.

Reno was a convenient stopping-off place for penniless travelers riding the rods between the East and West. Just outside the town there was a large hobo jungle. Many hungry Negroes from the East came through Reno in freight cars, heading for San Francisco where they thought times might be better. Others came through from the Coast, heading for Kansas City or Chicago where they thought times might be better. A few of these black wanderers settled for a while in Reno. But Reno really had no Negro section as such, although there was a scrubby little area across the railroad tracks where the Colored Club for gambling was located, not far from the Stockade in which the white prostitutes were segregated. This crib-area was a genuine stockade with a high wooden fence behind which the prostitutes worked—and where, of course, Negroes were denied entrance. Reno was then a very prejudiced town with no public places where Negroes could eat other than two cheap Chinese restaurants. I found a room in Reno in a Negro boardinghouse whose owner was on relief, as were most of her guests, so they pooled their relief supplies and served them at table. I never before ate so much canned bully-beef and Spam-like meat. But board and room was cheap there—and I was as poor as the others.

In Reno, and a few months later in Mexico, I had the only two "psychic" experiences I have ever had. At least, the happenings were of the sort that people term psychic. I do not know yet what to make of them, and I have no rational explanation for them. All I know is, they did happen. Both of the strange coincidences were related to death, and both were literary in nature. One concerned my father in Mexico to whom I had not written for several months, and the other took place in Mexico itself and concerned a friend in the States. My father and I had not gotten on well during the year I spent with him after my graduation from high school. Now I had not seen him for thirteen years. But I usually wrote him two or three times a year, and he would answer.

Every day in Reno, after a lengthy stint at the typewriter, in the afternoon I would take a long walk in the late-autumn sunshine. One day I decided to follow a road that led outside the city and up the dusty slope of a barren hillside where there were no houses or trees. Far in the distance on the side of this parched hill, near its crest I saw a forlorn little mountain cemetery with a log fence around it. Perhaps a cowboy cemetery, I thought to myself, still several hundred yards away from its scattered graves with their tiny slabs. As I came closer, I was startled to see on the cemetery gate—with no house or living person about—what looked to be a mailbox.

"How can that be?" I asked myself. "A mailbox for the dead?"

But when I came up to the gate, I saw that it was not a mailbox at all. One of the rough unpainted boards of which the gate was made had warped in the sun so that a portion of the board buckled out and looked in silhouette like the shape of a mailbox. As I came back down the hill in the sunset, I thought to myself, "What a striking title for a story," "Mailbox for the Dead." So I began to think of a situation to suit the title. When I got back to my rooming house, after our Home Relief supper that night, I sat down and wrote the first draft of a story. Several times during the evening as I wrote, I kept thinking about my father. This was unusual, as I did not think of him often. But before I went to sleep, I thought perhaps I ought to drop him a line. Still I went to bed without writing him. The next afternoon word came that my father had died that night. He was dying during the time I was writing my story called "Mailbox for the Dead."

## PERIOD TO A WILL

WHEN I got word that my father was dead, the word came at second-hand. What happened was that a wire in Spanish had come for me to Carmel. The Filipino houseboy had relayed it to a friend of mine, who attempted to translate it, and who, in turn, advised me by wire in English to Reno that my father had died and the estate awaited my claim. I had at that moment less than a hundred dollars, not nearly enough for a trip to Mexico City. The only other relative my father had to whom he wrote was a sister in Indianapolis. I phoned her and asked what she thought I should do. My aunt—Aunt Sallie—advised me to go to Mexico right away and see about the property. Since she could not speak Spanish, but might perhaps be an heir—indeed felt sure that she was—she would lend me the money for the trip.

Aunt Sallie wired me three hundred dollars. The next day I took my first plane flight—from Reno over the mountains to San Francisco. There I picked up the original wire from Mexico. In Spanish what it really said was not that the estate awaited my arrival to receive it, but that the reading of the will awaited my coming. Since my father and I never liked each other, I doubted he had left me anything. But, since I loved Mexico, I didn't mind going there again. Twenty-four hours outside of Mexico City, on the train, I suddenly remembered how much Mexicans go in for mourning. I had not even a dark suit nor a black tie to wear, let alone a mourning band on my arm. And I was my father's only son!

My father had lived in Mexico for thirty years. During that long period his best friends had been three very devout Catholic ladies, unmarried sisters, one of whom had looked after his real estate, and all of whom had cared for him during his illness. These gentle women had cared for me as a child, and I loved them. Each time that I had been to Mexico and had seen them, they had always been deep in mourning for somebody, all in black from head to toe—since Mexican women of the old school love to mourn for even very distant relatives. I knew these elderly sisters would expect me to be wearing black for my father. Since I was certain they would meet me at the station, my stomach began to turn over with anxiety. How could I avoid startling their sense of propriety when I got off the train in California sport clothes—with nothing black at all?

Fortunately, the train was scheduled to stop an hour at Guadalajara. I thought that there I could find a shop near the station and at least buy a black tie and a crepe band for my arm. But when we got to Guadalajara, it was a Saint's Day of some kind, so all the shops were closed. In desperation out of my luggage I took a dark blue tie with canary polka dots and, with the ink from my fountain pen, attempted to color the yellow dots black, so that I would at least be wearing a dark tie upon my arrival at the capital in the morning. Over my berth I hung the tie up to dry when I retired. The next day just before arriving in Mexico City, when I went to put the tie on, to my consternation the chemicals in the ink had only changed the canary-yellow polka dots to a bright green! When the three Patiño sisters met me at the station, all in black themselves and weeping, I had no semblance of mourning on. But when I got to their house, one of them quickly made for me a black arm band as they told me the circumstances of my father's death.

During his last years, as the result of a stroke, he had been partially crippled, and had made his home with them. He was able always to get about a bit. But one night he had become suddenly ill. They had rushed him to a hospital and had sent for a priest. All his life my father had been a most uncompromising and rather irritating atheist. These three darling old sisters had worried greatly about his soul. When my father, too ill to object, was given the last rites of the church as he lay dying, I am sure it made the women feel happier and did my father no harm. I was grateful to them for what they had done, and for being with him at the end. And I was happy myself to be back with them in their big, dark, old apartment after many years—with their saints, madonnas, candles, stiff white lace curtains, bitter black coffee and scurrying Indian servants. The three old women made me as welcome as a son, and vied with each other to see that I was comfortable.

To mention a will did not seem proper to any of us for several days. Then one day the youngest of the sisters, who took care of all the business for all of them, said that whenever I thought it wise, she would send for my father's lawyer and ask that he open and read to us my father's testament. Since it was almost Christmas, I suggested that we delay until after the New Year—for I dreaded the time when I would have to write my aunt in Indianapolis and probably have to tell her that she had inherited not a cent. I felt sure my father had left us nothing. He had had a large ranch in the mountains a hundred miles from Mexico City, and in the city itself a few tenements bringing in good rentals. But I coveted none. My aunt, however, had advanced *three hundred dollars* toward her interest in the contents of his will. That money I had already spent.

The day of the reading, however, finally came. An elderly pince-nezed lawyer, dressed all in black, arrived. Quite solemnly the sisters received him, and we seated ourselves stiffly in small chairs in the *sala*. The lawyer opened his brief case and took out a large parchment sealed with a medallion of red wax. The old man broke the seal and slowly opened the will. The oldest of the sisters wept a little. When she was quieted, the lawyer began to read. Although the paper was large, the margins were wide and the text of the will was brief. The properties were listed, then all were bequeathed to the three Patiño sisters. The youngest, who took care of business, was named executrix. My father's second wife had been a German woman in Mexico City, but they had been separated. Mexican law says that a wife must be mentioned in a will, even if the husband does not wish to leave her anything—otherwise she may legally contest it. At the very end of my father's will there was a single sentence: "I have a wife, Frau Berta Schultz Hughes." Period. That was all.

At the end of his testament in very black ink was my father's signature. Nowhere did it contain my name or my aunt's name.

Now I had to write my aunt in Indianapolis and tell her what was—or rather wasn't—in the document. This upset me a bit. Otherwise, for myself I was unperturbed. When the lawyer had finished, I said to the three elderly sisters that I was very happy my father had given them what he possessed, for nothing could really repay them for their kindness to him and to me—much less express what I felt was his gratitude, and mine, for their friendship and love over the years. In spite of my halting Spanish, they knew I meant each word sincerely. Then we all cried a little, I guess because we loved each other and we wanted everybody to be happy, and nobody embarrassed at what the lawyer had read. The three sisters said they wished to share everything with me, dividing the estate four ways, so that I would have a portion, too. To this I said, no, because I didn't think such an arrangement would have made my father happy.

In the end it was agreed that only the deposits on my father's bank account would be divided equally among the four of us. In pesos this money seemed like a considerable amount. But when my share was changed into American dollars, it came to little more than enough to repay my aunt her three hundred dollars. So I stayed in Mexico until I could make enough money from writing to come home.

## DIEGO, LUPE AND A LEPER

FOR me it was a delightful winter. I have an affinity for Latin Americans, and the Spanish language I have always loved. One of the first things I did when I got to Mexico City was to get a tutor, a young woman friend of the Patiños, and began to read *Don Quixote* in the original, a great reading experience that possibly helped me to develop many years later in my own books a character called Simple. I also began to translate into English a number of Mexican short stories and poems by young writers for publication in the United States. I met a number of painters, the sad Orozoco, the talkative Siqueros, and the genteel Montenegro, whose studio was across the street from where I lived.

Every Sunday there were the bullfights. After the regular season in the big ring, young fighters at Vista Alegre were pitted by unscrupulous promoters against enormous bulls, their bodies tossed, trampled and gored with frequency by animals too swift and tricky for beginners. I watched two boys killed. Every week after such a spectacle, I would swear each Sunday night never to attend another bullfight. But the next Sunday afternoon I'd be there before the gates opened. From the days of my adolescence when I first saw the famous Mexican matador, Rudolfo Gaona, and the great Spaniard, Sanchez Mejias (of Lorca's *Five O'Clock in the Afternoon*), I have been fascinated with bullfights—to my mind the most beautiful and dangerous of sports in the world.

At Lupe Marin's home I met the young Spanish matador, Juan Luis de la Rosa, a handsome lad who was having a rough time with the Mexican public. Armillita and Domingo Ortega were the favorites at the big ring, El Toreo, and Alberto Balderos was a runner-up until he was viciously gored as, after a beautiful pass, he turned to walk away. The bull caught Balderos in the seat of his golden trousers, lifted him high on a single horn, and tossed him halfway across the arena. Juan Luis de la Rosa fought more carefully, and so was more popular at parties than in the ring. One Sunday Lupe Marin gave a big dinner for de la Rosa—the traditional Mexican turkey with *mole*, a sauce that takes days to make. But Juan Luis did not show up. Hostess and guests waited, waited and waited. Finally, Lupe, instead of blessing the succulent bird on the table, with carving knife poised delivered a few choice words concerning bullfighters and their worthless mothers, then we all fell to and demolished the fowl.

By spring I had sold a few stories so, with a young French photographer, Henri Cartier-Bresson and a Mexican poet, Andres Henestrosa, I took a tiny ground-floor flat near the Lagunilla Market across from the stalls of the coffin merchants, and continued to have a wonderful time. The darling old-school Patiño sisters had not approved of the artists, writers, models and bullfighters who sometimes came by their house looking for me. As young ladies, my father's friends had worshiped President Porfirio Diaz. They hated the leaders of the Mexican revolution, as well as all its art and artists. The mere name, Diego Riviera, caused them to turn pale and cross themselves for protection. When the three sisters learned that I had been to Diego's studio at San Angel, they were horrified. And one day when his former wife, Lupe Marin, came by to call for me with some other friends, they looked at Lupe without smiling and spoke only with formal politeness to this exotic Mexican whose lips were a bright red and who dressed in so colorful and careless a way. To make matters worse, however, Lupe was entranced by the three Patiño sisters, whom she thought were like quaint figurines under glass, lovely leftovers of distant days beyond even Diaz. So Lupe came back to their house especially to see them and to admire the precious lace mantillas they wore about their shoulders in the chilly stone rooms where candles before the madonnas provided the only warmth.

The Patiños liked Miguel Covarrubias and Cartier-Bresson a little, but the others of my friends not at all. It was mostly for this reason that in the spring I sometimes stayed with the three sisters, but more often in the flat near the market where no one was embarrassed by bohemian company.

With a photographer and a poet as roommates, and none of us with any money to speak of, I recall no period in my life when I've had more fun with less cash. From our poor neighbors we learned how to cut down on electricity. Instead of allowing lights to burn on the meter, the neighbors taught us how to attach our wires to a long, heavy, copper wire with a hook at one end. At night, through our grilled window, with the aid of a broom handle, this attachment could be looped over the power line that ran across the courtyard. Thus one had lights for nothing. None of the other tenants got electrocuted. We didn't either.

Henri Cartier-Bresson had come to Mexico from Paris on a sight-seeing trip and had liked it so much that he did not want to return home when the francs his father gave him for his vacation ran out. His father wrote that Henri might stay in Mexico then and starve if he chose! He did not send him any more money. But Cartier, in love with a camera, still managed to take pictures. And in March he had a joint exhibition of his photographs with Manuel Alvarez Bravo at the Palacio de Bellas Artes. This was Cartier-Bresson's first major showing of his photographs. Some of the pictures that hung in this show were taken in our Lagunilla courtyard, and in the streets surrounding the market. When the show came down, Cartier generously gave Andres and me several of the prints.

Andres Henestrosa was a little Indian—a white Indian from Oaxaca—a poet and transcriber of folk tales, who was busy beginning to make the first dictionary of his own Indian language. He later completed this at Columbia University, and then went on to become a politician and a congressman in his native Mexico. Andres was courting a beautiful and much-photographed Indian girl, dark brown in complexion, whom he later married. And Cartier was in love with another Indian beauty from Tehuantepec who went barefooted. My favorite girl was a tortilla maker's daughter named Aurora. All three of us in the Lagunilla flat were interested in the folk dances, songs and night life of the Mexican capital. When our daytime work was done, if there were no parties to which we were invited, we would often seek out the little bars and clubs where the *mariachis* played their guitars and wailed their *corridos* and *huapangos*. Once I went with Cartier to the hot springs on a picture-taking trip. Aside from that, other than one excursion to Guadalajara to see the Rivera frescoes, one to Taxco, and another to my old home of Toluca, I remained in the capital.

The artist, Miguel Covarrubias and his wife, Rose Rolando, I had known in New York in the days when Harlem was in vogue. For my first book, *The Weary Blues*, Miguel had done the jacket, and he had tried several times to do a caricature of me, but finally said I wasn't caricaturable. He and his wife had a charming house outside Mexico City where more and more Miguel was turning toward serious painting and serious writing, documenting the history, folk life and Indian art of his country. It was Covarrubias who introduced me to Diego Rivera, that mountain of a man, darker than I am in complexion. When I told Diego he looked more like an American Negro than a Mexican Indian, Rivera said, "One of my grandmothers was a Negro."

Then he and Covarrubias told me about the African strains to be found in Mexican blood, particularly in the Vera Cruz section of the coast where many of the people are dark indeed. Certainly, Diego Rivera had large and quite Negroid features and a deep bronze complexion. But fortunately in Mexico color did not matter as it does in the United States. My father had gone to Mexico when I was a baby, to escape the color line in Oklahoma, where he had been refused permission, because of race, to take the law examination for the bar. He practiced in Mexico City instead, and came back only once in thirty years to his native land. When my father wanted a vacation, he went to Europe instead. He hated Jim Crow, and thought I must be crazy to live in the United States. But then my father, although himself a Negro, was not fond of Negroes. He felt that they were too passive in the face of prejudice. In Mexico City I missed Negroes in large numbers. There were some there, long-time residents as my father had been, but most of them had so merged into the Mexican community that they were hard to find. However, one old friend of my father's, a successful colored business man named Butch Lewis, owned the largest and most popular (next to Sanborn's) American-style restaurant in Mexico City. Mr. Lewis finally dug up a few other Negroes for me, when I convinced him that I really wanted to find some. That winter, too, I met the boxer, Henry Armstrong, when he came down to fight Casanova. And José Antonio Fernandez de Castro, my journalist friend from Havana, had become a diplomat in Mexico, so he introduced me to the Cuban Negro drummers about town, since both of us could listen to bongos for hours.

But José Antonio, when he found out I was in Mexico, immediately began broadcasting to the Mexican press what an (in his view) "important" writer I was, and he himself wrote a long piece about my poetry, which was published. The result was for me a number of newspaper interviews, sessions with photographers and artists, and translators asking me how to translate the syncopated rhythms and Harlem slang of my poems into Mexican idioms and Spanish meters. Javier Villarrutia, José Mancisidor, and Heliodoro Valle, among others, wrote articles about my work. The big newspaper, El Nacional, published a page of my poems with my photograph in its Sunday supplement. Requests for me to speak at literary soirees began to come in. And for a while it looked as if I were going to be lionized—which I never liked very much. I get embarrassed. So in the late spring I began to think about going back to California to find peace for writing again.

I never lived in Greenwich Village in New York, so its bohemian life—in the old days when it was bohemian—was outside my orbit. Although once I lived for a year in Montmartre in Paris, I lived there as a worker, not an artist. So the nearest I've ever come to la vie de boheme was my winter in Mexico when my friends were almost all writers and artists like Juan de la Cabada, Maria Izquierdo, Luis Cardoza y Aragon, Manuel Bravo, Rufino Tamayo and Francesca and Nellie Campobello. Most of my friends were almost always broke, or very nearly so. But then we didn't care. Henri declared his father in Paris—whom rumor said was a wealthy industrialist—could keep his money. He, Henri, would get along. Andres said he'd never had much money anyway, so no le hace. As for me, I'd often lived hand-to-mouth. But when I got really hungry, the gracious Patiños always set a good noonday table, and every evening had an enormous jarro of steaming chocolate and sugared rolls for supper. Sometimes José Antonio would invite me to dine in a good restaurant where foreign diplomats ate. Or Butch Lewis, my father's old friend, would see me passing the windows of his café on Calle 5 de Mayo and beckon me to come in and have some chicken. Or Andres might sell an article on Tehuantepec and all three of us would go to Las Casuelas—a restaurant with an open kitchen where you could look in the pots and see the food cooking. On Sundays after the bullfights, Lupe Marin might have a feast.

Once I went with Lupe to collect her alimony from Diego Rivera. We had been that day to luncheon with Miguel and Rose Covarrubias in suburban Tizapan. On the way back into town, Lupe said, "Let's go by San Angel and see Diego. He's behind on my payments. Maybe I can catch him."

But she did not find him. There was no one at his studio, a box of modern French architecture built high in the air on stilts of steel with the pipes of the plumbing exposed beneath. There was a similar companion studio a few yards away which Lupe said Rivera had built for Freda Kahlo, herself a fine artist. Some twenty feet up in the air connecting the two buildings, there was a little bridge.

"That," said Lupe, "is the catwalk. How it supports Diego's weight at night, I'll never know. Where is that big hunk of Mexican mud, anyhow?"

Both Lupe and Diego were famous for the names they called each other. The ample and voluptuous Lupe had been not only his wife, but for years his favorite model. Now, parted, they were fighting friends, or friendly fighters, according to their moods on meeting. Their alimony meetings were always dramatic, their friends said, and usually of sufficiently public a nature to furnish the capital's cocktail parties with a fresh supply of quotes and anecdotes every month. Lupe's language was often most vivid, but it does not stand up well in print. Many writers have tried to write about her, and she herself wrote one or two *Lives*, but none as alive as herself, by a long shot.

Anyway, having heard that she and her former husband sometimes indulged in head-on collisions, the day I went to San Angel with her and she called up to the open windows of Diego's studio, "Come out, you rock-hearted heathen idol!" and there was no answer, I thought maybe a picture might come flying down on our heads. (Gossip gave them credit for fantastic fights.) But nothing happened. Only silence, and the rustling of the eucalyptus leaves in the tall trees. Disappointed, Lupe gazed at the studio above her head, and spat at the pipes of the plumbing beneath it.

"I guess I'll have to climb those *malditas* steps," she said.

Up the stairs she went and flung open the door, which was not locked although there was nobody home.

"Look at this crap in here," said Lupe.

Large paintings and small paintings, sketches half finished and unfinished were all around—a fortune in Riveras—and nobody home.

"I can't stand the sight of these pictures," said Lupe. "None of them are of me. Let's go sit in the yard. He'll come. He scents me. Something always tells Diego when I'm around, so he'll come."

Sure enough, we had hardly been sitting in the eucalyptus shade ten minutes when down the road came a little car and out stepped a huge man, Diego Rivera. He greeted us jovially, but asked us to do him the favor of remaining in the yard "Because," he said, "look! Buyers!"

Trailing his car came a long luxurious motor with a well-dressed American couple of obvious means in the back. A chauffeur let them out. Diego had guided them in from the city to take a look at his paintings. They disappeared into the studio.

"They'll pay a year's fortune for something he painted in half an hour," said Lupe. "But I'm not going to wait while he entertains tourists. I'll be back, don't worry about that. Adios, pumpkin-belly!" she called.

Without further ceremony we drove off into town. I did not hear how or when she collected her month's alimony. But there was a story current that once when Diego thought he had no money, he simply gave Lupe a blank check which he signed and said, "Maybe there's a little something in the bank, Peso-eater, go get it."

That very morning it seems, according to the tale, without his knowledge, one of Diego's foreign dealers posted to his account a quite large sum of several thousand dollars. Lupe drew it all. Anecdotes about Diego and Lupe were as common in Mexico City then as were tall tales about Robinson and Una Jeffers at Carmel, or stories of the amazing doings of Mabel Dodge Luhan and Tony at Taos. Rivera and his ex-wife were favorite conversation pieces in the capital. But not with the Patiño sisters! My father's old friends would have none of them.

My last few weeks in Mexico I spent at the Patiño home, because I knew they would feel hurt if I didn't. I went to vespers with them every night in the old church just across the street, lighted by tall candles and smelling of incense. Sometimes I even got up early in the morning to attend mass. And I still cherish the lovely old rosaries they gave me. These sisters were very sweet, kindhearted women. But sometimes I thought their kindness was a little misspent. I was then all in favor of working to change the *basic* economics of the world, while they were engaged in little charities widely dispersed to help various indigents a *little*. From their small income they gave, in proportion, generously—five pesos here, ten there, two to this brotherhood, three to that sisterhood, one peso to one organization, a peso and a half to another—and regularly each week to the church. Then from their home they had their own little private dispensation every seventh day to the poor of the neighborhood.

This weekly ritual seemed touching, but very futile to me. There were literally thousands of poor people in the neighborhood, since the Patiños lived in the heart of Mexico City, not far from the Zocalo. In our block alone there were perhaps two or three hundred shoeless or nearly shoeless folks. Personal charity for a handful, I felt, was hardly a drop in the bucket for so great a need. But these elderly women had been doing this for years, so I said nothing to discourage them. Every Monday, early in the morning they would busy themselves, these three sisters, packaging in separate cones of newspapers little cups of beans, a tiny scoop of sugar, perhaps two or three onions, a bunch of grapes or an orange, and a small slice of laundry soap. Several dozen such little packets of each thing they would make. Then from eleven to twelve, just before midday dinner, the poor of the neighborhood would come to receive their gifts. To each who asked, a set of these tiny packets would be given at the door, with a "Bless you, Marianita! . . . Bless you, Luz!" as each filed past with open hands. But the food each got was not enough for even one good meal. And the tiny piece of soap would hardly wash anyone's hands and face more than a day.

But there was among the deserving poor in the neighborhood one woman who must have felt as I did—concerning this small donation—because she always stayed to dinner. After she got her tiny packages, she would squat on the floor just inside the dining-room door, and no one could move her until the three sisters sat down to eat their noonday meal and she was served on the floor, too. Her name was Carolina (pronounced Car-o-*lean*-a) and she was a leper—a very old, sick and repulsive-looking leper. Her hands were calcified and spotty with horrible gnarled fingers. Her face was peeling and her eyes were rheumy. Her distorted lips drooled. But she could talk very fast and quite continuously, and would do so until fed. She was hardly decorative to have around during dinner.

"God give me the grace to bear Carolina," Lola, the youngest of the Patiño sisters would sigh.

"Isn't she one of God's creatures? Isn't she one of God's creatures?" Fela, the eldest, would mutter rapidly with upturned eyes. "She belongs to God."

"That's right," Carolina would say. "I'm in God."

Cuca, the middle sister, who had a sly sense of humor, would murmur softly—so I could hear, but not her more serious sisters or *la pobre* Carolina, "Oh, would to God that He'd take care of you at the hour of our dinner!" I would bow my head to hide the laughter in my eyes. Carolina had a sense of humor, too, and knew well what she was doing—that she wryly amused Cuca and me while she irritated the more fastidious younger sister and the pious elder one. Sometimes the unrotted side of Carolina's mouth would flash Cuca and me a quick smile. Then her face would become woeful again as she lamented her plight, her poverty and her hunger, as she turned her pus-filled eyes on Lola and Fela. Carolina knew well that none of us would sit there in the name of God and eat a hot full-course meal and not give her some of it, too. Yet she wailed like a beggar as a preliminary to each course.

The problem was that the Patiños always had a really big dinner with several courses, a soup, a meat, two or three vegetables, tortillas, salad, the final customary plate of Mexican red beans, a dessert and coffee. Carolina had only one spoon and one eating utensil in her possession, a kind of large clay cup the size of a bowl, which she tied to her belt. She, being a leper, could not be served from any of the Patiño dishes. So all of her food had to go into this one cup—first soup, then a mixture of meat and vegetables, then salad and beans, then dessert. Carolina wanted some of everything—and chattered until she got it. Finally at the end, into the greasy and unwashed cup was poured her coffee. The servant would touch nothing belonging to Carolina for fear of contamination. No one could blame her—for this decaying leper was a sight to behold. Sometimes I would deliberately not be at home for Monday's dinner, just to miss looking at Carolina. But whenever I did see her, I always gave her a few pesos, and she gave me a smile from the good side of her mouth, plus a blessing. Once I went to help her up from the floor when she seemed weak, but the two serious sisters both cried aloud, "Don't touch her! For the love of God, don't touch her!"

They explained after Carolina left that touching a leper might give one leprosy. Cuca looked at me slyly and whispered under her breath, "You might get it quicker from just looking at her. Imagine Christians saying, 'For the *love* of God, don't touch her!'" Then mocking her older sister, she intoned aloud, "'Isn't she one of God's creatures, Fela? Isn't she one of God's creatures?'"

I once said to the Patiños that I thought it would be better, instead of giving once a week to so many people so many *little* bags of beans, if *all* those beans were put into one *big* bag and given to Carolina; she could live the whole week—then at least *one* person—and the most needy one—would be fed adequately. But they didn't see it that way. They prayed a lot for everyone, and gave a little to everyone, too.

## INVITATION TO PHILANTHROPY

WHEN I got back to California in June, I learned that Arna Bontemps and his family were in Los Angeles. Arna and I had written a children's book together which Macmillan's had published, a little story of Haiti called *Popo and Fifina*. We decided to try our hand at another juvenile, so I went out to suburban Watts to spend some time with the Bontemps in a little cottage there. Arna was then unemployed. He had a wife and several children. The depression was on, and I was, as usual, generally broke. We each put what we had into the pot and we lived—but on very simple fare.

Late one afternoon, after I had been in Los Angeles all day trying to sell an article to a paper, I got back to Watts at dinnertime to find a genteel grey-haired white lady waiting for me in the Bontemps parlor. She introduced herself—a three-way name like Mrs. Clara Kemble Penn—which I vaguely seemed to have heard or read. In a cultured but self-confident manner she began to tell me her mission.

She said that she had just heard that I had inherited a fortune in Mexico, and she was sure that I would be deeply interested in her proposal. For many years she had been concerned about the lack of cultural relations between the Negroes of America and those of Africa, particularly, she said, on the artistic level. Americans knew little of great African sculpture, almost nothing of her folk tales, and the Africans really had no knowledge of our contemporary writers, artists and musicians. For example, she said, a writer like myself should be known throughout Africa. It was her intention to set up a foundation to bring about such American-African interrelationships. In this she was sure I would be interested.

I said that I was interested indeed, and would be happy to lend my name and influence to such a project.

That, she said, was among the things she wanted to request of me, my name and my support. But the other request, she said, was for a sizable donation toward the initiation of this project—perhaps twenty or thirty thousand dollars.

I had never been so flattered in my life by being asked for so large a sum of money. All I could do was gasp. But when I finally got my breath back I hastened to inform this genteel woman that my father had left me not a cent, and that I had had barely the money to return to California from Mexico.

She said, well, in that case, since I'd had several books published, perhaps I would be willing to contribute a lesser sum to help set up the foundation—say five or ten thousand dollars. Again I was filled with pride to think that anyone would believe me so successful an author. But, I told her quite frankly that my books, though they were critical successes, were far from best sellers, and my royalty statements after the initial spurt were seldom in the hundreds, never in the thousands.

"How disappointing!" she said. "A fine writer like you. Your income should be a very solid one."

"Unfortunately, it isn't, I'm sorry to say."

"Then perhaps you could give me just a thousand dollars," she murmured.

Here I almost lost my patience. The Bontemps were sitting down in the kitchen eating, and I was very hungry, so I wanted to draw this unscheduled and by now preposterous interview to a close.

"Lady," I said, "I've never possessed a thousand dollars in cash all at once in my life." This was true. "And right now I wish someone would contribute just half that amount to me."

Undeterred, the dignified white woman said, "But I'm sure you realize the worth of a great cultural exchange between our great American Negroes and the great people of Africa. I know you do. And I know you would not want to miss being one of the founders of such a foundation—which eventually will receive the support of Rockefeller, Carnegie, Ford. But we must get it started—an office, letterheads. My own time I will give without recompense. But I must have stationery. For a hundred dollars we could——"

"But, lady, I haven't got a hundred dollars. Not even ten dollars. Nothing!"

"Mr. Hughes," she said, "I've taken my last penny to come all the way from Pasadena to see you about this project. Your interest I don't doubt, as I'm sure you do not doubt mine. Could you kindly let me have a dollar for carfare back to Pasadena?"

I put my hand into my pocket where I had only three or four dollars and gave her one of those. She rose, thanked me graciously, shook hands, and I bowed her out. The Bontemps had finished dinner when I got to the table. But in spite of growing children, they had managed to save a plate of beans for me. They listened in amazement to my tale of the well-dressed lady who'd begun by asking poverty-stricken me for twenty or thirty thousand dollars—but ended up accepting one dollar for carfare.

I later learned that this genteel white woman had been to many of the prominent colored business men in Los Angeles with her story, and to the few Negro movie actors who worked regularly. A number of them had given her small sums. The lady had once been quite prominent in social service movements in the East and had written on minor aspects of race relations and other social subjects for liberal journals. But she had fallen on evil days after marrying abroad a handsome European husband much younger than herself and transporting him to a California bungalow. It seemed that her husband did not work at all. So, in order to keep him well-dressed, his wife had been reduced to using the advanced funds for her proposed foundation to care for what her friends termed "a legal gigolo." At least those are the alleged facts which a young Negro newspaperwoman claimed she unearthed when the lady asked her to publish a story concerning the proposed Afro-American foundation's noble aims. Out of regard for amicable race relations and the woman's former prominence, the Negro paper published nothing at all.

## A WRITER AND A FIGHTER

I MET Jim Tully at a dinner given for me in Beverly Hills. The Irish hobo writer did not bring his company manners with him that night. Our charming hostess, Lillian Mae Ehrman, a friend of Noel Sullivan's whom I had met at Carmel, called me up one day to invite me to dinner. Her brother was a top Hollywood talent scout, who had discovered a number of young stars. Other relatives and many friends of Mrs. Ehrman's were connected with the motion-picture industry, so she herself knew everyone. Top executives and scintillating stars were her friends. She said she would have perhaps a half-dozen guests for dinner, and asked whom in Hollywood I would most like to meet. Immediately I said the writer, Jim Tully, whom I admired greatly. And, perhaps, if she knew her, Katharine Hepburn.

"Of course," said Mrs. Ehrman, "I would love to invite her."

But Mrs. Ehrman thought I had said on the phone *Theresa Helburn*. So it was the executive of the Theatre Guild that I met at dinner rather than the actress, Miss Hepburn. I was delighted, of course, to meet one of the founders of America's leading theatrical organization. But perhaps had the actress been there instead of Miss Helburn, the dinner might not have ended with the hostess unhappy.

Jim Tully had been to a cocktail party and arrived tardy at Mrs. Ehrman's home just as she was about to lead her guests into dinner.

Mr. Tully was somewhat unsteady on his feet as he came in, but nevertheless managed to shake my hand with an iron grip and to say that
he admired my writing as much as I said I admired his.

"You know damn well what you're doing when you write," he
roared as he rolled toward the table like the literary tough guy that he
pictured himself in his books, his body short and stocky, his round
pug-nosed face flushed, and the shock of hair on his head even redder
than his face. He scarcely acknowledged the introductions to the other
guests—a former Earl Carroll beauty being groomed as a star, a European dance choreographer of foreign fame, and Miss Helburn.

Hardly had we been seated at table and the soup served than
a most unpleasant discussion began to crackle across the table between
Jim Tully and Theresa Helburn. I had reminded Miss Helburn that
a play of mine had once been read at the Theatre Guild offices, and
Miss Helburn said that the play had some interesting qualities, but
seemed to her insufficiently developed. At this point Jim Tully cut in
to say that he did not see why Miss Helburn had the right to express
an opinion about anything in the theater. Naturally, everyone was
taken aback at his brusque comment.

Miss Helburn said, "Well, at the Guild we do examine a great
many plays a year."

Said Mr. Tully, "But what is the Theatre Guild? Nothing but a
great louse on the tree of the American theater!"

This aroused Miss Helburn's ire. Although she did not raise her
voice, she put up a spirited defense of the Theatre Guild across the
table. But her conversational tones were no match for Jim Tully's roar.

"A great louse, I say, that's what the Guild is, on the tree of the
theater. A Broadway bloodsucker! A commercial leech!"

"Why, Jim!" gasped the perturbed hostess, a pretty, gentle little
lady whose soft voice did not reach Tully's ears at all.

"Oh, my! Oh, my!" said the foreign choreographer, "could we
not discuss something else?"

"Have you seen Ruth Draper's latest program?" I asked. "She
was in Mexico City this spring and I thought she was wonderful—a
hundred characters in one."

"You don't need to be kind by trying to change the subject,
Langston Hughes," Jim Tully bellowed at me. "You look like a decent

man. But you don't need to protect the Theatre Guild—that blood-
sucking Broadway combine! You keep quiet."

"The Guild must have turned down a play of yours once," said
Miss Helburn acidly.

"You're not big enough to turn down a play of mine," snorted
Mr. Tully.

"Oh, dear," said our gentle hostess. "Dear, dear! Theresa, please
pay him no mind."

"What cocktails they must've served at that party where you
were, Mr. Tully!" laughed the Earl Carroll beauty.

"I know what I'm saying," shouted Mr. Tully. "The Guild is
nothing but a——"

"But they have done some beautiful plays," I cut in, trying to
save perhaps an even more dire description of the Guild from being
uttered. "And they first produced *Porgy*, which was beautiful."

"Langston Hughes," said Jim Tully solemnly, "you have no busi-
ness out here in Beverly Hills. These people will ruin you. And for
God's sake, Langston, stay away from Hollywood! Look at me! As a
writer, they've ruined me. Hollywood will buy you, and ruin you!
They ignore you until they find out you've got something they can
use. Then they buy you—and lynch you with money. Stay away from
Hollywood! Stay away from Beverly Hills! Stay down on Central
Avenue with your poor hurt niggers!"

At the word *nigger* everyone gasped, except myself. The hostess
reddened.

"Langston Hughes knows what I mean," said Jim Tully. "He's
got their souls in his hands. He writes about them. He knows what I
mean when I say niggers—as you people say it. As for the Theatre
Guild . . ."

Jim Tully turned his attention again to Miss Helburn across the
table. But at this point the hostess rose, and said, "Please, let's all go
in the living room for coffee."

The Earl Carroll beauty took Mr. Tully's arm in her perfumed
grip and managed to get his mind off the Guild. Miss Helburn said,
as we left the dining room, "I realize he's intoxicated, but nevertheless . . ."

"Oh, dear," said our gentle hostess, "I've known Jim for years and never seen him act quite like this."

Miss Helburn did not stay for coffee. For the rest of the evening, the young actress regaled us with gossip of the studios. Before I left for the long ride by tram back to the Negro section of Los Angeles, Jim Tully made me promise to come to his house for luncheon the following week. He said, "We've got things in common, you and I. We're both beaten up by life—but we fight back. That's what I like about you—you fight back, Langston! Call me up and tell me what day you can chow with me." I said I would.

Henry Armstrong was preparing for a fight then in Los Angeles. His brother and trainer, Harry, wanted to be a writer, and one day at the gym he showed me some interesting short stories. I thought, since Jim Tully had once been a boxer, and some of Harry's stories dealt with the fight arena, it might be interesting and perhaps helpful to the young writer to meet Tully. When I phoned, I asked if I might bring Harry Armstrong to luncheon with me. Tully said, "Sure."

Since it took about an hour and a half to get from downtown Los Angeles by interurban car to the section of Hollywood where Jim Tully lived, I went by Harry Armstrong's house long before noon so that we might start in ample time. But Harry said Henry was free that day and had offered to drive us out to Tully's in his little car. I said, "Oh, if I'd known that, I'd have asked Tully if Henry could be a luncheon guest, too."

But Henry said, "Don't worry about me. I ate a late breakfast. I'll just sit in the car and wait for you fellows."

So that is what he did, parked his car outside in the sunshine near Tully's house to wait for Harry and me. But when I told Jim Tully the young fighter was outside, Tully went out and brought Henry in to luncheon, too. As we ate, Tully talked with Harry and myself a little about writing, and with Henry a great deal more about fighting. They discussed the trials and tribulations of a ring career—for at that time Henry was not a triple world's champion, but still a preliminary fighter garnering very small purses, and most of his income went to his handlers. Tully said he was going to speak to Al Jolson about Harry, as well as to other big guys in Hollywood, and see if they couldn't help straighten things out for him. This Tully did. The writer and the two Armstrong boys became good friends. Several years later, in his book, A Dozen & One, along with chapters on Charlie Chaplin, George Jean Nathan, Walter Winchell, Clark Gable and other spotlighted names, Jim Tully included a very moving sketch of Harry Armstrong which begins with a description of our meal together that day.

## FIRST PLAY ON BROADWAY

WHEN Arna Bontemps and I had finished a draft of our children's book in Watts, I went on up the Coast to Carmel, intending to settle down for a summer of writing. But I had hardly gotten there when I received a very disturbing letter from my mother, saying that she was not at all well, was without funds, and had moved to Oberlin to live with some distant cousins. My mother was always finding new —but usually very distant—relatives. For this she had a genius. Her newly discovered kinfolks were almost always as poor, if not poorer than ourselves. Often my mother ended up helping her relatives, rather than they being of any help to her. The opposite of my father, my mother was very generous and kindhearted with everyone around her. But as she grew older and unable to work, it was the money which I sent her for her own support that she shared so sweetly. Then as quickly as it ran out, she would write me for more. My mother thought one's name on the cover of a book automatically meant a large income, even if the book were far, far from the best-seller list. I showed my mother my royalty statements, but the low figures seldom made any impression on her. When they did, she would say I ought to quit writing, and get a job with a steady income. What kind of job she thought I could find in the middle of the depression which would pay enough for three of us to live on—herself, my brother and me—I do not know. But sometimes I was inclined to agree with her that it would be good to have a regular weekly income, no matter how small, for it was frequently a long wait between story sales. Now my twice-yearly royalty statements reflected the depression's poverty, for most people could no longer afford to buy books.

My mother, as a great many poor mothers do, seemed to have the fixed idea that a son is born for the sole purpose of taking care of his parents as soon as possible. Even while I was still in high school, whenever my amiable but unpredictable stepfather would wander away, my mother would suggest that I quit school and get a job to help her.

"But, Mama," I would say, "with no training, what kind of job can I get that would pay enough to make it worth while leaving school? At least if I get a little education, I'll be better able to help you afterwards."

Other youngsters in our neighborhood, less determined than myself, were forced by their parents to quit school and go to work, anyway. But I managed to stick it out. Later, when I could earn enough from writing to send a little money home, my mother always found relatives more needy than herself whom she felt called upon to aid. I soon learned that even with a high-salaried job, it would have been impossible for me to look after *all* of our poor relations adequately, faced as most of them were with continual emergencies. With a very minor income from writing and an occasional fellowship, adequate help from me for our whole clan was not even conceivable. So my mother would write, "You ought to get a job and go to work, that's all." Like my father, she did not have very much faith in writing. But I liked my mother better than I did my father. He was very penurious. At least, my mother had a well-meaning heart, and was generous to a fault. Perhaps I was a bit like her, too, for during the periods I had spent in Mexico with my father, he always complained, "You're just like your mother, throwing your money away. You'll never have anything. Your mother didn't even look at money before she spent it. She had no respect for a dollar at all!"

I remember later when I was at Columbia, another fellow and myself went to a night club in Harlem. I'd just gotten twenty-five dollars from the sale of a poem. For fun I intended to spend *only* four or five dollars and keep the rest for campus expenses. But the other fellow, excited about a beautiful shake dancer, threw her a dollar as she undulated about the night-club floor. I threw her a dollar, too, since the dancer *was* good. But as the dance went on, my friend turned to me and cried, "Lend me five dollars."

I took out a twenty-dollar bill I had in my wallet and said, "Here, get this changed."

By then the drums were pounding so terrifically, and the dancer was shaking so frantically that my companion did not hear what I said, nor even look at the amount of the greenback I'd given him. He simply tossed it to the shake dancer. He hasn't paid me back yet. I think it is all right to be generous with one's own money, but not with some one else's. My mother was generous with her own and everybody else's, too. So I guess my father was right when he claimed she didn't have any respect for a dollar.

Since my return from the Soviet Union, I had not seen my mother. So when letters came to Carmel, telling she was not well, I thought I had better head East and find out exactly how things were at home—home now being Oberlin, where I had never been. That she had moved was not unusual, since for me, from childhood on, home had constantly shifted from one place to another—Joplin, Buffalo, Lawrence, Kansas City, Topeka, Mexico City, Colorado Springs, Lincoln, Illinois, Chicago, Cleveland—dozens of places I had called home. So it was not strange that now home should be a town to which I'd never been. I knew we had relatives in Oberlin, and my grandmother had been the first Negro woman to attend Oberlin College. There before the Civil War she had married Sheridan Leary who went off to die with John Brown. I was interested in seeing Oberlin. When I got there, I found it a pleasant little town, and our newly found relatives were good people.

My mother had cancer of the breast. She had visited a public health clinic where the doctor told her abruptly and brutally, without any preparation, what her ailment was. She was quite upset when I got home, and said she would not go again to what she called "charity doctors" where they talked to people like dogs. She also felt she had been treated so brusquely because she was colored. But in depression times, I learned that with the public health services overloaded with unemployed patients, white people also complained of discourtesy, lack of attention and the quick brush-off. Nevertheless, color or not being at the root of it, my mother insisted on having a private physician. She chose an excellent Negro doctor in Cleveland, who gave her sympathetic attention without unduly high fees. As reasonable as his charges were, however, my mother's illness took every penny I could make during the months that followed and used up most of the Guggenheim Fellowship I was awarded that year.

In the fall, I thought it might be wise for me to go to New York and re-establish some of my old contacts there that might be helpful in disposing of my new stories and articles, so I left Oberlin for a while. I had hardly come up out of the subway in Harlem on a bright September morning, when I ran into an acquaintance on the street who said, "Oh, so you've come to New York for the rehearsals of your play!"

"What play?" I asked.

"What do you mean, what play?" the friend said, thinking I was joking. "According to the *Times*, your *Mulatto* is in rehearsal to open soon."

That was the first I had heard of it, I assured him. My agent had had the play for five years, but had not notified me of any producer's taking it. Immediately I went into a corner phone booth and phoned the agency. Sure enough, I was told, my play was in rehearsal. The agent had just not gotten around to sending me a contract, or even letting me know. "But come in and you can sign the contracts today."

I signed them that afternoon. Then I went by the rehearsal hall. There I saw a group of white and Negro actors reading lines I had never written. But eventually a scene came up that I recognized as my own. It turned out that the producer had already made a number of changes in my play without a by-your-leave from myself, the author. When I rather timidly questioned this, I was told, "What do you know about the theater? This is your first play, isn't it? You play-wrights are a nuisance. Besides, I thought you were in California."

"But——" I objected softly, without getting any further that day, for the producer cut in.

"You want to make some money, don't you? Well, your play's not box-office as it stands. We're trying to make it box-office. Just sit down, keep quiet, and listen to the rehearsal."

I did. What I saw and heard amazed me, but intrigued me, too. *Mulatto*, concerned the son of a white plantation owner by his Negro housekeeper in the Deep South. This boy had been sent North to college and when he comes back home, he wants to use the front door

of his father's house—as he feels a son should, especially since he is
as light in complexion as his father and might easily pass for white.
The front door stands as a kind of symbol of equality in my drama,
which is a problem play on race relations. There is a clash between the
colored son and the white father in which the youth kills the plantation owner. A lynch mob comes. The boy commits suicide rather
than be humiliated by a mob and hung. At the final curtain, alone,
the mother goes mad. I intended the play as a tragedy of the American
South.

The play opens in the early fall just as the boy's younger sister, a
pretty teen-age girl, is going away to school. She leaves. To my astonishment, at the rehearsals in New York I found this girl still walking
about the plantation mansion throughout the second act. I asked how
she could be in the second act of the play when she had gone away
in the first act.

"Oh, we had her miss the train," I was told. "You have to have a
pretty girl all through a play on Broadway—for box-office."

"But what happens to her in the end?" I asked.

"According to the revised script, she gets raped by the white
overseer. That's part of the finale."

"But isn't that adding horror on top of horror?" I said. "I've
already got a murder, a suicide, a mob and a mad scene in the play."

"Rape is for sex," he said. "You have to have sex in a Broadway
show."

When I protested to my agent, a venerable former actor, he
pooh-poohed me and agreed with the producer, saying a melodramatic
hit with plenty of action would be better than an artistic flop. Over-
ridden on all sides, I sat and watched my first play—which I had conceived as a poetic tragedy—being turned into what the producer hoped
would be a commercial hit. Despite all of this, however, in the end
the basic meaning of the play was not altered. It was still quite clear
at the final curtain that race relations in the plantation states are not
all sweetness and light. The pretty girl was pretty, walking in and out
of the set all through the acts until rape time came. And Leon Janny,
who played the mulatto boy, looked like a matinee idol. The actress,
Rose McClendon, for whom I had first written the play at Jasper
Deeter's Hedgerow Theater, was magnificent as the mother. It was a

well-chosen cast. Chester Erskine was the director. The producer was Martin Jones.

Mr. Jones was a strange man of inherited wealth, whose hobby was the theater. He had had a big financial success with *White Cargo*, another drama of miscegenation laid in the South Seas. Mr. Jones quite frankly said he was not interested in the message of my play. What he hoped to have on his hands when it was molded into box-office form was another *White Cargo*. He implied that if I as author would just leave him alone, we might have a box-office hit. My agent assured me that Mr. Jones knew what he was doing, and that anyone so lucky as to have a first play headed for Broadway might well leave it in the experienced hands of men who knew the professional theater. He told me Martin Jones had been a backer of various Earl Carroll revues and knew the commercial stage.

Earl Carroll, tall, thin and debonair, came to the last afternoon run-through of *Mulatto* at the Vanderbilt Theater, just before the dress rehearsal scheduled for that evening. The producer asked Mr. Carroll to remain while the others went to supper. Then he requested Earl Carroll's assistance in the lighting of the play. Chester Erskine, the director, had already set the light cues, but Mr. Jones wanted some changes. He also thought it might be effective, he told Mr. Carroll, to have colored lights playing on the curtains between scenes as they did at musical shows. So, between five and seven that evening, I watched as Martin Jones and Earl Carroll worked out some very fancy lighting effects for my somber drama. A little after seven, Chester Erskine returned to the Vanderbilt by way of the lobby and paused at the back of the auditorium. Seeing a rainbow of lights playing on the stage and a tall man directing the electricians setting new light cues of which he, the director, knew nothing, Chester Erskine yelled, "Who in the hell is that man?"

Martin Jones turned to see his director standing in the aisle. He said, "This is Earl Carroll. I've asked him to help us with the lights."

"Who's directing this play?" cried Erskine angrily, "you, me, or Earl Carroll?"

Before Martin Jones could answer, Chester Erskine stalked in high dudgeon from the theater. I have not seen him since. The dress rehearsal was held without a director, and the New York playbills did not bear Mr. Erskine's name. The play opened for a series of previews. Then came the grand opening. At the opening the white members of the cast all found in their dressing rooms large linen envelopes containing an engraved invitation to a party on Park Avenue following the performance. None of the Negro members of the cast—nor I, the author—were invited to this party, not even Rose McClendon, who played the leading role.

My play ran for a year on Broadway and was listed among the twelve longest runs for 1935-36. It then played for two more seasons on the road all the way to the Coast, establishing a record for the number of performances in America of any play yet written by a Negro. During the Broadway run Rose McClendon became ill and died. Mercedes Gilbert took over the role of the mother, and later Abbie Mitchell played it on tour.

On account of its subject matter—and box-office sex—*Mulatto* was banned in Philadelphia. It came near being banned in Chicago, too, where the rape had to be toned down a great deal. A good press agent took advantage of all this to make the play front-page news in many cities. In New York he engaged a goateed Southern "Colonel" to picket the theater with a sign claiming the play libeled the South. Result—Southerners bought tickets in great numbers to see what was being said about them. Because the young mulatto died heroically protesting segregation, Negroes liked the play, so there was a large colored attendance. At first, at the Vanderbilt, the box office tried not to sell Negroes seats in the orchestra. When I learned of this, I not only protested, but I bought as many orchestra seats myself as I could afford in the very center of the theater. These I gave to the darkest Negroes I knew, including Claude McKay.

The management and I never got along very well. Several times I was asked to take a royalty cut. Once they asked me to waive royalty rights altogether. During the first six weeks I received no royalties. When I finally got the Dramatists Guild to collect the amount due, Martin Jones stopped speaking to me. He then added his name to mine on the playbills as author, several weeks after the play had opened. It took a Dramatists Guild arbitration to return the sole authorship to me. Again the management held up my royalties—and with my mother's illness requiring ever greater expenditures for X-rays, radium, and frequent hospital care, I badly needed the money. The correspondence between myself, the Dramatists Guild, my agent and the play's management eventually grew to such a number of pages that it was more than a hundred times the thickness of the actual manuscript of *Mulatto*. Eventually, however, my royalties were paid and the delaying tactics ceased.

Not being one to take business matters personally, however, I continued to greet my producer, Martin Jones, politely whenever I saw him. But Mr. Jones would pass me without a word, in the theater or out. After the Dramatists Guild intervention, he never broke his silence—until months later on my way to Spain, we ran into each other quite by accident in the lobby of the *Folies Bergères* in Paris. I did not know Martin Jones was in Europe, and he did not know I was there. We were both so astonished that we shook hands like old friends.

## PRELUDE TO SPAIN

WHEN I got on the boat to go to Europe, in the spring of 1937 to cover the Spanish Civil War, I could hardly speak above a whisper. The night before I left Cleveland, Joe Louis had become heavyweight champion of the world, so I had ridden around for hours in a car full of folks shouting and yelling after the news of Braddock's defeat came over the radio. I do not believe Negro America has ever before or since had a national hero like Joe Louis. As he went up the ladder toward the championship, and after he became champion, winning fight after fight, Louis became a kind of symbol of all that Negroes had always dreamed of in American life. Then, as the Nazi threat in Europe became more and more pronounced, he became for the Negro people through the world a champion of racial decency and achievement, the one who could and was giving the lie to the Hitler blood theory of white supremacy—which our own American Red Cross was later to adopt to the hurt and horror of black Americans.

Each time Joe Louis won a fight in those depression years, even before he became champion, thousands of colored Americans on relief or W. P. A., and poor, would throng out into the streets all across the land to march and cheer and yell and cry because of Joe's one-man triumphs. No one else in the United States has ever had such an effect on Negro emotions—or on mine. I marched and cheered and yelled and cried, too. A few years before, when Joe Louis had lost his first fight to Schmeling in Harlem, I had been a part of the hush and the sadness that fell over darker New York. After the fight, which I attended, I walked down Seventh Avenue and saw grown men weeping like children, and women sitting on the curbs with their heads in their hands. All across the country that night when the news came that Joe was knocked out, people cried.

Before I set out for Spain at the end of June, I stopped by the office in New York of my long-time friend and lawyer-without-fee, Arthur Spingarn, and made my first will. Not that I had anything to leave anybody—except possible potential royalties. But the papers were full of news of bombing raids on Spanish cities where the Germans and the Italians were trying out their new war planes, so I thought maybe I might not come back. Therefore, if any more royalties were collected from *Mulatto*, my mother should have them. I had been surprised one day to receive in Cleveland (where my mother had moved from Oberlin to be near her doctor) a letter from the *Baltimore Afro-American* asking me if I would consider going to Spain—since I spoke Spanish—to cover for that paper the activities of Negroes in the International Brigades. One of my dreams had always been to go to Spain. But at first I was not sure I wanted to go in the midst of a Civil War—with the part that I most wanted to see, Andalusia, in the hands of Franco. I had touched Spain briefly during my days as a seaman—Valencia and Alicante—but had not been able to go inland. I loved what I saw then of Spain. Very little money was coming from my writing that spring, and there were continual difficulties collecting from my play. Since the *Afro-American* offered me four to six months abroad at what seemed to me a good rate of pay, I made up my mind to accept. The *Cleveland Call Post* and *Globe* magazine also said they would pay for articles. So on very short notice I made ready for the trip.

First I paid my mother's rent for three months ahead. Then I opened an account for her at the bank in which I deposited, with the

*Mulatto* monies sent from New York just before sailing, enough for her and my brother to live on during the summer. The previous year I'd paid my brother's tuition for his first semester at Wilberforce, but he had been expelled before the end of the term for disobeying the Dean of Women's rules in regard to dating freshman girls. Forgiving this sin of youthful ardor, since he wanted to return for the midwinter term, I took what royalties I was then able to get, and again paid his tuition. But this spring report showed very low marks, and the Dean of Men reported him absent from the campus more often than he was present, enjoying himself in Columbus or Cincinnati. So it was agreed among us, him, my mother and me, that he would remain at home in Cleveland and work, and help our ailing mother around the house as much as he could while I was abroad. But I had hardly gotten to Spain before letters came from home asking for more money. I did not then know why, but later I learned that my brother had persuaded mother to let him go back to college again. Before I got home from Europe he had flunked out a second time—but said he had lots of fun in the process. I have never been one to object to fun. But when I learned that my mother had gone to the landlord and gotten back the three months rent I had paid to send with his application for readmission to college, I didn't think he really needed to have fun that badly. My mother was always goodhearted that way, though.

But what happened to the money in the bank, that it should all be gone before I even got to Madrid? Why did I have to send almost all my newspaper pay to Cleveland from Spain when I thought I'd left enough money at home for several months' expenses? That mystery was not solved until I got back to America. I was not told by letter of an emergency that arose. A cousin, fourth or fifth removed, whom I had never met, wrote my mother that her daughter had just graduated from high school. She said conditions were very bad where they were living, with no available jobs for Negro girls. She asked could not her daughter come to live with my mother in Cleveland, a big Northern city without prejudice where there surely must be work and opportunities for a colored youngster? My generous-hearted mother replied, surely send the dear girl to her. With me away and my brother returning to college, she had plenty of room and needed someone to help keep her company.

The girl arrived pregnant. Of this condition my mother had not been informed. It seemed the girl's parents wanted to get her away from the small town where they lived before the fact of her pregnancy became obvious. I never saw the girl, but my mother told me later that she was very bright and very pretty. My mother was sorry for her, but a bit put out when she showed up in a pregnant state, disturbed, moody, and unable to work. Unfortunately, this distant young relative, of whom up to that time I had only vaguely heard, became seriously ill in Cleveland and had a difficult miscarriage. Most of the money I'd left in the bank to provide for my ailing mother had to go toward caring for this strange relative my mother had taken into her home. The girl recovered before I returned from Spain, and went back to her parents. I still don't know what she looks like, since even yet I've never seen her. But that year my brother, plus this distant cousin, used up all the money I left at home and most that I airmailed or cabled from Europe. My mother had even sold some of our belongings—including an ancient Aztec statuette Miguel Covarrubias had given me in Mexico—for the sake of these young folks.

That such financial confusion would occur, of course, I did not know when I got on the *Aquitania* to cross the Atlantic. I had had a hard year in Cleveland trying to make ends meet, then the *Mulatto* difficulties further exhausted me, so I slept almost all the way across the ocean. But whenever I did go on deck I found someone I knew with whom to talk. An old friend of my grandmother's, Mary Church Terrell from Washington, was sailing for London to deliver a speech on "The Progress and Problems of Colored Women" before the International Assembly of the World Fellowship. Bishop J. A. Hamlett and his wife of Kansas City sailed to attend a religious conference at Oxford. There were several colored tourists aboard and, in the third class, two young men from the West Indies who did not announce their destination, but later I met them in Spain in the International Brigades.

No sooner had I gotten to Paris than I found Cartier-Bresson, who had returned from Mexico. I located Bricktop, too, at her night club on Rue Pigalle, and even found some old Parisian friends with whom I used to work more than a dozen years before in Montmartre. Cartier-Bresson continued to take pictures. He had married a beautiful little Javanese dancer, Retna Moerindiah, and they had a small flat just off the Grand Boulevards near the Opera. His tiny wife was a vegetarian, so Henri had become a vegetarian, too. So with them I often dined at vegetarian restaurants in Paris, which most people were surprised to know existed. A few days after I arrived, Retna (whom everyone called Elee) starred with Djemil-Anik in a colorful program of Javanese dances at the Comédie des Champs Elysées, and there I met Cartier-Bresson's charming mother, sister and brothers. On the fourteeth of July, Bastille Day, I carried Henri's camera case in order to follow the great military parade down the Champs Elysées. Now a full-fledged professional photographer, Cartier-Bresson had a newspaper pass through police lines, so I saw within arm's reach the President and all the dignitaries on the official reviewing stand, and was practically under the horses' feet when the famous Spahis came riding by. I was anxious to get a good view of the tall, colorful Moroccan troops in their flowing robes, and the giant Senegalese, jet-black in red fezzes. That afternoon we went to the Bastille and covered the workers' parade, and later we watched the boat fêtes on the Seine, where musicians with flutes and drums floated by, and on tiny boats men held athletic contests with lances and shields, trying to push each other in the water—the popular Joutes Nautiques de Sete, a sport worth seeing. That night with Henri, Elee and other friends we went dancing in the streets, stopping at all the firehouses where free refreshments were proffered the celebrants.

The novelist, Louis Aragon, introduced me that summer to Nancy Cunard, with whom I had corresponded when she was preparing her big anthology, Negro, but had never met, although she had been in America. I told Nancy I had come to France on a Cunard Line vessel, thinking it would please her, since I knew she was of that family. To my surprise, she had never set foot on a Cunard liner and never intended to do so, she said, because the line segregated Negroes. Instead, she traveled on the French boats. Nancy Cunard had a fondness for Negro music, so together we visited Bricktop's. That amazing little freckle-faced personality I had known from the day in 1925 when she first set foot in Paris to sing at the Grand Duc where I was working as a kitchen boy. She arrived in Montmartre broke, having lost her purse on the docks at Havre, and the club had few patrons to greet her arrival, so the night of her debut she came into the kitchen and cried. But now she was perhaps the most famous nightclub hostess on the Continent, with royalty—and Cole Porter—at her tables.

Mabel Mercer, an English chanteuse of color with a way with a song, was singing at Bricktop's that summer, too. Eddie South's Band had come over from New York to play at the Exposition Internationale, where the electric fountains were a sight to behold. There was also a big American Negro revue at the Moulin Rouge, and Adelaide Hall at the Big Apple. So in Paris I ran into a lot of people I knew and had so much fun that for two or three weeks I didn't do much about getting my passport validated for Spain. Jacques Roumain, the Haitian poet and diplomat whom I had met in Port au Prince, was then living in Paris where he was studying authropology at the Musee de l'Homme. Mercer Cook—the son of Abbie Mitchell, the actress then playing in my *Mulatto* at home—was also in Paris, studying, with his wife and sons. And shortly the Cuban poet, Nicolás Guillén, arrived from Havana. So I found a great many old friends in France and made a number of new ones. René Maran, the French Negro author of *Batouala*, entertained me at his home. And Josephine Baker, who was starring at the *Folies Bergères*, invited me to a performance there and received me afterwards in her dressing room. This stunning dancer from St. Louis spoke with me almost entirely in French.

"Her French is of the purest and best," said the old-time Negro musicians of Montmartre, "but her English ain't so good—which is why she don't speak it much."

The Negroes of Montmartre claimed that Josephine Baker, a toast of Paris almost from the moment of her arrival a dozen years before, had acquired perfect French by moving only in the highest artistic and social circles for so long. But her English, they said, was still Dixie Negro. True or not, I don't know. Certainly Miss Baker seemed to me one of the most cultivated and beautifully dressed women I had ever seen—every inch a star then, with a half-dozen attendants waiting on her hand and foot back stage. Just in front of me in the auditorium during the show at the *Folies Bergères* I noticed a whole row of turbanned Moroccans in flowing brown robes. When

I asked Miss Baker if she knew who they were, she said, "Oh, yes, the Sultan of Morocco and his aides. This is the fourteenth night straight they've reserved the same row."

At the International Writers' Congress in Paris that summer I met Stephen Spender and W. H. Auden from London, also John Strachey and the beautiful Rosamund Lehman, Pablo Neruda from Chile, José Bergamin from Spain, Michael Koltsov and Ilya Ehrenburg from Russia, and a great many French writers, including Tristan Tzara and André Malraux. At one of the sessions, the young actor, Jean-Louis Barrault, recited some of my poems in French. And there was a gala evening of music and dance at which the Negro performers from the Moulin Rouge appeared to climax the program. With Cartier-Bresson I went to the motorcycle races and to an enormous outdoor labor fete where Trenet was singing. With a Martiniquian friend, who had once been the doorman at the Grand Duc where we had both worked in the 'twenties, but was now a race-track gambler, I went several times to the races, to the stadium to see Panama Al Brown fight, and explored the little *boîtes* of Montmartre. I heard Eddie South's music at the Exposition and saw the fireworks at night. Paris was so alive that summer that I regretted having to leave it to fulfill my newspaper assignment in Spain. But finally I got on a train headed for Barcelona on the very day that the Paris papers reported the worst bombing of all so far of that war-torn Catalonian port. The latest German and Italian planes were just then beginning to be used in large numbers against the Loyalist cities. Several hundred people, so I heard on the radio as I was packing my bags, had been killed by Fascist aviation that day in Barcelona.

# 8
# WORLD WITHOUT END

### BOMBS IN BARCELONA

NICOLÁS GUILLÉN went with me to Spain as a correspondent for a Cuban paper. Since everybody said food in that war-torn country was scarce, we took along with us an enormous basket of edibles. But we ate it all on the train. Guillén was a jovial companion with whom to travel and on the way to Barcelona he entertained me with Cubanismos and folk songs:

> *Oyelo bien, encargada!*
> *Esta es la voz que retumba—*
> *Esta es la ultima rumba*
> *Que bailamos en tu morada.*

At the border between France and Spain there is a tunnel, a long stretch of darkness through which the night express from Paris passes in the early morning. When the train comes out into the sunlight, on the Spanish side of the mountain, with a shining blue bay where children swim in the Mediterranean, you see the village of Port Bou. The town seemed bright and quiet that morning. But as I left the train, I noticed that almost all of the windows of the station were shattered. There were machine-gun marks on the walls of the custom-house and several nearby houses were in ruins, gutted by bombs. In the winding streets of Port Bou there were signs, REFUGIO, pointing to holes in the mountains to be used in case of air raids. And on old walls there were new Loyalist posters. One read: "It's better to be the tail of a lion than the head of a rat." This was my first view of war-time Spain, this little town by the blue sea where travelers changed trains.

In the country they were harvesting the wheat, and as we chugged southward, men and women were swinging primitive scythes in the fields. The Barcelona train was very crowded that day and all around me folks kept up a rapid fire of conversation in various accents. Guillén and I were the only Negroes on the train, so I thought, until at one of the stations when we got out to buy fruit, we noticed a dark face leaning from a window of the coach ahead of us. When the train started again, we went forward to investigate. He was a brownskin boy from the Canary Islands in a red shirt and a blue beret. He had escaped from the Canaries by the simple expedient of getting into his fishing boat with the rest of her crew and sailing toward French Morocco. From there he had gotten to France. The Canary Islands were a part of Spain, he said, but the fishermen did not like the men who had usurped power, so many of them sailed their boats away and came to fight with the Loyalists. This young man spoke a strange Spanish dialect that was hard for Guillén to understand, but he told us that many folks in the Canaries are colored, mixed with African and Spanish blood.

What should have been a short trip from the French border to Barcelona, took all day and well into the night. When our blacked-out train pulled into the blacked-out city near midnight, Nicolás Guillén was so tired that he had stopped talking or singing, and wanted nothing so much as a good bed. There were no lights whatsoever on the platform of the Barcelona station, so we followed the crowd moving slowly like shadows into the station where one lone lantern glimmered behind a ticket wicket. I was loaded down as usual with bags, books, records and a typewriter. Guillén had sense enough to travel light with mostly just his songs and himself. He helped me carry things, and clung to what little remained of our hamper of food. We took a bus through pitch-black streets to a hotel on the Ramblas—there was no gas for taxis and only one bus met each train. I was so tired that night that I slept right through an air-raid alert. Hotel in-structions were that all guests were to assemble in the lobby when an alert sounded. Since the hotel had no basement, the ground floor was considered safest. But the so-called ground floor of this hotel was really several feet above street level. The lobby had enormous French doors and windows opening on a balcony. It did not look very safe to me. But I learned later that in a bombing no place was really safe, and that the Spaniards had two rather fatalistic theories about protection. One was during an air raid to go to the roof of a building and fall down with it if a bomb struck. The other was go to the ground floor and, in case of a hit, be buried at once under debris.

One could tell that Barcelona was jittery from the terrific bombing it had undergone the day before I arrived. But nothing happened during the first twenty-four hours I was there, so Guillén and I walked about, looking at the destruction and at the antiaircraft guns on most of the busy corners, the flower sellers on the tree-lined Ramblas, and the passing crowds everywhere, with folks clinging to the overcrowded street cars all day long. Sitting in the cafés, whenever the public radios started to blare out the latest war news, everybody would jump. Nerves were certainly on edge. But there were no planes overhead all day.

As Guillén and I sat at a sidewalk table on the Ramblas that afternoon, a dark young man passed, turned, looked back at me and spoke. He recognized me, he said, because he had heard me read my poems at the library in New York. He was a Puerto Rican named Roldan, who had come from Harlem to serve as an interpreter in Spain. At that moment he was on his way to a dance at a little club where the Cubans and other Spanish-speaking peoples from the Caribbean gathered. He invited us to come with him. The club had a beautiful courtyard and a little bar where rum drinks were mixed. The party that afternoon was in honor of the International Brigaders on leave, among them several Spanish-speaking Negroes and a colored Portugese. Catalonian soldiers and their girls mingled gaily with the Negro guests. And Guillén, lionized as Cuba's most famous poet, was in his element, surrounded by girls.

That night back at our hotel we knew it was wartime because, in the luxurious dining room with its tuxedoed waiters, there was only one fixed menu with no choice of food. The dinner was good, but not elaborate. Later we went to an outdoor café for coffee. Until midnight we sat watching the crowds strolling up and down the tiled sidewalks of the Ramblas. The fact that Barcelona was lightless did not keep people home on a warm evening. There was a wan bulb behind the bar inside to help the barman find his bottles, but other than that no visible light save for the stars shining brightly. The buildings were great grey shadows towering in the night, with windows shuttered everywhere and curtains drawn. There must be no visible lights in any windows to guide enemy aviators.

At midnight, the public radios on many corners began to blare the war news and people gathered in large groups to hear it. Then the café closed, and we went to the hotel. I had just barely gotten to my room and begun to undress when the low extended wail of a siren began, letting us know that Fascist planes were coming. They came, we had been told, from Mallorca across the sea at a terrific speed, dropped their bombs, then circled away into the night again. Quickly, I put on my shirt, passed Guillén's room, and together we started downstairs. Suddenly all the lights went out in the hotel. We heard people rushing down the stairs in the dark. A few had flashlights with them. Some were visibly frightened. In the lobby a single candle was burning, casting giantlike shadows on the walls. In an ever-increasing wail the siren sounded louder and louder, droning its deathly warning. Suddenly it stopped. By then the lobby was full of people, men, women and children, speaking in Spanish, English, French.

In the distance we heard a series of quick explosions.

"Bombs?" I asked.

"No, antiaircraft guns," a man explained.

Everyone became very quiet. Then we heard the guns go off again.

"Come here," a man called, leading the way. Several of us went out on the balcony where, in the dark, we could see the searchlights playing across the sky. Little round puffs of smoke from the antiaircraft shells floated against the stars. In the street a few women hurried along to public bomb-proof cellars.

Then for a long while nothing happened. No bombs fell. After about an hour, the lights suddenly came on in the hotel as a signal that the danger had ended. Evidently, the enemy planes had been driven away without having completed their mission. Everyone went back upstairs to bed. The night was quiet again. I put out my light, opened the window and, never being troubled with sleeplessness, I was soon sound asleep. The next thing I knew was that, with part of my clothes in my arms, I was running in the dark toward the stairs. A terrific explosion somewhere nearby had literally lifted me out of bed. Apparently I had slept through an alert, for almost all the other guests in the hotel had already assembled in the lobby, huddled in various stages of dress and undress. At the foot of the stairs I put my trousers on over my pajamas and sat down shaking like a leaf, evidently having been frightened to this dire extent while still asleep, because I had hardly realized I was afraid until I felt myself shaking. When I put one hand on the other, both hands were trembling. There were the sounds of what seemed like a major battle going on in the streets outside—but this was only the antiaircraft guns firing at the sky, so someone near me explained. Suddenly I developed the worst stomachache I've ever had in my life. I managed to find my way to a MEN'S ROOM about the time a distant explosion sounded, far away, yet near enough to cause the hotel to shake. When I came back, by the light of the single candle at the desk, I managed to find Guillén, sitting calmly like Buddha on a settee under a potted palm. He said, "Ay, chico, eso es!" Well, this is it! Which was of little comfort.

Gradually I began to be fully awake and less frightened, so I sat down, too, smoked a cigarette, and got acquainted with some of the other folks in the lobby. After perhaps a half hour, when the crackling of the antiaircraft batteries had died down, an all clear sounded, and the desk clerk said we might return to our beds. He blew out his candle before opening some of the French doors leading onto the balcony overlooking the Ramblas. Some of us went out on the balcony to see what was happening in the streets. An occasional military motor passed without lights, and a few people moved up and down—police and rescue workers, I supposed. As I stood there with the others a sudden crackle of shots rang out in our direction from across the corner square. Glass came down all over us from windows on the upper floors. A machine gun was firing directly at the hotel! We almost fell over each other getting back inside the lobby. Door and shutters were slammed again. Shortly some soldiers entered from the street and said that someone on an upper floor had turned on a light.

(Their orders were to fire at any exposed light in any building.) Sternly they mounted the stairs in search of the offender. Later I learned that some foreigner (not knowing the rules) had turned on a bedside bulb after he had opened his window for air. So the guards simply blasted away at the lighted room. The frightened guest was severely reprimanded. And I had cause to quake all over again. It was quite a while before I went back to sleep that night.

Eventually, however, I got used to air raids in Spain—the Junkers, Heinkels, Savoias and Capronis going over—and the sound and the feel of bombs bursting. But I never got used to the alerts—those baleful, high, eerie, wailing sirens of warning.

## SWEET WINE OF VALENCIA

SOMEWHERE along the line, the railroad to Valencia had been bombed, and no one knew just when the train service would be resumed. So Guillén and I, with others in the hotel who wished to go south, managed to hire a car to drive down the coast. Bright and early one morning through the Catalonian countryside we went speeding, through villages as old as the Roman Empire, and along the dancing Mediterranean, blue beneath the morning sky. We passed fields of wheat, groves of olives and oranges, and cities that recently had been bombed from the air or shelled from the sea. Sometimes elderly peasants in the fields lifted a clenched fist in the government salute. On walls half ruined by explosives, slogans were freshly painted hailing the People's Army. And in village squares young men were drilling to go to the front. The beautiful landscape of Spain rolled by as our car went down the road south, the Spain that had for more than a year occupied the front pages of the world, the Spain of the huge Madison Square Garden meetings in New York, the Spain that I had seen placarded in the main streets of cities like Buffalo and Denver and Salt Lake when I had lectured there: AID BESIEGED MADRID! . . . MILK FOR THE BABIES OF SPANISH DEMOCRACY! . . . MEDICAL SUPPLIES TO THE LOYALISTS! . . . The Spain to which had come from all over the world young men—including many Negroes—to fight in the International Brigades. The Spain that had brought up thousands of young Moors from Morocco as shock troops for Franco. Divided Spain, with men of color fighting on both sides. To write about them I had come to Spain.

Among the things I wanted to find out was what effect, if any, the bringing by Franco of dark troops to Spain from North Africa, had had on the people in regard to their racial attitudes. Had color prejudice been created in a land that had not known it before? What had been the treatment of Moorish prisoners by the Loyalists? Were wounded Moors segregated in the prison hospitals? Were there any Moors at all on the government side? How were American Negroes received in the cities of Spain when they came on furlough from the Brigades?

As I wondered about these things, our car began to slow down in the late afternoon for traffic was growing heavier on the road. Now burros, trucks and oxcarts mingled in increasingly long lines. Fords and oxen, peasants on muleback and soldiers in American trucks, the old and the new vied for dusty passage. On either side of us were orange groves as far as one could see. I thought of *Cuentos Valencianos* and the novel, *Entre Naranjos*, by Blasco-Ibáñez that I had read in Mexico. About sunset I saw in the distance medieval towers, mingling with tall modern structures. We were approaching a city, a big city.

"Valencia," the chauffeur said.

Ancient Mediterranean seaport, now the seat of the Spanish government. From my days as a merchant seaman, I had happy memories of Valencia. That night as I looked out the windows in the Hotel Londres with the crowded Plaza Castelos below, I was glad to find myself again in that pleasant coastal town. Valencia was a rest center for Loyalist troops and numbers of foreign sailors were in and out, too, including some Americans on boats bringing supplies to Spain. The cafés were full morning to night—even long after dark, for Valencia did not take care to black out as completely as Barcelona, although the city was shelled from the sea and bombed from the air with frequency. But the Valencians just didn't seem to care much. They had good wine and good food—fresh fish, melons and the sweetest of oranges and grapes—much more food than any other city I visited in Spain. And there were parks and bathing beaches, music and dancing, antiaircraft guns making fireworks in the sky every night, and tracer bullets arching like Roman candles in the air as Franco's bombs lighted up the port. The docks were miles from the heart of Valencia, so whenever an alert sounded, the citizens would say, "Oh, they're just going to bomb the port, not us." And they kept right on doing whatever they were doing. Nobody bothered much to seek shelter. People were always being nicked by bits of antiaircraft shrapnel showering down on them as they stood in the street or on rooftops trying to see the enemy planes when they should have been indoors.

I spent a week or so in Valencia before moving on to Madrid and the battle fronts. Word of our coming had already been sent ahead from Paris to the House of Culture in Valencia, so the poet, Miguel Hernandez and several other writers made Guillén and me welcome, and soon found for us a guesthouse where we might stay much cheaper than at a hotel. But the day we arrived the House of Culture was draped in mourning and the body of Gerda Taro, young Hungarian photographer, was lying in state there. Taking pictures at the front during an attack, she had been smashed between a tank and a truck the day before. She was Robert Capa's friend in Spain, and like him took wonderful photographs, everyone said. Valencia honored her as the first foreign newspaperwoman to die in battle during the war.

From Valencia I wrote a long letter to the girl I was in love with then, Elsie Roxborough, in Detroit. Elsie had staged a play of mine, *Emperor of Haiti*, and was ambitious to become a director in the professional theater, radio, or motion pictures. She was a lovely-looking girl, ivory-white of skin with dark eyes and raven hair like a Levantine. Each time that we met in Detroit or Cleveland or Chicago, Elsie would tell me about her dreams, and wonder whether or not it would be better for her to pass for white to achieve them. From what I knew of the American entertainment field and how Negroes were then almost entirely excluded from the directorial or technical aspects of it, I agreed with her that it was difficult for any colored person to gain entrance except as a performer—as a director or technician, almost impossible—and for a colored woman I would think it harder even than for a man. Elsie was often mistaken for white in public places, so it would be no trouble at all for her to pass as white. While I was in Spain she wrote me that she had made up her mind to do so. She intended to cease being colored. The intervals between her letters to me gradually became greater, until finally no letter came at all. When I got back to the United States, Elsie had disappeared into the white world. None of her friends saw her any more, nor did I. But every Christmas for several years she sent me a carefully chosen little present —with no return address on the packet.

That summer in Spain the beach at Valencia was as lively as Coney Island on the Fourth of July. The sand and surf were crowded with soldiers on leave and their girls. In the surf I saw one afternoon an ebony-dark young man, bathing with a party of Spaniards. Thinking he was perhaps an American or a Jamaican from one of the International Brigades, when he came out of the water I spoke to him in English, but he replied in Spanish. He was an African from Guinea on the West Coast, who had come to study in Spain before the war. He had enlisted in the People's Army, he told me, but having been a university student, he was assigned to the officers' school in Valencia to study for a commission.

I asked this young African what he thought about the war. He said, "I hope the government wins because the new Republic stands for a liberal colonial policy with a chance for my people in Africa to become educated. On Franco's side are all the old dukes and counts and traders who have exploited the colonies so long, never giving us schools or anything else. Now they are making the Africans fight against the Spanish people—using the Moors and my own people, too, to try to crush the Republic. And the same Italians who dropped bombs on Ethiopia now come over here to help Franco bomb Spaniards. You can pick up shrapnel in Valencia with Italian markings on it."

When he learned I was from New York, he wanted to know all about Harlem, and if I had ever met Joe Louis. He said he would like to come to America some day.

"To stay?" I asked him.

"No," he said, "just to visit. I like Spain. My wife is Spanish."

"I like Spain, too," I said, "only I miss the bullfights."

"I never saw one," he said, "and now all the famous matadors have run away to Franco where the money is. They are not as brave at fighting fascists as they are at facing bulls."

A common saying in Valencia was, "All the best bullfighters and all the best whores have gone over to the enemy—but we'll get along without them." That summer I did not see any bullfighters, but the few remaining prostitutes were making a fortune. Valencia, like all Mediterranean seaports, had had a great many houses of pleasure when I was there on a freighter in the early 'twenties. Now there were not nearly so many, although the city was full of soldiers on leave and sailors with bonus pay to spend, looking for agreeable girls. What houses of ill-fame there were now operated only from four in the afternoon until seven in the evening. But during these three hours of operation, the houses were as crowded as a New York subway train at rush hour, and the women did a rushing business. Unlike American soldiers visiting such houses, the Spaniards did not queue up and take their proper turns. Instead, they pushed, shoved and crowded by the hundreds into the parlors of the houses, charging boisterously but amiably like young bulls after each girl who came into view. As soon as a woman was free, she was mobbed by as many men as could reach her at once. Finally the girl would manage to untangle one eager customer from the mob and disappear, to return in a few minutes for another. When the doors were closed at seven, the girls of the houses remained at work until all those within the gates were accommodated.

Such after-hours courtesies, however, did not exist in Madrid, I learned later in the summer. There the houses of prostitution like every other business, had to close promptly on time; unserved patrons, no matter how long they had been waiting, had to leave. Madrid was a fighting city, not a center of furlough pleasures; so the black-out and curfew were strictly enforced. But in Madrid after dark the ladies of the evening took to the streets. In For Whom the Bell Tolls, Ernest Hemingway has a vivid description of nocturnal love-making along the avenues of the besieged capital. But I do not recall that he described one of its most picturesque areas. After dark just off the Puerta del Sol in the heart of Madrid, in the block behind the Telefonica— the city's only skyscraper and a favorite target for Franco's artillery— numerous prostitutes and hundreds of soldiers off duty congregated.

On moonlight nights these human shadow shapes, milling about, could see other only dimly in the moonlight. On nights of no moon, in the inky blackness between the tall buildings, no one could see anything. But the darkness up and down the street would be pin-pointed by the tiny flames of dozens and dozens of matches being lighted by the soldiers to peer into the faces of the prostitutes walking in the dark. The blacked-out canyon of the street danced with little flames of hope, burning briefly, then flung to the ground as some young soldier, lighting a match at the sound of a seductive voice, found himself peering into a broken-down witch's face.

"Caramba! You're older than my grandmother!" was a not infre-quent exclamation as the match dropped to the pavement and the soldier in disgust moved on to the next feminine voice calling in the dark. But sometimes an artillery shell gave a sudden burst of light, enough for a soldier to see a woman clearly, and perhaps pick out a partner for his needs.

Concerning the nice girls of the town, there was a very sad story going the rounds of Madrid that year. In pre-revolutionary Spain, good maidens did not go out with young men until they were engaged, and only then accompanied by a chaperon. Such girls remained virgin until married. If it were rumored otherwise, and chastity were doubted, a girl might never get a good husband. But when the Franco troops besieged Madrid in overwhelming numbers early in the days of the Civil War, and when it seemed that the city could hold out no longer, word spread that if Madrid fell to Franco his Moorish legions would rape all the women in the city. This pleasure, without hindrance, Franco had promised them. Rather than be raped, many of the good girls of Madrid decided to give themselves to their sweethearts—the gallant young men who expected to die anyway, within a few days, in defense of the city. So, under the thunder of Franco guns and the bombs of foreign planes, one thunderous night shaken by gunfire, a sort of mass submission of the decent maidens of Madrid to their beloveds took place. But due to the miracle of "No pasaron!"—They Shall Not Pass!—the city did not fall—not that week, nor that month, nor that year. Madrid held out. Then, even in the eyes of their own lovers, thousands of the nice girls of Madrid, since they were no longer virgins, were held in contempt.

In Madrid, when I went to visit the famous bull ring, it was empty save for antiaircraft guns mounted in the arena. Madrid's famous *majas* with their mantillas were gone, too, and the ladies of the evening were mostly homely hags. The great actors and actresses and musicians—except for a very few courageous artists—had all fled to San Sebastián, Salamanca, or Seville along with the rich industrialists and the Franco generals. But one great artist remained, the flamenco singer, La Niña de los Peines. She refused to leave the city she loved. When I learned in Valencia that La Niña was still singing in Madrid under fire, I decided it was time I got my permit validated for the front. Madrid was the front.

## BREAKFAST IN MADRID

MY first Sunday in Madrid, having heard that La Niña de los Peines was singing, I found the theater. The performance was at eleven o'clock in the morning—why that odd hour I never knew—but the place was already crowded when I arrived to discover on a bare stage a group of Gypsy guitarists and dancers clapping hands and tapping heels as I entered. In their midst on a wooden kitchen chair sat a middle-aged woman. The performers were not dressed in traditional Gypsy clothing—as in a professional theater presentation—but wore the ordinary working clothes of poor Madrileños. There was nothing visually colorful or picturesque about them. They might have been people out of the audience sitting on the barren stage with no special lighting and no curtains, and without a spotlight, fooling around with a few guitars. Never having seen La Niña before, I asked if she were there. My seat neighbor said, "Yes. The old one in the middle on the chair, that's her."

La Niña de los Peines, Pastora Pavón. She was clapping her hands with the others, but someone else was singing when I sat down. Shortly, without any introduction or fanfare, she herself sat up very straight in her chair and, after a series of quavering little cries, began to half-speak, half-sing a *solea*—to moan, intone and cry in a Gypsy Spanish I did not understand, a kind of raw heartbreak rising to a crescendo that made half the audience cry aloud with her after the rise and fall of each phrase. The guitars played behind her, but you forgot the guitars and heard only her voice rising hard and harsh, wild, lonely and bitter-sweet from the bare stage of the theater with the unshaded house lights on full. This plain old woman could make the hair rise on your head, could do to your insides what the moan of an air-raid siren did, could rip your soul-case with her voice. I went to hear La Niña many times. I found the strange, high, wild crying of her flamenco in some ways much like the primitive Negro blues of the deep South. The words and music were filled with heartbreak, yet vibrant with resistance to defeat, and hard with the will to savor life in spite of its vicissitudes. The poor of Madrid adored La Niña de los Peines—this old Girl with the Combs—who refused to leave her besieged city, and whose voice became part of the strength of Madrid's stubborn resistance under the long-range guns, a few miles away.

The Franco batteries shelled the city almost daily. I wondered, when I first arrived in Madrid, why I was offered my choice of the large and beautifully furnished front rooms on the top floor of the Alianza de Intelectuales, instead of the much smaller former servant's room at the back of the house. With living quarters very scarce in Madrid, and the clubhouse crowded, I wondered why someone was not already occupying these spacious front rooms with a lovely view of the city. Gratefully I accepted one. Guillén, much wiser, took a servant's room belowstairs. I soon learned that my room, being a high corner room, was the room most exposed to shellings in the whole house. In fact, its windows on one side, directly faced the Fascist guns. At night I could see the flash of enemy fire when shells poured into the city. But once I'd moved in, I stayed. Another American and I were the only tenants on the top floor. The Spanish writers, thinking that all Americans were like Ernest Hemingway, anyhow, believed we loved to live facing guns.

My fellow American was away at the front when I arrived. But when he came back, I found him a well-bred Princetonian named Harry Dunham, a young cameraman for Pathé News, who had been in the thick of several battles and had taken some daring sequences. We became quite good friends and he gave me a picture of himself riding atop an armored car with his camera. Some years later Harry was killed in the American Army in the South Pacific. But neither of us were struck by shells that summer in our exposed bedrooms of the Alianza.

The poet, Rafael Alberti and his wife, Maria Teresa Leon, were in charge of the Alianza de Intelectuales at Marques del Duero 7. They lived reasonably safe from shells in a little apartment on the sub-street level of the mansion, an apartment that probably had been occupied by a governess or a tutor. The actual servants' rooms were in a two-story wing of their own, and were very small. When I asked Guillén if he did not wish to share my large light airy chamber on the top floor, Guillén said, no, he would keep his servant's room with its one window. Mine, he said, had too much glass to shatter in case a shell struck the house. Guillén said he would hate to be blown up and cut up by glass also. With Dunham away most of the time making newsreels, on that third floor all by myself, it was lonely, especially during shellings.

This Alianza was the writers' and artists' club. Few foreigners lived there—Dunham, Guillén and I being the only ones then. It was a richly furnished house of some fifty rooms, the former home of a rebel marquis whose family fortune was derived from the slave trade in the days of the Spanish Main. The walls of the living room were hung with priceless Goyas, El Grecos, and other famous paintings. There were rare medieval tapestries, enormous porcelain vases, and much antique furniture, including real Louis XV chairs. The marquis had been a great bullfight fan and possessed chests full of spangled toreador suits. Other trunks were filled with ruffled skirts and beautiful lace mantillas, which smart Spanish women sometimes wore to corridas and the Feria at Sevilla. There was an entire room full of old armor and suits of mail, too, such as Don Quixote wore. Sometimes on chilly nights when we had nothing better to do, the men would all dress up in matador jackets and the women in dresses from Seville of old and have, to my jazz records, an impromptu costume ball. But we were careful to put everything back properly in the basement, for some of the things were priceless, and we knew they would probably go to a museum when the war was over.

The military bus that brought Guillén and me to Madrid over a shell-scarred road had arrived at night after a thirteen-hour trip from

Valencia. Dinner at the Alianza was over, and we were told that there
were no restaurants open after dark in the whole city. Anyway, with
a curfew no one was allowed abroad late at night without a military
pass. I went to bed very hungry. But I slept right through the breakfast hour the next morning. At the Alianza there were only two meals
a day, breakfast at nine in the morning and dinner at eight at night.
There was not a scrap of food to be found in the house between
meals. There were no railroads running into Madrid, and only one
highway for the transportation of food—the military road over which
our bus had come. A city of a million people was fed entirely by this
one road. No wonder there was almost nothing to eat for sale anywhere, nothing on the shelves of the food shops, and restaurants—
what few there were—were strictly rationed, with a food card required
of each diner.

But on that morning of intense hunger, I refused to believe it
would be my fate to starve my first day in Madrid. Guillén had already
gotten up and gone out, as had Alberti. So I ventured into the streets
alone and found my way through the morning sunlight to the Grand
Via. Fortunately, speaking Spanish fairly well, I was able to ask of
almost every passer-by where a restaurant might be. Most people
looked at me in complete amazement and said they knew of none in
operation at that hour anywhere in town. With supplies so short,
Madrid restaurants opened only at dinner time. A few food stores
were pointed out to me, but they had nothing edible to sell, even if I
had had a ration card—which I'd not yet secured.

Soon I reached the Puerta del Sol, the Times Square of Madrid,
all of whose shops were sandbagged, with just a hole between sandbags for an entrance. There were many broken windows, some boarded
up and some not. But I was too hungry to pay much attention to the
ravages of war. I felt certain there must be *somewhere* in that city
something to eat. I determined to find it. At last I did. A man in the
Puerta del Sol told me that each day in a bar near the Telefonica,
they opened a keg of beer at noon—and with the beer there were
usually appetizers.

I headed post haste for the bar. It was crowded to the doors, but
I managed to wedge my way inside. The keg of beer had not yet been
opened. Finally noon came, and the crowd of soldiers and civilians

surged toward it. I was in the forefront and managed to get, if not at the bar, at least near it, as the mugs of beer were put on the counter. I got one. That was my breakfast juice. But where were the tidbits, the morsels, the appetizers? Everyone else seemed to be waiting hungrily, for most eyes were turned expectantly toward a door that led to the kitchen. At last that door opened and two waiters emerged, each bearing a big, round tray piled high with I knew not what, since the contents of their trays were obscured by clouds of steam that rose from them. The waiters put the trays down, one at either end of the bar. I lost no time getting to the nearest one. Everyone reached out and took a handful of whatever was on the trays. I stretched over a man's shoulder and plunged my hand into the tray, too. My hand came up full of warm hard grey little objects which turned out to be tiny swirling little shells. I discovered I had a handful of snails!

I knew that people in the Latin lands ate snails, but I had never intended to eat one myself. However, at this point I was so hungry that I did not hesitate, nor even stop to think. I simply pulled a snail out of its shell and ate it. In fact, as fast as I could, I pulled snails from their shells and ate them—then I reached just in time for another handful before the tray was emptied. Steamed snails were my first meal in Madrid.

## HARLEM SWING AND SPANISH SHELLS

ONE of Franco's ways of getting back at besieged Madrid for holding out so tenaciously was to broadcast daily, from his powerful radio towers at Burgos or Seville, the luncheon and dinner menus of the big hotels there, the fine food that the Falangists were eating, and the excellent wines they drank. (Rioja and the best of wine areas were in Fascist hands.) One could almost hear rebel diners smacking their lips on the radio.

Since food was scarce in Madrid, I did not torture myself listening to Franco's succulent broadcasts. But I found myself thinking a great deal about hamburgers, hot dogs, sugared doughnuts and ice cream—things one can get on almost any American corner—not to speak of more substantial items like steak. In Madrid, when I got there, even with the proper ration cards, there was next to nothing to buy. The city was almost surrounded by Franco's troops, who were trying to starve the people out. I, after missing my first breakfast in the city, never missed another one.

Breakfast at the Alianza consisted of a single roll and "Malta coffee"—burnt grain, pulverized and brewed into a muddy liquid. Sometimes there was milk, but no sugar. Guillén and I had brought from Paris several bottles of saccahrin tablets which we shared with the others as a sweetener. After breakfast one had the whole day uninterrupted by meals. I spent much of my time trying to discover bars that served tidbits with drinks. There were several that tried to do so each day, circumstances permitting, so by making the rounds between bombardments, I could manage sometimes to eat a small lunch of knick-knacks before night. One very sedate old wine house on Alcala Zamora was still serving ancient expensive sherry—for very rare old sherry was all it had left in its cellars. Here they would attempt every day at five to serve something to go with the sherry—often only chestnuts or green almonds. But sometimes from the slaughter house, the venerable proprietor would secure the hearts, liver and lights of various animals and boil them, then slice them into little hunks to be speared with a toothpick. Each person might have a small saucer of these innards with his sherry. Almost all the writers at the Alianza were to be found in this dusky wood-paneled old bar in the late afternoon talking about literature and trying not to seem unduly disturbed if the proprietor was unable to furnish anything that day but rare old sherry.

Dinner at the Alianza was beautifully served every evening and delicious, for the club had an excellent cook, who did her best to make what little she could purchase appetizing. She could create a wonderful soup out of almost nothing but a pot of water, a few herbs and some rancid olive oil. It became a very special soup if someone left a few crumbs or crusts of bread on the breakfast table. She would toast and fry these in olive oil at night and put them into the soup. Beans she could flavor superbly. Once in a blue moon we might have meat, a little cube, or a very thin slice for each person. Sometimes, but rarely, there was fresh fish from Valencia. I shall never forget one night when we had fish; we had also a very special guest. He was a venerable Spanish scholar, soft-spoken and grey-haired, who had arrived in Madrid from Valencia, probably on the same truck that brought the city's ration of fish that day. Our distinguished guest had not been in Madrid before during the Civil War, so he had never experienced such slim food rations, since in Valencia people still ate fairly well. And there, of course, came plenty of fish directly from the sea.

When our ration of fish arrived on the table at the Alianza—a dozen beautifully fried but quite small smelts—and the platter was passed to our distinguished guest first, he simply raked all the fish into his own plate, thinking them a single service. As polite as Spaniards generally are, at this moment two or three persons at the table could not resist a groan of anguish. Someone even blurted out before thinking, "Ay, Señor, you've taken all the fish."

Our hostess, Maria Teresa Leon, who presided over the table, quickly and graciously said, "Oh, but they're yours, sir, prepared just for you." However, the bewildered guest could not help but notice the sad faces at the table, so he said, "But won't you all share mine?"

By now everyone had gotten their company manners back, and politely refused. "Oh, thank you, no, those are for you, dear friend, sweet visitor. *Bon apetit!* Eat well!"

A dozen little fish normally would have been a rather small serving for even one person in Spain—just a starter preceding the meat course. In Valencia one person might even in war time have that many fish for a meal. But in Madrid, where everything had to come into the city by trucks using precious gasoline, and over a shell-raked road, it was another matter. Our embarrassed guest entreated in vain that we share his fish. No, we would not! We stuck to the fiction that they were prepared *just* for him. Fortunately, a bowl of *garbanzos*, big old Spanish cowpeas, arrived on the table, so we each had a helping of those for dinner, plus an onion. I never ate so many raw onions in my life as I did that summer. Onions and grapes were the only things to eat that were at all plentiful in Madrid. Sometimes the grapes were very sour and green, but we ate them voraciously.

Beans and onions and grapes at the Alianza were all elegantly brought to table in priceless old china belonging to the marquis who was with Franco in Burgos. I suppose he has gotten all his beautiful dishes back now after the war, as well as his lovely tapestries and priceless El Grecos on the walls. As head of the Alianza, Rafael Alberti, was most careful of its belongings. And everybody's heart bled when a cup or something was broken, which didn't happen often, but when it did the fault usually lay with the club's collective son, Luis, a war orphan the Alianza had adopted. Luis was a gentle boy of sixteen who tried to be as careful as he could, but it seemed his fate to almost always be tripping over a rung near a Venetian mirror, dropping something, or tearing the page of an old book just by looking at it. The writers and artists in the house nicknamed the boy, El Destroyer. But because he had seen his whole family wiped out in a bombing raid on his village, nobody scolded him. Usually Maria Teresa just asked him to *please* be very careful.

At first I thought perhaps the youngster was just careless, until I saw a series of little mishaps, one after another, overtake him through no fault of his own; the lad was accident prone. One night I witnessed what must have been for an adolescent, the most embarrassing moment of his life. This was the evening when the main salon of the mansion, seldom used, had been opened in honor of the visit to Madrid of two American Congressmen, Henry O'Connell of Montana and James T. Bernard from Minnesota. For these American dignitaries the intellectuals of wartime Madrid held a reception at the Alianza. Everybody put on their best clothes for the occasion. After we had all shaken hands with the visiting Americans, there was to be an hour of music. The large drawing room was crowded with visitors, including General Miaja, the defender of Madrid. All went well until the very moment when the music was to begin. As the Congressmen took their seats, the rest of the assemblage found places, too, including El Destroyer. He sat down unobtrusively on one of the little antique golden Louis XV chairs in an out-of-the-way corner near the tail of the grand piano. This chair, generations old, must have held many people in its time. But of all nights, tonight was the night the chair decided to cease performing its function. Just as the first note was about to be struck on the piano and the dignified soprano faced her quiet listeners, with an unduly loud splintering of its tiny legs, the Louis XV chair suddenly gave way beneath the young Spaniard.

It sank to the floor with a loud crash, carrying with it an astonished adolescent.

El Destroyer loved American jazz. But fortunately my records were locked away safe from breakage, with the marquis's symphonies in the recreation house across the courtyard from the mansion itself. This room had a splendid record player with modern amplification and was seldom used except during a very heavy shelling of the city. The shells generally came from the west where Franco's artillery was situated. This recreation house was on the western side of the court, protected by a much taller building adjoining it. Shells would have to penetrate this larger building before striking the recreation rooms. So this house was considered by the residents of the Alianza as the safest place to be during a *bombardeo*. When heavy shells began to whistle too near our mansion, or explode within wall-trembling distance, Maria Teresa would get the key to the game room and we would all gather there and listen to music until the bombardment ceased. Before I came, Harry Dunham told me, they had listened mostly to Beethoven, Brahms, or Wagnerian overtures. But when I appeared with a box full of swing music, folks would call for Benny Goodman, Duke Ellington, Lunceford or Charlie Barnet. Certainly in intensity and volume my records were much better than the marquis's symphonies for drowning out the sound of Franco's shells exploding in the streets outside.

The first heavy night shelling of Madrid after my arrival occurred at about two o'clock in the morning. Busy on an article for the *Afro-American*, I had not yet gone to bed, and was rather fascinated to watch from my window artillery flashes in the distance, then a split second later to hear a shell whistling overhead. Artillery bombardments never frightened me nearly so much as air raids. There were no baleful warning sirens, screeching eerily, to make the flesh crawl as there were before air raids. The big guns simply started to go off— and that was that. But this night shells soon began to fall near the Alianza. Suddenly a projectile landed at our very corner with a terrific explosion, like a thousand tons of dynamite. I jumped up from my typewriter and started downstairs.

Usually at the Alianza no one bothered to get out of bed during a late bombardment. But this bombardment was so intense that almost everyone gathered for company across the court in the recreation hall. As usual, someone began to play records to drown out the sound of the explosions. The amplifier was turned up very loud—so loud in fact, that unless a shell had fallen in the courtyard, we could hardly have heard it. The automatic record player would repeat a disc innumerable times if one wished. So that night of the big bombardment, the Jimmie Lunceford record we kept going continuously until almost dawn was "Organ Grinder's Swing."

## DEATH AND LAUGHTER

THE rebel gunners seemed to love to fire on Madrid in the middle of the night, but sometimes there were bombardments in the daytime, too. There were no air raids directly on the city while I was there, but enemy planes were used on nearby troop concentrations and on the bridges and highways in the surrounding countryside. The one road leading into Madrid was frequently bombed in an attempt to disrupt its traffic. But just for fun, it seemed, artillery batteries showered Madrid almost every day, sometimes taking the Telefonica for a target and dropping shells all around that skyscraper into the heart of the town. At other times, instead of concentrating on the business section, the big guns would be trained fanwise, spraying destruction over a wide area of the city. Sometimes, it seemed to me that enemy gunners just shot up in the air and let their projectiles fall at random for no military reason except to terrorize people. But the people of Madrid, having lived under fire for a year, had gotten over terror by the time I arrived. Most bombardments they treated like showers of rain, simply crossing to the opposite side of the street from that toward which the guns were firing—as one does when the rain is slanting the wrong way and shelter is drier on the other sidewalk.

My first visit to the famous Hotel Florida was to pay a call on Sherwood Eddy, the sixty-five-year-old Y. M. C. A. executive whom I had known in New York. I had run into him the day before, bustling about Madrid in an old overseas cap from World War I, which he said he had put on to make him feel at home under fire.

Together that day, Sherwood Eddy and I toured various floors of the Hotel Florida where Ernest Hemingway lived, and where up to that time some twenty artillery shells had penetrated the walls. The street entrance to the Florida was well protected with sandbags. But since it was impossible to sandbag nine stories, some of the front upper floors now had no complete walls at all. Not many guests accepted front rooms anyway any more, and suites with a view were not in demand— since the view from the rise on which the Florida sat was a full panorama of enemy territory just beyond the Casa de Campo. From shattered windowpanes one did not need binoculars to see the enemy trenches.

The Hotel Alfonso, another important hostelry a few blocks from the Florida, had several large shell holes through its four walls, too. Sometimes a shell came in one side and went right on through the other. One of the corridors on an upper floor of the Alfonso led straight into space—its French doors, balcony and all having been shot away. In an unused bedroom I looked slantingly down three floors into the street through an opening made by a projectile that had struck the roof and plowed its way downward to the sidewalk. On the hotel's marble staircase two persons had been killed by shrapnel a few days before.

The safest hotel seemed to be the Victoria, not so near the firing lines. There, Herbert Matthews of *The New York Times* and many other foreign journalists lived. The Victoria had not been struck by shell fire up to the time I left Madrid. But any of its inhabitants who had been in the city long could tell you of narrow escapes in other parts of town. Some journalists I knew, covering a special dinner for a distinguished foreign delegation, had to flee to the cellar of the restaurant with the guests when the big guns started to fire. Shortly a bus boy came down into the basement with a table leg in his hands. A member of the foreign delegation asked, "What's that?"

"That's the table where you were eating," replied the bus boy.

The citizens of Madrid themselves had thousands of humorous tales with a macabre twist. One concerned a man who went into a barbershop to get his hair cut entirely bald, since there was no soap for shampoos and he wished to avoid lice. As he sat in the chair, a shell fell in the street just outside, a sharp piece of shrapnel flew through the window, and he got his *head* cut off instead of his hair. The barber was unharmed—except that he didn't get paid for the haircut.

Another story concerned a Franco projectile that landed with a hiss and a boom one busy afternoon on a sidewalk of the Puerta del Sol. Fortunately, no one was killed. But when the smoke cleared away, people saw a man lying on the sidewalk stunned and speechless, with one leg of his trousers ripped from belt to ankle. Sympathetic strangers crowded around him. "An ambulance right away! Get the poor fellow to a hospital."

But the man, having regained his senses, jumped to his feet, angrily looked at his torn trousers, and cried, "Hospital, hell! I want a tailor."

There were certain sections of Madrid more dangerous than the actual front-line trenches, so people said, since they were more frequently exposed to direct artillery fire. But in spite of the bombardments in the city traffic usually kept on moving and, while I was there, the streetcar service was seldom disrupted. But during a shelling, motormen seemed to have a tendency to increase their speed. So when shells fell, I would often see trams whizzing faster than ever through the streets. A few cars had been hit and passengers killed, so if any passenger wished to get off and take shelter, the motorman would stop the car for him. But the general feeling was that a person was as safe on a streetcar as in a shelter. The car might be struck, but so might the shelter. The streetcar men of Madrid had sent a whole company of their own to the front. Sometimes those at work relieved the men at the front so that they might come back to town and take a turn on leave at running the cars again.

During that second year of the war, there were said to be almost a hundred thousand children in Madrid. Certainly one saw many youngsters playing in the streets, picking up shrapnel for fun, and playing hide-and-seek in shell holes. But mothers in the more exposed sections of the city usually called their children into the house at the first boom of the cannon. The children, often more expert than the grownups in recognizing the sounds of artillery and from just which direction the shells were coming, were sometimes loath to obey. I heard a small boy yell from the street to his mother in an upper window one day, as he kept on playing, "Aw, those are our guns, ma, shooting the other way. Can't you tell by the sound?"

In the early days of the war Madrid was frequently bombed from the air. But after the first few months, the rebels no longer wasted their aviation on nonmilitary targets. However, by that time whole areas of Madrid had already been destroyed. Now the artillery continued the destruction. By 1937, the beautiful Arguelles section of new villas and modern apartment houses was a shambles. One enormous apartment house, covering a whole block, was known as the House of Flowers, because, in its planning, each window had been designed with a window box for plants, and each balcony had its rows of potted flowers or vines. But when I saw this huge dwelling house, it was empty and desolate, with great shell holes in the walls, its window boxes broken and its balconies smashed. But a few flowers were still blooming in some of the windows, and from a number of balconies little green vines still hung. Although the taller buildings, being excellent targets for artillery, were empty, a number of cottages were still occupied. One day in Arguelles, I was told, a shell fell in the study of a bearded old professor of Greek. His wife and daughter came running to see if anything had happened to him. They found the old gentleman standing in the center of the floor, holding a portion of the shell in his hand and shaking his head quizzically.

"This little thing," he said, "this inanimate object, can't do any more than kill us. It's the philosophy that lies behind this little fragment, wife, that is so dangerous."

The Cuban poet, Alejo Carpentier, who had been living in Arguelles, told me that one morning after an especially heavy shelling, he had passed a house, a considerable portion of whose front wall was lying in the yard. A shell had passed through the roof the night before and carried with it not only a portion of the living room wall but the top corner of the family piano as well. Then the shell buried itself in the garden. Nevertheless, early that morning Carpentier saw the little daughter of the house seated at the damaged piano, very clean and starched, her hair brushed and braided, her face shining. Diligently, she was practicing scales from a music book in front of her. The fact that the top corner of the piano had been shot away in the night and that the living room had no wall did not seem to affect the child's concentration. In answer to the Cuban's good morning and his question as to what had happened, the little girl said, "Oh, a shell came through our house last night. I'm going to help clean up after a while, but I have to practice first. Today's the day my music teacher comes."

Madrid, you wondrous city!

were words the Brigade boys had to put to an old Spanish folk song, "Mamita Mia." The Madrileños had previously put wartime Spanish words to it, too, about the way their city was holding out under siege:

> Madrid, que bien resistes!
> Madrid, que bien resistes,
> Mamita, mia, los bombardeos!

The will to live and laugh in this city of over a million people under fire, each person in constant danger, was to me a source of amazement. One could forget the possibility of imminent death, but it was impossible not to be cold as winter came, or always half hungry. At the Alianza sometimes, when transportation had been disrupted and our food shop had no rations for our dinner, there would be nothing at meal time but bread soup with bread. The writers around the table would repeat an old Spanish proverb, "Bread with bread—food for fools." Then we would all laugh and tighten our belts as we got up to keep our stomachs from feeling so empty.

I was an American who could go home anytime I wanted to. But the others were Spaniards who lived in Madrid. How much longer could they resist like this, I wondered. Yet it seemed certain that they would never be starved out—perhaps not even shelled out or bombed out, unless overwhelming military forces were unleashed against them. Hemingway and Matthews, Leland Stowe and all the other American journalists in the city agreed that there were no signs of surrender. Yet there were no heroics, no mass meetings, no bands, no great speeches about it. City without heroics, Madrid, que bien resistes!

One night that summer, in the center of the city, in one of the larger motion-picture theaters the audience avidly followed the progress of an American-made film. Suddenly a shell fell in the street outside with a tremendous detonation—but nobody moved from his seat. The film continued. Shortly another shell fell, nearer and louder than before, shaking the whole building. The manager of the theater went into the lobby and looked up and down the Grand Via. He saw a billowing tower of smoke at the corner. Overhead the whine of one shell after another caused him to decide to stop the show so that people might seek refuge. He had the film halted and mounted the stage to announce his decision to the audience, and say that in view of the intensity of the shelling, he thought it best to call off the rest of the picture. Before he had gotten the words out of his mouth, he was greeted with such hissing and booing and stamping of feet and calls for the show to go on—plus cried of "Coward!" hurled in his direction—that he shrugged his shoulders, signaled the operator to continue, and left the stage. The magic of Hollywood resumed its spell. While enemy shells whistled dangerously over the theater to crash in nearby streets, the film went its make-believe way to a thrilling climax—a climax in which gunfire played a prominent part. Artillery fire outside and machine-gun fire on the screen mingled, one hardly distinguishable from the other. The picture was *Terror in Chicago*.

## BODY HERE, LEG THERE

JUST after the big battle of Brunete near the city, I reached Madrid. This was the battle in which the Loyalist troops experienced the heaviest concentration of aerial bombs yet used up to that time anywhere in the world. For more than twenty-four hours, Spanish, Italian and German aviation bombed the government trenches. The whole earth shook, and its trembling was felt all day and all night in Madrid itself. Brunete was an outpost of the defense of Madrid. To go with one of the first groups of American newspapermen to visit that front after the battle, was my good fortune—journalistically speaking. I had never been on any war front before, so I was lucky to be going with experienced men, for the reporters with whom I traveled were Leland

Stowe and Richard Mowrer. We went in Mowrer's car, driving over shell-pocked roads until we came within sight of Quijorna on the Brunete front. At the top of a rise a sentry stopped us.

He said, "You'd better leave the car here. Down there in the hollow the road is within range of fascist guns. They might machine-gun a car. If you walk, they'll only snipe."

"Maybe they won't even bother to do that," said Stowe. "Anyway, we'll walk."

So we left the car and started down the road in the brilliant sunlight. The leaves on the trees along the road had all been shot away, and the branches were splintered and broken. This was the first time I'd ever seen battle-scarred trees. While I was looking up at the trees, it seemed that ever so often I heard a bird cheep. But I could not see any birds. Finally I asked my companions, "Where are the birds I keep hearing?"

"Birds?" Stowe said, "There's no birds. Those are sniper bullets whistling by."

"Firing at us?" I exclaimed.

"Certainly," said Stowe. "There's nobody else on this road to fire at."

"I never knew bullets sounded like birds cheeping before."

"Well, now you know," Mower grinned. "And there's no use to duck. Anyhow, they're probably just shooting at us for fun."

Perhaps for my comfort, Stowe said, "I can tell by the sound, the bullets are over our heads."

Chee-eep! . . . Chee-eep! . . . Chee-eep! I didn't know just where the cheep came from, so soft and swift, but Stowe's words were of little comfort. I could see spurts of dust fly up every so often in the road where an occasional bullet landed too near for a feeling of safety.

I was glad when we had crossed that declivity and went up the next rise and down into the outskirts of the ruined village toward which we were headed. Had there been a hotel, or any shelter standing whole, I probably would not have gone back to Madrid until the snipers cleared out. I had never been a *personal* target before, and I did not relish the thought of being a target again that day.

The little town was a scene of complete desolation. Nobody

remained there, but there were still portions of the dead in the streets. Whole bodies had been cleared away, but hands, arms, fingers and legs were still lying around, protruding from piles of rubble, smelling not good in the sun. There were no soldiers about, nobody at all, so one could walk into any of the shell-battered houses and bombed-out buildings and take whatever one wished. In some houses books and furniture had not been harmed. In others, everything was smashed, scorched, or otherwise damaged. The records at the little city hall were scattered all over the place in the rubble of its shattered walls. Maybe it had been a very old building, two or three hundred years old, but now it was in ruins. I picked up an old ledger with a leather back, its faint pages indicating records of marriages more than eighty years ago.

There wasn't much to see in the village except ruination, and the stench of death was not pleasant. After I'd ventured into one quite pretty little villa, only partly destroyed, to find a dead man sprawled just inside the door, his left leg a yard or two away from his body, I was none too eager to explore any more of the deserted town. Stowe and Mowrer wanted to check up on the full extent of aerial destruction, so I let them go ahead. It didn't take more than a quick look on my part to verify that it had been devastating, a kind of preview of what happened later to other larger and more famous European cities in World War II—to which some of the newsmen in Madrid predicted Spain was but a prelude.

Some of the men in the International Brigades had told me they came to Spain to help keep war and fascism from spreading. "War and fascism"—a great many people at home in America seemed to think those words were just a left-wing slogan. War and fascism! He was not just a slogan, that dead man sprawled on the floor of his house; not just a slogan the chee-eep, chee-eep, chee-eep of what I thought were birds singing; certainly not a slogan the streets I had to traverse through that smashed village with a leg here, a hand there, to get back to the road exposed to snipers' fire to reach our car to return to Madrid.

"Death does not smell good at all," I thought, a little sick at the stomach as I walked away from that Spanish town where nobody lived any more on account of war and fascism.

## GENERAL FRANCO'S MOORS

"IMAGINE," said the Madrileños, "that rebel Franco bringing Mohammedans to Spain to fight Christians! The Crusaders would turn over in their graves. The Moors are back in Spain."

With Dick Mowrer and Leland Stowe, I visited a prison hospital in Madrid and saw my first Moor. We had gone to interview some captured German aviators and Italian ground troops. The Germans were in one ward and the Italians in another. The Italians were the most talkative. They said they had come to Spain because Mussolini had sent them. They had no choice in the matter, and they seemed to have no idea what the war was about—or if they did have, they were careful not to express themselves. They were amiable young fellows, stocky and rough-looking, probably peasants at home or unskilled workers. The Germans, on the other hand, were much less communicative. They had been sent to fight communism, they said, and yes, they bombed cities full of women and children. An airman had to take orders, *nein?* But one of them said that now he knew what a bombardment felt like, as he lay there in this prison hospital that had been struck by fourteen shells.

It was a hot day and smelly in the hospital wards. Since I didn't understand German or Italian well, and the other reporters were dragging out their interviews a very long time, I decided to walk down the corridor and see if I could find some water. If I missed anything, Stowe or Mowrer would tell me later. The hospital hall was empty. But as I got almost to the end where the hall turned, around the corner came one of the darkest, tallest men I have ever seen in my life. His blackness was accentuated by a white hospital gown flopping about his bare legs, and a white bandage around his head. Not having seen a Negro since I'd been in Madrid, the sudden sight of this very dark face almost startled me out of my wits. There at the corner of the corridor the man and I would have collided, had I not stopped in my tracks as he passed me without a word, silently like a black ghost.

I was a bit ashamed of myself for having been startled at the unexpected sight of a dark face in a hospital I had thought filled only with white prisoners. I thought of how once, when I had been walking with some other fellows along a bayou in Louisiana, a white woman had looked out of her hut and cried, "You colored boys get away from here. I'm scared of you." Now, here I was—a Negro myself— suddenly frightened by another dark face!

When I got back to the German ward and asked the nurse about the man I had seen, she said there were a number of Moors in another part of the hospital. While Mowrer and Stowe continued to talk to the Germans, I went with the nurse to find them. In a big room with three rows of cots, a number of Moors sat on their beds in white wrappings and bandages, while others lay suffering quietly, too badly wounded to be up. It was almost impossible for me to carry on any sort of conversation with them. They spoke little or no Spanish and I had no interpreter with me. But finally I came across a small boy who had been wounded at the Battle of Brunete. He looked to be a lad of ten or eleven, a bright smiling child, who spoke Spanish.

"Where did you come from?" I asked.

He named a town I'd never heard of in Morocco.

"How old are you?"

"Thirteen," he said.

"And how did you happen to be fighting in Spain?"

"I came with my mother," he said.

"Your mother?" I exclaimed, for that was the first time I had heard of Moorish women being brought to Spain. The rebels, I learned later, imported women as well as men—women to accompany the troops, to wash and cook for them behind the lines.

"What happened to your mother?"

The little boy closed his eyes. "She was killed at Brunete," he said.

The Moorish troops were colonial conscripts, or men from the Moroccan villages enticed into the army by offers of what seemed to them very good pay. Franco's personal bodyguard consisted of Moorish soldiers, tall picturesque fellows in flowing robes and winding turbans. Before I left home American papers had carried photographs of turbanned Mohammedan troops marching in the streets of Burgos,

Seville and Malaga. And a United Press dispatch from Gibraltar that summer said:

> Arabs have been crossing the Straits of Gibraltar from Spanish Morocco to Algeciras and Malaga at the rate of 300 to 400 a day, according to reliable information reaching here. General Franco intends to mass 50,000 new Arab troops in Spain so that he can maintain the strength of the Nationalist army should the Italian volunteers be withdrawn.

According to Madrid papers these shiploads of Moorish mercenaries from Larache provided a strange union of the Cross and the Crescent against Spanish democracy. The Falangist papers reaching Madrid were most religious, even running in their advertisements slogans such as VIVA CRISTO REY! VIVA FRANCO! as if Christ and the General were of equal importance. On the cover of the book, *Espana en la Cruz*, published in rebel territory, the map of Spain was pictured crucified on an enormous cross by the nails of Marxism, Judaism and Masonry, which the book claimed formed the core of the Loyalist government. Yet the Franco insurrectionists, in spite of their Christian cast, had encamped thousands of pagan Moors at Casa del Campo. And General Queipo de Llano was said to have promised one girl in Madrid to each twenty Moors. But I could not find that the enemy's use of these colored troops had brought about any increased feeling of color consciousness on the part of the people of Spain. I was well received everywhere I went, and the Negroes in the International Brigades reported a similar reception.

Negroes were not strange to Spain, nor did they attract an undue amount of attention. In the cities no one turned around to look twice. Most Spaniards had seen colored faces, and many are quite dark themselves. Distinct traces of Moorish blood from the days of the Mohammedan conquest remain in the Iberian Peninsula. Copper-colored Gypsies like La Niña de los Peines are common. There were, too, quite a number of colored Portugese living in Spain. And in both Valencia and Madrid I saw pure-blooded Negroes from the colonies in Africa, as well as many Cubans who had migrated to Spain.

All the Negroes, of whatever nationality, to whom I talked, agreed that there was not the slightest trace of color prejudice in Spain. In that respect they said it was even better than France because in Paris, charming city that it is, some of the big hotels catering to tourists will not register dark-skinned guests. Negro jazz musicians told me that they enjoyed performing in Spain where audiences are most cordial. I found, shortly after my arrival, that one of the most popular variety stars in Madrid was El Negro Aquilino, a Cuban, who played both jazz and flamenco on the saxophone. Aquilino was then in his third month at the Teatro Calderon, and appeared on the same bill with the famous Pastora Imperio, the great dancer who remained on the Loyalist side. Aquilino traveled all over government Spain, and was a great favorite with the soldiers for whom he played at the front. When I went backstage to interview him for my paper, I asked him about color in Spain. He said, "Color? *No le hace nada en Espana—* it doesn't matter."

Sometimes, amusingly enough, American Negroes in Brigade uniforms were asked if they were Moors fighting on the Loyalist side. One young Negro, Walter Cobb, had a big scare behind the lines on the Aragon front where he was the only American with a French brigade. Cobb spoke both French and Spanish.

"I have to keep in practice with my languages in this man's country," he said. "If I hadn't known Spanish in the last action, I'd have been taken for a Moor and made a prisoner. Man, I was driving a captured Franco truck that we took at Belchite one night, bringing it back behind our own lines to be repaired, and I hadn't had a chance to paint out the Falangist markings on it. I hadn't gone but a few kilometers in the dark before some Loyalist soldiers on patrol duty, Spanish boys, stopped me at a crossroads and threw their flashlights on the truck. When they saw me, dark as I am, and saw that truck with those Fascist insignias on it, they thought sure I was a Moor that had got lost and come across the lines by accident. They yelled at me to jump down quick with my hands up, and they held their guns cocked at my head until I got off that truck. Man, I started talking Spanish right away, explained I was an International. So they let me show them my papers and tell them how we captured that truck from the Fascists, and that it belonged to us now. Then, man, they almost hugged me! But suppose I didn't keep in practice with my Spanish?

As much like a Moor as I look, I might have been dead, driving a Franco truck! It pays to *habla espanol*."

In Arguelles, I saw two posters in a classroom for the Spanish soldiers of the 14th Battalion training to fight the Moors. One poster said: LIKE THE SPANISH PEASANTS, THE INDUSTRIOUS AND DECENT MOOR DOES NOT TAKE UP A GUN, HE TILLS THE SOIL. And the other poster declared: THE MOORS ON THE SIDE OF THE FALANGISTS DO NOT KNOW THEY ARE FIGHTING AGAINST THE REAL SPANISH REVOLUTION. WORKERS, HELP US! RESPECT THE MOORISH PRISONERS.

The International Brigaders were, of course, aware of the irony of the colonial Moors—victims themselves of oppression in North Africa—fighting against a Republic that had been seeking to work out a liberal policy toward Morocco. To try to express the feelings of some of the Negro fighting men in this regard, I wrote these verses in the form of a letter from an American Negro in the Brigades to a relative in Dixie:

International Brigades, Lincoln Battalion, Somewhere in Spain, 1937

> Dear Brother at home:
> We captured a wounded Moor today.
> He was just as dark as me.
> I said, Boy, what you doin' here,
> Fightin' against the free?
> He answered something in a language
> I couldn't understand.
> But somebody told me he was sayin'
> They grabbed him in his land
> And made him join the Fascist army
> And come across to Spain.
> And he said he had a feelin'
> He'd never get back home again.
> He said he had a feelin'
> This whole thing wasn't right.
> He said he didn't know
> These folks he had to fight.
> And as he lay there dyin'
> In a village we had taken,
> I looked across to Africa

And I seen foundations shakin'—
For if a free Spain wins this war,
The colonies, too, are free—
Then something wonderful can happen
To them Moors as dark as me.
I said, Fellow, listen,
I guess that's why old England
And I reckon Italy, too,
Is afraid to let Republic Spain
Be good to me and you—
Because they got slaves in Africa
And they don't want 'em free.
Listen, Moorish prisoner—
Here, shake hands with me!
I knelt down there beside him
And I took his hand,
But the wounded Moor was dyin'
So he didn't understand.

## CITATION FOR BRAVERY

MUSSOLINI'S invasion of Ethiopia in 1936 caused a number of young Negroes, so some of them in the Brigades told me, to come to Loyalist Spain. By fighting against Franco they felt they were opposing Mussolini. Others said they had come to Spain to fight against the kind of people who oppress Negroes in the American South. Others said they had come to oppose fascism, and help prevent its spread in the world. Certainly they had not come because they had been forced to come, or because they were well paid, or because there was a great deal of prestige or glory attached to coming. Indeed, many would find it dangerous to go back home after having fought in Spain. Why then were these men in the Brigades? With so many unsolved problems in America, I wondered why would a Negro come way over to Spain to help solve Spain's problems—perhaps with his very life. I don't know. I wondered then. I wonder still. But in my heart I salute them. And I tried to find the answers.

I met in Spain two colored kids hardly sixteen, Al Chisolm and George Waters, from the U. S. A. I met a very elderly Negro cooking beans for the Loyalist troops. I met several young married men with children who had left their families to fight at Brunete, Lerida, Teruel, and places they had never heard the names of before they came to Spain. I met some Negroes who, I was told, had been at the Lenin School in Moscow. And I met others who had only the vaguest idea what communism was, or socialism either. I met all kinds of Negroes in Spain, just as I'd met all kinds in Harlem. I couldn't type the men in Spain any more than I've been able to type Negroes anywhere else. Some were smart and some were dumb. Some had been to college, others hardly to grammar school. Some were pleasant, some rude. And some—in Spain of all places—were even "a disgrace to the race"—at least, to hear others tell it.

Just before I got to Madrid, perhaps the greatest "disgrace to the race" of all had occurred at Brunete. A colored officer in charge of a mixed unit of several nationalities in the Brigades, so I was told, had taken shelter with his men in a hillside cave during a terrible day-long Fascist bombardment. As the foreign planes dropped high-test explosives from the skies hour after hour after hour, and the Franco artillery pounded away at the Loyalist positions, the whole countryside shook. Deathly thunder! Smoke and fire everywhere! Nevertheless, the order came into the shelters and caves for the Brigaders to charge. The various units went out under fire to attack—that is, all but the unit commanded by the Negro officer in the cave. To his men he gave no orders to charge. Finally, some of his subordinates asked if he did not intend to obey the command. They were, they said, ready to charge.

"Charge on, then," the Negro officer is reported to have said. "Charge on! But if anybody thinks I am going to charge—out there under those bombs—they're crazy."

A junior officer took command of the unit, and the men charged —most of them to their deaths. The Negro officer in the cave survived to walk up Lenox Avenue in Harlem again—of course, disgraced—but alive. In Spain he was stripped of his rank, and sent back to the U. S. A. The Brigaders took it hard, particularly the Negroes among them. When I suggested that perhaps the man was shell shocked, they said, "Shell shocked nothing! If it just hadn't been a *mixed* unit —white boys and all—waiting to obey his orders! Imagine! And him sitting back there in that cave saying damn if he's going to charge! A disgrace to the race, that's what he is!"

But such behavior was not true of Oliver Law, the Brigade Commander killed at Brunete, and proclaimed a National Hero by the Loyalist Government. It was not true of Milton Herndon who died in action at Fuentes de Ebro; or of Lt. Walter Garland or Sgt. Bunny Rucker who lived to come home; or Alonzo Watson or Douglass Roach or Otto Reeves, who didn't come back; or Ralph Thornton, who took four prisoners at Belchite and was cited for bravery beyond the call of duty; or of Abraham Lewis, who cooked hundreds of meals on the battle front under fire; or of Thaddeus Battle, the Howard University student, fighting on the Madrid sector. And somehow I don't think the man in the cave was too much of a disgrace to the race. At least, *he was there* at the front. At least, he went to Spain.

I was introduced to Ralph Thornton in the improvised office of the mimeographed bulletin of the Washington-Lincoln Battalion in the ruined city of Quinto. Artillery and air bombs had left few buildings standing whole. The Brigade library, post office and bulletin had taken possession of one of the least demolished houses. Ralph Thornton was the acting clerk there when I met him. We sat in the sunlight near the door and I tried to get him to tell me why he had just been cited for bravery.

Thornton, a light brownskin fellow from Pittsburgh, a former newsboy, was loath to talk about himself. "It wasn't much," he insisted. "We just took four prisoners, that's all. Me and two other boys captured them."

Luckily, other members of Thornton's outfit were sitting with us and they weren't bashful in talking about Thornton. The story was that after the taking of Belchite, during which Thornton led a successful charge on a rebel-held building, he and two white comrades, Ben Findley and Carl Geiser, were given several blocks of houses to inspect in the captured city. Many of the houses were in ruins, but some stood intact. From upper windows, snipers still operated. Behind barred doors and closed blinds, rebels who had been unable to escape crouched in hiding. Inspecting these ominously quiet houses was no gentle task. You could easily get a hand grenade in the face.

The Americans went up the narrow stone stairs of an ancient

house with walls three feet thick, and dark cold silence everywhere. But on the top floor, when Thornton opened the door to a front room, the silence was suddenly perfumed with the scent of powder and acrid smoke stung him in the eyes and burned his throat. A man moved in the dark, then jumped to his feet crying, "Salud!" At the same time he threw his rifle down. The gun was still hot when Thornton picked it up. The man was a Fascist who had been lying there sniping at government soldiers. The captured sniper turned out to be the vice-president of the local Falangists, and one of the most active enemies of republicanism in that section of Aragon. "A Spanish klansman," Thornton said, "I should've shot him." Further inspection of the house revealed several cupboards filled with gold and hidden jewels.

Nearby, in another house whose inhabitants had been unable to flee, the three Americans found an old woman sitting at a window. They asked her if there was anyone hiding in the house. She said, "No." But a search of the premises revealed a concealed opening leading to a tunnel where an Italian soldier was hiding. The Italian probably thought he was in Ethiopia by mistake when he saw Thornton's dark face inviting him to surrender.

Before the three Americans went back to staff headquarters that morning, Thornton and his comrades had taken two other prisoners, and had made sure that there were no more snipers in the blocks of houses they had been sent to inspect. Because of Thornton's valor at Belchite in the storming of a rebel-held building, followed by the importance of the prisoners he took, the whole Brigade united in the presentation to him of a watch on the day his citation arrived.

## MY ONE AND ONLY WOUND

SEVERAL times in Spain I thought I might not live long. One of those times when I felt my end had come was at University City. My nearness to death came about because of a "wartime tourist," as the Brigade boys termed the endless stream of do-gooders coming to Madrid that year, who immediately wanted a conducted tour of the front. These do-gooders from almost all over the world were well-meaning people, some of whom had done effective propaganda work for Loyalist Spain in their homelands, or raised large sums of money for Spanish causes, sent milk for children and supplies for hospitals. But when they came to Madrid, they sometimes innocently got in the way of more urgent activities, and took up the time of the city's fighting citizens and soldiers with repetitious and silly requests for autographs. On the other hand, some visitors came quietly, like Dorothy Parker, and went away quietly. Others made a lot of noise to let everybody know they were there—willing to give their *all*. But the trouble was that, whereas their *all* perhaps meant a lot in terms of what they could do for Spain at home, in Madrid under siege, their zeal was of little immediate value. But Spain that summer was very popular. A trip to besieged Madrid became almost as important to visitors as seeing Seville at Easter had been to peacetime tourists. I made the mistake of going to University City one day with such a group of eager wartime sight-seers.

The group included a woman from the American Midwest who wore a large white hat. The women of Madrid did not wear hats— perhaps because there were no hats there to buy during the war. Milliners had gone out of business. At any rate, American women with hats seemed to attract a lot of attention in the streets, so usually, after the first day or two in town, they would become aware of this and leave their hats at the hotel. But that day when we went to University City, the sun was shining very brightly so, the American woman wore her large-brimmed, lacy, rather floppy white hat as a sunshade.

I was typing in my room at the Alianza when the Spanish writer, Vincente Salas Viu, called to ask me if I would like to take a ride out to the University. They had, he said, two cars to carry the ladies of some foreign committee out there to see the Clinic. This famous *Clinica*—a modern structure of several stories belonging to the Medical College—had been written about a great deal in the European and American press as unique in the annals of warfare since, for some time, the Fascists held the wings at one end of the building, and the Loyalists held the wings at the other end. And right through the campus the front-line trenches ran. One part of the grounds belonged to the government, the other to the rebels. Sometimes they took potshots at each other. But generally in the daytime, University City was a quiet front, with little firing. Most of the activity was at night. Then it consisted mainly of tunneling under each other's trenches to plant explosives and blow sky-high a machine-gun emplacement or an outlook post. Sometimes, in my room at the Alianza after midnight I could hear a tremendous explosion in the University City sector. The *dinameteros* were at work.

People could take the subway to this unique front at the edge of the city, so I had been there before. Like most visitors to Madrid, since it had become so famous, the first thing I wanted to see was University City. But since I had seen it several times by now, I really had no good reason to leave my typewriter that day to ride out there again.

"But some of the ladies are Americans," Salas Viu said. "My English is very bad. Come along and entertain them." So I went—to my sorrow. It was such a beautiful summer day, the sky very clear and blue, that it was good to get out of doors. Besides, I thought, those ladies might have some chocolate bars from the outside world in their pocketbooks. They did not have any chocolate bars, but they were good women, seriously interested in raising funds for Spanish war relief in their various countries. And the American women were acquainted with people I knew in Pittsburgh and Chicago. The ride out to the campus was a pleasant one.

At the University we went into the Clinic to look through sand-bagged holes in walls toward the rebels behind their sandbags in opposite wings. By keeping quiet, you could sometimes hear the enemy laughing and talking. Then we paid a visit to the ground fortifications where we saw a trench school for the many Spanish soldiers who could hardly read and write. These trench schools were a part of the government's campaign against illiteracy. I told the women how I had visited such a trench school a few weeks before on the very day when a soldier had just learned to sign his name in full for the first time. The man was so proud of this achievement that he stuck the paper up on the platoon bulletin board and he and his fellow soldiers made quite a happy occasion of it—*his whole name* written in his own hand by himself for the first time in his life!

The women were not happy just being in a school in a quiet

dugout only a few yards inside a trench. Where were the guns? The Spanish corporal assigned to guide us, took us a few hundred yards further. We passed a few lookout men on guard with rifles. But when we came to the communications trench, the young corporal stopped and indicated that we should turn back. I could see that the women were disappointed with their uneventful tour. It was so quiet, not a shot being fired in the trenches. Nothing was happening. University City, for all its fame, did not seem as exciting to them as the Alfonso Hotel where they were stopping in Madrid.

"Couldn't we just go a little further?" one of the women asked.

The corporal shook his head, and a higher officer standing there agreed, "No."

"Why, from here we can't even see the Fascist lines," said the woman in the big white hat. "Couldn't we go right on up to the front?"

I had found the Spaniards almost always obliging, and I knew if these women kept on asking, they might even land in rebel territory. Personally, I was none too anxious to follow them when, finally, the officer shrugged and the young corporal agreed to lead us through the communications corridor to the next line of trenches.

"But," suggested the Spanish officer, "would madame please take off her hat?"

"Why?" asked the lady, for the sun was beating down on the open trench where she stood.

"It might attract attention," said the officer.

"Oh, who can see us down here in this hole?" laughed the woman. "Come on, let's go. I'll keep my head down." The Spaniard said no more.

The trenches were rather shallow and, from the tall buildings about, perhaps the enemy could see us moving. But we reached the forward trenches without incident. There, the corporal said, if we cared to climb on the high platform where a machine gun rested, we could look through the sandbagged opening directly across to the Fascist trenches a few hundred yards away. Three or four people could stand around the machine gun at one time, so I climbed up to look out along with the lady in the white hat and a couple of others. I had just pulled my head back from the opening and was about to step down into the trench again when all of a sudden the crackle of rifle fire aimed our way rang out from the rebel trenches. A bullet whizzed through the opening. Another struck the side of a sandbag, sending a stinging spray of sand all over us. Suddenly I felt a sting in the crook of my arm, and the muscle there begin to tremble.

The women screamed. One of them almost fell backward into the trench as the rest scrambled down. I had on only a sport shirt that day, and when I looked down at my bare arm I saw a little stream of blood trickling toward my wrist. Salas Viu had flecks of blood all over his face.

"Come! Hurry!" said the little corporal, leading us rapidly back through the communications trench. "Heads down! Señora, please, take off your hat."

But the woman had already taken off her hat, bent very low running as fast as she could toward the exit. I held a handkerchief to my arm to stop the blood. And Salas Viu kept wiping his bloody face with his coat sleeve. Fortunately none of the women were harmed, only badly frightened. But presently they were more frightened still, for the rebels threw a well-aimed trench mortar. It narrowly missed the trench, but landed near enough to send a mighty spray of earth and sand high into the air. Pebbles and dirt scattered all over us, and the noise was deafening.

"What are they doing?" one of the women screamed.

"Jugando,"—playing, said the little corporal.

"They play like that sometimes," Salas Viu said, "just for fun, Madame."

This was true. University City was a dull front, so sometimes the men shot at each other for lack of anything else to do.

We stopped at a first-aid station beyond the trenches where a dressing was put on my arm. "A piece of dum-dum bullet nicked you," said the nurse. "But it didn't penetrate the flesh much. The bleeding will soon stop."

Salas Viu was treated for the cuts on his face, full of tiny little abrasions from the stinging sand where an explosive bullet had hit the sandbag. He was advised to go to a hospital when he got back to Madrid just in case there were bits of metal embedded in his skin.

As for the woman in the white hat—well, none of the other

tourists spoke to her on the way back to the city. Some of the other women had already repeated in her presence several times, "They asked her to take off that target on her head and she wouldn't listen—until we got shot at! That nice young Spaniard asked her to take off her hat!" But by the time the early shock of the first fright had passed, the women in the cars riding back to Madrid became quite silent, probably realizing how close someone had come to being killed. Perhaps the rebels were *just* playing that afternoon—but their bullets were real.

## A HEMINGWAY STORY

NOT given to frequenting the Algonquin in New York, I never met many famous writers. During the months that I was in Spain I became acquainted with more white American writers than at any other period in my life. Ernest Hemingway and Martha Gellhorn were in Madrid when I got there, as were Herbert Matthews and Leland Stowe. Dorothy Parker came that summer, and Malcolm Cowley, and Lillian Hellman, as well as Elliot Paul, Meyer Levin, Louis Fischer, Joseph North, Seymour Waldman, Richard Watts, Jr., Thyra Edwards and Vincent Sheean. The Negro short-story writer, Lucius McDaniel, and the poet, Edwin Rolfe, were members of the International Brigades, and Alvah Bessie joined them later. Of the English writers, the novelist Ralph Bates, and the poet, Tom Wintringham, were Brigade members. There as correspondents were Tom Driberg from London, Sylvia Townsend Warner and Nancy Cunard, who came in and out from Paris several times. Stephen Spender visited Spain, too.

Among the non-English-speaking writers I encountered were André Malraux, Juan de la Cabada and Andres Iduarte whom I had known in Mexico; Pablo Neruda, Alfred Kantorowicz, Ludwig Renn, Ernst Toller, Gustav Regler, Ilya Ehrenburg, Michael Koltsov, Jef Last, and a number of others from Middle Europe and Scandinavia whose names I can't remember now. But some of them, we were told at the Alianza, were very famous in their own countries, just as Nicolás Guillén was famous in Cuba.

The night that Lillian Hellman made her broadcast to America from the Madrid radio, a shell tore half the cornice off the front of the building from which she was talking. At the Alianza a few blocks away, we heard it strike like a million giant firecrackers exploding simultaneously in one spot—a quick, dry, loud BANG! of terrific power. But Miss Hellman kept right on talking. Her broadcast was already twenty-four hours late because the night before Madrid had experienced an even bigger shelling. Then more than a hundred projectiles crashed into the city, so Miss Hellman could not leave her hotel to go to the radio station. The following evening in her talk she said of the bombardment of the night before, "You are quiet when a shelling comes because the bravery of these people who have seen so much, and will see so much more, reaches you and makes you quiet. And maybe you get quiet because you, too, are angry; you can't believe in a world which allows foreign dictators to wreck a city by carefully picking the poorest and most crowded part of that city, where the houses are the flimsiest and the children play most, then shell it and shell it with monotonous regularity. You would think the human heart would turn and make them stop."

Lillian Hellman closed her radio talk with a little anecdote about a truck full of évacués one day on the Madrid-Valencia road. She said, "When in most other places of the world it would have been time for lunch, an old man took out his one loaf of bread. He looked around at the others and said, 'If nobody has bread, then I have bread for all.' "

I had found the people of Spain most generous with what little food they had—and with their belongings or services. Once in Madrid I took my shoes to be repaired. When I went back to get them the shoemaker refused payment. He said, "You, a foreigner, would not be here in besieged Madrid if you had not come to help us. I will not take money from you for my work." And he would not take it.

Certainly the most celebrated American in Spain was Ernest Hemingway. I found him a big likable fellow whom the men in the Brigades adored. He spent a great deal of time with them in their encampments. Hemingway himself had been under fire more than once, and he lived in one of the most vulnerable buildings of Madrid, the Hotel Florida. I ran into him and the golden-haired Martha Gellhorn from time to time, and spent a whole day with Hemingway in the late summer at the Brigade Auto Park on the edge of the city where my friends, Rucker and Battle, were stationed. I don't remember now what we talked about, nothing very profound, I'm sure, and there was a lot of kidding as we shared the men's food.

I did not frequent the same bar as did Hemingway—the bar which he made famous in his stories about Spain. It was too expensive for me, being the only bar in town that had any Scotch whisky left, and not much else. Most of the foreign correspondents frequented it, as well as some of the better-heeled Spaniards and military men. And the pretty Moorish girl that all the men liked was always there at cocktail time. This bar—the Aquarium—aside from being expensive, was probably the most dangerous café in Madrid, for it was in the very middle of the Grand Via between the Puerta del Sol and Cibeles, and shells were sometimes falling all around it. To make matters worse, its walls were glass like a fish bowl. But while I was there a shell never hit it, so far as I know, nor even shattered its glass panels. Its fourth-estate patrons, men used to covering wars and catastrophies all over the globe, led a charmed life. After endless cocktail hours in this glass-walled café in the heart of bombed Madrid, most of the correspondents I knew who frequented the place are still living.

But one evening there was a mighty ducking and dodging in this bar, so I was told, for at its most crowded hour a man pulled out his pistol and fired several times at another, killing him. Hemingway turned the incident into a short story, later published in *Esquire*. I was not involved. But immediately afterwards, two of the people present in the bar, who became characters in Hemingway's story, told me about the shooting.

They were a young English couple in charge of the English-language broadcasts for the Madrid radio. The man was a slightly built fellow with whom Hemingway had had a disagreement, so I was told, that became a fist fight which Hemingway won. Since that time, the author and the English couple had not been on speaking terms, although they saw each other often in the Aquarium Café. The English girl was stocky with short black hair. Hemingway in his short story did not name the couple, but he described them so pointedly that no one who was in Madrid at the time could mistake whom he meant. In the story, he exaggerated the man's slightness and the woman's stockiness, and in the fiction version of the incident, he had the man hiding under a table as the shots rang out, leaving his wife unprotected. The Englishman in reality claimed he pushed his wife into the kitchen and himself got behind a door only after he had seen that she was protected. I was not there, so I do not know. I was waiting at the Hotel Victoria for some other newspapermen to come and have dinner. But the police had locked the doors of the bar and would let nobody out until after their investigation, so almost everyone was late dining that evening.

What led up to the shooting that afternoon was that a ragged little Spaniard of middle age had wandered drunkenly into the de luxe bar filled with foreigners, top-echelon army men and government officials. In his hands he had, of all things, a flit gun. With alcoholic good humor, the little man began to spray people with flit. Some Spaniard at the bar objected to this. When the man kept on, an argument developed. The little drunk called the other man a few bad names. Spanish cursing is vile indeed. We have nothing like it in English. The Spaniard at the bar drew a pistol and shot the little drunk dead. From this real-life episode Hemingway fashioned a fictional story, adding to the episode a wedding feast earlier that afternoon when the little drunk's son had gotten married, and where his father with the flit gun had imbibed too much.

In many of my stories I have used real situations and actual people as a starting point, but have tried to change and disguise them so that in fiction they would not be recognizable. I was interested in observing what Hemingway did to real people in his story, some of whom he described almost photographically.

## HAIL AND FAREWELL

TARAZONA, an English-speaking training base for the International Brigades, was hung with flags on the autumn morning that I arrived. They were celebrating the end of the first year of the formation of the Brigades. Big doings were coming off: a military parade, a sports festival, boxing matches, a banquet and, in the afternoon, a visit from the American Congressmen, Bernard and O'Connell. At night there was to be a mass meeting in the town hall, followed by a party at staff headquarters for Lieutenant Walter Garland, the Negro in charge of this training base, who was returning soon to America.

Garland, only twenty-four years old, was one of the youngest commissioned officers in the Brigades, tall, brown-skinned, efficient-looking in his officer's uniform. He stood at the entrance to head-quarters that autumn afternoon with the members of his staff, all white besides himself, to receive the American Congressmen as they drove into camp followed by a car full of newspapermen. Later at the reviewing stand in the ancient village square, the mayor of Tarazona and the members of the City Council received the visitors. Then the signal for the beginning of the military review was given. Lieutenant Garland and his officers took their places in front of the stand and, for the last time, the men whose training he had supervised, passed in review before him. Marching in squads in long ranks, steel-helmeted, in brown uniforms, they came out of the narrow village streets, passed the stand, turned, and lined up in the square before their officers in the brilliant sunshine.

These Internationals from all of the Americas and England stood in formation before their young Negro officer, who presented the men to the American Congressmen and, in turn, the Congressmen to the troops.

In the speeches that followed, the American visitors paid their respects to the International Brigades. Of the volunteers, Congressman Bernard said, "I have the greatest admiration for every one of you. . . . You represent the cause of world democracy, and the success of that cause will be a blow to Mussolini and Hitler." Congressman O'Connell of Montana declared, "We have only the highest praise for your bravery and for the cause for which you carry on." At the close of the speeches the American ranks broke into the "Star Spangled Banner" and the square full of soldiers stood at salute. Following the ceremonies, Lieutenant Walter Garland formally turned his command over to the new officer in charge, Major Johnson, a white American.

Garland entered the International Brigades as a private. He became a sergeant, was wounded at Jarama, and spent two months in the hospital with a bullet wound in the stomach. Then he entered Officers' Training School. During the Brunete offensive, as First

Lieutenant, Garland led his men into action under the heaviest bombardment from the air that a modern army had ever known up to that time. Here he was wounded again and forced to retire from the lines. Upon his second recovery, he was sent to a post at the Tarazona Training Base, and rose to the position of commander. During the time of his directorship, various innovations were made. One, of great importance, was the setting up of the technical facilities for the reproduction of military maps in a more accurate fashion than had yet been known in Spain. The writing of the first manual in English for the use of the International Brigades was begun. And the mechanisms for the training of radio and telephone operators and observers were developed.

I asked Garland how he accounted for his sudden ability for things military, since at home he had been a musician. Did music, I wondered, have any connection with warfare? Garland laughed and said he didn't think so.

That night at staff headquarters, his fellow officers and friends gave a farewell party for him—a party full of warmth and friendship. There was wine and food, the old songs of various countries, and the new songs the soldiers had made up in Spain. Then somebody asked Joe Taylor, a Negro scout just out of the trenches, to sing a spiritual. He sang "Were You There When They Crucified My Lord?" Then Joe Kelly, veteran of the Irish revolution, sang an Irish song as hauntingly beautiful in its way as the Negro lament that had gone before. Then those who had been Garland's closest co-workers and friends, his staff officers who had served under him, English and American, Irish and Spanish, made short speeches of farewell to their fellow soldier whose work at that particular post was done. And I, who did not know that soldiers cried, saw some of them cry. The next day Garland left for the United States to try to tell the folks at home what the Spanish struggle meant.

## HAND GRENADES AND RATIONS

WHEN the 1st Regiment de Train of the 15th Brigade was at rest not far from Madrid in the fall, their camp was near a road. The tents

were so cleverly camouflaged, painted a zigzag green and brown, and
so carefully hidden under trees that, from the highway, it was difficult
to know there was a camp there. One day the enemy bombers had
come over and dropped a few bombs, but they landed in the woods
and did no damage. The Madrid front, a few kilometers away, was
near enough for the wind to bring with it the sound of heavy artillery
beyond the Casa del Campo and exploding mines at University City.
The first day I visited the Brigades Auto Camp there was a steady
rumble in the air.

Thaddeus Battle, one of the two Negro members of the Regiment, was a student at Howard University, a major in Political
Science, before he came to Spain. He was a mild-mannered, quiet
young man, wearing glasses, who busied himself studying Spanish
and French during his spare time.

"Student movements in America are beginning to carry some
weight in national life," he told me as he sat smoking in his tent that
chilly autumn afternoon. "Negro students must be a part of these
movements."

Outside we heard what seemed to be the hum of planes. We
stuck our heads out of the tent and looked up, but nothing was in
sight, so we went on with our conversation.

"Negro college students must realize the connection between the
international situation and our problems at home," Battle continued.
"Right here in Madrid, I've seen how Fascists destroy schools and
libraries. University City, a million-dollar educational center in ruins!
Why gain culture only to see it destroyed? Franco tears down what it
has taken people years to build. He burns books and closes schools
and stifles education. In America our students, Negro and white, must
stand up against all the forces that point toward a Fascist social order.
And our Negro campuses should play a much more vital role in in-
fluencing government policy than they have done in the past."

We talked until the big gong for supper sounded and we got in
line before the cook tent. Three Spanish women were ladling out a
savory rabbit stew. The line of soldiers forming there was a typical
section of the English-speaking units of the International Brigades:
Irish and Cockney lads, a Southern father and son from Oklahoma,
two cousins from a wealthy old family in California, an Australian

school teacher, and two colored troupers—one Thaddeus Battle, standing behind me, and Bernard Rucker, from Ohio.

It was Rucker, whom the fellows called Bunny, who drove me back to Madrid that night in one of the Brigade trucks. On the way we talked. He told me that he had played basketball on the Beatty Park team back home in Columbus, and that when he got out of school in the middle of the depression, he had gotten a government relief job on W. P. A. and was a member of the Workers' Council of the Urban League, active in the National Association for the Advancement of Colored People, and acted in the Y. M. C. A. Theatre Guild plays. Bunny said that he had come to Spain to show good will toward the Loyalist cause, since he felt that Negroes should become more international in their viewpoint and activities, then they would understand their own problems better, and see their relationship to similar problems elsewhere in the world.

Bunny said that for several months he had been a driver in this Brigade shock unit, taking troops and supplies to the front, often working under fire and sometimes strafed by enemy planes. Peasant women and children he had seen machine-gunned in the fields, and once Bunny and the men in his transport unit helped put out a fire in a wheat field to save the grain from going up in flames. During the Brunete offensive his convoy was caught in a heavy bombardment, and he saw a bombing plane crash into a tower of flames only a few hundred yards from his truck.

As we reached the outskirts of Madrid, several times Bunny had to show his papers to sentries who flagged down his speeding truck. When we got to the Alianza, it was almost dark. He would have to drive back to the Auto Park without lights. Military drivers seemed to have little regard for speed limits and, in the blacked-out streets of Madrid at night, there were frequent crashes. So I warned Bunny to be careful as I said goodbye. He grinned, then disappeared in the twilight like a bat out of hell, taking the corner as fast as his truck would go.

Inside the Alianza some of the residents said, smiling, that they had missed my company at dinner.

"But I'll bet you ate my food," I answered, which was a sort of customary reply at such mock solicitousness—for at mealtime at the

Alianza de Intelectuales nobody ever really missed anyone else. An absent boarder meant a little more to eat for all around the table. If at breakfast, someone announced he would not be back for dinner that evening, you could almost hear the silent cheers. Everybody was glad I had eaten with the Transport Brigade.

Certainly I was happy to know the boys in the Transport unit because they were helpful to me in getting about. The high-powered foreign correspondents, representing big papers or important wire services, all had cars in Madrid, or were able to rent them, and to acquire gas—which was more difficult to get than a car. With no trains running in or out of the city, and with no car, I had to depend on the kindness of others to travel, or wait until I heard of a military convoy going someplace that I wanted to go. One of the places I wanted to go was the American Hospital at Villa Paz. I also wanted to visit Campesino's headquarters at Acala de Henares where Cervantes was born. Attached to Campesino's headquarters were a number of Cubans of color.

Nicolás Guillén and I finally got to Campesino's camp. While we were talking to him outside headquarters, an officer threw a hand grenade up into the air just for fun and it came down near us with a loud explosion. Campesino laughed fit to kill at seeing us jump. He liked such pranks, and was famous throughout Spain as the daredevil general of the war. Campesino wanted us to meet his favorite Cuban officer, Captain Cueria.

"Ven aca, Cueria," he called. I do not recall any salutes being exchanged as the captain approached the general under the trees where we were standing near headquarters. Basilio Cueria was a big fine-looking brownskin Cuban in his thirties, a former baseball player who had been in the United States, and who spoke English well. He was the captain of a machine-gun company made up entirely of Spanish gunners. When General Miaja inspected the Campesino troops, Cueria and his company gave a lightning demonstration on the field of how quickly a machine gun might be assembled from the parts each man carried, and they were singled out for a special citation by the general staff. Cueria's men were also the best baseball players in Spain, Campesino said. Cueria had taught them the game.

In Campesino's mess hall I had one of the best meals I had eaten in Spain. "How do you get such good food?" I wondered.

"*Como crees, chico?*" he asked, using the intimate *tu* form as if he had known me all my life. "How do you think, kid?" Grinning, his hand pulled a grenade from his belt. "I always get my proper rations. When they see me coming in a commissary, they begin to load up my trucks right away before I start playing ball with this."

## HOW A MAN DIED

IN order to get permission to visit the Ebro front in the northeast where it was rumored the next major battle was to take place, and where a number of Negro Internationals were stationed, it was necessary for me to go to the Brigade headquarters at Albacete.

The trip to Valencia was without incident. But the troop train to Albacete was packed to the door with soldiers returning from leave, many of them drunk and exhausted. When I got to the station that night, the train was already crowded. The coaches were third class with wooden benches. I was lucky to get a seat on the rail of a bench, for soon the aisles were packed with standees. The trip took all night. Most of the way the coaches were blacked out, the lights being turned on only at stations. During long waits in the pitch-black countryside, men would stick their heads out the windows to see if enemy planes were overhead. To move about in that train, one had to walk over sleeping men prone in the aisles or under benches. Some fell asleep standing up. Finally I got so sleepy myself that I lay down with my body partially under a bench. For the rest of the night, fellows were walking all over my feet, but usually I slept on.

Albacete was a madhouse, filled with troops, recruits drilling, bustling military offices, and officials so busy it took hours to see any of them. I stayed there only one night—that was enough! The hotels were all packed and jammed, but I was given permission to sleep in a Spanish barracks on the outskirts of town, a big greystone building filled with double-decker wooden bunks where hundreds of men were sleeping when I got there around midnight. The *responsable* told me to take any bunk I saw. If there was none empty, just wait until somebody got up for guard duty or something, he said. Men were coming and going and moving about in the barracks all night. I found an empty bunk, the top tier of a double-decker, and lay down with all my clothes on—for it was a chilly night. When I went to sleep, I was so tired that I thought nothing could wake me up. But I did wake up to find my whole body crawling with bedbugs. The insect I loathe most in the world is a bedbug—their cold brown bodies and horrible smell when they are mashed, and the bloody little stains they leave on bedding and clothing! I sat up and looked at the bugs crawling in and out of my coat sleeves. I pulled up my trouser legs to scratch and dozens of bugs were on my legs. The whole bunk was covered with bedbugs. When I looked at the man sleeping below me, he was covered with them, too. To try to kill them would have been futile, there were too many. Besides I hated their smashed odor. But I swore, if I ever got back to a nice clean bed in the U. S. A., I would never leave again. Finally I went to sleep.

From Albacete a Brigade truck carrying machine-gun parts to the Canadian Mackenzie-Papineau Battalion, took me along, too, to the front, where a Loyalist attack was in progress. In this attack, so I learned in Albacete, Milton Herndon, one of the Negroes I had hoped to see, had just been killed. North of Valencia, a few miles out of Vinaros the truck in which I was riding broke down and refused to budge. We were due at the front in time for supper, but we never made it. While the fellows worked on the truck, I was stuck there on the road until long after midnight. It was dawn before we reached Pueblo de Hijar, and from there set out to find the tents of the Brigade battalion's new field headquarters where I was to sleep. But we learned from a sentry on the road that enemy artillery had located it during the night and blasted it out. A young officer and two other men had been killed and seven seriously wounded, including a doctor. It was a good thing for me that our truck had broken down on the road and I had not slept at headquarters the night before. I might have been blown out of this world.

That morning in the drizzling rain, we located the new position of the battalion staff several miles further away now behind a ridge.

Dave Doran, political commissar of the 15th Brigade greeted me, gave me something to eat and a blanket and showed me a tent in which I might spread it to get a little daytime sleep, since I had been up most of the night. I slept until noon. The Negroes in the area were all off in dugouts and trenches three or four miles away, and so widely scattered that Doran felt it would not be wise in bad weather and under battle conditions for me to try to seek them out. Besides, he had no one he could assign to the task of conducting me into the lines on that fluid front where at any moment new battles might break out. I was disappointed, but asked if there were any way I might see some of the men from the machine-gun unit with which the slain Milton Herndon had served. Doran said he would try to find out where these men were located, and perhaps take me there.

Milton Herndon's younger brother, Angelo Herndon, whom I had met in New York, had given me a copy of his autobiography, *Let Me Live*, which told the story of his part in a relief demonstration in Atlanta. He had been arrested and sentenced by an all-white jury to twenty years on the chain gang under an old Georgia law designed to prevent slave insurrections. That ancient statute of ante-bellum days had been dug up and applied to the street demonstration against the relief commissioners which was termed "rebellion." When I first met Angelo, he was free on fifteen thousand dollars bail, and had come to New York to make a speech about his harsh sentence which had created almost as much newspaper comment around the world as the famous Scottsboro Case of a few years before. "When Negroes ask for bread in Georgia, the only answer is the chain gang and death," Angelo said in his speech. He told me that his brother, Milton, was in Spain, and he said if I should see him, to be sure to say hello for him. But I missed Milton by a few days. So the least I could do when I got back home, I thought, would be to tell Angelo how his brother died.

The rain kept up all day, dreary and cold, and toward evening it began to come down in a steady torrent. It was quiet on the Ebro front. No action, just silence in the pitch-black dark of a rainy night in a valley where perhaps twenty thousand men lay in trenches and dugouts, behind barricades in ruined villages, squatting beside machine guns, or gathered around field pieces. Rain and silence. Then after dark, sporadic rifle fire. Occasionally, for a few seconds, a machine gun spitting a row of bullets into space. Then long blanks of silence again. Afar, the boom of cannon, steady for maybe a half hour. Perhaps the Loyalist guns trained on Zaragossa, as the rebel guns were trained on Madrid. Then silence again. And the rain coming down in a soft steady drizzle.

Where the headquarters tent sags, water drips down and spatters on the table. Two candles burn. Men come in and out with messages for members of the Geenral Staff, papers to sign, calls to the field telephone in a dugout on the side of a hill. The pop of a motorcycle. A courier arriving or departing for the lines. When the tent flap is lifted, you see the sentry outside with his gun on his shoulder, scarcely visible in the darkness, his capelike coat touching the ground. He stands there silent, on guard in the rain. Dave Doran comes in. "Sorry," he says, "but we can't go to the Mac-Pap's tonight. Too much rain. Too difficult for you to see the men on a night like this. Besides, that Battalion's the furthest away, a couple of miles or more through the trenches—once you get to the trenches. They're the last in our lines. Instead of you going, I've telephoned for two of the members of Herndon's section to come in and talk to you."

The rain seemed to come down harder than ever. Rain and the dull boom of artillery. It was cold so I went into the next tent to look for my overcoat. One of my tentmates was spreading down a ground cloth with a flashlight, preparatory to making our pallets on the damp earth.

"We've just dug a little trench around our tent so the water'll run off," he said. "You know, this is the first night the *Estado Mayor's* been located here."

"Yes," I said, "I know about the shelling. I'd been in it myself, if we hadn't been delayed on the road."

"Lucky you!" said the soldier.

This was my first visit to an International unit in action under battle conditions. They were on the Aragon sector, specifically, Fuentes de Ebro—which means the village of Fuentes located on the River Ebro. The Loyalist troops, including the English-speaking battalions, had taken Belchite and Quinto only a short time before, important victories for the government. Now the Brigade lines lay just outside the town of Fuentes de Ebro. In the attack on Fuentes, Milton Herndon was killed. Now, two of his comrades were coming to field headquarters behind the lines to tell me about it.

I put on my heavy coat and went back to the busy staff tent to wait. Two or three hours passed, and they did not come. Meanwhile, there was a meeting of the Political Commissars from the various International companies, English, Canadian, Irish and Spanish-speaking. I was invited to sit in and listen to the problems and interests of the men whom the Commissars were commissioned to look after.

Nine o'clock came, ten, eleven. Still the men hadn't arrived from the Mackenzie-Papineau Battalion where Sergeant Herndon had served. The meeting of Commissars broke up. It was raining very hard, so Doran decided to telephone for a truck to carry the men back to the nearest trenches where, even then, some would have an hours' or two hours' walk to reach their companies.

"Something must have happened that they couldn't leave," Doran said to me regarding the men from the Mac-Pap's. "But I'll phone again and see."

I followed him out into the rain. On our way to the communications dugout, we ran into two dark shapes moving in the dark on the side of the hill.

"Johnson! Sankari!" they called out, identifying themselves.

"What happened to you," Doran asked. "We'd given you up."

"Snipers must have heard us coming out," one of them answered, "so they kept picking at us all around until we had to stop."

"So many bullets kept whizzing by for a while that we had to lay down in a ditch and stay there more'n an hour."

"Then in the rain, we couldn't find the path up here since you've moved. We weren't sure where you were."

But they had finally arrived. Two men from the 4th Company of the Mackenzie-Papineau Battalion who had served under Sergeant Herndon in his machine-gun section. They were big fellows, standing there in the dark. Dave Doran introduced me: Aaron Johnson of Los Angeles, Hjalmar Sankari of New York. When we got inside the candle-lighted tent, I saw that one was a colored boy, Johnson. And the other was a Scandinavian-American, Sankari.

"You'd better go back in the truck we're sending for now," Dave Doran advised them as he started out to phone, "so there won't be much time for you to talk."

The two men wiped the rain from their faces and we sat down on the square rim of a bank of earth that had been dug out to make a hollow seat around the table. The others left us alone in the tent. I began to ask questions about Herndon and his life in Spain. But, at first, it was a rather halting interview. I knew that no fighter likes to talk much about a comrade who's just been killed. But these men were his friends, and they had come to tell me about him.

"Milt Herndon! He died like this," they said. Sometimes one talked, sometimes the other. One answered a question, another added a phrase. Two voices in the night, a Negro voice and a white voice. Two American voices telling how Milton Herndon of Atlanta died.

"He died like this," they said. "He was taking the second machine gun over the top. He was the Sergeant, the section leader. He had three guns under him. He was taking the second gun over the top with his men. We went about three hundred metres up a little rise—when the Fascists opened up. We had to stop. A regular rain of bullets. They hit one of our comrades, Irving Schatz, his name was. He fell just ahead of us on top of the ridge in full view of the Fascist fire. Irving was wounded in the leg and couldn't move. The man nearest to him, Smitty, raised up to drag him back, and a bullet got Smitty in the heart. Got him right in the heart. Then Herndon crawled up the slope to rescue the wounded boy. They got Herndon, too—through the head, through the mouth—two bullets, just like that! And Herndon and Smitty both died. The other boy lived. Irving's in the hospital now. But Herndon and Smitty were killed right there. It was October thirteenth, our first day in the lines. At one o'clock we went over the top."

The rain came down in torrents on the little tent where we were sitting. A motor truck drew up outside. We heard the fellows piling in for their return to the trenches. Someone came to say that the others would wait for us to finish our conversation. But I did not like to keep a whole truck full of men standing in the rain.

"Tell me a little of what he was like," I said, "before you go. I know Angelo, but I never knew Milton."

"He used to talk a lot about Angelo," Sankari said. "He was proud of his brother for what he did in Atlanta. Milton was smart, too —he knew what lies behind this war. He knew what's up Hitler's sleeve. He worked hard in the company and in his section. Good machine gunner. Fine soldier. The men liked him. He had both Americans and English guys under him, and we all liked him."

"Two of us are colored in the company besides Herndon," Johnson said, rising. "Myself and Charlie Lewis from New York. We all liked Herndon. He worked hard. Milt was good-natured. He was a good cardplayer, too. A good fellow."

"He wanted to be a dynamiter," the Scandinavian added as he lifted the tent flap. "Herndon, he was a big tall guy, used to be a coal miner, and he would have been in one of the Spanish companies as a dynamiter if he could've spoken Spanish. He was a good singer. Everybody liked him."

"He and Smitty were both fine fellows," Johnson said. "They were good friends, too. Smitty was white. They're buried together."

"Out in No-Man's-Land, over by Fuentes, we buried them that night," Sankari said.

"You know, our machine-gun company was named after Frederick Douglass," Johnson added as they left the tent. "Herndon suggested the name, and when we named it the Frederick Douglass Machine-Gun Company, Milt made a speech on the connection between Negro rights at home and the fight here in Spain. He said, 'Yesterday, Ethiopia, Czechoslovakia—today, Spain—tomorrow, maybe America. Fascism won't stop anywhere—until we stop it.' That's what he said."

Their truck rumbled slowly away in the blackness of the downpour, its headlights out. With it went these two Americans, one white, one Negro. Together they had come through the rain, hiding in roadside ditches from the bullets, in order to tell me how two other Americans, one white and one black, had died to stop fascism. At the moment of their death, they saved a wounded comrade.

On my pallet that night on the soggy ground under a dripping tent at the Ebro front, I remembered long ago it was written, "Greater love hath no man than this, that a man lay down his life for his friends." I thought how Milton Herndon had died there at the Ebro not only to save a friend—and a land not his own, Spain—but all of us.

## NEGROES IN SPAIN

AT Pueblo de Hijar in an abandoned mill the night before I left the front, I gave a program of my poems for a group of the Brigaders, and I read some of the *Letters from Spain* in verse that I had written. Afterwards there was a discussion, punctuated by the occasional roar of artillery. Some of the Internationals sitting around on the cold stone floor of the mill objected to the lack of correct grammar and the slightly broken English that I had used in these *Letters*. They said that many of their Negro comrades in arms were well educated; furthermore, I might mistakenly be aiding in perpetuating a stereotype. I answered that, of course, most of the Negroes in the Brigades spoke grammatically, but that others—and plenty of whites, as well— had had but little formal education and did not speak as if they were college men. Like the colonial Moors on Franco's side who had had meager, if any, opportunities for education, Negroes from states like Georgia, Alabama and Mississippi had attended very poor schools at best, and in some communities they had none. Anyway, one of the things I was trying to show in my poems was that even the least privileged of Americans, the Southern Negroes, were represented in the International Brigades, fighting on the side of the Spanish peasants and workers to help them preserve a government that would give the peasants and workers—as were most Negroes, too—a chance at schools and the learning of grammar.

With a French reporter, Mathieu Gorman, I went to captured Quinto. We found the Mexican painter, Antonio Pujol, sitting in a battalion kitchen that had been set up in a storage house with piles of licorice root stacked in the corners. Pujol was trying to keep warm. A Cuban boxer, Raul Rojas, came in and showed us the knife with which he had killed the Fascist hero of Toledo, Santa Pau, in hand-to-hand fighting at Belchite a few days before. The dead man's dried blood was still on the knife handle. This didn't help to make a damp chilly afternoon any more cheerful. But at the receiving hospital two American nurses brewed a big pot of tea, and gave us some tinned biscuits, which made me feel better. As usual, I was hungry.

A truck headed south before dawn took me as far as a bridge in the middle of Spain where the road across a river divided into two forks, one of which led into the Madrid-Valencia highway. I hadn't the least idea that morning where I was when they dropped me off at the near end of the bridge from which, the driver said, I would have the best chance of hitchhiking a ride into Madrid. The sentry guarding the bridge, who stopped all cars to examine papers, said he would help me get a ride. He was a teen-age Spaniard who told me that almost every day a Fascist plane or two came over and tried to bomb the bridge. He pointed out some big holes along the almost dry river bed where he said bombs had fallen. Sure enough, it wasn't any time before we heard a plane, and I looked up to see it high in the distance. I looked around, wondering which way to seek shelter. There were woods on either side of the road.

"Shall we go into the wood?" I asked, thinking it wise, in any case, to get away from the bridge which was a bombing target.

"Never into the woods," said the little Spaniard. "Come with me —we go under the bridge."

"Under the bridge?" I cried, feeling myself being blown sky high.

"Sure," he said, "they always aim at the bridge, but never hit it. Most times their bombs fall in the woods." But before we had time to get under the bridge, the plane had come over, and no bombs fell. Just a reconnaissance flight, I guess.

An hour or two passed, and finally a car came hurtling down the road with some Spanish soldiers in it, and they carried me on to Madrid, speeding through the country as fast as their car would go. I got back to the Alianza in time for dinner.

It was cold in Madrid at the end of October, and there was no fuel for heating purposes, so it was more comfortable to keep on the move. Since I could not visit Seville or Cordova, the cities I most wanted to see in Spain, as they were in rebel hands, I settled for a trip to the ancient Escorial which the Alianza arranged, requisitioning a car for me from the Ministry of War, as was at times its cultural privilege. One of the great sights of the world, this sixteenth-century monastery, church and royal palace where once lived Phillip II, has over a thousand fantastic windows and hundreds of doors. Twenty-four miles from Madrid in the Guadarrama Mountains, where some of the worst fighting took place in the early days of the war, the Escorial itself was untouched. At least the rebels did not bomb it. They respected this national treasure, so the Spanish kings buried in its dusky Panteon still slept in peace, and the hand-illuminated scrolls in the monastery library were intact. After a trip through the Escorial, climbing up and down stairs, with Maria Teresa Leon stopping to explain the history of every object to me, I was more fatigued that day than if I had taken a tour of an entire battle front. Even though there was much of interest and beauty at the Escorial, museums always tire me out.

A trip to Tarazona later, while not exciting in any memorable way, gave me a chance to meet one of the Negro Internationals I had heard a great deal of, and about whom I wanted to do a piece for the *Cleveland Call-Post*. When I got to Tarazona at midnight (and it was fortunate for me, I did not arrive later or I would have missed him), the man I wanted to see was about to start out with two trucks on a food purchasing tour for the various kitchens at the Anglo-American Training Base. He had little time to talk to me as the trucks were about to get under way, but while the chauffeurs were gassing up for the journey, he told me briefly something of his work in Spain.

Abraham Lewis was his name. He came from Cleveland, where he was one of the active workers in the Future Outlook League. He had been in Spain almost a year. At first he was attached to a transport regiment. Now he was the chief quartermaster at the English-speaking Training Base, with a large staff of various nationalities under him. His responsibilities included the feeding, clothing, sanitary and recreational facilities of the entire base. Lieutenant Lewis, however, was not without experience in such work. He was formerly chief steward on an American boat and there acquired the knowledge of handling food and preparing menus. In Spain, though, the feeding of Internationals was no simple problem. In the first place, the Spaniards cook with olive oil, a procedure not agreeable to the pallet of most foreigners. Lewis had to find available substitutes for this oil that would appeal to the International tastes at his tables in a land where lard or butter were not easily to be gotten. Then there was the problem of cooks. Very few of the International Brigaders wanted to serve as cooks. They wanted to fight. So Lewis had to train Spanish cooks in American ways of cooking, stressing sanitation and efficiency—especially in the matter of time, having food ready *exactly* at the hour when it should be served. Since most of his kitchen workers could neither read nor write, written orders and listed menus were at first impossible. Out of twenty-seven cooks and helpers only seven were literate. So Lewis organized classes for them. Already seventeen had learned to read. For this achievement the U. G. T. Trade Unions, to which the Spanish kitchen employees belonged, complimented Lewis in an official letter.

The International Brigades in Spain were integrated several years before American military services started mixing Negroes and whites, and there were Negro officers in the Brigades with white men serving under them. The units of the American Medical Bureau in Spain were mixed, too. There were several colored ambulance drivers, including two teen-age kids, George Waters and Al Chisholm, who got there, I have no idea how, since they should have been home in high school. But they were driving ambulances up to the fronts under fire and bringing back the wounded. At the charming white villas of the International Convalescent Center at Benicasim there was jovial Ted Gibbs from Chicago, who chauffeured a big evacuation ambulance; and talkative Julius Rodriquez from Harlem, who drove ambulatory patients to the movies or to the country for picnics, and was in charge of the office work for the entire ambulance transport group. On the days when hospital trains filled with wounded pulled into Benicasim, these Negroes sometimes worked a twenty-four-hour shift. Among the wounded when I was there was Otto Reeves, a fine youngster from Dayton, who asked me to tell his parents he was O.K. when I got back to Ohio. But before I got home, Otto had returned to the Ebro front and was killed.

At the American Base Hospital at Villa Paz to which serious cases were evacuated, there were graduate nurses from all over the United States, among them a Negro girl, Salaria Kee. Dr. Arnold Donawa of Harlem was in charge of rebuilding the faces of soldiers there whose jaws were splintered, teeth shattered, or chins blown away. This tall, kindly colored man, a favorite with the patients, stayed in Spain until near the end of the war, and brought back with him a group of wounded Americans. Dr. Donawa showed me one of his patients at Villa Paz, a Spanish boy, whose lower jaw had been torn away by an explosive bullet and who had to be fed with a tube. Dr. Donawa told me the explosive bullets used by the Franco troops were the kind that explode inside a wound and leave splinters of metal in flesh and bone. They are generally used, he said, only for big game hunting in Africa, not on human beings.

The nurse, Salaria Kee, was a slender chocolate-colored girl. When Mussolini's troops invaded Ethiopia, Salaria was one of the initiators of the fund-raising campaign in Harlem which sent a seventy-five-bed field hospital to Ethiopia. When she had the chance to come to Spain to help the Loyalist government repel an Italian-aided insurrection, she came.

"What! You're going to Spain in wartime?" she said her friends in Harlem exclaimed in amazement. "And alone?"

"Sure," Salaria answered. "I wasn't born twins. I have to go alone."

When I met her at Villa Paz, she had been there for six months, and had just become Mrs. John Joseph O'Reilly. On October second, she had married an Irish ambulance driver. An old judge with handlebar mustaches from the nearby village of Salices had performed the ceremony, the village band had played at her wedding, and a blinded American soldier, Robert Raven, had made a speech.

Salaria told me of some of the problems of the American Hospital at Villa Paz. In spite of the fact that it had recently been a royal palace, sometimes the plumbing did not work, and the water pressure had been so low that often water would not run at all, so the nurses and doctors had recently chipped in and bought a gasoline pump. But sometimes that did not work either. One day in caring for a patient who had to have a diet of soft-boiled eggs at regular intervals, when no water would come out of any faucets in the building, Salaria took a bottle of wine from the Spanish workers' table, and boiled the eggs in wine. Another time on a bitter cold day when a wounded French soldier, after long exposure, was brought in out of the rain with a mangled leg that had to be amputated immediately, the doctor ordered the chilled soldier surrounded at once by hot-water bags, otherwise he might die. But there was no hot water ready for such an emergency, and the diluted kerosene in the oil stove in the operating room would not light. Suddenly it occurred to Salaria that it was almost lunch time and they always had soup for luncheon. She rushed into the kitchen and filled a half-dozen water bags from a boiling pot of soup, and thus kept the soldier warm until the operation.

At Villa Paz I saw also Ed White, one of the first two men of color to come to Spain in the original Lincoln Brigade. The other, Alonzo Watson, had been the first Negro slain in the Spanish War. In the hospital at Quinto I talked with Crawford Morgan of New York. Under treatment at Benicasim were Frank Alexander of Los Angeles, George Waters from San Francisco, Andrew Mitchell of Pittsburgh, Jeff Wideman and Henry George of Philadelphia, and Nathaniel Dickson of Chicago. In the various transport units there were a number of St. Louis Negroes—Tom Brown, Frank Warfield, Jimmy Cox, Larry Dukes, Walter Callum. At Tarazona, I ran into Bert Jackson of Brooklyn and Vaughn Love from Harlem. At Albacete, I saw Oscar Hunter, a former social worker at Karamu House in Cleveland, William Baker from Honolulu, Canute Frankson, and several more whose names I did not put down. With the John Brown Heavy Artillery Battery, I met a French Algerian Negro named Frazal, and a former pitcher with the Cuban Giants, Domingo, also Gowldyn, a New Yorker from the 369th Infantry unit of the National Guard in Harlem. I met Tommy Paige from the Cordova front, Joe Taylor from the Ebro, and Tomas Callado in a Madrid hospital. With Campesino I'd seen Eugene Gavin of Youngstown, a tall machine gunner who lost an eye at Teruel. There had been four Negro aviators in Spain, including James Peck, but they had been invalided home shortly before I arrived. And among the men I never knew because they had been killed, were Milton Herndon, Morris Wickman, Norman Lisberg, Alonzo Watson, and the man whom the Brigaders spoke of very often, Oliver Law.

Who were these Negroes who, like Law, Herndon, Garland, Donowa, and Abe Lewis, left their peaceful U. S. A. for a war zone in a foreign country, coming of their own free will to Spain? Nobody made them come. They were not conscripts like the Moors, or mercenaries—the money was next to nothing. They were not professional soldiers like the Germans, or draftees like the Italians. They came of their own free will. A number of them died there.

Who were they? There were a hundred or so that I talked with in the various hospitals, or on the Ebro front, at Albacete, Valencia, Tarazona and Madrid. I put their names in my notebooks. Yet their names cannot tell us who they really were, nor could any additional pages I might write about them. But they were there in Spain in 1937-38, American Negroes. History has recorded it. Before that time, the leading ambassadors of the Negro in Europe were jazz-band musicians, concert artists, dancers, or other performers. But these Negroes in Spain were fighters—*voluntary fighters*—which is where history turned another page.

## ARTISTS UNDER SEIGE

*Cuidadito, compa' gallo, cuidadito!*
*Cuidadito, compa' gallo, cuidadito!*

*TAKE care, brother rooster, take care!* Guillén used to sing as he came up the stairs to my Alianza room. But one day in late November, he came up shivering. "Damn, man," he sputtered in his Cuban Spanish, "it's getting too cold in Madrid for Papa Gallo to crow any more. But I hear it's still warm in Valencia."

"When are you cutting out?" I asked.

"As soon as I can crowd into a military bus," said Guillén, his teeth chattering.

I knew it was time for me to be leaving, too, but I hated to quit that city I had grown to love. Like the Madrileños, even under doom, I did not want to leave. A year or so earlier, when the citizens of Madrid could have gone and, in fact, the government had begged as many of them as possible to evacuate the city, they wouldn't go. Now that they couldn't go, since there was no transportation, they wouldn't go anyway. But there was no real reason for me, an American, to stay there any longer, eating up their meager food, taking up their fighting time. I had gotten the stories for my paper, overstayed the time for which the editor had agreed to pay me, and seen almost all there was to see. Still I wanted to remain. It was mid-December before I left. Franco was threatening to sever the Madrid-Valencia road—and even more than that, to divide Loyalist Spain into two parts, cutting off the north from the south, by a drive through Teruel to the coast. The Americans in Madrid said it would be wise to leave before the city was entirely surrounded and a starvation blockade in force. I brought no winter clothes to Spain and should have gone home before the cold set in. But the longer I stayed in Madrid, the more I liked it. I might get hungry there, but I never got bored. And certainly there were abnormal deprivations plus the normal and great poverty—but not the dull relief W. P. A. kind of worried existence we had at home in Cleveland—with little hope in sight. Here in Madrid, where people had next to nothing—with the guns pointed at them every day to take that little away—they expected soon to have everything. At the Alianza poets were making poems about it, musicians making songs, artists painting pictures ,and Maria Teresa Leon preparing plays.

To get tickets to the crowded Madrid theaters was difficult without standing in line a long time, but fortunately through Maria Teresa I was able to see a number of plays, and could always attend the Teatro Lope de Vega, which she administered, or the Zarzuela where she performed and directed an excellent student company in Spanish and other European plays. Maria Teresa Leon, Alberti's wife, was a buxom blonde with a handsome face and a commanding personality. Her hair was very long, her complexion clean and wholesome, and her Spanish very clear and positive. She dressed well. And in Spain, where men always turn around to look at a woman, she was an eye-catcher.

There is an old Spanish custom taken for granted that a man may whistle or even speak to a pretty girl on the street without offense. But if the girl so much as turns here eyes, then—but only then—she may be insulted by a direct proposition. So long as the woman does not notice the admiration of the unknown male, she is safe from intrusion, but may hear after she has passed a whispered compliment to her pretty legs. Only loose women ever turn around to acknowledge such compliments. But with revolutionary zeal, some of the more ardent Loyalist ladies in Spain set out to put an end to what they felt was "intrusive and uncomradely" in this traditional Spanish way of flirting. Women, they said, were workers and citizens just like men, not mere objects of sex, and so should not be subjected to personal remarks from unknown admirers on the public streets. In Paris, London, New York, and other truly cultured centers where she had been, Maria Teresa said, such behavior on the part of men toward women was unknown. The new Spain should not tolerate it either.

One day, walking alone down the Paseo de Recoletos in Madrid, Maria Teresa was the subject of a passing soldier's ardent compliments, "Wow! What a blonde! Gee, *chica*, you're pretty!" Most women, secretly pleased, would have walked straight on, eyes ahead without the flicker of a lash. But Maria Teresa decided to teach the young soldier a lesson. She turned her head to tell him that that was no way for any comrade in Loyalist Spain to behave toward another—since he did not even know her name. But before she got the words out of her mouth, the young soldier took for granted that, having turned her head, she was a streetwalker, so he playfully slapped her on her shapely behind. Maria Teresa screamed indignantly. The corner policeman recognized the popular actress and immediately laid hands on the young soldier for daring to strike her, and she permitted the bewildered youth to be hauled off to police court.

That night at dinner, when Maria Teresa told the assembled diners about it, the few women there, of course, voiced indignation concerning the amorous soldier's uncouth behavior. But the men all looked embarrassed, and even Maria's husband did not support her position very strongly. Spanish males were all for preserving the right to whistle at a pretty face or figure in passing, and to give vent to a few fleeting sidewalk compliments.

But at the Alianza de Intelectuales, whose president was the Catholic writer, José Bergamin, and Alberti the executive secretary, women were on a par with men. There were few amorous doings there anyway. Everybody was too busy working: making posters for the war effort or the liquidation of illiteracy campaign, or editing and publishing books. I was busy translating, with the aid of Rafael Alberti and Manuel Altolaguirre, the "Gypsy Ballads" of Federico Garcia Lorca, and his play, *Bodas de Sangre*. Alberti, Altolaguirre, and Arturo Barea had known Lorca well and still grieved for his execution at the hands of the Fascists. With workshops at the Alianza, Miguel Prieto had established a satirical puppet theater, La Tarumba, touring the trenches right up to the front lines. But most male members of the Alianza were soldiers and so able to work at art only when in Madrid on leave. The leading man at Maria Teresa's theater came in from the trenches at University City to play his roles, then went back to the front after his performance.

Maria Teresa's student group presenting Lorca's *Mariana Pineda* often took their play to the battle fronts to perform in the open for the soldiers, many of the men standing throughout the whole show. Maria Teresa told me of a peasant soldier watching the play who suddenly exclaimed, "All my life I have done nothing but dig in the earth. Now here I am like a lord watching a play." After a performance the actors and the director made it a point to mingle with the soldiers and discuss the play with them.

"What we want to do—our theater groups," Maria Teresa Leon told me, "is make the peasants and workers, even while they are soldiers, realize that they too can learn to make up plays, direct plays, and act in them. The soldiers can talk with our actors if they want to, and they can become actors themselves."

Alberti added, "What the members of the Alianza want to do is make art life, and life art, with no gulf between the artists and the people. After all, as Lorca said, 'The poem, the song, the picture is only water drawn from the well of the people, and it should be given back to them in a cup of beauty so that they may drink—and in drinking, understand themselves.' Now our art is at the service of the Republic to help win the war, since we do not want the books we write to be burned in public squares by Fascists, or blown into bits on library shelves by bombs, or censored until all their meaning is drained away. That is why we artists help to hold Madrid against Franco."

## HOW TO EAT A CAT

MIGUEL HERNANDEZ, a young poet in peasants' shoes, came from Valencia to visit us at the Alianza for a week. He had been a shepherd boy. The Cuban writer, Pablo de la Torriente-Brau, had

passed by the house earlier that year on his way to the trenches where
he was killed. Miguel Hernandez, who had fought with him in the
same regiment, told us about it. Louis Aragon from Paris and Egon
Ervin Kish from Central Europe had visited the Alianza, too, and the
painter, Alfredo Siquieros from Mexico. But since the Alianza was
more a work place than a center of entertainment, not too many
foreign writers dropped by during their visits to the beleaguered city,
for there was no food and little drink to offer a guest. If a guest came,
and pesetas were available, the guest might be taken in the late afternoon to the old bar that had the good sherry. There, when other
knick-knacks were lacking, a big bowl of walnuts or almonds might be
placed on the table along with several little hammers. Sometimes at
the cocktail hour, the cracking of nuts at tables was louder than the
gunfire at the front. There being less and less food in Madrid as fall
became winter, one did not leave a single kernel of a single nut
uneaten.

Late at night I could hear the emaciated lions roaring in the
Madrid Zoo just beyond the Retiro near the Alianza. I always wondered what they fed these animals. Some said they fed them the
skinny horses that dropped dead of starvation. At the nearly abandoned American Embassy there was a famous dog, a great Dane, that
some foreigner had left behind in the embassy's care. The dog could
eat more meat than a whole family of people. The Spanish caretakers
at the embassy slighted themselves to feed this dog the little that they
were able to give him during the war. The dog was still surviving
when I left the city, looking at visitors with big sad eyes.

The Gypsy dancers were still dancing in the music halls and El
Niño Perez playing his guitar. Albacin, son of Madrid's prettiest
Gypsy flower seller, was appearing in La Copla Andaluza. Don Juan
Tenorio was playing at the Español. And at the Calderon Pastora
Imperio, the famous Argentinita, had just come back from two hundred performances for the soldiers in the trenches. In the early fall a
delegation of Mexican writers and painters brought to Madrid a stunning exhibition of art and posters. Every evening during the Mexican
exhibition there were literary programs in which Spanish poets like
Rafael Alberti and Leon Felipe took part, as well as the visiting Mexican writers, Jorge Mansisidor, Maria Luisa Vera, Juan de la Cabada,

and the young poet, Octavia Paz. Silvestre Revueltas conducted the Madrid Symphony Orchestra in a program of his works. I found the jovial Revueltas a likable man, very simple in manner, and almost as stout as Diego Rivera. Revueltas set my "Song for a Dark Girl" to music, and it was later published in New York with both the English and Spanish text.

Revueltas, like most Mexicans I've known, had a keen sense of humor. He enjoyed the ironic anecdotes and wry jokes about the bombardments, the war, Franco, Mola and Queipo de Llano that continually went the rounds of Madrid. One joke concerned the pregnant wife of an African savage who asked her husband what they should name their son, Lion, Hyena or Leopard. The husband answered, "None of those, wife, they're not savage enough. We'll call him Mussolini." Another tale was that when Franco went to make a speech to a division of his troops at Cordova, as he stood up before them, he asked, "Does anybody here know Spanish?" And a little story that the Madrileños thought very funny concerned a soldier who, after weeks of eating nothing but rice in the trenches, came home on leave and his mother prepared a surprise dish for him for dinner. When she put it on the table, it was a pot of rice! In an almost lunchless city a common question was, "What did you have for lunch?" The answer might be, "Boiled mule's tongue." Whereupon, the questioner, not to be outdone, would say, "Why, we had fried pony."

The bombardments that fall seemed heavier than ever in the city and the hard metallic bang of exploding shells clearer and sharper in the cold autumn air. Loyalist Intelligence Agents said the rebels were now trying out new model Krupp cannons, firing on Madrid from the Garabitas Hills a few miles beyond the city limits. The government was answering back from Carabanchel with the same old guns they had been depending upon for months. In the Plaza de Castelar just down the street from the Alianza, a shell had broken the nose off of one of the lions hitched to the chariot of the Goddess of the Fountain of Cibeles. Now that the fountain had been belatedly covered with sandbags, the wits of Madrid called her, "Beauty Under Covers."

With a Spanish soldier friend who came into town often on

leave, I went to visit his parents in the Cuartro Caminos section of Madrid, a poor neighborhood East of University City. There every house had been damaged by shrapnel or flying shells. But the neighborhood was still thickly populated, with children scampering in the streets, women washing clothes in courtyards, and old men sitting in the chilly sunlight to absorb what warmth was left before the freezing weather came. My friend, Vincente, gave me packs of "draft killers," the hard little black cigarettes supplied the troops, which he lighted from one end of a fuselike rope-lighter he wound about his waist. He said its long smoldering tip was used to touch off dynamite charges at the front. I in turn gave Vincente saccharin tablets to sweeten the family coffee. He introduced me to the little bodegas, wineshops, in Antocha, a roughneck section of Madrid near the railroad yards where every night seemed like Saturday, in spite of the frequent crack of rifle fire, the staccato run of machine guns, and the boom of trench mortars and hand grenades on the Madrid front. When the enemy artillery opened up on the town and you knew again you weren't just *near* action, but *in* it, the folks in Antocha simply closed the wineshop doors to keep flying shell fragments from bursting a wine keg—and the good times kept on. What people, those Madrileños!

The sixteen-story Telefonica had closed down operations on its upper floors since they were riddled with shell holes, and no elevators were running, but the lower five floors were still in use. The telephone girls still sat at their switchboards, and you could put through a call to Paris if you wished. The Madrid Post Office near the Alianza had hardly any windows left, but the mail went out on schedule by plane to Valencia. Across the plaza from the post office, the flower stand that had been at the curb for years still did business, in spite of the fact that the Ministry of War, at which the Fascists regularly aimed a shell or two, was only a few hundred yards away.

Ralph Heinzen, the United Press man in Madrid called the siege of the city one of the most notable of modern times, and one "that will go down in history with the sieges of Troy, Sagunto, Paris and Verdun." During the months that I was there, it was estimated that more than three thousand shells fell in Madrid, almost a thousand people were killed, some three thousand wounded, and twenty-seven hundred buildings rendered uninhabitable, many totally demolished.

By the end of the war there were to be six thousand civilian dead and some twenty thousand Madrileños wounded. The Associated Press correspondent whom I knew, Charles P. Nutter, wrote, "*They Shall Not Pass* (*no pasaron*) still remains the blood-stained motto of war-battered Madrid, cold, hungry, forlorn, the capital of Spain."

War and hunger were daily companions there. With the coming of autumn and the scarcity of fresh vegetables from the country, even onions became less plentiful. Potato peelings and sausage skins were boiled in Madrid to make soup. At the Alianza even horse meat became a luxury, its coarse-grained flesh prepared to look as much like pot roast as possible by our skillful cook. She was adept at making gravies to cover up the peculiar looks of things. With lentils in one of the beautiful antique bowls belonging to the marquis, horse meat in gravy made a right nice dinner.

In extremely poor sections like Antocha and Quarto Caminos, it was said that people sometimes ate their cats. I asked my friend, Vincente, about this. He shrugged. "*Quien sabe?* Might be," he said. "But I wouldn't eat a cat by itself, would you? The best way to eat a cat is stewed with a rabbit—then you don't know when you have a mouthful of what. Each time you take a bite, you can imagine it's rabbit."

## SALUD MADRID

ON my last night in Madrid I did not go to bed at all. I had intended to go to bed, but I neglected to pack any of my belongings before I went out into the streets—and once out, I did not get back home until after three in the morning. The bus for Valencia left at five from a point a long way from the Alianza. On my return I had to pack hurriedly and start walking, for, with all the things I had to carry, I knew it would take me a long time to get to the bus stand. There was no transportation available save my own feet, no taxis, not even a push cart.

Herbert Matthews, Ernest Hemingway, and some of the other newspapermen were giving a little farewell party for me at the Hotel

Victoria that night about ten. Earlier in the evening Bunny Rucker had come in town from the Auto Camp to say goodbye and invited me out for a drink. We went to a café off the Puerto del Sol and when it closed, it being not quite time to go to the Victoria, I started to walk with Bunny to the point where his truck was parked. He was due back at camp by ten. One of the heaviest shellings I'd encountered in Madrid began while we were groping our way through a pitch-dark side street on the way to the truck. It was the hour for the theaters and cafés to close that the enemy often chose to shell Madrid in order to terrorize the throngs headed home from what little public pleasures were available in that city after dark. In the chill December air, the clarity of the preliminary BOOM! and whiz and SPANG! of shells passing, then striking the stone of a building or the concrete pavement, made each hit seem very near. No doubt, some were very near. Bunny and I took refuge in a wineshop that we found still open. Tables and counter were crowded with Spaniards who greeted us with friendly *Saluds!*

"Internationals, welcome!" they said. Almost all the men in the place insisted on buying us wine, glass after glass.

SPANG! . . . BANG! . . . SPANG! . . . The shells continued to fall, mostly toward the center of the city, it seemed, but often so near that their vibrations were distinctly felt inside the little bodega.

Some of the men at a long table began to sing, folk songs and flamenco, and everybody turned to listen while they drank. One husky, hairy Spaniard with a range from bass to high falsetto, threw back his head and cried some verses that were almost as frightful in their intensity as the crash of the shells. Flamenco and explosives on my last night in Madrid became an unforgettable combination! Wine and two candles burning in the crowded little wine house, and Bunny saying, "I guess I won't get back to camp by ten o'clock tonight." BANG! . . . One of the men began to sing:

> Madrid, que bien resistes,
> Madrid, que bien resistes,
> Mamita mia, los bombardeos!

This everyone knew, and when the contemporary wartime stanzas were exhausted, they sang together the old folk verses about the four mule drivers. Then they asked us to sing something in our language. I, who could never carry a tune, was unable to oblige. But Bunny sang "Go down, Moses, and tell old Pharaoh to let my people go." The men stamped and shouted for more, so he sang another spiritual, and another. Then the Spaniards sang some more, and the singing and drinking kept up all the time the shells were falling. Each time that there was a lull in the firing and I thought we could leave, by the time another farewell round was set up, the Franco batteries had turned loose on the city again. It was past eleven o'clock before Bunny and I, both far from sober, left the bar. We shook hands on a pitch-black corner in a canyon of enormous darkened buildings; then I found my way to the Victoria. Six or eight journalists were waiting for me there with wine and bottles of Scotch on the table. Later a few others who had been delayed by the shelling arrived, and we sat talking and drinking until after two o'clock. Hemingway and some others headed for the Florida or the Alfonso, so we shook hands on a dark corner, and I went down the Grand Via in the opposite direction toward the Alianza.

The lightless streets of Madrid were quite deserted, except for military patrols. The sandbagged shops and offices were solid walls of darkness, their roof tops dim silhouettes against an inky sky. An occasional sentry at a crossing watched me as I went by, but only one stopped me as I passed the Banco de Espana and asked to see my permit to be abroad after the curfew.

He said, "Pase, comarada. Salud!"

"Salud," I said. "Salud, Madrid!" I knew this was the last time I would walk through the main streets of this city. "Salud, Madrid!"

A shell earlier in the evening must have grazed the corner of a building just across the street for there was scattered rubble and the fallen stone of what looked like a broken cornice all over the sidewalk as I went up the Paseo past the War Ministry toward the street where I lived. Guillén, who was catching the bus, too, was in bed sleeping soundly, his single bag already packed and sitting ready just inside his door. I did not wake him but went on to my room to gather my various belongings into some portable form. Because I had so little time, I stuffed my suitcases carelessly and quickly as full as I could get them. Then I stood in the middle of the floor puzzled as to what I should do with all the other things I had to carry—books by the dozens which various writers had given me, warmly inscribed; gifts and souvenirs, including a handsome pair of bullfight banderillas that a famous torero had placed in the neck of a bull at a great corrida and which a friend presented to me when he learned that I was an *aficionado*; a bottle of wine in a wicker holder another friend had brought me to drink on the way to Valencia; a box of pieces of shrapnel I had picked up in the streets after shellings, and a ledger from the rubble of the city hall at Quijorna; a lace mantilla one of the women of the Alianza was sending to my mother; and my typewriter and manuscripts! The situation looked hopeless, for I had no transportation to get me to the bus a mile away, and no porters to help me lug so much. Besides, I was drunk.

The wine of the bodega, and the Scotch of the Victoria's party had finally gone to my head. I observed my belongings through an alcoholic fog. Drunk or sober, it was hard to figure out at that late hour what to discard. I couldn't bear to part with the banderillas, so I tied them together with a string. Of the books and ledger and manuscripts, I made a single heavy package. I stuffed my overcoat pockets full of shrapnel and other souvenirs. And I decided to hang the wine bottle around my neck. With two bags, the enormous package, my typewriter, the banderillas, and the bottle, I had no recourse but to hope that the amiable Guillén would not object to being a pack mule. Fortunately, he didn't, so about four o'clock, both of us, loaded down, started on foot toward the distant bus. I was so tired, so sleepy, and so unsteady on my legs, and the things I had in my hands, under my arms, and in my pockets were so heavy that I had to stop every few hundred yards and put everything down to rest. Guillén declared we were going to miss the bus if I didn't hurry. To get another permit for another bus on another date from the military authorities might take weeks. I replied that I didn't care—to go ahead if he wanted to— just drop my stuff on the ground and leave me.

"*Caramba, chico*," Guillén cried, "Madrid might be cut off from the rest of the world soon—you might never get out."

"*Nichevo*," I said. "*Que le hace?* Damn if I care! I can't walk any faster with this stuff—and I'm *not* going to leave my typewriter here, and these books the writers have given me, nor my banderillas, and my few clothes I've got. So go ahead."

But Guillén stuck with me, and we finally reached the bus, standing in the dark almost ready to depart and already crowded. When the motor began to sputter and bark and backfire, and the bus took off with a jerk and lurched through the dusky streets before dawn and past the bull ring at the edge of town, from the wine and the whisky, the weariness and the flamenco and the shells and the goodbyes of the night before to the men and women with whom I'd shared for so long the dangers of Madrid—plus the sadness of leaving a city that I loved—I began to feel sick at my stomach and in my soul. I rode the long way to Valencia all day until well after dark feeling very sick.

Filled with refugees from the ruined villages and towns near the fronts, Valencia was more crowded than ever. But the weather was mild and sunny, and there was still much more to eat than in Madrid. Some of the hotels even had hot water for a hot bath. But the nights were enlivened with sirens and air raids, searchlights cutting across the sky, bombs falling, and occasional shellings from the sea, and the air was full of desperate rumors. It was said that the government was preparing to move to Barcelona. Months ago it had moved from Madrid to Valencia. Now in the eventuality that Loyalist Spain were cut in two, it intended to move to Barcelona. Said the maid at my hotel, "The big shots can always go, señor. Governments can always move, *but the people have to stay.*"

For a week or so it looked as if I might have to stay in Valencia, too. There was no transportation available to the north. The trains to Catalonia were booked up for weeks ahead and crowded to the gunwales. Ticket queues were unending at the station, and there were no more tickets available for Barcelona for a month. People of means were streaming northward toward the French border—just in case. Cars could no longer be rented, since all transport now belonged to the military. Even Constancia de la Mora, the charming aristocrat in charge of the Government Press Bureau, to whom members of the foreign press appealed for everything, could be of no immediate help to me.

"So many people all of a sudden seem to want to go to Paris," said Constancia. (Everyone called her by her first name.) "Maybe after the rush is over, I can get you a seat on a train, perhaps by Christmas."

I had thought I might spend Christmas at home in Cleveland with my folks, but that hope grew dimmer as the days passed. Finally, an idea occurred to me. Almost every day I passed the downtown office of Cook's Travel Service. But no one ever seemed to be going in or out of the travel bureau, and it did not appear to be doing any business. There were no tourists coming to Valencia, and the posters in Cook's unwashed windows were all old and dusty. But the door was open. I knew that the night train for Barcelona carried one de luxe *wagon-lit* coach. I had, of course, asked at the station about a berth on this coach long ago, and was told that usually all its space was taken by the government for diplomats or military men. The stationmaster said that there was a long civilian waiting list for any free space in this car for weeks ahead.

Guillén wanted to get to Barcelona, too, where he intended to remain a few weeks doing some pieces on the Catalonians for his paper. So I said one day, "Guillén, I think I'll try Cook's." But Guillén laughed at the idea of a mere tourist bureau being able to get us tickets, when the Government Press Bureau itself could not.

"Cook's is open," I said. "They must be open for *some* reason, so no harm to try."

My one previous experience with Cook's Travel Service had been an unpleasant one. The first time I had gone to Havana from New York, I had sought to purchase a steamship ticket and make hotel reservations at the Fifth Avenue office of Cook's in New York, first phoning for information, and being assured that space was available both on the boats and in the hotels. But when I went to the office, an astonished clerk, seeing that I was colored, hurried off to confer with others, and came back to tell me in a somewhat embarrassed manner that Cook's was not equipped to give Negroes service in the Caribbean areas.

"But Cubans are all mixed with Negroes," I said. "Havana is full of colored people."

The clerk reddened and stammered, and said he was sorry. But I did not get my ticket to Cuba from Cook's nor from any American steamship agency or line. I sailed from New York on a British cruise boat and sought out my own hotel after I got to Havana.

In Valencia, however, I did not expect to find any such color difficulties. And there were none. I simply walked into Cook's bureau one morning and asked if there were two places available on the Barcelona *wagon-lit* any night that week.

The English clerk asked, "When would you like to go?"

I said, "Tomorrow."

He said, "Yes, I can give you a compartment for two."

It was that simple. I had heard from many travelers that the British-controlled Cook's was wonderfully dependable all around the world, and I had never heard of anyone having difficulties with them except Negroes in the color-conscious United States. When I found that Cook's in Valencia had tickets to Barcelona—when no one could get them for love or money—and the clerk made no fuss about it, but quite nonchalantly stamped them, I thought, "What a firm!"

Guillén was amazed when I got back to the hotel with the tickets, although a bit astonished at the price for such de luxe accommodations. We traveled the following night to Barcelona in style in a private room with plenty of space, while in other coaches people were packed in like sardines.

When I bought the morning papers at a stand on the Rambla de las Flores, I noticed the Barcelona Symphony Orchestra—the Orquesta Simfonica Catalana—would be performing that evening George Gershwin's "Rhapsody in Blue." I went to the concert and heard it beautifully played with Maria Campmany at the piano. The other numbers were "Scheherezade," "La Revoltosa," and the "Overture to Tannhauser." And, for once, no air-raid warnings sounded during the concert. The following afternoon I went to a music hall to see some Basque dancers. At the top of the printed programs there was a notice signed by Spain's two great labor unions to this effect:

JUST A MOMENT, COMRADE

The United Syndicate of Public Spectacles begs you to have the greatest respect for all the comrades you are going to see on the stage. They are workers just as you are. DON'T DISTURB the show and spoil its performance. Take art as it should be taken.

The Joint Committee

of

CNT——UGT

The CNT, the National Confederation of Labor, was an anarchist union, and the UGT, the General Union of Workers, was Socialist-Communist controlled. They had formerly been bitter rivals, and even now in the midst of war, they did not always see eye to eye. Certainly, a visitor did not have to be in Loyalist Spain long to see that it was not a Communist land, as many outside Spain claimed it to be. If there were Russians fighting in Spain, I never saw them. I saw German Nazis and Italian Fascists in Madrid's Prison Hospital, but of the thousands of Russians some papers said were aiding the Loyalists, I saw not a one. The only Russian whom I came across in Spain, other than reporters like Kolsov, was a nurse in one of the hospitals. In the cabinet of the Republican coalition government, when I was there, if I remember correctly, only one post was occupied by a Communist, that of the Ministry of Agriculture. In Madrid, Valencia and Barcelona, it was easy to tell from the press and the daily conversations of the people that political opinions varied widely. In fact, it seemed to me a major weakness of Loyalist Spain that, even in regard to the conduct of the war, action and opinion varied so greatly between the Socialist, Communist, Anarchist, and Republican parties as to cause not infrequent confusion in military plans. The Communists, although an important party, by no means controlled the government, the military forces, the press, the arts, or anything else so far as I could see. At Maria Teresa's theater in Madrid, for example, the actors and stagehands belonged to the UGT, and the members of the orchestra to the CNT. At one performance which I attended, the lights in the orchestra pit were turned on full during a scene on the stage that required darkness. When I asked Maria Teresa why that was, she said, "Because the CNT musicians union will not co-operate with the actors who belong to the UGT." Even to an outsider like myself, not only in the theater was such disunity evident, but in much else in government Spain. Alvarez del Vayo, Socialist Minister of Foreign Affairs, once asked, "Why is it Spain's people are so great, but her leaders so small?"

On one thing, however, all parties seemed united. That was to lift the cultural level of the peasants and workers, teach them to read and write, have good manners, appreciate their national arts, and take care of public property—including the churches. Some had wanted to destroy the churches—particularly the Anarchists, who took advantage in the early days of the Civil War to try to settle by violence their long feud with Catholicism. But in the trench schools I had visited there were teachers of all parties working with the illiterates. And in the public parks of Madrid—where the antiaircraft batteries were stationed under the trees—there were also signs that read:

CITIZENS, how we respect plants and animals is an index of culture. Trees, plants and flowers have life, just as do men and women. Look upon them as we do ourselves. A sincere regard for nature will lead you to respect all its works.

On a visit to a kindergarten in Barcelona, I found the children being told not to mark with their crayons on the walls of the buildings. Walls that the enemy did not mind marring with ten-ton bombs were being protected from children with chalk.

After a few days in Barcelona, I left Guillén there, and went on alone across the border to Tour de Carol, a charming French village in the Pyrenees. There I took the night express to Paris, bags, banderillas, books, typewriter, shrapnel and all still intact. But I no longer had any phonograph records to lug. Those I left with my friends in Madrid to play during the bombardments.

Out of earshot of shells and bombs for the first time in six months, at Tour de Carol that day high in the snow-covered mountains I sat down in the station buffet and ordered an enormous meal. Just across the border on the Spanish side, there had been nothing at all to eat. Now, less than a mile away, there was everything: fat cheeses, smoked turkey, hanging hams overhead, tarts, cakes and all sorts of pastries, long loaves of crackly French bread protruding from a wicker basket on the floor, a dozen brands of cigarettes and packets of chocolates on the newsstand counter. What a difference a border makes: on one side of an invisible line, food; on the other side, none. On one side, peace. On the other side, war. On one side, quiet in the sunlight. On the other side the dangerous chee-eep, chee-eep, chee-eep that was not birds, the BANG! of shells, the whine of sirens, and the bursting of bombs over crowded cities.

I stood alone on the platform of the little station at Tour de Carol that bright December day and looked down the valley into

Spain and wondered about borders and nationalities and war. I wondered what would happen to the Spanish people walking the bloody tightrope of their civil struggle. In the last few years I had been all around the embattled world and I had seen people walking tightropes everywhere—the tightrope of color in Alabama, the tightrope of transition in the Soviet Union, the tightrope of repression in Japan, the tightrope of the fear of war in France—and of war itself in China and in Spain—and myself everywhere on my tightrope of words.

Anybody is liable to fall off a tightrope in any land, I thought, and God help you if you fall the wrong way.

## HAPPY NEW YEAR

I ARRIVED in Paris just in time for Christmas. The holidays were pleasant. Some Negro friends invited me to Christmas dinner—a wonderful home-cooked dinner it was, too. During the holiday week I saw the Cartier-Bressons, Nancy Cunard, Bricktop and the Roumains. Louis Aragon introduced me to George Adam, who had begun to translate my short stories into French, and I met Pierre Seghers, my publisher. For almost five years now I had earned a living from writing, so my dream was beginning to come true—to be a professional writer—and it had been my good fortune so far not to have to write anything I did not really want to write. Meanwhile, my interests had broadened from Harlem and the American Negro to include an interest in all the colored peoples of the world—in fact, in *all the people* of the world, as I related to them and they to me.

I liked being a writer, traveling, meeting people, and looking at main events—like the depression in America, the transition from serfdom to manhood in Soviet Asia, and the Civil War in Spain—in it all, but at the same time apart from things, too. In the Soviet Union I was a visitor. In the midst of a dreary moral-breaking depression in America, I lived in a bright garden cottage at Carmel with a thoroughbred dog and a servant. In the Civil War in Spain I am a writer, not a fighter. But that is what I want to be, a writer, recording what I see, commenting upon it, and distilling from my own emotions a personal interpretation.

Unconsciously, in doing this I found that music helped me, and everywhere I looked for it, and listened. All over Paris that winter there was Negro music—Comptom Glover at Harry's New York Bar, Maceo Jefferson at the Big Apple, Georgie Johnson at the Boeuf sur le Toit, and anybody and everybody dropping by to play piano or blow a horn at Frisco's place—the popular coal-black Negro with the lighthouse smile. Una Mae Carlisle, Rollin Smith and Valaida Snow were singing at Montmartre clubs, and French jazz bands all over town were trying their best to beat it out like the Negroes. Meanwhile, I went to see Mauriac's *Asmodée* at the Comédie Française, and to hear the ancient Yvette Guilbert and Damia at the music halls, and Maurice Rostand reciting his poems, and to the Boule Blanche on the Left Bank to watch the Africans dancing.

But Paris did not seem as happy that winter as it had been in the summer. There was much talk of war in the air—not just war in Spain. The Parisian intellectuals declared Spain was only a training ground for Hitler and Mussolini, a place to try out Nazi bombing planes and educate Fascist pilots. The coming war, they predicted, would be everywhere. The charming but sad Jacques Roumain said, "I expect the world will end."

"I doubt it," I answered, "and if it does, I intend to live to see what happens."

He smiled, "You Americans!" he said.

But many Americans felt then as apprehensive as did the Europeans. A number of long-time residents of Paris were considering packing up to come home. I myself had wanted to spend the winter in France, but I'd had to send most of my money to Cleveland. Letters from my mother said that she was no better and that since my brother was back in college at Wilberforce, she hated to live alone, so she wrote that she had given up the house to move with some cousins. A great woman for linking her fate with cousins, my mother! But her illness worried me, so I thought I'd better go straight home and see about her. There wasn't much choice, anyhow, as I had just about enough money left to pay my passage. But this was not the first time I'd found myself in Paris practically penniless. I'd been so during my first weeks in the city long ago when I jumped ship and came there in 1924 looking for work. And since then I had been broke or almost broke in so many other cities around the world—and still had fun—that my personal predicament didn't worry me much. Sitting one night in the Bar Boudon on rue Douai, where the Negro musicians gathered, I remembered once during my childhood in Kansas my grandmother had given me an apple that had been bruised and so had a brown spot on it. I didn't want to eat the apple.

My grandmother said, "What's the matter with you, boy? You can't expect every apple to be a perfect apple. Just because it's got a speck on it, you want to throw it away. Bite that speck out and eat that apple, son. It's still a good apple."

That's the way the world is, I thought, if you bite the specks out, it's still a good apple.

In Paris, I stayed at an Ethiopian hotel—the only "colored" hotel in town—which amazed the Negro newspaperman, John Davis, when he stopped in Montmartre on his way to interview the Emperor Haille Selassie in exile near London.

"In Paris," he said, "of all places to stay in a colored hotel! Why?"

"For fun," I said. The hotel was amusing, with bushy-haired Ethiopians, Sudanese, Algerians and other non-Parisian characters coming in and out, and a panorama of Montmartre from its windows.

John Davis said he had to interview Haille Selassie the next morning at nine at His Highness's country place in England, so he took a night plane for London. But I learned from Davis later in New York that, when he arose very early the next day in London to drive out to see the Emperor, and got there promptly at nine, he was told that the appointment was for nine o'clock *Ethiopian time*—which meant four that afternoon. "Damn it all," said Davis, "I could have had an extra night in Paris!"

Before his departure from Paris we had gone night-clubbing along rue Pigalle and had met a charming girl who said she was from Java, part Dutch and part Javanese, but who spoke hesitant English and broken French with a Georgia drawl. John Davis whispered to me over the champagne he had bought that he was sure she was colored, from somewhere in Dixie, passing for Javanese in Paris, which amused him greatly. The girl was so exotic-looking that I doubted she was American, and disputed his insistence on it. I was wrong. Later I ran into the girl in New York talking perfectly good Harlemese, and not passing for anything on Lenox Avenue where she was quite at home.

On New Year's Eve I went to the Paris Opera alone. Why I chose to hear *Samson and Delilah* that particular night, I don't remember now. Perhaps it was the only evening that I could get a ticket at the Opera before sailing for America. I didn't enjoy the performance much. My seat in the gallery was very high, far away from the stage and behind a pillar. The music rose beautifully to my location, but the singers and the ballet seemed miles off. The sets were ponderous and old-fashioned. When Samson pushed the temple down, each piece seemed to take a full minute to descend separately on quite visible wires into a heap of obviously artificial scenery. Visually the *Folies Bergères* did a thousand times better on sets. The Opera Comique was better, too, to observe from the gallery. I wondered why I had not gone there instead of to the *Grand Opera*.

After the Opera, I had intended locating a party that some Martinique friends of the French Guiana poet, Leon Damas, a protégé of Gide's, were giving in the Latin Quarter. But when I started down into the Metro, I found that I had left the address of the party at my hotel. Rather than go back to the hotel and get it, since it was nearly midnight, I decided not to go to the party. Instead, I walked down the almost deserted Boulevards toward the Madeleine, thinking there might perhaps be a midnight mass there with organ music in honor of the New Year. Midway between the Opera and the Madeleine, I noticed a slightly limping figure approaching me, head down in his overcoat collar for it was cold. I remembered that limp from Moscow. It was Seki Sano, the Japanese theater director I had met at a Meyerhold rehearsal. We were surprised to see each other. To exchange news, we went into the glass enclosure of a sidewalk café and ordered drinks. All but one of the tables on the glass-encircled winter terrace were empty. At that table a rather pretty woman sat alone. Through the glass outside we could see the lights of the lonely boulevard, for very few people were passing in the chilly darkness. Quite unlike New York on New Year's Eve, downtown Paris as midnight approached was very quiet. The French remain home on holidays.

Seki Sano said, "I read a year or two ago in the Moscow papers about your being expelled from Japan. I'm sorry that happened to you in my country. But I am expelled, too. I cannot go back."

"I'm sure someday you can go back," I said, "and I, too, if I want to go."

But Seki Sano was not so optimistic. "There are too many people wandering around the world now who can't go home," he said. "Lots of them are in Moscow. More are in Paris—people from the Hitler countries, from the South American dictatorships, from China, from my own Japan. No exiles from America—though I wouldn't be surprised if the day didn't come."

"That's one nice thing about America," I said, "I can always go home—even when I don't want to."

"*Bonne année!*" said the waiter bringing our drinks. "It's the New Year!"

Sure enough, faintly, somewhere out in the Paris night, we could hear bells tolling the entrance of 1938, so we lifted our glasses. But the woman at the nearby table suddenly began to cry.

Seki Sano said, "Pardon, madam, but won't you join us?"

The woman sobbed *thank you* in an accent that was not French. Russian, maybe? Or German? We did not know. An exile, too, like Seki Sano? We did not ask her. She had been drinking coffee. The waiter brought her cup to our table as she rose.

The woman finally managed a smile. She sat with us quietly until the bells stopped ringing, then thanked us again and said good night. She disappeared alone down the boulevard toward the Madeleine. Seki Sano and I shook hands and parted at the corner across from the Café de la Paix. He was going to the Left Bank and I to Montmartre.

Slowly I walked through the lightly falling snow that had begun to sift down over the Paris rooftops in scattered indecisive flakes. The streets were very lonely as I passed the Galleries Lafayette and the Gare Saint Lazare and turned up the slight incline leading to Montmartre. Even the little clubs and bars along the way were quiet.

Where could everybody be, I wondered. How still it was in this old, old city of Paris in the first hour of the New Year.

The year before, I had been in Cleveland. The year before that in San Francisco. The year before that in Mexico City. The one before that at Carmel. And the year before Carmel in Tashkent. Where would I be when the next New Year came, I wondered? By then, would there be war—a major war? Would Mussolini and Hitler have finished their practice in Ethiopia and Spain to turn their planes on the rest of us? Would civilization be destroyed? Would the world really end?

"Not my world," I said to myself. "My world will not end."

But worlds—entire nations and civilizations—do end. In the snowy night in the shadows of the old houses of Montmartre, I repeated to myself, "My world won't end."

But how could I be so sure? I don't know.

For a moment I wondered.